George Gordon Byron

Letters

1804-1813

George Gordon Byron

Letters
1804-1813

ISBN/EAN: 9783744713245

Printed in Europe, USA, Canada, Australia, Japan

Cover: Foto ©Thomas Meinert / pixelio.de

More available books at **www.hansebooks.com**

THE WORKS OF
LORD BYRON

EDITED BY

WILLIAM ERNEST HENLEY

Letters, 1804-1813

LONDON
WILLIAM HEINEMANN
1897

To

THE MARCHIONESS OF GRANBY

IN MEMORY OF

TWO ANNIVERSARIES

MUSWELL HILL, *Sept. 4th*, 1896.   W. E. H.

EDITOR'S PREFACE

THE present Edition of Byron's prose is divided into
(1) Letters; (2) Journals and Memoranda; and (3)
Miscellanies—as the epistle to Roberts, the *Vampire*
fragment, the *Observations upon ' Observations,'* and
the like. The Text is reprinted from Moore, from
Dallas, Leigh Hunt, J. T. Hodgson, and the rest,
and, incomplete as probably it is, it is practically the
first reissue on novel and peculiar lines which has
been attempted for close on seventy years.

For the Notes.—There is a sense in which Byron
is grossly over-annotated. There is also a sense
in which his work cries out for annotation. In
preparing my commentary, I have drawn when I
could on Moore and the others; so that a certain
proportion of it also is not new. But when the
Life and Letters was published in 1830-31, many
allusions were plain which are now obscure, or
worse; so that there was a very great deal to be

done—as not a little still remains to do—in the way
of elucidation pure and simple. More: the years
whose voice-in-chief was Byron, have always seemed
to me among the most personal (so to speak), as they
are certainly the worst understood, in the national
existence. They were years of storm and triumph
on all the lines of human destiny; and they gave to
history a generation at once dandified and truculent,
bigoted yet dissolute, magnificent but vulgar (or so
it seems to us), artistic, very sumptuous, and yet
capable of astonishing effort and superb self-sacrifice.
It was a generation bent above all upon living its life
to the utmost of its capacity; and, though there are
still those living who can remember when its master-
poet—(for that, I take it, the singer of Lara and Juan
was)—was gathered to his fathers, so great a change
has come upon his England in the interval between
the obsequies at Hucknall Torkard and the writing
of this Preface, that it is practically not less remote
from ours than the England of Spenser and Raleigh.
Rightly or wrongly, then, I have written on the
theory that to know something of Byron, one should
know something of the aims and lives and personalities of contemporary men and women, with something of the social and political conditions which

made him and his triumph possible. I cannot believe that this first instalment, for all its bulk, will go far towards the accomplishment of such an end. But I confess to cherishing a hope that, by the time I have finished my task, I shall be found to have formed a collection of facts and portraitures, which, by making for a juster apprehension of the quality and temper of Byron's environment, will make for a more intimate understanding of Byron's character and Byron's achievement. Both these are extraordinary; neither can be explained, or shouted, or sniffed away; and it is merely futile to attempt an estimate of either till one can do so with some knowledge of relevant and significant circumstances, and with a certain sympathy (or the reverse, if it must be so) with the influences under which the character was developed and the achievement done.

It will be found, I think, that in the course of my work I have made acknowledgments wherever they were due. In this place I have pleasure in tendering peculiar thanks to Mr. Alfred Morrison for permission to copy certain pieces in his unrivalled Collection of Autographs, and to Mr. James Fitzmaurice-Kelly, as to Mr. Daniel Conner, for the communication of results, of lasting moment to this contribution to the literature which has accumulated, and must go on accumulating, round the sole English poet—(for Sir Walter conquered in prose)—bred since Milton to live a master-influence in the world at large.

W. E. H.

23rd November 1896.

CONTENTS

1804

LETTERS

CONTENTS

LETTERS

xiv

CONTENTS

LETTERS

CONTENTS

1813

LETTERS

CONTENTS

LETTERS

Burgage Manor, August 29, 1804.

I received the arms, my dear Miss Pigot, and am *i* very much obliged to you for the trouble you have taken. It is impossible I should have any fault to find with them. The sight of the drawings gives me great pleasure for a double reason,—in the first place, they will ornament my books, in the next, they convince me that *you* have not entirely *forgot* me. I am, however, sorry you do not return sooner—you have already been gone an *age*. I perhaps may have taken my departure for London before you come back ; but, however, I will hope not. Do not overlook my watch-riband and purse, as I wish to carry them with me. Your note was given me by Harry, at the play, whither I attended Miss L—— and Dr. S—— ; and now I have sat down to answer it before I go to bed. If I am at Southwell when you return,— and I sincerely hope you will soon, for I very much regret your absence,—I shall be happy to hear you sing my favourite, *The Maid of Lodi*. My mother, together with myself, desires to be affectionately remembered to Mrs. Pigot, and, believe me, my dear Miss Pigot, I remain your affectionate friend,

BYRON.

LETTERS

P.S.—If you think proper to send me any answer to this, I shall be extremely happy to receive it. Adieu.

P.S. 2nd.—As you say you are a novice in the art of knitting, I hope it don't give you too much trouble. Go on *slowly*, but surely. Once more, adieu.

TO HENRY ANGELO

Trinity College, Cambridge,
May 16, 1806.

Sir,—You cannot be more indignant, at the insolent and unmerited conduct of Mr. Mortlock, than those who authorised you to request his permission. However, we do not yet despair of gaining our point, and every effort shall be made to remove the obstacles, which at present prevent the execution of our project. I yesterday waited on the Master of this College, who having a personal dispute with the Mayor, declined interfering, but recommended an application to the Vice-Chancellor, whose authority is paramount in the University. I shall communicate this to Lord Altamont, and we will endeavour to bend the obstinacy of the *upstart* magistrate, who seems to be equally deficient in justice and common civility. On my arrival in town, which will take place in a few days, you will see me at Albany Buildings, when we will discuss the subject further. Present my remembrance to the Messrs. Angelo, junior, and believe me, we will yet *humble* this *impertinent* bourgeois.—I remain, Sir, your obedient servant,

BYRON.

2

TO MR. PIGOT

TO MR. PIGOT

16 *Piccadilly, August* 9, 1806.

My dear Pigot,—Many thanks for your amusing *iii*
narrative of the last proceedings of my amiable
Alecto, who now begins to feel the effects of her
folly. I have just received a penitential epistle, to
which, apprehensive of pursuit, I have despatched a
moderate answer, with a *kind* of promise to return in
a fortnight ;—this, however (*entre nous*), I never mean
to fulfil. Her soft warblings must have delighted her
auditors, her higher notes being particularly musical,
and on a calm moonlight evening would be heard to
great advantage. Had I been present as a spectator,
nothing would have pleased me more ; but to have
come forward as one of the *dramatis personæ*—St.
Dominic defend me from such a scene ! Seriously,
your mother has laid me under great obligations, and
you, with the rest of your family, merit my warmest
thanks for your kind connivance at my escape from
' Mrs. Byron *furiosa.*'

Oh ! for the pen of Ariosto to rehearse, in epic, the
scolding of that momentous eve,—or rather, let me
invoke the shade of Dante to inspire me, for none
but the author of the *Inferno* could properly preside
over such an attempt. But, perhaps, where the pen
might fail, the pencil would succeed. What a group !
—Mrs. B. the principal figure ; you cramming your
ears with cotton, as the only antidote to total deafness ; Mrs. —— in vain endeavouring to mitigate
the wrath of the lioness robbed of her whelp ; and
last, though not least, Elizabeth and *Wousky,*—won-

3

derful to relate!—both deprived of their parts of speech, and bringing up the rear in mute astonishment. How did S. B. receive the intelligence? How many *puns* did he utter on so *facetious* an event? In your next inform me on this point, and what excuse you made to A. You are probably, by this time, tired of deciphering this hieroglyphical letter;—like Tony Lumpkin, you will pronounce mine to be 'a d——d up and down hand.' All Southwell, without doubt, is involved in amazement. Apropos, how does my blue-eyed nun, the fair ——? Is she '*robed in sable garb of woe*'?

Here I remain at least a week or ten days; previous to my departure you shall receive my address, but what it will be I have not determined. My lodgings must be kept secret from Mrs. B. You may present my compliments to her, and say any attempt to pursue me will fail, as I have taken measures to retreat immediately to Portsmouth, on the first intimation of her removal from Southwell. You may add, I have now proceeded to a friend's house in the country, there to remain a fortnight.

I have now *blotted* (I must not say written) a complete double letter, and in return shall expect a *monstrous budget*. Without doubt the dames of Southwell reprobate the pernicious example I have shown, and tremble lest their *babes* should disobey their mandates, and quit, in dudgeon, their mammas on any grievance. Adieu. When you begin your next, drop the 'lordship,' and put 'Byron' in its place.—Believe me yours, etc.   BYRON.

TO MISS PIGOT

London, August 10, 1806.

My dear Bridget,—As I have already troubled *iv* your brother with more than he will find pleasure in deciphering, you are the next to whom I shall assign the employment of perusing this second epistle. You will perceive from my first, that no idea of Mrs. B.'s arrival had disturbed me at the time it was written; *not* so the present, since the appearance of a note from the *illustrious cause* of my *sudden decampment* has driven the 'natural ruby from my cheeks,' and completely blanched my woe-begone countenance. This gunpowder intimation of her arrival (confound her activity!) breathes less of terror and dismay than you will probably imagine, from the volcanic temperament of her ladyship; and concludes with the comfortable assurance of all *present motion* being prevented by the fatigue of her journey, for which my *blessings* are due to the rough roads and restive quadrupeds of his Majesty's highways. As I have not the smallest inclination to be chased round the country, I shall e'en make a merit of necessity; and since, like Macbeth, 'they've tied me to the stake, I cannot fly,' I shall imitate that valorous tyrant, and 'bear-like fight the course,' all escape being precluded. I can now engage with less disadvantage, having drawn the enemy from her intrenchments, though, like the *prototype* to whom I have compared myself, with an excellent chance of being knocked on the head. However, 'Lay on,

Macduff, and d——d be he who first cries, Hold, enough.'

I shall remain in town for, at least, a week, and expect to hear from *you* before its expiration. I presume the printer has brought you the offspring of my *poetic mania*. Remember in the first line to read '*loud* the winds whistle,' instead of 'round,' which that blockhead Ridge has inserted by mistake, and makes nonsense of the whole stanza. Addio!—Now to encounter my *Hydra*.—Yours ever.

TO MR. PIGOT

London, Sunday, midnight,
August 10, 1806.

v   Dear Pigot,—This *astonishing* packet will, doubtless, amaze you; but having an idle hour this evening, I wrote the enclosed stanzas, which I request you will deliver to Ridge, to be printed *separate* from my other compositions, as you will perceive them to be improper for the perusal of ladies; of course, none of the females of your family must see them. I offer 1000 apologies for the trouble I have given you in this and other instances.—Yours truly.

TO MR. PIGOT

Piccadilly, August 16, 1806.

vi   I cannot exactly say with Cæsar, '*Veni, vidi, vici*': however, the most important part of his laconic account of success applies to my present situation; for, though Mrs. Byron took the *trouble* of '*coming*,' and '*seeing*,' yet your humble servant proved the *victor*. After an obstinate engagement of some hours, in which we suffered considerable damage, from the quickness of the enemy's fire, they at length retired in confusion, leaving behind the artillery, field equipage, and some prisoners: their defeat is decisive for the present campaign. To speak more intelligibly, Mrs. B. returns immediately, but I proceed, with all my laurels, to Worthing, on the Sussex coast; to which place you will address (to be left at the post-office) your next epistle. By the enclosure of a second *gingle of rhyme*, you will probably conceive my muse to be *vastly prolific*; her inserted production was brought forth a few years ago, and found by accident on Thursday among some old papers. I have recopied it, and, adding the proper date, request that it may be printed with the rest of the family. I thought your sentiments on the last bantling would coincide with mine, but it was impossible to give it any other garb, being founded on *facts*. My stay at Worthing will not exceed three weeks, and you may *possibly* behold me again at Southwell the middle of September.

Will you desire Ridge to suspend the printing of my poems till he hears further from me, as I have determined to give them a new form entirely. This prohibition does not extend to the two last pieces I have sent with my letters to you. You will excuse the *dull vanity* of this epistle, as my brain is a *chaos* of absurd images, and full of business, preparations, and projects.

LETTERS

I shall expect an answer with impatience ;—believe me, there is nothing at this moment could give me greater delight than your letter.

TO MR. PIGOT

London, August 18, 1806.

vii   I am just on the point of setting off for Worthing, and write merely to request you will send that *idle scoundrel* **Charles** with my horses immediately; tell him I am excessively provoked he has not made his appearance before, or written to inform me of the cause of his delay, particularly as I supplied him with money for his journey. On *no* pretext is he to postpone his *march* one day longer ; and if, in obedience to the caprices of Mrs. B. (who, I presume, is again spreading desolation through her little monarchy), he thinks proper to disregard my positive orders, I shall not, in future, consider him as my servant. He must bring the surgeon's bill with him, which I will discharge immediately on receiving it. Nor can I conceive the reason of his not acquainting Frank with the state of my unfortunate quadrupeds. Dear Pigot, forgive this *petulant* effusion, and attribute it to the idle conduct of that *precious* rascal, who, instead of obeying my injunctions, is sauntering through the streets of that *political Pandemonium,* Nottingham. Present my remembrances to your family and the Leacrofts, and believe me, etc.

P.S.—I delegate to *you* the unpleasant task of despatching him on his journey—Mrs. B.'s orders to the contrary are not to be attended to : he is to pro-

8

ceed first to London, and then to Worthing, without delay. Everything I have *left* must be sent to London. My *Poetics you* will *pack up* for the same place, and not even reserve a copy for yourself and sister, as I am about to give them an *entire new form* : when they are complete, you shall have the *first fruits.* Mrs. B. on no account is to *see* or touch them. Adieu.

TO MR. PIGOT

Little Hampton, August 26, 1806.

I this morning received your epistle, which I was viii obliged to send for to Worthing, whence I have removed to this place, on the same coast, about eight miles distant from the former. You will probably not be displeased with this letter, when it informs you that I am £30,000 richer than I was at our parting, having just received intelligence from my lawyer that a cause has been gained at Lancaster Assizes, which will be worth that sum by the time I come of age. Mrs. B. is, doubtless, acquainted of this acquisition, though not apprised of its exact *value*, of which she had better be ignorant ; for her behaviour under any sudden piece of favourable intelligence, is, if possible, more ridiculous than her detestable conduct on the most trifling circumstances of an unpleasant nature. You may give my compliments to her, and say that her detaining my servant's things shall only lengthen my absence : for unless they are immediately dispatched to 16 Piccadilly, together with those which have been so long

LETTERS

delayed, belonging to myself, she shall never again behold my *radiant countenance* illuminating her gloomy mansion. If they are sent, I may probably appear in less than two years from the date of my present epistle.

Metrical compliment is an ample reward for my strains: you are one of the few votaries of Apollo who unite the sciences over which that deity presides. I wish you to send my poems to my lodgings in London immediately, as I have several alterations and some additions to make; *every* copy must be sent, as I am about to *amend* them, and you shall soon behold them in all their glory. I hope you have kept them from that upas tree, that antidote to the arts, Mrs. B. *Entre nous,*—you may expect to see me soon. Adieu.—Yours ever.

TO MISS PIGOT

August 26, 1806.

ix My dear Bridget,—I have only just dismounted from my *Pegasus*, which has prevented me from descending to *plain* prose in an epistle of greater length to your *fair* self. You regretted, in a former letter, that my poems were not more extensive; I now, for your satisfaction, announce that I have nearly doubled them, partly by the discovery of some I conceived to be lost, and partly by some new productions. We shall meet on Wednesday next; till then believe me yours affectionately,   BYRON.

P.S.—Your brother John is seized with a poetic

10

mania, and is now rhyming away at the rate of three
lines *per hour*—so much for *inspiration*! Adieu !

TO MR. PIGOT.

Southwell, Jan. 13, 1807.

I ought to begin with *sundry* apologies, for my *x*
own negligence, but the variety of my avocations in
prose and *verse* must plead my excuse. With this
epistle you will receive a volume of all my *Juvenilia*,
published since your departure : it is of considerably
greater size than the *copy* in your possession, which I
beg you will destroy, as the present is much more
complete. That *unlucky* poem to my poor Mary
has been the cause of some animadversion from
ladies in years. I have not printed it in this collection, in consequence of my being pronounced a most
profligate sinner, in short, a '*young Moore*,' by ——,
your . . . friend. I believe, in general, they have
been favourably received, and surely the age of their
author will preclude *severe* criticism. The adventures
of my life from sixteen to nineteen, and the dissipation into which I have been thrown in London, have
given a voluptuous tint to my ideas ; but the occasions which called forth my Muse could hardly
admit any other colouring. This volume is *vastly*
correct and miraculously chaste. Apropos, talking
of love, ...

If you can find leisure to answer this farrago of
unconnected nonsense, you need not doubt what
gratification will accrue from your reply to yours
ever, etc.

LETTERS

Southwell, Notts, February 6, 1807.

xi My dearest Clare, — Were I to make all the apologies necessary to atone for my late negligence, you would justly say you had received a petition instead of a letter, as it would be filled with prayers for forgiveness; but instead of this, I will acknowledge my *sins* at once, and I trust to your friendship and generosity rather than to my own excuses. Though my health is not perfectly re-established, I am out of all danger, and have recovered everything but my spirits, which are subject to depression. You will be astonished to hear I have lately written to Delawarr, for the purpose of explaining (as far as possible without involving some *old friends* of mine in the business) the cause of my behaviour to him during my last residence at Harrow (nearly two years ago), which you will recollect was rather '*en cavalier.*' Since that period, I have discovered he was treated with injustice both by those who misrepresented his conduct, and by me in consequence of their suggestions. I have therefore made all the reparation in my power, by apologising for my mistake, though with very faint hopes of success; indeed I never expected any answer, but desired one for form's sake; *that* has not yet arrived, and most probably never will. However, I have *eased* my own *conscience* by the atonement, which is humiliating enough to one of my disposition; yet I could not have slept satisfied with the reflection of having, *even unintentionally,* injured any individual.

I have done all that could be done to repair the injury, and there the affair must end. Whether we renew our intimacy or not is of very trivial consequence.

My time has lately been much occupied with very different pursuits. I have been *transporting* a servant, who cheated me, — rather a disagreeable event ;—performing in private theatricals ;—publishing a volume of poems (at the request of my friends, for their perusal) ;—making love ;—and taking physic. The two last amusements have not had the best effect in the world; for my attentions have been divided amongst so many fair damsels, and the drugs I swallow are of such variety in their composition, that between Venus and Æsculapius I am harassed to death. However, I have still leisure to devote some hours to the recollections of past, regretted friendships, and in the interval to take the advantage of the moment, to assure you how much I am, and ever will be, my dearest Clare, your truly attached and sincere   BYRON.

TO MR. WILLIAM BANKES

Southwell, March 6, 1807.

Dear Bankes,—Your critique is valuable for many reasons : in the first place, it is the only one in which flattery has borne so slight a part ; in the *next*, I am *cloyed* with insipid compliments. I have a better opinion of your judgment and ability than your *feelings*. Accept my most sincere thanks for your kind decision, not less welcome, because totally unexpected. With regard to a more exact estimate, I need not remind you how few of the *best poems*, in our language, will stand the test of *minute* or *verbal* criticism: it can, therefore, hardly be expected the effusions of a boy (and most of these pieces have been produced at an early period) can derive much merit either from the subject or composition. Many of them were written under great depression of spirits, and during severe indisposition :—hence the gloomy turn of the ideas. We coincide in opinion that the '*poësies érotiques*' are the most exceptionable; they were, however, grateful to the *deities*, on whose altars hey were offered—more I seek not.

The portrait of Pomposus was drawn at Harrow, after a *long sitting* ; this accounts for the resemblance, or rather the *caricatura*. He is *your* friend, he *never was mine*—for both our sakes I shall be silent on this head. The *collegiate* rhymes are not personal—one of the notes may appear so, but could not be omitted. I have no doubt they will be deservedly abused—a just punishment for my unfilial treatment of so excellent an *Alma Mater*. I sent you no copy, lest *we* should be placed in the situation of Gil Blas and the Archbishop of Grenada ; though running some hazard from the experiment, I wished your *verdict* to be unbiassed. Had my '*Libellus*' been presented previous to your letter, it would have appeared a species of bribe to purchase compliment. I feel no hesitation in saying, I was more anxious to hear your critique, however severe, than the praises of the *million*. On the same day I was honoured with the encomiums of *Mackenzie*, the celebrated author of the *Man of*

TO MR. PIGOT

Feeling. Whether *his* approbation or *yours* elated me most, I cannot decide.

You will receive my *Juvenilia,*—at least all yet published. I have a large volume in manuscript, which may in part appear hereafter; at present I have neither time nor inclination to prepare it for the press. In the spring I shall return to Trinity, to dismantle my rooms, and bid you a final adieu. The *Cam* will not be much increased by my *tears* on the occasion. Your further remarks, however *caustic* or bitter, to a palate vitiated with the *sweets of adulation,* will be of service. Johnson has shown us that *no poetry* is perfect; but to correct mine would be an Herculean labour. In fact I never looked beyond the moment of composition, and published merely at the request of my friends. Notwithstanding so much has been said concerning the *genus irritabile vatum,* we shall never quarrel on the subject—poetic fame is by no means the 'acme' of my wishes.—Adieu.
Yours ever,   BYRON.

TO MR. PIGOT

Southwell, April 1807.

My dear Pigot,—Allow me to congratulate you on xiii the success of your first examination—' *Courage, mon ami.*' The title of Doctor will do wonders with the damsels. I shall most probably be in Essex or London when you arrive at this d——d place, where I am detained by the publication of my *rhymes.*

Adieu.—Believe me yours very truly,

BYRON.

P.S.—Since we met, I have reduced myself by

15

violent exercise, *much* physic, and *hot* bathing, from
14 stone 6 lb. to 12 stone 7 lb.   In all I have lost
27 pounds.   Bravo!—what say you?

TO MR. WILLIAM BANKES

*   *   *   *   *

For my own part, I have suffered severely in the
decease of my two greatest friends, the only beings I
ever loved (females excepted); I am therefore a
solitary animal, miserable enough, and so perfectly a
citizen of the world, that whether I pass my days in
Great Britain or Kamschatka, is to me a matter of
perfect indifference.   I cannot evince greater respect
for your alteration than by immediately adopting it
—this shall be done in the next edition.   I am sorry
your remarks are not more frequent, as I am certain
they would be·equally beneficial.   Since my last, I
have received two critical opinions from Edinburgh,
both too flattering for me to detail.   One is from
Lord Woodhouselee, at the head of the Scotch literati,
and a most *voluminous* writer (his last work is a life
of Lord Kaimes); the other from Mackenzie, who
sent his decision a second time, more at length.   I
am not personally acquainted with either of these
gentlemen, nor ever requested their sentiments on the
subject: their praise is voluntary, and transmitted
through the medium of a friend, at whose house they
read the productions.

Contrary to my former intention, I am now preparing a volume for the public at large: my amatory
pieces will be exchanged, and others substituted in

their place. The whole will be considerably enlarged, and appear the latter end of May. This is a hazardous experiment; but want of better employment, the encouragement I have met with, and my own vanity, induce me to stand the test, though not without *sundry palpitations.* The book will circulate fast enough in this country, from mere curiosity, what I prin——

*   *   *   *   *

TO MR. FALKNER

Sir,—The volume of little pieces which accompanies *xv* this, would have been presented before, had I not been apprehensive that Miss Falkner's indisposition might render such trifles unwelcome. There are some errors of the printer which I have not had time to correct in the collection: you have it thus, with 'all its imperfections on its head,' a heavy weight, when joined with the faults of its author. Such *Juvenilia,* as they can claim no great degree of approbation, I may venture to hope, will also escape the severity of uncalled for, though perhaps *not* undeserved, criticism.

They were written on many and various occasions, and are now published merely for the perusal of a friendly circle. Believe me, sir, if they afford the slightest amusement to yourself and the rest of my *social* readers, I shall have gathered all the *bays* I ever wish to adorn the head of yours, very truly,

Byron.

P.S.—I hope Miss F. is in a state of recovery.

June 11, 1807.

xvi Dear Queen Bess,—*Savage* ought to be *immortal*: —though not a *thorough-bred bull-dog*, he is the finest puppy I ever *saw*, and will answer much better; in his great and manifold kindness he has already bitten my fingers, and disturbed the *gravity* of old Boatswain, who is *grievously discomposed*. I wish to be informed what he *costs*, his *expenses*, etc. etc., that I may indemnify Mr. G——. My thanks are *all* I can give for the trouble he has taken, make a *long speech*, and conclude it with 1 2 3 4 5 6 7.   I am out of practice, so *deputize* you as a legate,—*ambassador* would not do in a matter concerning the *Pope*, which I presume this must, as the *whole* turns upon a *Bull*.—Yours,   BYRON.

   P.S.—I write in bed.

Cambridge, June 30, 1807.

xvii 'Better late than never, Pal,' is a saying of which you know the origin, and as it is applicable on the present occasion, you will excuse its conspicuous place in the front of my epistle.   I am almost superannuated here.   My old friends (with the exception of a very few) all departed, and I am preparing to follow them, but remain till Monday to be present at three *Oratorios*, two *Concerts*, a *Fair*, and a Ball.   I find I am not only *thinner* but *taller* by an inch since my last visit.   I was obliged to tell every body my *name*, nobody having the least recollection of my *visage*, or person.   Even the hero of *my*

Cornelian (who is now sitting *vis-à-vis*, reading a volume of my *Poetics*) passed me in Trinity walks without recognising me in the least, and was thunderstruck at the alteration which had taken place in my countenance, etc. etc. Some say I look *better*, others *worse*, but all agree I am *thinner*,—more I do not require. I have lost two pounds in my weight since I left your *cursed*, *detestable*, and *abhorred* abode of *scandal*, where, excepting yourself and John Becher, I care not if the whole race were consigned to the *Pit* of *Acheron*, which I would visit in person rather than contaminate my *sandals* with the polluted dust of Southwell. *Seriously*, unless obliged by the *emptiness* of my purse to revisit Mrs. B., you will see me no more.

On Monday I depart for London. I quit Cambridge with little regret, because our *set* are *vanished*, and my *musical protégé* before mentioned has left the choir, and is stationed in a mercantile house of considerable eminence in the metropolis. You may have heard me observe he is exactly to an hour two years younger than myself. I found him grown considerably, and, as you will suppose, very glad to see his former *Patron*. He is nearly my height, very *thin*, very fair complexion, dark eyes, and light locks. My opinion of his mind you already know;—I hope I shall never have occasion to change it. Every body here conceives me to be an *invalid*. The University at present is very gay from the fêtes of divers kinds. I supped out last night, but eat (or ate) nothing, sipped a bottle of claret, went to bed at two, and rose at eight. I have commenced early rising, and find it agrees with me. The Masters and the Fellows all very *polite*, but look a little *askance*—don't much admire *lampoons* — truth always disagreeable.

Write, and tell me how the inhabitants of your *Menagerie* go *on*, and if my publication goes *off* well : do the quadrupeds *growl*? Apropos, my bulldog is deceased—'Flesh both of cur and man is grass.' Address your answer to Cambridge. If I am gone, it will be forwarded. Sad news just arrived— Russians beat—a bad set, eat nothing but *oil*, consequently must melt before a *hard fire*. I get awkward in my academic habiliments for want of practice. Got up in a window to hear the oratorio at St. Mary's, popped down in the middle of the *Messiah*, tore a *woeful* rent in the back of my best black silk gown, and damaged an egregious pair of breeches. Mem.—never tumbled from a church window during service. Adieu, dear ——! do not remember me to anybody :—to *forget* and be forgotten by the people of Southwell is all I aspire to.

TO MISS PIGOT

Trin. Coll. Cam. July 5, 1807.

xviii   Since my last letter I have determined to reside *another year* at Granta, as my rooms, etc. etc. are finished in great style, several old friends come up again, and many new acquaintances made; consequently my inclination leads me forward, and I shall return to college in October if still *alive*. My life here has been one continued routine of dissipation—out at different places every day, engaged to more dinners, etc. etc. than my *stay* would permit me to fulfil. At this moment I write with a bottle of claret in my *head* and *tears* in my *eyes*; for I have just parted with my '*Cornelian*,' who spent the evening with me. As it was our last interview, I postponed my engagement to devote the hours of the *Sabbath* to friendship:—Edleston and I have separated for the present, and my mind is a chaos of hope and sorrow. To-morrow I set out for London: you will address your answer to 'Gordon's Hotel, Albemarle Street,' where I *sojourn* during my visit to the metropolis.

I rejoice to hear you are interested in my *protégé*; he has been my *almost constant* associate since October, 1805, when I entered Trinity College. His *voice* first attracted my attention, his *countenance* fixed it, and his *manners* attached me to him for ever. He departs for a *mercantile house* in *town* in October, and we shall probably not meet till the expiration of my minority, when I shall leave to his decision either entering as a *partner* through my interest, or residing with me altogether. Of course he would in his present frame of mind prefer the *latter*, but he may alter his opinion previous to that period;—however, he shall have his choice. I certainly love him more than any human being, and neither time nor distance have had the least effect on my (in general) changeable disposition. In short, we shall put *Lady E. Butler* and *Miss Ponsonby* to the blush, *Pylades* and *Orestes* out of countenance, and want nothing but a catastrophe like *Nisus* and *Euryalus* to give *Jonathan* and *David* the 'go by.' He certainly is perhaps

LETTERS

more attached to *me* than even I am in return.
During the whole of my residence at Cambridge we
met every day, summer and winter, without passing
one tiresome moment, and separated each time with
increasing reluctance. I hope you will one day see
us together. He is the only being I esteem, though
I *like* many.

The Marquis of Tavistock was down the other
day; I supped with him at his tutor's—entirely a
Whig party. The opposition muster strong here
now, and Lord Hartington, the Duke of Leinster,
etc. etc. are to join us in October, so every thing
will be *splendid*. The *music* is all over at present.
Met with another '*accidency*'—upset a butter-boat in
the lap of a lady—look'd very *blue*—*spectators* grinned
—'curse 'em!' Apropos, sorry to say, been *drunk*
every day, and not quite *sober* yet—however, touch
no meat, nothing but fish, soup, and vegetables, consequently it does me no harm—sad dogs all the
Cantabs. Mem.—*we mean* to reform next January.
This place is a *monotony of endless variety*—like it—
hate Southwell. Has Ridge sold well? or do the
ancients demur? What ladies have bought?

Saw a girl at St. Mary's the image of Anne ——,
thought it was her—all in the wrong—the lady
stared, so did I—I *blushed*, so did *not* the lady,—
sad thing—wish women had *more modesty*. Talking
of women, puts me in mind of my terrier Fanny—
how is she? Got a headach, must go to bed, up
early in the morning to travel. My *protégé* breakfasts with me; parting spoils my appetite—excepting
from Southwell. Mem.—*I hate Southwell.*—Yours, etc.

TO MISS PIGOT

TO MISS PIGOT

Gordon's Hotel, July 13, 1807.

You write most excellent epistles—a fig for other *xix*
correspondents, with their nonsensical apologies for
'*knowing nought about it*,'—you send me a delightful
budget.   I am here in a perpetual vortex of dissipation (very pleasant for all that), and, strange to tell,
I get thinner, being now below eleven stone considerably.   Stay in town a *month*, perhaps six weeks,
trip into Essex, and then, as a favour, *irradiate*
Southwell for three days with the light of my
countenance; but nothing shall ever make me *reside*
there again.   I positively return to Cambridge in
October; we are to be uncommonly gay, or in truth
I should *cut* the University.   An extraordinary circumstance occurred to me at Cambridge; a girl so
very like —— made her appearance, that nothing but
the most *minute inspection* could have undeceived
me.   I wish I had asked if *she* had ever been at
H——

What the devil would Ridge have? is not fifty in
a fortnight, before the advertisements, a sufficient
sale?   I hear many of the London booksellers have
them, and Crosby has sent copies to the principal
watering places.   Are they liked or not in Southwell? . . . I wish Boatswain had *swallowed* Damon !
How is Bran? by the immortal gods, Bran ought to
be a *Count* of the *Holy Roman Empire.*

The intelligence of London cannot be interesting
to you, who have rusticated all your life—the annals
of routs, riots, balls and boxing-matches, cards and
crim. cons., parliamentary discussion, political details,

masquerades, mechanics, Argyle Street Institution
and aquatic races, love and lotteries, Brookes's and
Buonaparte, opera singers and oratorios, wine, women,
wax-work, and weathercocks, can't accord with your
insulated ideas of decorum and other *silly expressions*
not inserted in *our vocabulary*.

Oh! Southwell, Southwell, how I rejoice to have
left thee, and how I curse the heavy hours I dragged
along, for so many months, among the Mohawks
who inhabit your kraals!—However, one thing I do
not regret, which is having *pared off* a sufficient
quantity of flesh to enable me to slip into 'an eel-
skin,' and vie with the *slim* beaux of modern times;
though I am sorry to say, it seems to be the mode
amongst *gentlemen* to grow *fat*, and I am told I
am at least fourteen pound below the fashion.
However, I *decrease* instead of enlarging, which is
extraordinary, as *violent* exercise in London is impracticable; but I attribute the *phenomenon* to our
evening squeezes at public and private parties. I
heard from Ridge this morning (the 14th, my letter
was begun yesterday): he says the poems go on as
well as can be wished; the seventy-five sent to town
are circulated, and a demand for fifty more complied
with, the day he dated his epistle, though the advertisements are not yet half published. Adieu.

P.S.—Lord Carlisle, on receiving my poems, sent,
before he opened the book, a tolerably handsome
letter:—I have not heard from him since. His
opinions I neither know nor care about: if he is
the least insolent, I shall enrol him with Butler
and the other worthies. He is in Yorkshire, poor

24

man! and very ill! He said he had not had time
to read the contents, but thought it necessary to
acknowledge the receipt of the volume immediately.
Perhaps the Earl '*bears no brother near the throne,*'
—*if so*, I will make his *sceptre* totter *in his hands.*—
Adieu!

TO MR. CROSBY

Stationers' Court, July 21, 1807.

Sir,—I have sent, according to my promise, some *xx*
stanzas for *Literary Recreations*; the insertion I leave
to the option of the editors, they have never appeared
before. I should wish to know whether they are
admitted or not, and when the work will appear, as
I am desirous of a copy, etc. etc.   BYRON.

P.S.—Send your answer when convenient.

TO MISS PIGOT

August 2, 1807.

London begins to disgorge its contents—town is *xxi*
empty—consequently I can scribble at leisure, as
occupations are less numerous. In a fortnight I
shall depart to fulfil a country engagement; but
expect two epistles from you previous to that period.
Ridge does not proceed rapidly in Notts—very
possible. In town things wear a more promising
aspect, and a man whose works are praised by
reviewers, admired by *duchesses*, and sold by every
bookseller of the metropolis, does not dedicate much
consideration to *rustic readers*. I have now a review
before me, entitled *Literary Recreations*, where my
bardship is applauded far beyond my deserts. I

know nothing of the critic, but think *him* a very discerning gentleman, and *myself* a devilish *clever* fellow. His critique pleases me particularly, because it is of great length, and a proper quantum of censure is administered, just to give an agreeable *relish* to the praise. You know I hate insipid, unqualified, common-place compliment. If you would wish to see it, order the 13th Number of *Literary Recreations* for the last month. I assure you I have not the most distant idea of the writer of the article—it is printed in a periodical publication—and though I have written a paper (a review of Wordsworth), which appears in the same work, I am ignorant of every other person concerned in it—even the editor, whose name I have not heard. My cousin, Lord Alexander Gordon, who resided in the same hotel, told me his mother, her Grace of Gordon, requested he would introduce my *Poetical* Lordship to her *Highness*, as she had bought my volume, admired it exceedingly, in common with the rest of the fashionable world, and wished to claim her relationship with the author. I was unluckily engaged on an excursion for some days afterwards; and, as the Duchess was on the eve of departing for Scotland, I have postponed my introduction till the winter, when I shall favour the lady, *whose taste I shall not dispute*, with my most sublime and edifying conversation. She is now in the Highlands, and Alexander took his departure, a few days ago, for the same *blessed* seat of '*dark rolling winds.*'

Crosby, my London publisher, has disposed of his second importation, and has sent to Ridge for a *third*—at least so he says. In every bookseller's window I see my *own name*, and *say nothing*, but enjoy my fame in secret. My last reviewer kindly requests me to alter my determination of writing no more: and 'A Friend to the Cause of Literature' begs I will *gratify* the *public* with some new work 'at no very distant period.' Who would not be a bard? —that is to say, if all critics would be so polite. However, the others will pay me off, I doubt not, for this *gentle* encouragement. If so, have at 'em! By the by, I have written at my intervals of leisure, after two in the morning, 380 lines in blank verse, of *Bosworth Field*. I have luckily got Hutton's account. I shall extend the poem to eight or ten books, and shall have finished it in a year. Whether it will be published or not must depend on circumstances. So much for *egotism*! My *laurels* have turned my brain, but the *cooling acids* of forthcoming criticisms will probably restore me to *modesty*.

Southwell is a damned place—I have done with it—at least in all probability; excepting yourself, I esteem no one within its precincts. You were my only *rational* companion; and in plain truth, I had more respect for you than the whole *bevy*, with whose foibles I amused myself in compliance with their prevailing propensities. You gave yourself more trouble with me and my manuscripts than a thousand *dolls* would have done. Believe me, I have not forgotten your good nature in *this circle* of *sin*, and one day I trust I shall be able to evince my gratitude. Adieu, yours, etc.

P.S.—Remember me to Dr. P.

LETTERS

London, August 11, 1807.

xxii   On Sunday next I set off for the Highlands. A friend of mine accompanies me in my carriage to Edinburgh. There we shall leave it, and proceed in a *tandem* (a species of open carriage) through the western passes to Inverary, where we shall purchase *shelties*, to enable us to view places inaccessible to *vehicular conveyances*. On the coast we shall hire a vessel, and visit the most remarkable of the Hebrides; and, if we have time and favourable weather, mean to sail as far as Iceland, only 300 miles from the northern extremity of Caledonia, to peep at *Hecla*. This last intention you will keep a secret, as my nice *mamma* would imagine I was on a Voyage of *Discovery*, and raise the accustomed *maternal warwhoop*.

Last week I swam in the Thames from Lambeth through the two bridges, Westminster and Blackfriars, a distance, including the different turns and tacks made on the way, of three miles ! You see I am in excellent training in case of a *squall* at sea. I mean to collect all the Erse traditions, poems, etc. etc., and translate, or expand the subject to fill a volume, which may appear next spring under the denomina- of *The Highland Harp*, or some title equally *picturesque*. Of *Bosworth Field*, one book is finished, another just began. It will be a work of three or four years, and most probably never *conclude*. What would you say to some stanzas on Mount Hecla? they would be written at least with *fire*. How is

28

the immortal Bran? and the Phœnix of canine quadrupeds, Boatswain? I have lately purchased a thorough-bred bull-dog, worthy to be the coadjutor of the aforesaid celestials—his name is *Smut!*— 'Bear it, ye breezes, on your *balmy* wings.'

Write to me before I set off, I conjure you, by the fifth rib of your grandfather. Ridge goes on well with the books—I thought that worthy had not done much in the country. In town they have been very successful; Carpenter (Moore's publisher) told me a few days ago they sold all theirs immediately, and had several enquiries made since, which, from the books being gone, they could not supply. The Duke of York, the Marchioness of Headfort, the Duchess of Gordon, etc. etc., were among the purchasers; and Crosby says, the circulation will be still more extensive in the winter, the summer season being very bad for a sale, as most people are absent from London. However, they have gone off extremely well altogether. I shall pass very near you on my journey through Newark, but cannot approach. Don't tell this to Mrs. B., who supposes I travel a different road. If you have a letter, order it to be left at Ridge's shop, where I shall call, or the post-office, Newark, about six or eight in the evening. If your brother would ride over, I should be devilish glad to see him—he can return the same night, or sup with us and go home the next morning—the Kingston Arms is my inn.—Adieu, yours ever,

BYRON.

Trinity College, Cambridge
October 26, 1807.

xxiii   My dear Elizabeth,—Fatigued with sitting up
till four in the morning for the last two days at
hazard, I take up my pen to inquire how your
highness and the rest of my female acquaintance at
the seat of archiepiscopal grandeur go on. I know
I deserve a scolding for my negligence in not writing more frequently; but, racing up and down the
country for these last three months, how was it
possible to fulfil the duties of a correspondent?
Fixed at last for six weeks, I write, as *thin* as
ever (not having gained an ounce since my reduc-
tion), and rather in better humour;—but, after all,
Southwell was a detestable residence. Thank St.
Dominica, I have done with it: I have been twice
within eight miles of it, but could not prevail on
myself to *suffocate* in its heavy atmosphere. This
place is wretched enough—a villanous chaos of din
and drunkenness, nothing but hazard and burgundy,
hunting, mathematics, and Newmarket, riot and
racing. Yet it is a paradise compared with the
eternal dulness of Southwell. Oh! the misery of
doing nothing but make *love*, *enemies*, and *verses*.

Next January (but this is *entre nous* **only,** and pray
let it be so, or my maternal persecutor will be throw-
ing her tomahawk at any of my curious projects),
I am going to *sea* for four or five months, with my
cousin Captain Bettesworth, who commands the
Tartar, the finest frigate in the navy. I have seen

30

most scenes, and wish to look at a naval life. We are going probably to the Mediterranean, or to the West Indies, or—to the d——l; and if there is a possibility of taking me to the latter, Bettesworth will do it; for he has received four-and-twenty wounds in different places, and at this moment possesses a letter from the late Lord Nelson, stating Bettesworth as the only officer in the navy who had more wounds than himself.

I have got a new friend, the finest in the world, a *tame bear*. When I brought him here, they asked me what I meant to do with him, and my reply was, ' He should *sit for a fellowship.*' Sherard will explain the meaning of the sentence, if it is ambiguous. This answer delighted them not. We have several parties here, and this evening a large assortment of jockeys, gamblers, boxers, authors, parsons, and poets, sup with me,—a precious mixture, but they go on well together; and for me, I am a *spice* of everything except a jockey; by the by, I was dismounted again the other day.

Thank your brother in my name for his treatise. I have written 214 pages of a novel,—one poem of 380 lines, to be published (without my name) in a few weeks, with notes,—560 lines of *Bosworth Field*, and 250 lines of another poem in rhyme, besides half a dozen smaller pieces. The poem to be published is a Satire. *Apropos*, I have been praised to the skies in the *Critical Review*, and abused greatly in another publication. So much the better, they tell me, for the sale of the book; it keeps up controversy, and prevents it being forgotten.

Besides, the first men of all ages have had their share, nor do the humblest escape ;—so I bear it like a philosopher. It is odd, two opposite critiques came out on the same day ; and out of five pages of abuse, my censor only quotes *two lines* from different poems in support of his opinion. Now, the proper way to *cut up* is to quote long passages, and make them appear absurd, because simple allegation is no proof, On the other hand, there are seven pages of praise, and more than *my modesty* will allow, said on the subject. Adieu.

P.S.—Write, write, write ! ! !

TO THE REV. HENRY DRURY

Dorant's Hotel, Jan. 13, 1808.

xxiv My dear Sir,—Though the stupidity of my ser-vants, or the porter of the house, in not showing you upstairs (where I should have joined you directly), prevented me the pleasure of seeing you yesterday, I hoped to meet you at some public place in the evening. However, my stars decreed otherwise, as they generally do, when I have any favour to request of them. I think you would have been surprised at my figure, for, since our last meeting, I am reduced four stone in weight. I then weighed fourteen stone seven pounds, and now only *ten stone and a half.* I have disposed of my *superfluities* by means of hard exercise and abstinence.

Should your Harrow engagements allow you to visit town between this and February, I shall be most happy to see you in Albemarle Street. If I

am not so fortunate, I shall endeavour to join you
for an afternoon at Harrow, though, I fear, your
cellar will by no means contribute to my cure. As
for my worthy preceptor, Dr. B., our encounter would
by no means prevent the *mutual endearments* he and
I were wont to lavish on each other. We have only
spoken once since my departure from Harrow in
1805, and then he politely told Tatersall I was not
a proper associate for his pupils. This was long
before my strictures in verse; but, in plain *prose*,
had I been some years older, I should have held
my tongue on his perfections. But, being laid on
my back, when that schoolboy thing was written—
or rather dictated—expecting to rise no more, my
physician having taken his sixteenth fee, and I his
prescription, I could not quit this earth without
leaving a memento of my constant attachment to
Butler in gratitude for his manifold good offices.

I meant to have been down in July; but thinking
my appearance, immediately after the publication,
would be construed into an insult, I directed my steps
elsewhere. Besides, I heard that some of the boys
had got hold of my *Libellus*, contrary to my wishes
certainly, for I never transmitted a single copy till
October, when I gave one to a boy, since gone, after
repeated importunities. You will, I trust, pardon
this egotism. As you had touched on the subject,
I thought some explanation necessary. Defence I
shall not attempt, '*Hic murus aheneus esto, nil con-
scire sibi*'—and 'so on' (as Lord Baltimore said on
his trial for a rape)—I have been so long at Trinity
as to forget the conclusion of the line; but though

I cannot finish my quotation, I will my letter, and entreat you to believe me, gratefully and affectionately, etc.

P.S.—I will not lay a tax on your time by requiring an answer, lest you say, as Butler said to Tatersall (when I had written his reverence an impudent epistle on the expression before mentioned), viz. 'that I wanted to draw him into a correspondence.'

TO MR. DALLAS

Dorant's Hotel, Albemarle Street,
Jan. 20, 1808.

xxv Sir,—Your letter was not received till this morning, I presume from being addressed to me in Notts, where I have not resided since last June; and as the date is the 6th, you will excuse the delay of my answer.

If the little volume you mention has given pleasure to the author of *Percival* and *Aubrey*, I am sufficiently repaid by his praise. Though our periodical censors have been uncommonly lenient, I confess a tribute from a man of acknowledged genius is still more flattering. But I am afraid I should forfeit all claim to candour, if I did not decline such praise as I do not deserve; and this is, I am sorry to say, the case in the present instance.

My compositions speak for themselves, and must stand or fall by their own worth or demerit: *thus far* I feel highly gratified by your favourable opinion. But my pretensions to virtue are unluckily so few, that though I should be happy to merit, I cannot accept your applause in that respect. One passage

34

in your letter struck me forcibly : you mention the two Lords Lyttleton in the manner they respectively deserve, and will be surprised to hear the person who is now addressing you has been frequently compared to the *latter*. I know I am injuring myself in your esteem by this avowal, but the circumstance was so remarkable from your observation, that I cannot help relating the fact. The events of my short life have been of so singular a nature, that, though the pride commonly called honour has, and I trust ever will, prevent me from disgracing my name by a mean or cowardly action, I have been already held up as the votary of licentiousness, and the disciple of infidelity. How far justice may have dictated this accusation, I cannot pretend to say ; but, like the *gentleman* to whom my religious friends, in the warmth of their charity, have already devoted me, I am made worse than I really am. However, to quit myself (the worst theme I could pitch upon), and return to my poems, I cannot sufficiently express my thanks, and I hope I shall some day have an opportunity of rendering them in person. A second edition is now in the press, with some additions and considerable omissions ; you will allow me to present you with a copy. The *Critical, Monthly*, and *Anti-Jacobin Reviews* have been very indulgent ; but the *Eclectic* has pronounced a furious Philippic, not against the *book* but the *author*, where you will find all I have mentioned asserted by a reverend divine who wrote the critique.

Your name and connection with our family have been long known to me, and I hope your person will be not less so : you will find me an excellent compound of a 'Brainless' and a 'Stanhope.' I am afraid you will hardly be able to read this, for my hand is almost as bad as my character; but you will find me, as legibly as possible, your obliged and obedient servant, BYRON.

TO MR. DALLAS

Dorant's, January 21, 1808.

xxvi Sir,—Whenever leisure and inclination permit me the pleasure of a visit, I shall feel truly gratified in a personal acquaintance with one whose mind has been long known to me in his writings.

You are so far correct in your conjecture, that I am a member of the University of Cambridge, where I shall take my degree of A.M. this term; but were reasoning, eloquence, or virtue, the objects of my search, Granta is not their metropolis, nor is the place of her situation an *El Dorado*, far less an Utopia. The intellects of her children are as stagnant as her Cam, and their pursuits limited to the church—not of Christ, but of the nearest benefice.

As to my reading, I believe I may aver, without hyperbole, it has been tolerably extensive in the historical department; so that few nations exist, or have existed, with whose records I am not in some degree acquainted, from Herodotus down to Gibbon. Of the classics, I know about as much as most school-boys after a discipline of thirteen years; of the law of the land as much as enables me to keep 'within the statute'—to use the poacher's vocabulary. I did study the *Spirit of Laws* and the *Laws of Nations*; but when I saw the latter violated every

36

month, I gave up my attempts at so useless an accomplishment:—of geography, I have seen more land on maps than I should wish to traverse on foot;—of mathematics, enough to give me the headache without clearing the part affected;—of philosophy, astronomy, and metaphysicks, more than I can comprehend; and of common sense so little, that I mean to leave a Byronian prize at each of our *Almæ Matres* for the first discovery,—though I rather fear that of the longitude will precede it.

I once thought myself a philosopher, and talked nonsense with great decorum: I defied pain, and preached up equanimity. For some time this did very well, for no one was in *pain* for me but my friends, and none lost their patience but my hearers. At last, a fall from my horse convinced me bodily suffering was an evil; and the worst of an argument overset my maxims and my temper at the same moment: so I quitted Zeno for Aristippus, and conceive that pleasure constitutes the τὸ καλόν. In morality, I prefer Confucius to the Ten Commandments, and Socrates to St. Paul, though the two latter agree in their opinion of marriage. In religion, I favour the Catholic emancipation, but I do not acknowledge the Pope: and I have refused to take the sacrament, because I do not think eating bread or drinking wine from the hand of an earthly vicar will make me an inheritor of heaven. I hold virtue, in general, or the virtues severally, to be only in the disposition, each a *feeling*, not a principle. I believe truth the prime attribute of the Deity, and death an eternal sleep, at least of the body. You have here a brief compendium of the sentiments of the *wicked* George Lord Byron; and, till I get a new suit, you will perceive I am badly cloathed.—I remain, etc.

TO MR. HARNESS

Dorant's Hotel, Albemarle Street,
Feb. 11, 1808.

xxvii   My dear Harness,—As I had no opportunity of returning my verbal thanks, I trust you will accept my written acknowledgments for the compliment you were pleased to pay some production of my unlucky muse last November,—I am induced to do this not less from the pleasure I feel in the praise of an old school-fellow, than from justice to you, for I had heard the story with some slight variations. Indeed, when we met this morning, Wingfield had not undeceived me; but he will tell you that I displayed no resentment in mentioning what I had heard, though I was not sorry to discover the truth. Perhaps you hardly recollect, some years ago, a short, though, for the time, a warm friendship between us. Why it was not of longer duration I know not. I have still a gift of yours in my possession, that must always prevent me from forgetting it. I also remember being favoured with the perusal of many of your compositions, and several other circumstances very pleasant in their day, which I will not force upon your memory, but entreat you to believe me, with much regret at their short continuance, and a hope they are not irrevocable,— Yours very sincerely, etc.,   BYRON.

TO MR. BECHER

TO MR. BECHER

Dorant's Hotel, Feb. 26, 1808.

My dear Becher,—Now for Apollo. I am happy *xxviii* that you still retain your predilection, and that the public allow me some share of praise. I am of so much importance that a most violent attack is preparing for me in the next number of the *Edinburgh Review*. This I had from the authority of a friend who has seen the proof and manuscript of the critique. You know the system of the Edinburgh gentlemen is universal attack. They praise none ; and neither the public nor the author expects praise from them. It is, however, something to be noticed, as they profess to pass judgment only on works requiring the public attention. You will see this when it comes out ;—it is, I understand, of the most unmerciful description ; but I am aware of it, and hope *you* will not be hurt by its severity.

Tell Mrs. Byron not to be out of humour with them, and to prepare her mind for the greatest hostility on their part. It will do no injury whatever, and I trust her mind will not be ruffled. They defeat their object by indiscriminate abuse, and they never praise except the partisans of Lord Holland and Co. It is nothing to be abused when Southey, Moore, Lauderdale, Strangford, and Payne Knight share the same fate.

I am sorry—but *Childish Recollections* must be suppressed during this edition. I have altered, at your suggestion, the *obnoxious allusions* in the sixth stanza of my last ode.

LETTERS

And now, my dear Becher, I must return my best acknowledgments for the interest you have taken in me and my poetical bantlings, and I shall ever be proud to show how much I esteem the *advice* and the *adviser.*—Believe me most truly, etc.

TO MR. BECHER

Dorant's, March 28, 1808.

xxix   I have lately received a copy of the new edition from Ridge, and it is high time for me to return my best thanks to you, for the trouble you have taken in the superintendence. This I do most sincerely, and only regret that Ridge has not seconded you as I could wish,—at least, in the bindings, paper, etc., of the copy he sent to me. Perhaps those for the public may be more respectable in such articles.

You have seen the *Edinburgh Review*, of course. I regret that Mrs. Byron is so much annoyed. For my own part, these 'paper bullets of the brain' have only taught me to stand fire ; and, as I have been lucky enough upon the whole, my repose and appetite are not discomposed. Pratt, the gleaner, author, poet, etc. etc., addressed a long rhyming epistle to me on the subject, by way of consolation ; but it was not well done, so I do not send it, though the name of the man might make it go down. The E. R^s. have not performed their task well ; at least the literati tell me this ; and I think *I* could write a more sarcastic critique on *myself* than any yet published. For instance, instead of the remark,—ill-natured enough, but not keen,—about Macpherson, I (*quoad* Reviewers)

40

could have said, 'Alas, this imitation only proves the assertion of Dr. Johnson, that many men, women, and *children*, could write such poetry as Ossian's.'

I am *thin* and in exercise. During the spring or summer I trust we shall meet. I hear Lord Ruthyn leaves Newstead in April. As soon as he quits it for ever, I wish much you would take a ride over, survey the mansion, and give me your candid opinion on the most advisable mode of proceeding with regard to the *house*. *Entre nous*, I am cursedly dipped; my debts, *every* thing inclusive, will be nine or ten thousand before I am twenty-one. But I have reason to think my property will turn out better than general expectation may conceive. Of Newstead I have little hope or care; but Hanson, my agent, intimated my Lancashire property was worth three Newsteads. I believe we have it hollow; though the defendants are protracting the surrender, if possible, till after my majority, for the purpose of forming some arrangement with me, thinking I shall probably prefer a sum in hand to a reversion. Newstead I may *sell*;—perhaps I will not,—though of that more anon. I will come down in May or June.—Yours most truly, etc.

TO MR. BECHER

Newstead Abbey, Notts, September 14, 1808.

My dear Becher,—I am much obliged to you for *xxx* your inquiries, and shall profit by them accordingly. I am going to get up a play here; the hall will constitute a most admirable theatre. I have settled the *dram. pers.*, and can do without ladies, as I have

some young friends who will make tolerable substi-
tutes for females, and we only want three male
characters, beside Mr. Hobhouse and myself, for the
play we have fixed on, which will be the *Revenge*.
Pray direct Nicholson the carpenter to come over to
me immediately, and inform me what day you will
dine and pass the night here.—Believe me, etc.

TO MR. JACKSON
N. A., Notts, September 18, 1808.

xxxi Dear Jack,—I wish you would inform me what has
been done by Jekyll, at No 40 Sloane Square, concerning the pony I returned as unsound.

I have also to request you will call on Louch at
Brompton, and inquire what the devil he meant by
sending such an insolent letter to me at Brighton;
and at the same time tell him I by no means can
comply with the charge he has made for things pre-
tended to be damaged.

Ambrose behaved most scandalously about the
pony. You may tell Jekyll if he does not refund the
money, I shall put the affair into my lawyer's hands.
Five-and-twenty guineas is a sound price for a pony,
and by ——, if it costs me five hundred pounds, I
will make an example of Mr. Jekyll, and that immediately, unless the cash is returned.—Believe me,
dear Jack, etc.

TO MR. JACKSON
N. A., Notts, October 4, 1808.

xxxii You will make as good a bargain as possible with
this Master Jekyll, if he is not a gentleman. If he is

a *gentleman*, inform me, for I shall take very different steps. If he is not, you must get what you can of the money, for I have too much business on hand at present to commence an action. Besides, Ambrose is the man who ought to refund,—but I have done with him. You can settle with L. out of the balance, and dispose of the bidets, etc., as you best can.

I should be very glad to see you here; but the house is filled with workmen, and undergoing a thorough repair. I hope, however, to be more fortunate before many months have elapsed.

If you see Bold Webster, remember me to him, and tell him I have to regret Sydney, who has perished, I fear, in my rabbit warren, for we have seen nothing of him for the last fortnight.—Adieu.—Believe me, etc.

TO THE HONOURABLE MRS. BYRON

Newstead Abbey, Notts, October 7, 1808.

Dear Madam,—I have no beds for the H——'s xxxiii or anybody else at present. The H——'s sleep at Mansfield. I do not know that I resemble Jean Jacques Rousseau. I have no ambition to be like so illustrious a madman—but this I know, that I shall live in my own manner, and as much alone as possible. When my rooms are ready I shall be glad to see you: at present it would be improper, and uncomfortable to both parties. You can hardly object to my rendering my mansion habitable, notwithstanding my departure for Persia in March (or May at farthest), since *you* will be *tenant* till my return; and in case of any accident (for I have already arranged my will to be drawn up the moment I am twenty-one), I have taken care you shall have the house and manor for *life*, besides a sufficient income. So you see my improvements are not entirely selfish. As I have a friend here, we will go to the Infirmary Ball on the 12th; we will drink tea with Mrs. Byron at eight o'clock, and expect to see you at the ball. If that lady will allow us a couple of rooms to dress in, we shall be highly obliged;— if we are at the ball by ten or eleven, it will be time enough, and we shall return to Newstead about three or four. Adieu.—Believe me, yours very truly,

BYRON.

TO THE HONOURABLE MRS. BYRON

Newstead Abbey, November 2, 1808.

xxxiv Dear Mother,—If you please, we will forget the things you mention. I have no desire to remember them. When my rooms are finished, I shall be happy to see you; as I tell but the truth, you will not suspect me of evasion. I am furnishing the house more for you than myself, and I shall establish you in it before I sail for India, which I expect to do in March, if nothing particularly obstructive occurs. I am now fitting up the *green* drawing-room; the red for a bedroom, and the rooms over as sleeping-rooms. They will be soon completed;—at least I hope so.

I wish you would inquire of Major Watson (who is an old Indian) what things will be necessary to pro-

44

vide for my voyage. I have already procured a
friend to write to the Arabic Professor at Cambridge
for some information I am anxious to procure. I
can easily get letters from Government to the ambassadors, consuls, etc., and also to the governors at
Calcutta and Madras. I shall place my property and
my will in the hands of trustees till my return, and I
mean to appoint you one. From Hanson I have
heard nothing—when I do, you shall have the particulars.

After all, you must own my project is not a bad
one. If I do not travel now, I never shall, and all
men should one day or other. I have at present no
connections to keep me at home ; no wife, no un-
provided sisters, brothers, etc. I shall take care of
you, and when I return I may possibly become a
politician. A few years' knowledge of other countries
than our own will not incapacitate me for that part.
If we see no nation but our own, we do not give
mankind a fair chance; it is from *experience*, not
books, we ought to judge of them. There is nothing
like inspection, and trusting to our own senses.—
Yours, etc.

TO MR. HODGSON

Newstead Abbey, Notts, Nov. 3, 1808.

My dear Hodgson,—I expected to have heard ere *xxxv*
this the event of your interview with the mysterious
Mr. Haynes, my volunteer correspondent. However,
as I had no business to trouble you with the adjust-
ment of my concerns with that illustrious stranger,
I have no right to complain of your silence.

LETTERS

You have of course seen Drury, in all the pleasing palpitations of anticipated wedlock. Well! he has still something to look forward to, and his present extacies are certainly enviable. ' Peace be with him and with his spirit,' and his flesh also, at least just now. . . .

Hobhouse and your humble are still here. Hobhouse hunts, etc., and I do nothing; we dined the other day with a neighbouring Esquire (not Collet of Staines), and regretted your absence, as the Bouquet of Staines was scarcely to be compared to our last ' feast of reason.' You know, laughing is the sign of a rational animal; so says Dr. Smollett. I think so too, but unluckily my spirits don't always keep pace with my opinions. I had not so much scope for risibility the other day as I could have wished, for I was seated near a woman, to whom, when a boy, I was as much attached as boys generally are, and more than a man should be. I knew this before I went, and was determined to be valiant, and converse with *sang froid*; but instead I forgot my valour and my nonchalance, and never opened my lips even to laugh, far less to speak, and the lady was almost as absurd as myself, which made both the object of more observation than if we had conducted ourselves with easy indifference. You will think all this great nonsense; if you had seen it, you would have thought it still more ridiculous. What fools we are! We cry for a plaything, which, like children, we are never satisfied till we break open, though like them we cannot get rid of it by putting it in the fire.

TO MR. HODGSON

I have tried for Gifford's *Epistle to Pindar*, and the bookseller says the copies were cut up for *waste paper*; if you can procure me a copy I shall be much obliged.—Adieu.—Believe me, my dear Sir, yours ever sincerely.

TO MR. HODGSON

Newstead Abbey, Notts, Nov. 27, 1808.

My dear Sir,—Boatswain is to be buried in a vault xxxvi waiting for myself. I have also written an epitaph, which I would send, were it not for two reasons: one is, that it is too long for a letter; and the other, that I hope you will some day read it on the spot where it will be engraved.

You discomfort me with the intelligence of the real orthodoxy of the ' Arch-fiend's' name, but alas! it must stand with me at present; if ever I have an opportunity of correcting, I shall liken him to Geoffrey of Monmouth, a noted liar in his way, and perhaps a more correct prototype than the Carnifex of James II.

I do not think the composition of your poem 'a sufficing reason' for not keeping your promise of a Christmas visit. Why not come? I will never disturb you in your moments of inspiration; and if you wish to collect any materials for the *scenery*, Hardwicke (where Mary was confined for several years) is not eight miles distant, and, independent of the interest you must take in it as her vindicator, is a most beautiful and venerable object of curiosity. I shall take it very ill if you do not come; my mansion is improving in comfort, and, when you require solitude, I shall have an apartment devoted to the purpose of receiving your poetical reveries.

I have heard from our Drury ; he says little of the Row, which I regret : indeed I would have sacrificed much to have contributed in any way (as a school-boy) to its consummation ; but Butler survives, and thirteen boys have been expelled in vain. Davies is not here, but Hobhouse hunts as usual, and your humble servant 'drags at each remove a lengthened chain.' I have heard from his Grace of Portland on the subject of my expedition : he talks of diffi-culties ; by the gods ! if he throws any in my way I will next session ring such a peal in his ears,

> That he shall wish the fiery Dane
> Had rather been his guest again.

You do not tell me if Gifford is really my com-mentator : it is too good to be true, for I know nothing would gratify my vanity so much as the reality ; even the idea is too precious to part with.

I still expect you here ; let me have no more excuses. Hobhouse desires his best remembrance. We are now lingering over our evening potations. I have extended my letter further than I ought, and beg you will excuse it ; on the opposite page I send you some stanzas I wrote off on being questioned by a former flame as to my motives for quitting this country. You are the first reader. Hobhouse hates everything of the kind, therefore I do not show them to him. Adieu !—Believe me yours very sincerely,

BYRON.

TO MR. JACKSON.

N. A., Notts, December 12, 1808.

My dear Jack,—You will get the greyhound from *xxxvii* the owner at any price, and as many more of the same breed (male or female) as you can collect.

Tell D'Egville his dress shall be returned—I am obliged to him for the pattern. I am sorry you should have so much trouble, but I was not aware of the difficulty of procuring the animals in question. I shall have finished part of my mansion in a few weeks, and if you can pay me a visit at Christmas, I shall be very glad to see you.—Believe me, etc.

TO MR. HODGSON

Newstead Abbey, Notts, Dec. 17, 1808.

My dear Hodgson,—I have just received your *xxxviii* letter, and one from B. Drury, which I would send, were it not too bulky to despatch within a sheet of paper; but I must impart the contents and consign the answer to your care. In the first place, I cannot address the answer to him, because the epistle is without date or direction; and in the next, the contents are so singular that I can scarce believe my optics, ' which are made the fools of the other senses, or else worth all the rest.'

A few weeks ago, I wrote to our friend Harry Drury of facetious memory, to request he would prevail on his brother at Eton to receive the son of a citizen of London well known unto me as a

pupil; the family having been particularly polite
during the short time I was with them, induced me
to this application. 'Now mark what follows,' as
somebody or Southey sublimely saith : on this day,
the 17th December, arrives an epistle signed B.
Drury, containing not the smallest reference to tuition
or *in*tuition, but a *petition* for *Robert Gregson*, of
pugilistic notoriety, now in bondage for certain
paltry pounds sterling, and liable to take up his everlasting abode in Banco Regis.   Had this letter been
from any of my *lay* acquaintance, or, in short, from
any person but the gentleman whose signature it
bears, I should have marvelled not.   If Drury is
serious I congratulate pugilism on the acquisition
of such a patron, and shall be happy to advance
any sum necessary for the liberation of the captive
Gregson ; but I certainly hope to be certified from
you or some reputable housekeeper of the fact, before
I write to Drury on the subject.   When I say the *fact* I
mean of the *letter* being written by *Drury*, not having
any doubt as to the authenticity of the statement.
The letter is now before me, and I keep it for your
perusal.   When I hear from you I shall address my
answer to him, under *your care* ; for as it is now the
vacation at Eton, and the letter is without *time* or
place, I cannot venture to consign my sentiments on
so *momentous* a *concern* to chance.

To you, my dear Hodgson, I have not much to
say. If you can make it convenient or pleasant to
trust yourself here, be assured it will be both to me.

50

Reddish's Hotel, Jan. 25, 1809.

My dear Sir,—My only reason for not adopting xxxix
your lines is because they are *your* lines. You will
recollect what Lady Wortley Montague said to Pope:
'No touching, for the good will be given to you, and
the bad attributed to me.' I am determined it shall
be all my own, except such alterations as may be
absolutely requisite; but I am much obliged by the
trouble you have taken, and your good opinion.

The couplet on Lord C. may be scratched out,
and the following inserted:

> Roscommon! Sheffield! with your spirits fled,
> No future laurels deck a noble head.
> Nor e'en a hackney'd Muse will deign to smile
> On minor Byron, nor mature Carlisle.

This will answer the purpose of concealment. Now,
for some couplets on Mr. Crabbe, which you may
place after 'Gifford, Sotheby, M'Neil':

> There be who say, in these enlighten'd days,
> That splendid lies are all the Poet's praise;
> That strain'd invention, ever on the wing,
> Alone impels the modern Bard to sing.
> 'Tis true that all who rhyme, nay, all who write,
> Shrink from that fatal word to genius, trite:
> Yet Truth will sometimes lend her noblest fires,
> And decorate the verse herself inspires.
> This fact in Virtue's name let Crabbe attest;
> Though Nature's sternest painter, yet the best.

I am sorry to differ with you with regard to the

title, but I mean to retain it with this addition : *The (British) English Bards and Scotch Reviewers* ; and, if we call it a *Satire*, it will obviate the objection, as the Bards also were Welch. Your title is too humorous ;—and as I know a little of ——, I wish not to embroil myself with him, though I do not commend his treatment of ——.

I shall be glad to hear from you, or see you, and beg you to believe me yours very sincerely,

BYRON.

TO MR. DALLAS

February 7, 1809.

xl   My dear Sir,—Suppose we have this couplet—

> Though sweet the sound, disdain a borrow'd tone,
> Resign Achaia's lyre, and strike your own :

or,

> Though soft the echo, scorn a borrow'd tone,
> Resign Achaia's lyre, and strike your own.

So much for your admonitions ; but my note of notes, my solitary pun, must not be given up—no, rather

> ' Let mightiest of all the beasts of chace
> That roam in woody Caledon '

come against me ; my annotation must stand.

We shall never sell a thousand ; then why print so many? Did you receive my yesterday's note? I am troubling you, but I am apprehensive some of the

TO MR. DALLAS

lines are omitted by your young amanuensis, to whom, however, I am infinitely obliged.—Believe me, yours very truly, Byron.

February 11, 1809.

I wish you to call, if possible, as I have some *xli* alterations to suggest as to the part about Brougham.

B.

TO MR. DALLAS

February 12, 1809.

Excuse the trouble, but I have added two lines *xlii* which are necessary to complete the poetical character of Lord Carlisle :—   B.

> . . . . . in his age
> His scenes alone had damn'd our sinking stage ;
> But Managers for once cried, ' hold, enough !'
> Nor drugg'd their audience with the tragic stuff.

—Yours, etc.,   B.

TO MR. DALLAS

February 15, 1809.

I wish you much to call on me, about *One*, not *xliii* later, if convenient, as I have some thirty or forty lines for addition.—Believe me, etc.

February 16, 1809.

xliv   *Ecce iterum Crispinus !*—I send you some lines to be placed after ' Gifford, Sotheby, M'Neil.' Pray call to-morrow any time before two, and believe me, etc.,

B.

P.S.—Print soon, or I shall overflow with more rhyme.

TO MR. DALLAS

February 19, 1809.

xlv   I enclose some lines to be inserted, the first six after ' Lords too are bards, etc.,' or rather immediately following the line :

' Ah ! who would take their titles with their rhymes.'

The four next will wind up the panegyric on Lord Carlisle, and come after 'tragic stuff.'—Yours truly,

> In these our times with daily wonders big,
> A letter'd Peer is like a letter'd Pig :
> Both know their alphabet, but who from thence
> Infers that Peers or Pigs have manly sense ?
> Still less that such should woo the graceful Nine ?
> Parnassus was not made for Lords and Swine.
> Roscommon, Sheffield, etc., etc.
>
>   *   *   *   *   *   *
>
> .   .   .   .   .   .   tragic stuff.

TO MRS. BYRON

Yet at their judgment let his Lordship laugh,
And case his volumes in congenial calf:
Yes, doff that covering where morocco shines,
'And hang a calf-skin on those recreant' lines.

TO MR. DALLAS

February 22, 1809.

A cut at the opera.—*Ecce signum !* from last night's xlvi
observation, and inuendos against the Society for the
suppression of Vice. The lines will come well in
after the couplets concerning Naldi and Catalani.—
Yours truly,   BYRON.

TO THE HONOURABLE MRS. BYRON

8 *St. James's Street, March* 6, 1809.

Dear Mother,—My last letter was written under xlvii
great depression of spirits from poor Falkland's
death, who has left without a shilling four children
and his wife. I have been endeavouring to assist
them, which, God knows, I cannot do as I could
wish, from my own embarrassments and the many
claims upon me from other quarters.

What you say is all very true: come what may,
Newstead and I *stand* or fall together. I have now
lived on the spot, I have fixed my heart upon it, and
no pressure, present or future, shall induce me to
barter the last vestige of our inheritance. I have
that pride within me which will enable me to
support difficulties. I can endure privations; but

could I obtain in exchange for Newstead Abbey the first fortune in the country, I would reject the proposition. Set your mind at ease on that score; Mr. Hanson talks like a man of business on the subject, —I feel like a man of honour, and I will not sell Newstead.

I shall get my seat on the return of the affidavits from Carhais, in Cornwall, and will do something in the House soon : I must dash, or it is all over. My Satire must be kept secret for a *month* ; after that you may say what you please on the subject. Lord Carlisle has used me infamously, and refused to state any particulars of my family to the Chancellor. I have *lashed* him in my rhymes, and perhaps his lordship may regret not being more conciliatory. They tell me it will have a sale ; I hope so, for the bookseller has behaved well, as far as publishing well goes.—Believe me, etc.

P.S.—You shall have a mortgage on one of the farms.

TO MR. HARNESS

8 *St. James's Street, March* 18, 1809.

xlviii There was no necessity for your excuses : if you have time and inclination to write, 'for what we receive, the Lord make us thankful,'—if I do not hear from you, I console myself with the idea that you are much more agreeably employed.

I send down to you by this post a certain Satire

lately published, and in return for the three and sixpence expenditure upon it, only beg that if you should guess the author, you will keep his name secret; at least for the present. London is full of the Duke's business. The Commons have been at it these last three nights, and are not yet come to a decision. I do not know if the affair will be brought before our House, unless in the shape of an impeachment. If it makes its appearance in a debatable form, I believe I shall be tempted to say something on the subject.—I am glad to hear you like Cambridge: firstly, because, to know that you are happy is pleasant to one who wishes you all possible sublunary enjoyment; and, secondly, I admire the morality of the sentiment. *Alma Mater* was to me *injusta noverca*; and the old beldam only gave me my M.A. degree because she could not avoid it.—You know what a farce a noble Cantab. must perform.

I am going abroad, if possible, in the spring, and before I depart I am collecting the pictures of my most intimate schoolfellows; I have already a few, and shall want yours, or my cabinet will be incomplete. I have employed one of the first miniature painters of the day to take them, of course, at my own expense, as I never allow my acquaintance to incur the least expenditure to gratify a whim of mine. To mention this may seem indelicate; but when I tell you a friend of ours first refused to sit, under the idea that he was to disburse on the occasion, you will see that it is necessary to state these preliminaries to prevent the recurrence of any similar mistake. I shall see you in time, and will carry you to the *limner*. It will be a tax on your patience for a week; but pray excuse it, as it is possible the resemblance may be the sole trace I shall be able to preserve of our past friendship and acquaintance. Just now it seems foolish enough; but in a few years, when some of us are dead, and others are separated by inevitable circumstances, it will be a kind of satisfaction to retain in these images of the living the idea of our former selves, and to contemplate, in the resemblances of the dead, all that remains of judgment, feeling, and a host of passions. But all this will be dull enough for you, and so good-night; and to end my chapter. or rather my homily, believe me, my dear H., yours most affectionately.

TO MR. DALLAS

April 25, 1809.

xlix   Dear Sir,—I am just arrived at Batt's Hotel, Jermyn Street, St. James's, from Newstead, and shall be very glad to see you when convenient or agreeable. Hobhouse is on his way up to town, full of printing resolution, and proof against criticism.—Believe me, with great sincerity, yours truly,

BYRON.

TO MRS. BYRON

Falmouth, June 22, 1809.

Dear Mother,—I am about to sail in a few days; *t* probably before this reaches you. Fletcher begged so hard, that I have continued him in my service. If he does not behave well abroad, I will send him back in a *transport.* I have a German servant (who has been with Mr. Wilbraham in Persia before, and was strongly recommended to me by Dr. Butler of Harrow), Robert, and William; they constitute my whole suite. I have letters in plenty:—you shall hear from me at the different ports I touch upon; but you must not be alarmed if my letters miscarry. The Continent is in a fine state—an insurrection has broken out at Paris, and the Austrians are beating Buonaparte—the Tyrolese have risen.

There is a picture of me in oil, to be sent down to Newstead soon.—I wish the Miss Pigots had something better to do than carry my miniatures to Nottingham to copy. Now they have done it, you may ask them to copy the others, which are greater favourites than my own. As to money matters, I am ruined—at least till Rochdale is sold; and if that does not turn out well, I shall enter into the Austrian or Russian service—perhaps the Turkish, if I like their manners. The world is all before me, and I leave England without regret, and without a wish to revisit any thing it contains, except *yourself* and your present residence.—Believe me, yours ever sincerely.

P.S.—Pray tell Mr. Rushton his son is well, and doing well; so is Murray, indeed better than I ever saw him; he will be back in about a month. I ought to add the leaving Murray to my few regrets, as his age perhaps will prevent my seeing him again. Robert I take with me; I like him, because, like myself, he seems a friendless animal.

TO THE REV. DR. DRURY

Falmouth, June 25, 1809.

li   My dear Drury,—We sail to-morrow in the Lisbon packet, having been detained till noon by the lack of wind and other necessaries. These being at last procured, by this time to-morrow evening we shall be embarked on the vide vorld of vaters, vor all the vorld like Robinson Crusoe. The Malta vessel not sailing for some weeks, we have determined to go by way of Lisbon, and, as my servants term it, to see 'that there *Portingale*'; thence to Cadiz and Gibraltar, and so on our old route to Malta and Constantinople; if so be that Captain Kidd, our gallant, or rather gallows, commander understands plain sailing and Mercator, and takes us on our voyage all according to the chart. . . . Will you tell Dr. Butler that I have taken the treasure of a servant, Friese, the native of Prussia Proper, into my service from his recommendation? He has been all among the worshippers of Fire in Persia, and has seen Persepolis and all that.

Hobhouse has made woundy preparations for a

TO MR. HODGSON

book at his return; 100 pens, two gallons Japan Ink,
and several volumes best blank is no bad provision
for a discerning public. I have laid down my pen,
but have promised to contribute a chapter on the
state of morals, and a further treatise on the same
to be intituled '. . . *Simplified, or . . . Proved to be
Praiseworthy from Ancient Authors aud Modern
Practice.*'

Hobhouse further hopes to indemnify himself in
Turkey for a life of exemplary chastity at home
by . . . the whole Divan. Pray buy his missellingany, as the Printer's Devil calls it. I suppose 'tis
in print by this time. Providence has interposed in
our favour with a fair wind to carry us out of its
reach, or he would have hired a Faqui to translate
it into the Turcoman Lingo.

> The Cock is crowing
> I must be going
> And can no more.
> *Ghost of Gaffer Thumb.*

Adieu.—Believe me yours as in duty bound.

P.S.—We have been sadly fleabitten at Falmouth.

TO MR. HODGSON

Falmouth, June 25, 1809.

Before this reaches you, Hobhouse, two officers' *lii*
wives, three children, two waiting-maids, ditto subal-
terns for the troops, three Portuguese esquires, and
domestics, in all nineteen souls, will have sailed in

61

the Lisbon packet with the noble Captain Kidd, as
gallant commander as ever smuggled an anker of
right Nantz. We are going to Lisbon first, because
the Malta packet has sailed, d'ye see? from Lisbon
to Gibraltar, Malta, Constantinople, and 'all that,'
as Orator Henley said when he put the Church and
'all that' in danger.

This town of Falmouth, as you will partly conjecture, is no great way from the sea. It is defended on
the sea-side by tway castles, St. Mawes and Pendennis,
extremely well calculated for annoying everybody
except an enemy. St. Mawes is garrisoned by an able-
bodied person of fourscore, a widower. He has the
whole command and sole management of six most
unmanageable pieces of ordnance, admirably adapted
for the destruction of Pendennis, a like tower of
strength on the opposite side of the channel. We
have seen St. Mawes, but Pendennis they will not
let us behold, save at a distance, because Hobhouse
and I are suspected of having already taken St.
Mawes by a *coup de main.*

The town contains many Quakers and salt fish;
the oysters have a taste of copper, owing to the soil
of a mining country; the women (blessed be the
corporation therefor) are flogged at the cart's tail
when they pick and steal, as happened to one of
the fair sex yesterday noon. She was pertinacious
in her behaviour, and damned the mayor.

This is all I know of Falmouth, nothing of note
occurred in our way down, except that on Hartford
Bridge we changed horses at an inn, where the great
apostle of pederastry, Beckford, sojourned for the

night. We tried in vain to see the martyr of prejudice, but could not. What we thought singular,
though you perhaps will not, was that Ld Courtney
travelled the same night on the same road, only one
stage *behind* him.

Hodgson, remember me to the Drury, and remember
me to yourself when drunk. I am not worth a sober
thought. Look to my satire at Cawthorn's, Cockspur
Street, and look to the Miscellany of the Hobhouse.
It has pleased Providence to interfere in behalf of a
suffering public by giving him a sprained wrist, so that
he cannot write, and there is a cessation of ink-shed.

I don't know when I can write again, because it
depends on that experienced navigator, Captain
Kidd, and the 'stormy winds that (don't) blow' at
this season. I leave England without regret, I shall
return to it without pleasure. I am like Adam, the
first convict, sentenced to transportation, but I have
no Eve, and have eaten no apple but what was sour
as a crab; and thus ends my first chapter.

TO MR. HODGSON

Lisbon, July 16, 1809.

Thus far have we pursued our route, and seen all *liii*
sorts of marvellous sights, palaces, convents, etc.;—
which, being to be heard in my friend Hobhouse's
forthcoming *Book of Travels*, I shall not anticipate
by smuggling any account whatsoever to you in a
private and clandestine manner. I must just observe,
that the village of Cintra in Estremadura is the most
beautiful, perhaps, in the world.

LETTERS

I am very happy here, because I loves oranges, and talks bad Latin to the monks, who understand it, as it is like their own,—and I goes into society (with my pocket-pistols), and I swims in the Tagus all across at once, and I rides on an ass or a mule, and swears Portuguese, and have got a diarrhœa and bites from the musquitoes. But what of that? Comfort must not be expected by folks that go a-pleasuring.

When the Portuguese are pertinacious, I say, *Carracho!*—the great oath of the grandees, that very well supplies the place of 'Damme,'—and when dissatisfied with my neighbour, I pronounce him *Ambra di merdo*. With these two phrases, and a third, *Avra bouro*, which signifieth 'Get an ass,' I am universally understood to be a person of degree and a master of languages. How merrily we lives that travellers be!—if we had food and raiment. But, in sober sadness, anything is better than England, and I am infinitely amused with my pilgrimage as far as it has gone.

To-morrow we start to ride post near 400 miles as far as Gibraltar, where we embark for Melita and Byzantium. A letter to Malta will find me, or to be forwarded, if I am absent. Pray embrace the Drury and Dwyer, and all the Ephesians you encounter. I am writing with Butler's donative pencil, which makes my bad hand worse. Excuse illegibility.

Hodgson! send me the news, and the deaths and defeats and capital crimes and the misfortunes of one's friends; and let us hear of literary matters, and the controversies and the criticisms. All this,

TO MR. HODGSON

will be pleasant.—*Suave mari magno,* etc. Talking
of that, I have been sea-sick, and sick of the sea.
Adieu.—Yours faithfully, etc.

TO MR. HODGSON

Gibraltar, August 6, 1809.

I have just arrived at this place after a journey *liv*
through Portugal, and a part of Spain, of nearly 500
miles. We left Lisbon and travelled on horseback
to Seville and Cadiz, and thence in the *Hyperion*
frigate to Gibraltar. The horses are excellent—we
rode seventy miles a day. Eggs and wine, and
hard beds, are all the accommodation we found,
and, in such torrid weather, quite enough. My
health is better than in England.

Seville is a fine town, and the Sierra Morena, part
of which we crossed, a very sufficient mountain; but
damn description, it is always disgusting. Cadiz,
sweet Cadiz!—it is the first spot in the creation.
The beauty of its streets and mansions is only
excelled by the loveliness of its inhabitants. For,
with all national prejudice, I must confess the women
of Cadiz are as far superior to the English women in
beauty as the Spaniards are inferior to the English in
every quality that dignifies the name of man. Just
as I began to know the principal persons of the city,
I was obliged to sail.

You will not expect a long letter after my riding
so far 'on hollow pampered jades of Asia.' Talking
of Asia puts me in mind of Africa, which is within
five miles of my present residence. I am going over
before I go on to Constantinople.

Cadiz is a complete Cythera. Many of the grandees who have left Madrid during the troubles reside there, and I do believe it is the prettiest and cleanest town in Europe. London is filthy in the comparison. The Spanish women are all alike, their education the same. The wife of a duke is, in information, as the wife of a peasant,—the wife of peasant, in manner, equal to a duchess. Certainly they are fascinating ; but their minds have only one idea, and the business of their lives is intrigue.

I have seen Sir John Carr at Seville and Cadiz, and, like Swift's barber, have been down on my knees to beg he would not put me into black and white. Pray remember me to the Drurys and the Davies, and all of that stamp who are yet extant. Send me a letter and news to Malta. My next epistle shall be from Mount Caucasus or Mount Sion. I shall return to Spain before I see England, for I am enamoured of the country.—Adieu, and believe me, etc.

TO THE HONOURABLE MRS. BYRON

Gibraltar, August 11, 1809.

lv   Dear Mother,—I have been so much occupied since my departure from England, that till I could address you at length I have forborne writing alto-gether. As I have now passed through Portugal, and a considerable part of Spain, and have leisure at this place, I shall endeavour to give you a short detail of my movements. We sailed from Falmouth on the 2nd of July, reached Lisbon, after a very favourable passage of four days and a half, and took up our abode in that city. It has often been described without being worthy of description; for, except the view from the Tagus, which is beautiful, and some fine churches and convents, it contains little but filthy streets and more filthy inhabitants. To make amends for this, the village of Cintra, about fifteen miles from the capital, is, perhaps in every respect, the most delightful in Europe; it contains beauties of every description, natural and artificial. Palaces and gardens rising in the midst of rocks, cataracts, and precipices; convents on stupendous heights—a distant view of the sea and the Tagus; and, besides (though that is a secondary consideration), is remarkable as the scene of Sir H. D.'s convention. It unites in itself all the wildness of the western highlands, with the verdure of the south of France. Near this place, about ten miles to the right, is the palace of Mafra, the boast of Portugal, as it might be of any country, in point of magnificence without elegance. There is a convent annexed; the Monks, who possess large revenues, are courteous enough, and understand Latin, so that we had a long conversation: they have a large library, and asked me if the *English* had *any books* in their country. I sent my baggage and part of the servants by sea to Gibraltar, and travelled on horseback from Aldea Galhega (the first stage from Lisbon, which is only accessible by water) to Seville (one of the most famous cities in Spain), where the government called the Junta is now held. The distance to Seville is nearly four hundred miles, and to Cadiz almost ninety further towards the coast. I had

orders from the government, and every possible accommodation on the road, as an English nobleman,
in an English uniform, is a very respectable personage in Spain at present. The horses are remarkably
good, and the roads (I assure you upon my honour,
for you will hardly believe it) very far superior to the
best British roads, without the smallest toll or turn-
pike. You will suppose this when I rode post to
Seville in four days, through this parching country, in
the midst of summer, without fatigue or annoyance.
Seville is a beautiful town ; though the streets are
narrow they are clean. We lodged in the house of
two Spanish unmarried ladies, who possess *six* houses
in Seville, and gave me a curious specimen of Spanish
manners. They are women of character, and the
eldest a fine woman, the youngest pretty, but not so
good a figure as Donna Josepha. The freedom of
manner which is general here astonished me not a
little ; and in the course of further observation I find
that reserve is not the characteristic of the Spanish
belles, who are, in general, very handsome, with large
black eyes, and very fine forms. The eldest honoured
your *unworthy* son with very particular attention, em-
bracing him with great tenderness at parting (I was
there but three days), after cutting off a lock of his
hair, and presenting him with one of her own, about
three feet in length, which I send, and beg you will
retain till my return. Her last words were, ' *Adios tu
hermoso! me gusto mucho.*'—' Adieu, you pretty
fellow, you please me much.' She offered a share
of her apartment, which my *virtue* induced me to
decline : she laughed, and said I had some English

amante (lover), and added that she was going to be married to an officer in the Spanish army. I left Seville, and rode on to Cadiz, through a beautiful country. At *Xeres*, where the sherry we drink is made, I met a great merchant, a Mr. Gordon, of Scotland, who was extremely polite, and favoured me with the inspection of his vaults and cellars, so that I quaffed at the fountain-head. Cadiz, sweet Cadiz, is the most delightful town I ever beheld, very different from our English cities in every respect except cleanliness (and it is as clean as London), but still beautiful, and full of the finest women in Spain, the Cadiz belles being the Lancashire witches of their land. Just as I was introduced, and began to like the grandees, I was forced to leave it for this cursed place; but before I return to England I will visit it again. The night before I left it, I sat in the box at the opera with Admiral Cordova's family; he is the commander whom Lord St. Vincent defeated in 1797, and has an aged wife and a fine daughter, Sennorita Cordova; the girl is very pretty in the Spanish style, in my opinion by no means inferior to the English in charms, and certainly superior in fascination. Long black hair, dark languishing eyes, *clear* olive complexions, and forms more graceful in motion than can be conceived by an Englishman used to the drowsy, listless air of his countrywomen, added to the most becoming dress, and, at the same time, the most decent in the world, render a Spanish beauty irresistible. I beg leave to observe that intrigue here is the business of life; when a woman marries she throws off all restraint, but I believe their conduct is chaste

69

enough before. If you make a proposal, which in
England would bring a box on the ear from the
meekest of virgins, to a Spanish girl, she thanks you
for the honour you intend her, and replies: 'Wait
till I am married, and I shall be too happy.' This is
literally and strictly true. Miss C. and her little
brother understood a little French, and, after regretting my ignorance of the Spanish, she proposed to
become my preceptress in that language. I could
only reply by a low bow, and express my regret that
I quitted Cadiz too soon to permit me to make the
progress which would doubtless attend my studies
under so charming a directress. I was standing at
the back of the box, which resembles our Opera
boxes (the theatre is large, and finely decorated, the
music admirable), in the manner in which Englishmen generally adopt for fear of incommoding the
ladies in front, when this fair Spaniard dispossessed
an old woman (an aunt or a duenna) of her chair
and commanded me to be seated next herself, at a
tolerable distance from her mamma. At the close of
the performance I withdrew, and was lounging with
a party of men in the passage, when, *en passant*, the
lady turned round and called me, and I had the
honour of attending her to the admiral's mansion.
I have an invitation on my return to Cadiz, which I
shall accept, if I repass through the country on my
return from Asia. I have met Sir John Carr, Knight
Errant, at Seville and Cadiz. He is a pleasant man.
I like the Spaniards much. You have heard of the
battle near Madrid, and in England they will call it a
victory—a pretty victory! Two hundred officers and

5000 men killed, all English, and the French in as great force as ever. I should have joined the army, but we have no time to lose before we get up the Mediterranean and Archipelago. I am going over to Africa to-morrow; it is only six miles from this fortress. My next stage is Cagliari in Sardinia, where I shall be presented to His Majesty. I have a most superb uniform as a court dress, indispensable in travelling.

August 13.

I have not yet been to Africa; the wind is contrary; but I dined yesterday at Algesiras, with Lady West-morland, where I met General Castanos, the cele-brated Spanish leader in the late and present war: to-day I dine with him; he has offered me letters to Tetuan in Barbary, for the principal Moors; and I am to have the house for a few days of one of the great men, which was intended for Lady W., whose health will not permit her to cross the Straits.

August 15.

I could not dine with Castanos yesterday, but this afternoon I had that honour; he is pleasant, and, for aught I know to the contrary, clever. I cannot go to Barbary. The Malta packet sails to-morrow, and myself in it. Admiral Purvis, with whom I dined at Cadiz, gave me a passage in a frigate to Gibraltar, but we have no ship of war destined for Malta at present. The packets sail fast, and have good accom-modations. You shall hear from me on our route.

Joe Murray delivers this. I have sent him and the boy back; pray show the lad any kindness, as he is my great favourite. I would have taken him on, *

* * * * * * *

* * * * * * *

* * Say this to his father, who may otherwise think he has behaved ill. I hope this will find you well.—Believe me yours ever sincerely,

BYRON.

P.S.—So Lord Gay is married to a rustic! Well done! If I wed, I will bring you home a Sultana, with half a dozen cities for a dowry, and reconcile you to an Ottoman daughter-in-law with a bushel of pearls, not larger than ostrich eggs, or smaller than walnuts.

TO MR. RUSHTON

Gibraltar, August 15, 1809.

lvi Mr. Rushton,—I have sent Robert home with Mr. Murray, because the country which I am about to travel through is in a state which renders it unsafe, particularly for one so young. I allow you to deduct five-and-twenty pounds a year for his education for three years, provided I do not return before that time, and I desire he may be considered as in my service. Let every care be taken of him, and let him be sent to school. In case of my death I have provided enough in my will to render him independent. He has behaved extremely well, and has travelled a great deal for the time of his absence. Deduct the expense of his education from your rent.

BYRON.

TO MRS. BYRON

Malta, September 15, 1809.

Dear Mother,—Though I have a very short time *lvii*
to spare, being to sail immediately for Greece, I
cannot avoid taking an opportunity of telling you
that I am well. I have been in Malta a short time,
and have found the inhabitants hospitable and
pleasant. This letter is committed to the charge of
a very extraordinary woman, whom you have doubtless heard of, Mrs. Spencer Smith, of whose escape
the Marquis de Salvo published a narrative a few
years ago. She has since been shipwrecked, and
her life has been from its commencement so fertile
in remarkable incidents, that in a romance they
would appear improbable. She was born at Constantinople, where her father, Baron Herbert, was
Austrian Ambassador; married unhappily, yet has
never been impeached in point of character; excited
the vengeance of Buonaparte by a part in some con-
spiracy; several times risked her life; and is not yet
twenty-five. She is here on her way to England, to
join her husband, being obliged to leave Trieste,
where she was paying a visit to her mother, by the
approach of the French, and embarks soon in a ship
of war. Since my arrival here, I have had scarcely
any other companion. I have found her very pretty,
very accomplished, and extremely eccentric. Buonaparte is even now so incensed against her, that her
life would be in some danger if she were taken
prisoner a second time.

You have seen Murray and Robert by this time,

73

and received my letter—little has happened since that date. I have touched at Cagliari, in Sardinia, and at Girgenti, in Sicily, and embark to-morrow for Patras, from whence I proceed to Yanina, where Ali Pacha holds his court, so I shall soon be among the Mussulmans. Adieu.—Believe me, with sincerity, yours ever, BYRON.

TO THE HONOURABLE MRS. BYRON

Prevesa, November 12, 1809.

lviii My dear Mother,—I have now been some time in Turkey: this place is on the coast, but I have traversed the interior of the province of Albania, on a visit to the Pacha. I left Malta in the *Spider*, a brig of war, on the 21st of September, and arrived in eight days at Prevesa. I thence have been about 150 miles as far as Tepaleen, his Highness's country palace, where I staid three days. The name of the Pacha is *Ali*, and he is considered a man of the first abilities, he governs the whole of Albania (the ancient Illyricum), Epirus, and part of Macedonia. His son, Velly Pacha, to whom he has given me letters, governs the Morea, and he has great influence in Egypt ; in short, he is one of the most powerful men in the Ottoman empire. When I reached Yanina, the capital, after a journey of three days over the mountains, through a country of the most picturesque beauty, I found that Ali Pacha was with his army in Illyricum, besieging Ibrahim Pacha in the castle of Berat. He had heard that an Englishman of rank was in his dominions, and had left orders in Yanina

with the commandant to provide a house, and supply
me with every kind of necessary *gratis* ; and, though
I have been allowed to make presents to the slaves,
etc., I have not been permitted to pay for a single
article of household consumption.   I rode out on
the vizier's horses, and saw the palaces of him and
his grandsons : they are splendid, but too much
ornamented with silk and gold.   I then went over
the mountains through Zitza, a village with a Greek
monastery (where I slept on my return), in the most
beautiful situation (always excepting Cintra in Portugal) I ever beheld.   In nine days I reached Tepaleen.
Our journey was much prolonged by the torrents that
had fallen from the mountains, and intersected the
roads.   I shall never forget the singular scene on
entering Tepaleen at five in the afternoon, as the sun
was going down : it brought to my mind (with some
change of *dress* however) Scott's description of
Branksome Castle in his *Lay*, and the feudal system.
The Albanians in their dresses (the most magnificent
in the world, consisting of a long *white kilt*, gold-
worked cloak, crimson velvet gold-laced jacket and
waistcoat, silver-mounted pistols and daggers), the
Tartars with their high caps, the Turks in their vast
pelisses and turbans, the soldiers and black slaves
with the horses, the former in groups in an immense
large open gallery in front of the palace, the latter
placed in a kind of cloister below it, two hundred
steeds ready caparisoned to move in a moment,
couriers entering or passing out with dispatches, the
kettle-drums beating, boys calling the hour from the
minaret of the mosque, altogether, with the singular

appearance of the building itself, formed a new and delightful spectacle to a stranger. I was conducted to a very handsome apartment, and my health inquired after by the vizier's secretary, *à la mode Turque*. The next day I was introduced to Ali Pacha. I was dressed in a full suit of staff uniform, with a very magnificent sabre, etc. The vizier received me in a large room paved with marble; a fountain was playing in the centre; the apartment was surrounded by scarlet ottomans. He received me standing, a wonderful compliment from a Mussulman, and made me sit down on his right hand. I have a Greek interpreter for general use, but a Physician of Ali's, named Femlario, who understands Latin, acted for me on this occasion. His first question was, why, at so early an age, I left my country?—(the Turks have no idea of travelling for amusement.) He then said, the English minister, Captain Leake, had told him I was of a great family, and desired his respects to my mother; which I now, in the name of Ali Pacha, present to you. He said he was certain I was a man of birth, because I had small ears, curling hair, and little white hands, and expressed himself pleased with my appearance and garb. He told me to consider him a father whilst I was in Turkey, and said he looked on me as his son. Indeed, he treated me like a child, sending me almonds and sugared sherbet, fruit and sweetmeats, twenty times a day. He begged me to visit him often, and at night, when he was at leisure. I then, after coffee and pipes, retired for the first time. I saw him thrice afterwards. It is singular, that the

Turks, who have no hereditary dignities, and few great families, except the Sultans, pay so much respect to birth; for I found my pedigree more regarded than my title.

His Highness is sixty years old, very fat, and not tall, but with a fine face, light blue eyes, and a white beard; his manner is very kind, and at the same time he possesses that dignity which I find universal amongst the Turks. He has the appearance of anything but his real character; for he is a remorseless tyrant, guilty of the most horrible cruelties, very brave, and so good a general, that they call him the Mahometan Buonaparte. Napoleon has twice offered to make him King of Epirus; but he prefers the English interest, and abhors the French, as he himself told me. He is of so much consequence, that he is much courted by both; the Albanians being the most warlike subjects of the Sultan, though Ali is only nominally dependent on the Porte. He has been a mighty warrior; but is as barbarous as he is successful, roasting rebels, etc. etc. Buonaparte sent him a snuff-box, with his picture; he said the snuff-box was very well, but the picture he could excuse, as he neither liked it nor the original. His ideas of judging of a man's birth from ears, hands, etc., were curious enough. To me he was, indeed, a father, giving me letters, guards, and every possible accommodation. Our next conversations were of war and travelling, politics and England. He called my Albanian soldier, who attends me, and told him to protect me at all hazard. His name is Viscillie, and, like all the Albanians, he is brave, rigidly honest, and faithful; but they are cruel, though not treacherous; and have several vices, but no meannesses. They are, perhaps, the most beautiful race, in point of countenance, in the world; their women are sometimes handsome also, but they are treated like slaves, *beaten*, and, in short, complete beasts of burthen; they plough, dig, and sow. I found them carrying wood, and actually repairing the highways. The men are all soldiers, and war and the chase their sole occupation. The women are the labourers, which, after all, is no great hardship in so delightful a climate. Yesterday, the 11th of November, I bathed in the sea; to-day it is so hot that I am writing in a shady room of the English Consul's, with three doors wide open, no fire, or even *fire-place* in the house, except for culinary purposes. To-day I saw the remains of the town of Actium, near which Antony lost the world, in a small bay where two frigates could hardly manœuvre: a broken wall is the sole remnant. On another part of the gulf stand the ruins of Nicopolis, built by Augustus in honour of his victory. Last night I was at a Greek marriage; but this, and a thousand things more, I have neither time nor *space* to describe. I am going to-morrow, with a guard of fifty men, to Patras in the Morea, and thence to Athens, where I shall winter. Two days ago, I was nearly lost in a Turkish ship of war, owing to the ignorance of the captain and crew, though the storm was not violent. Fletcher yelled after his wife, the Greeks called on all the Saints, the Mussulmans on Alla; the captain burst into tears and ran below deck, telling us to call on God; the sails were split, the main-yard shivered, the wind blowing fresh, the night setting in, and all our chance was to make Corfu, which is in possession of the French, or (as Fletcher pathetically termed it) 'a watery grave.' I did what I could to console Fletcher, but finding him incorrigible, wrapped myself up in my Albanian capote (an immense cloak), and lay down on deck to wait the worst. I have learnt to philosophize in my travels, and if I had not, complaint was useless. Luckily the wind abated, and only drove us on the coast of Suli, on the mainland, where we landed, and proceeded, by the help of the natives, to Prevesa again; but I shall not trust Turkish sailors in future, though the Pacha had ordered one of his own galliots to take me to Patras. I am therefore going as far as Missolonghi by land, and there have only to cross a small gulf to get to Patras. Fletcher's next epistle will be full of marvels: we were one night lost for nine hours in the mountains in a thunderstorm, and since nearly wrecked. In both cases Fletcher was sorely bewildered, from apprehensions of famine and banditti in the first, and drowning in the second instance. His eyes were a little hurt by the lightning, or crying (I don't know which), but are now recovered. When you write, address me at Mr. Strané's, English Consul, Patras, Morea.

I could tell you I know not how many incidents that I think would amuse you, but they crowd on my mind as much as they would swell my paper; and I can neither arrange them in the one, or put them down in the other, except in the greatest confusion. I like the Albanians much; they are not all Turks;

some tribes are Christians; but their religion makes
little difference in their manner or conduct: they are
esteemed the best troops in the Turkish service. I
lived on my route, two days at once, and three days
again, in a barrack at Salora, and never found soldiers
so tolerable, though I have been in the garrisons of
Gibraltar and Malta, and seen Spanish, French,
Sicilian, and British troops in abundance. I have
had nothing stolen, and was always welcome to their
provision and milk. Not a week ago an Albanian
chief (every village has its chief, who is called Prim-
ate), after helping us out of the Turkish galley in her
distress, feeding us, and lodging my suite, consisting
of Fletcher, a Greek, two Athenians, a Greek Priest,
and my companion, Mr. Hobhouse, refused any compensation but a written paper stating that I was well
received; and when I pressed him to accept a few
sequins, 'No,' he replied; 'I wish you to love me,
not to pay me.' These are his words. It is astonishing how far money goes in this country. While I
was in the capital I had nothing to pay by the Vizier's
order; but since, though I have generally had sixteen
horses, and generally six or seven men, the expense
has not been *half* as much as staying only three weeks
in Malta, though Sir A. Ball, the Governor, gave
me a house for nothing, and I had only *one servant*.
By-the-by, I expect Hanson to remit regularly; for
I am not about to stay in this province for ever. Let
him write to me at Mr. Strané's, English Consul,
Patras. The fact is, the fertility of the plains is
wonderful, and specie is scarce, which makes this
remarkable cheapness. I am going to Athens to

study modern Greek, which differs much from the ancient, though radically similar. I have no desire to return to England, nor shall I, unless compelled by absolute want, and Hanson's neglect; but I shall not enter into Asia for a year or two, as I have much to see in Greece, and I may perhaps cross into Africa, at least the Egyptian part. Fletcher, like all Englishmen, is very much dissatisfied, though a little reconciled to the Turks by a present of eighty piastres from the Vizier, which, if you consider everything, and the value of specie here, is nearly worth ten guineas English. He has suffered nothing but from cold, heat, and vermin, which those who lie in cottages and cross mountains in a cold country must undergo, and of which I have equally partaken with himself; but he is not valiant, and is afraid of robbers and tempests. I have no one to be remembered to in England, and wish to hear nothing from it, but that you are well, and a letter or two on business from Hanson, whom you may tell to write. I will write when I can, and beg you to believe me your affectionate son,   BYRON.

P.S.—I have some very *magnifique* Albanian dresses, the only expensive articles in this country. They cost fifty guineas each, and have so much gold, they would cost in England two hundred. I have been introduced to Hussim Bey and Mahmont Pacha, both little boys, grandchildren of Ali, at Yanina. They are totally unlike our lads, have painted complexions like rouged dowagers, large black eyes, and features perfectly regular. They are the prettiest little animals I ever saw, and are broken into the court ceremonies already. The Turkish salute is a slight inclination of the head, with the hand on the breast. Intimates always kiss. Mahmont is ten years old, and hopes to see me again. We are friends without understanding each other, like many other folks, though from a different cause. He has given me a letter to his father in the Morea, to whom I have also letters from Ali Pacha.

TO THE HONOURABLE MRS. BYRON

Smyrna, March 19, 1810.

lix Dear Mother,—I cannot write you a long letter; but as I know you will not be sorry to receive any intelligence of my movements, pray accept what I can give. I have traversed the greatest part of Greece, besides Epirus, etc. etc., resided ten weeks at Athens, and am now on the Asiatic side on my way to Constantinople. I have just returned from viewing the ruins of Ephesus, a day's journey from Smyrna. I presume you have received a long letter I wrote from Albania, with an account of my reception by the Pacha of the province.

When I arrive at Constantinople I shall determine whether to proceed into Persia or return, which latter I do not wish, if I can avoid it. But I have no intelligence from Mr. Hanson, and but one letter from yourself. I shall stand in need of remittances whether I proceed or return. I have written to him repeatedly, that he may not plead ignorance of my situation for neglect. I can give you no account of anything, for I have not time or opportunity, the frigate sailing immediately. Indeed, the further I go the more my laziness increases, and my aversion to letter-writing becomes more confirmed. I have written to no one but to yourself and Mr. Hanson, and these are communications of business and duty rather than of inclination.

Fletcher is very much disgusted with his fatigues, though he has undergone nothing that I have not shared. He is a poor creature; indeed English servants are detestable travellers. I have, besides him, two Albanian soldiers and a Greek interpreter, all excellent in their way. Greece, particularly in the vicinity of Athens, is delightful;—cloudless skies and lovely landscapes. But I must reserve all account of my adventures till we meet. I keep no journal, but my friend Hobhouse scribbles incessantly. Pray take care of Murray and Robert, and tell the boy it is the most fortunate thing for him that he did not accompany me to Turkey. Consider this as merely a notice of my safety, and believe me, yours, etc. etc.,

BYRON.

TO THE HONOURABLE MRS. BYRON

Smyrna, April 10, 1810.

Dear Mother,—To-morrow, or this evening, I sail for Constantinople in the *Salsette* frigate of thirty-six guns. She returns to England with our ambassador, whom she is going up on purpose to receive. I have written to you short letters from Athens, Smyrna, and a long one from Albania. I have not yet mustered courage for a second large epistle, and you must not be angry, since I take all opportunities of apprizing you of my safety; but even that is an effort, writing is so irksome. I have been traversing Greece, and Epirus, Illyria, etc. etc., and you see by my date, have got into Asia. I have made but one excursion lately to the ruins of Ephesus. Malta is the rendez-vous of my letters, so address to that island. Mr. Hanson has not written, though I wished to hear of the Norfolk sale, the Lancashire law-suit, etc. etc. I am anxiously expecting fresh remittances. I believe you will like Nottinghamshire, at least my share of it. Pray accept my good wishes in lieu of a long letter, and believe me, yours sincerely and affectionately,

BYRON.

TO THE HONOURABLE MRS. BYRON

'Salsette' frigate, off the Dardanelles,
April 17, 1810.

lxi   Dear Madam,—I write at anchor (in our way to Constantinople) off the Troad, which I traversed two days ago. All the remains of Troy are the tombs of her destroyers, amongst which I see that of Anti-lochus from my cabin window. These are large mounds of earth, like the barrows of the Danes in your island. There are several monuments, about twelve miles distant, of the Alexandrian Troas, which I also examined; but by no means to be compared with the remnants of Athens and Ephesus. This will be sent in a ship of war bound with despatches for Malta. In a few days we shall be at Con-stantinople, barring accidents. I have also written from Smyrna, and shall, from time to time, transmit

TO REV. H. DRURY

short accounts of my movements, but I feel totally
unequal to long letters.—Believe me, yours very
sincerely,   BYRON.

P.S.—No accounts from Hanson !!! Do not complain of short letters; I write to nobody but yourself
and Mr. H.

TO THE REV. HENRY DRURY

'Salsette' frigate, May 3, 1810.

My dear Drury,—When I left England nearly a lxii
year ago, you requested me to write to you—I will
do so.   I have crossed Portugal, traversed the south
of Spain, visited Sardinia, Sicily, Malta, and thence
passed into Turkey, where I am still wandering.   I
first landed in Albania, the ancient Epirus, where we
penetrated as far as Mount Tomarit—excellently
treated by the chief Ali Pacha,—and, after journeying through Illyria, Chaonia, etc., crossed the Gulf
of Actium, with a guard of fifty Albanians, and
passed the Achelous in our route through Acarnania
and Ætolia.   We stopped a short time in the Morea,
crossed the Gulf of Lepanto, and landed at the foot
of Parnassus;—saw all that Delphi retains, and so
on to Thebes and Athens, at which last we remained
ten weeks.

His Majesty's ship *Pylades* brought us to Smyrna,
but not before we had topographised Attica, including of course Marathon and the Sunian promontory.   From Smyrna to the Troad (which we
visited when at anchor, for a fortnight, off the tomb
of Antilochus) was our next stage; and now we are

85

in the Dardanelles, waiting for a wind to proceed to Constantinople.

This morning I *swam* from *Sestos* to *Abydos*. The immediate distance is not above a mile, but the current renders it hazardous;—so much so that I doubt whether Leander's conjugal affection must not have been a little chilled in his passage to Paradise. I attempted it a week ago, and failed,— owing to the north wind and the wonderful rapidity of the tide,—though I have been from my childhood a strong swimmer. But, this morning being calmer, I succeeded, and crossed the 'broad Hellespont' in an hour and ten minutes.

Well, my dear sir, I have left my home, and seen part of Africa and Asia, and a tolerable portion of Europe. I have been with generals and admirals, princes and pachas, governors and ungovernables,— but I have not time or paper to expatiate. I wish to let you know that I live with a friendly remembrance of you, and a hope to meet you again; and if I do this as shortly as possible, attribute it to anything but forgetfulness.

Greece, ancient and modern, you know too well to require description. Albania, indeed, I have seen more of than any Englishman (except a Mr. Leake), for it is a country rarely visited, from the savage character of the natives, though abounding in more natural beauties than the classical regions of Greece, —which, however, are still eminently beautiful, particularly Delphi and Cape Colonna in Attica. Yet these are nothing to parts of Illyria and Epirus, where places without a name, and rivers not laid down in maps, may, one day, when more known, be justly esteemed superior subjects, for the pencil and the pen, to the dry ditch of the Ilissus and the bogs of Bœotia.

The Troad is a fine field for conjecture and snipe-shooting, and a good sportsman and an ingenious scholar may exercise their feet and faculties to great advantage upon the spot;—or, if they prefer riding, lose their way (as I did) in a cursed quagmire of the Scamander, who wriggles about as if the Dardan virgins still offered their wonted tribute. The only vestige of Troy, or her destroyers, are the barrows supposed to contain the carcasses of Achilles, Antilochus, Ajax, etc.;—but Mount Ida is still in high feather, though the shepherds are nowadays not much like Ganymede. But why should I say more of these things? are they not written in the *Boke* of *Gell*? and has not Hobhouse got a journal? I keep none, as I have renounced scribbling.

I see not much difference between ourselves and the Turks, save that we have . . . . and they have none, that they have long dresses, and we short, and that we talk much, and they little. They are sensible people. Ali Pacha told me he was sure I was a man of rank, because I had *small ears* and *hands*, and *curling hair*. By-the-by, I speak the Romaic, or modern Greek, tolerably. It does not differ from the ancient dialects so much as you would conceive; but the pronunciation is diametrically opposite. Of verse, except in rhyme, they have no idea.

I like the Greeks, who are plausible rascals,—

with all the Turkish vices without their courage.
However, some are brave, and all are beautiful, very
much resembling the busts of Alcibiades ; the women
not quite so handsome.   I can swear in Turkish ;
but, except one horrible oath, and 'pimp,' and
'bread,' and 'water,' I have got no great vocabulary
in that language.   They are extremely polite to
strangers of any rank, properly protected ; and as I
have two servants and two soldiers, we get on with
great *éclat*.   We have been occasionally in danger of
thieves, and once of shipwreck,—but always escaped.

Of Spain I sent some account to our Hodgson,
but have subsequently written to no one, save notes
to relations and lawyers, to keep them out of my
premises.   I mean to give up all connection, on my
return, with many of my best friends—as I supposed
them—and to snarl all my life.   But I hope to have
one good-humoured laugh with you, and to embrace
Dwyer, and pledge Hodgson, before I commence
cynicism.

Tell Dr. Butler I am now writing with the gold
pen he gave me before I left England, which is the
reason my scrawl is more unintelligible than usual.
I have been at Athens, and seen plenty of these
reeds for scribbling, some of which he refused to
bestow upon me, because topographic Gell had
brought them from Attica.   But I will not describe,
—no—you must be satisfied with simple detail till
my return, and then we will unfold the floodgates of
colloquy.   I am in a thirty-six gun frigate, going up
to fetch Bob Adair from Constantinople, who will
have the honour to carry this letter.

And so Hobhouse's *boke* is out, with some sentimental sing-song of my own to fill up,—and how
does it take, eh? and where the devil is the second
edition of my Satire, with additions? and my name
on the title-page? and more lines tagged to the end,
with a new exordium and what not, hot from my
anvil before I cleared the Channel? The Mediterranean and the Atlantic roll between me and
criticism; and the thunders of the Hyperborean
Review are deafened by the roar of the Hellespont.

Remember me to Claridge, if not translated to
college, and present to Hodgson assurances of my
high consideration. Now, you will ask, what shall I
do next? and I answer, I do not know. I may
return in a few months, but I have intents and
projects after visiting Constantinople.—Hobhouse,
however, will probably be back in September.

On the 2nd of July we have left Albion one year
—*oblitus meorum obliviscendus et illis.* I was sick
of my own country, and not much prepossessed in
favour of any other; but I 'drag on my chain'
without 'lengthening it at each remove.' I am like
the Jolly Miller, caring for nobody, and not cared
for. All countries are much the same in my eyes.
I smoke, and stare at mountains, and twirl my
mustachios very independently. I miss no comforts,
and the musquitoes that rack the morbid frame of
H. have, luckily for me, little effect on mine, because
I live more temperately.

I omitted Ephesus in my catalogue, which I
visited during my sojourn at Smyrna; but the
Temple has almost perished, and St. Paul need not

trouble himself to epistolise the present brood of Ephesians, who have converted a large church built entirely of marble into a mosque, and I don't know that the edifice looks the worse for it.

My paper is full and my ink ebbing—good afternoon! If you address to me at Malta, the letter will be forwarded wherever I may be. H. greets you; he pines for his poetry,—at least, some tidings of it. I almost forgot to tell you that I am dying for love of three Greek girls at Athens, sisters. I lived in the same house. Teresa, Mariana, and Katinka are the names of these divinities, all of them under fifteen. Your ταπεινοτατος δουλος, BYRON.

TO MR. HODGSON

'Salsette' frigate, in the Dardanelles, off Abydos,
May 5, 1810.

lxiii   I am on my way to Constantinople, after a tour through Greece, Epirus, etc., and part of Asia Minor, some particulars of which I have just communicated to our friend and host, H. Drury. With these, then, I shall not trouble you; but as you will perhaps be pleased to hear that I am well, etc., I take the opportunity of our ambassador's return to forward the few lines I have time to despatch. We have undergone some inconveniences, and incurred partial perils, but no events worthy of communication, unless you will deem it one that two days ago I swam from Sestos to Abydos. This, with a few alarms from robbers, and some danger of shipwreck in a Turkish galliot six months ago, a visit to a Pacha, a passion for a married woman at Malta, a challenge to an officer, an attachment to three Greek girls at Athens, with a great deal of buffoonery and fine prospects, form all that has distinguished my progress since my departure from Spain.

Hobhouse rhymes and journalises; I stare and do nothing—unless smoking can be deemed an active amusement. The Turks take too much care of their women to permit them to be scrutinised; but I have lived a good deal with the Greeks, whose modern dialect I can converse in enough for my purposes. With the Turks I have also some male acquaintances —female society is out of the question. I have been very well treated by the Pachas and Governors, and have no complaint to make of any kind. Hobhouse will one day inform you of all our adventures—were I to attempt the recital, neither *my* paper nor *your* patience would hold out during the operation.

Nobody, save yourself, has written to me since I left England; but indeed I did not request it. I except my relations, who write quite as often as I wish. Of Hobhouse's volume I know nothing, except that it is out; and of my second edition I do not even know *that*, and certainly do not, at this distance, interest myself in the matter. I hope you and Bland roll down the stream of sale with rapidity, and that you have produced a new poem.

Of my return I cannot positively speak, but think it probable Hobhouse will precede me in that respect. We have now been very nearly one year abroad. I should wish to gaze away another, at least, in these evergreen climates; but I fear business, law business, the worst of employments, will recall me previous to that period, if not very quickly. If so, you shall have due notice.

I hope you will find me an altered personage,—I do not mean in body, but in manner, for I begin to find out that nothing but virtue will do in this d——d world. I am tolerably sick of vice, which I have tried in its agreeable varieties, and mean, on my return, to cut all my dissolute acquaintance, leave off wine and carnal company, and betake myself to politics and decorum. I am very serious and cynical, and a good deal disposed to moralise ; but fortunately for you the coming homily is cut off by default of pen and defection of paper.

Good morrow ! If you write, address to me at Malta, whence your letters will be forwarded. You need not remember me to anybody, but believe me, yours with all faith, BYRON.

Constantinople, May 15, 1810.

P.S.—My dear H.,—The date of my postscript will 'prate to you of my whereabouts.' We anchored between the Seven Towers and the Seraglio on the 13th, and yesterday settled ashore. The ambassador is laid up ; but the secretary does the honours of the palace, and we have a general invitation to his table. In a short time he has his leave of audience, and we accompany him in our uniforms to the Sultan, etc., and in a few days I am to visit the Captain Pacha with the commander of our frigate. I have seen enough of their Pachas already ; but I wish to have a view of the Sultan, the last of the Ottoman race. Of Constantinople you have Gibbon's description, very correct as far as I have seen. The mosques I shall have a firman to visit. I shall most probably (*Deo volente*), after a full inspection of Stamboul, bend my course homewards; but this is uncertain. I have seen the most interesting parts, particularly Albania, where few Franks have ever been, and all the most celebrated ruins of Greece and Ionia. Of England I know nothing, hear nothing, and can find no person better informed on the subject than myself. I this moment drink your health in a bumper of hock; Hobhouse fills and empties to the same; do you and Drury pledge us in a pint of any liquid you please—vinegar will bear the nearest resemblance to that which I have just swallowed to your name; but when we meet again the draught shall be mended and the wine also.—Yours ever, B.

TO THE HONOURABLE MRS. BYRON

Constantinople, May 18, 1810.

Dear Madam,—I arrived here in an English frigate *lxiv* from Smyrna a few days ago, without any events worth mentioning, except landing to view the plains of Troy, and afterwards, when we were at anchor in the Dardanelles, *swimming* from Sestos to Abydos, in imitation of Monsieur Leander, whose story you no doubt know too well for me to add anything on the subject, except that I crossed the Hellespont without so good a motive for the undertaking. As I am just going to visit the Captain Pacha, you will excuse the brevity of my letter. When Mr. Adair takes leave, I .am to see the Sultan and the mosques, etc.—Believe me yours ever, BYRON.

LETTERS

Constantinople, May 24, 1810.

lxv Dear Mother,—I wrote to you very shortly the other day on my arrival here; and as another opportunity avails, take up my pen again, that the frequency of my letters may atone for their brevity. Pray did you ever receive a picture of me in oil by *Sanders* in *Vigo Lane*, London? (a noted limner); if not, write for it immediately—it was paid for, except the frame (if frame there be) before I left England. I believe I mentioned to you in my last, that my only notable exploit lately has been swimming from Sestos to Abydos on the third of this month, in humble imitation of *Leander*, of amorous memory, though I had no *Hero* to receive me on the other shore of the Hellespont. Of Constantinople you have of course read fifty descriptions by sundry travellers, which are in general so correct that I have nothing to add on the subject. When our ambassador takes his leave, I shall accompany him to see the Sultan, and afterwards probably return to Greece. I have heard nothing of Mr. Hanson, but one remittance without any letter from that legal gentleman. If you have occasion for any pecuniary supply, pray use my funds as far as they *go* without reserve, and, lest this should not be enough, in my next to Mr. Hanson I will direct him to advance any sum you want, leaving it to your discretion how much, in the present state of my affairs, you may think proper to require. I have already seen the most interesting parts of Turkey in Europe and Asia

Minor, but shall **not proceed further till I** hear from
England : **in the meantime I** shall expect occasional
supplies according to circumstances ; and **shall** pass
my summer amongst my friends, the Greeks of the
Morea. You will direct to Malta, where my letters
are forwarded ; and believe **me to be,** with **great**
sincerity, **yours** ever, BYRON.

P.S.—Fletcher **is well ; pray take care of** my boy
Robert, and the old man Murray. It is fortunate
they returned ; neither the youth of the one, nor the
age of the other, would have suited the changes of
climate and **fatigue of** travelling.

TO THE REV. HENRY DRURY

Constantinople, June 17, 1810.

Though I wrote to you so recently, I break in upon *lxvi*
you again to congratulate you on a child being born,
as a letter from Hodgson apprizes me of that event,
in which I rejoice.

I am just come from an expedition through the
Bosphorus to the Black Sea and the Cyanean Sym-
plegades, up which last I scrambled with as great risk
as ever the Argonauts escaped in their hoy. You
remember the beginning of the nurse's dole in the
Medea, of which I beg you to take the following
translation, done on the summit :—

> Oh how I wish that an embargo
> Had kept in port the good ship *Argo* !
> Who, still unlaunched from Grecian docks,
> Had never passed the Azure rocks ;
> But now I fear her trip will be a
> Damn'd business for my Miss Medea, etc. etc.,

as it very nearly was to me;—for, had not this sublime passage been in my head, I should never have
dreamed of ascending the said rocks, and bruising
my carcass in honour of the ancients.

I have now sat on the Cyaneans, swam from Sestos
to Abydos (as I trumpeted in my last), and, after
passing through the Morea again, shall set sail for
Santa Maura, and toss myself from the Leucadian
promontory;—surviving which operation, I shall
probably join you in England. Hobhouse, who will
deliver this, is bound straight for these parts; and, as
he is bursting with his travels, I shall not anticipate
his narratives, but merely beg you not to believe one
word he says, but reserve your ear for me, if you have
any desire to be acquainted with the truth.

I am bound for Athens once more, and thence to
the Morea; but my stay depends so much on my
caprice, that I can say nothing of its probable duration.
I have been out a year already, and may stay another;
but I am quicksilver, and say nothing positively. We
are all very much occupied doing nothing, at present.
We have seen everything but the mosques, which we
are to view with a firman on Tuesday next. But of
these and other sundries let H. relate, with this pro-
viso, that *I* am to be referred to for authenticity; and
I beg leave to contradict all those things whereon he
lays particular stress. But, if he soars at any time
into wit, I give you leave to applaud, because that is
necessarily stolen from his fellow-pilgrim. Tell Davies
that Hobhouse has made excellent use of his best
jokes in many of his Majesty's ships of war; but add,
also, that I always took care to restore them to the

right owner; in consequence of which he (Davies) is
no less famous by water than by land, and reigns unrivalled in the cabin as in the 'Cocoa Tree.'

And Hodgson has been publishing more poesy.—
I wish he would send me his *Sir Edgar*, and Bland's
Anthology, to Malta, where they will be forwarded.
In my last, which I hope you received, I gave an outline of the ground we have covered. If you have not
been overtaken by this despatch, Hobhouse's tongue
is at your service. Remember me to Dwyer, who
owes me eleven guineas. Tell him to put them in
my banker's hands at Gibraltar or Constantinople. I
believe he paid them once, but that goes for nothing,
as it was an annuity.

I wish you would write. I have heard from Hodgson frequently. Malta is my post-office. I mean to
be with you by next Montem. You remember the
last,—I hope for such another; but after having swum
across the 'broad Hellespont,' I disdain Datchett.
Good afternoon! I am yours, very sincerely,

BYRON.

TO THE HONOURABLE MRS. BYRON

Constantinople, June 28, 1810.

My dear Mother,—I regret to perceive by your *lxvii*
last letter that several of mine have not arrived,
particularly a very long one, written in November
last from Albania, when I was on a visit to the Pacha
of that province. Fletcher has also written to his
spouse perpetually. Mr. Hobhouse, who will forward or deliver this, and is on his return to England,
can inform you of our different movements, but I am

very uncertain as to my own return. He will probably be down in Notts some time or other; but Fletcher, whom I send back as an incumbrance (English servants are sad travellers) will supply his place in the interim, and describe our travels, which have been tolerably extensive. I have written twice briefly from this capital, from Smyrna, from Athens, and other parts of Greece; from Albania, the Pacha of which province desired his respects to my mother, and said he was sure I was a man of high birth, because I had small ears, curling hair, and white hands!!! He was very kind to me, begged me to consider him as a father, and gave me a guard of forty soldiers through the forests of Acarnania. But of this and other circumstances I have written to you at large, and yet hope you will receive my letters.

I remember Mahmout Pacha, the grandson of Ali Pacha, at Yanina (a little fellow of ten years of age, with large black eyes which our ladies would purchase at any price, and those regular features which distinguish the Turks), asked me how I came to travel so young, without anybody to take care of me. This question was put by the little man with all the gravity of threescore. I cannot now write copiously; I have only time to tell you that I have passed many a fatiguing, but never a tedious moment; and that all I am afraid of is, that I shall contract a gypsy-like wandering disposition, which will make home tiresome to me: this, I am told, is very common with men in the habit of peregrination, and indeed I feel it so. On the third of May I swam from *Sestos* to *Abydos*. You know the story of Leander, but I had no *Hero* to receive me at landing. I also passed a fortnight in the Troad : the tombs of Achilles and Æsyetes still exist in large barrows, similar to those you have doubtless seen in the north. The other day I was at Belgrade (a village in these environs) to see the house built on the same site as Lady Mary Wortley's—by-the-by, her ladyship, as far as I can judge, has lied, but not half so much as any other woman would have done in the same situation. I have been in all the principal mosques by the virtue of a firman : this is a favour rarely permitted to Infidels, but the ambassador's departure obtained it for us. I have been up the Bosphorus into the Black Sea, round the walls of the city, and indeed I know more of it by sight than I do of London.

I hope to amuse you some winter's evening with the details, but at present you must excuse me ; I am not able to write long letters in June. I return to spend my summer in Greece. I shall not proceed further into Asia, as I have visited Smyrna, Ephesus, and the Troad. I write often, but you must not be alarmed when you do not receive my letters ; consider we have no regular post further than Malta, where I beg you will in future send your letters, and not to this city. Fletcher is a poor creature, and requires comforts that I can dispense with : he is very sick of his travels, but you must not believe his account of the country. He sighs for ale, and idleness, and a wife, and the devil knows what besides. I have not been disappointed or disgusted. I have lived with the highest and the lowest. I have been for days in a Pacha's palace, and have passed many a

night in a cow-house, and I find the people inoffen-
sive and kind. I have also passed some time with
the principal Greeks in the Morea and Livadia, and,
though inferior to the Turks, they are better than the
Spaniards, who, in their turn, excel the Portuguese.
Of Constantinople you will find many descriptions in
different travels; but Lady Wortley errs strangely
when she says 'St. Paul's would cut a strange figure
by St. Sophia's.' I have been in both, surveyed
them inside and out attentively. St. Sophia's is undoubtedly the most interesting from its immense
antiquity, and the circumstance of all the Greek
emperors, from Justinian, having been crowned there,
and several murdered at the altar, besides the Turkish
Sultans who attend it regularly. But it is inferior in
beauty and size to some of the mosques, particularly
'Soleyman, etc.,' and not to be mentioned in the
same page with St. P.'s (I speak like a *Cockney*).
However, I prefer the Gothic Cathedral of Seville to
St. P.'s, St. Sophia's, and any religious building I
have ever seen. The walls of the seraglio are like
the walls of Newstead Gardens, only higher, and
much in the same *order*; but the ride by the walls
of the city on the land side is beautiful. Imagine
four miles of immense triple battlements, covered
with ivy, surmounted with 218 towers, and on the
other side of the road Turkish burying-grounds (the
loveliest spots on earth), full of enormous cypresses.

I have seen the ruins of Athens, of Ephesus, and
Delphi; I have traversed great part of Turkey, and
many other parts of Europe, and some of Asia; but
I never beheld a work of nature or art which yielded

an impression like the prospect on each side from the Seven Towers to the end of the Golden Horn. Now for England. You have not received my friend Hobhouse's volume of poesy : it has been published several months ; you ought to read it. I am glad to hear of the progress of *E. Bards*, etc. Of course you observed I have made great additions to the new edition. Have you received my picture from Sanders, Vigo Lane, London ? It was finished, and paid for, long before I left England : pray send for it. You seem to be a mighty reader of magazines : where do you pick up all this intelligence, quotations, etc. etc.? Though I was happy to obtain my seat without the assistance of Lord C., I had no measures to keep with a man who declined interfering as my relation on that occasion, and I have done with him, though I regret distressing Mrs. Leigh, poor thing ! I hope she is happy. It is my opinion that Mr. B—— ought to marry Miss R——. Our first duty is not to do evil ; but alas ! that is impossible : our next is to repair it, if in our power. The girl is his equal : if she were his inferior, a sum of money and provision for the child would be some, though a poor compensation : as it is, he should marry her. I will have no gay deceivers on my estate, and I shall not allow my tenants a privilege I do not permit myself, *that* of debauching each other's daughters. God knows, I have been guilty of many excesses ; but, as I have laid down a resolution to reform, and lately kept it, I expect this Lothario to follow the example, and begin by restoring this girl to society, or, by the beard of my father! he shall hear of it. Pray take some notice of Robert,

who will miss his master; poor boy, he was very
unwilling to return. I trust you are well and happy.
It will be a pleasure to hear from you.—Believe me,
yours very sincerely,   BYRON.

P.S.—How is Joe Murray?

P.S.—I open my letter again to tell you that
Fletcher having petitioned to accompany me into the
Morea, I have taken him with me, contrary to the
intention expressed in my letter.

TO MR. HODGSON

Constantinople, July 4, 1810.

lxviii   My dear Hodgson,—Twice have I written—once
in answer to your last, and a former letter when I
arrived here in May. That I may have nothing to
reproach myself with, I will write once more—a very
superfluous task, seeing that Hobhouse is bound for
your parts full of talk and wonderment. My first
letter went by an ambassadorial express; my second
by the *Black John* lugger; my third will be conveyed
by Cam, the miscellanist. I shall begin by telling
you, having only told it you twice before, that I
swam from Sestos to Abydos. I do this that you
may be impressed with proper respect for me, the
performer; for I plume myself on this achievement
more than I could possibly do on any kind of glory,
political, poetical, or rhetorical. Having told you
this I will tell you nothing more, because it would
be cruel to curtail Cam's narrative, which, by-the-
by, you must not believe till confirmed by me, the
eye-witness. I promise myself much pleasure from

contradicting the greatest part of it. He has been plaguily pleased by the intelligence contained in your last to me respecting the reviews of his hymns. I refreshed him with that paragraph immediately, together with the tidings of my own third edition, which added to his recreation. But then he has had a letter from a Lincoln's Inn Bencher full of praise of his harpings, and vituperation of the other contributions to his *Missellingany*, which that sagacious person is pleased to say must have been put in as FOILS (*horresco referens !*); furthermore he adds that Cam 'is a genuine pupil of Dryden,' concluding with a comparison rather to the disadvantage of Pope. . . . I have written to Drury by Hobhouse; a letter is also from me on its way to England intended for that matrimonial man. Before it is very long I hope we shall again be together; the moment I set out for England you shall have intelligence, that we may meet as soon as possible. Next week the frigate sails with Adair; I am for Greece, Hobhouse for England. A year together on the 2nd July since we sailed from Falmouth. I have known a hundred instances of men setting out in couples, but not one of a similar return. Aberdeen's party split; several voyagers at present have done the same. I am confident that twelve months of any given individual is perfect ipecacuanha.

The Russians and Turks are at it, and the Sultan in person is soon to head the army. The Captain Pacha cuts off heads every day, and a Frenchman's ears; the last is a serious affair. By-the-by I like the Pachas in general. Ali Pacha called me his son, desired his compliments to my mother, and said he was sure I was a man of birth, because I had 'small ears and curling hair.' He is Pacha of Albania, six hundred miles off, where I was in October—a fine portly person. His grandson Mahmout, a little fellow ten years old, with large black eyes as big as pigeon's eggs, and all the gravity of sixty, asked me what I did travelling so young without a Lala (tutor)?

Good-night, dear H. I have crammed my paper, and crave your indulgence. Write to me at Malta.

I am, with all sincerity, yours affectionately,

BYRON.

TO THE HONOURABLE MRS. BYRON

Athens, July 25, 1810.

lxix Dear Mother,—I have arrived here in four days from Constantinople, which is considered as singularly quick, particularly for the season of the year. Your northern gentry can have no conception of a Greek summer; which, however, is a perfect frost compared with Malta and Gibraltar, where I reposed myself in the shade last year, after a gentle gallop of four hundred miles, without intermission, through Portugal and Spain. You see, by my date, that I am at Athens again, a place which I think I prefer, upon the whole, to any I have seen.

My next movement is to-morrow into the Morea, where I shall probably remain a month or two, and then return to winter here, if I do not change my plans, which, however, are very variable, as you may suppose; but none of them verge to England.

TO MRS. BYRON

The Marquis of Sligo, my old fellow-collegian, is here, and wishes to accompany me into the Morea. We shall go together for that purpose, but I am wofully sick of travelling companions, after a year's experience of Mr. Hobhouse, who is on his way to Great Britain. Lord S. will afterwards pursue his way to the capital; and Lord B., having seen all the wonders in that quarter, will let you know what he does next, of which at present he is not quite certain. Malta is my perpetual post-office, from which my letters are forwarded to all parts of the habitable globe :—by-the-by, I have now been in Asia, Africa, and the east of Europe, and, indeed, made the most of my time, without hurrying over the most interesting scenes of the ancient world. Fletcher, after having been toasted and roasted, and baked, and grilled, and eaten by all sorts of creeping things, begins to philosophise, is grown a refined as well as a resigned character, and promises at his return to become an ornament to his own parish, and a very prominent person in the future family pedigree of the Fletchers, who I take to be Goths by their accomplishments, Greeks by their acuteness, and ancient Saxons by their appetite. He (Fletcher) begs leave to send half a dozen sighs to Sally his spouse, and wonders (though I do not) that his ill-written and worse spelt letters have never come to hand; as for that matter, there is no great loss in either of our letters, saving and except that I wish you to know we are well, and warm enough at this present writing, God knows. You must not expect long letters at present, for they are written with the sweat of my brow, I assure you. It is rather singular that Mr. Hanson has not written a syllable since my departure. Your letters I have mostly received, as well as others; from which I conjecture that the man of law is either angry or busy.

I trust you like Newstead, and agree with your neighbours; but you know *you* are a *vixen*—is not that a dutiful appellation? Pray, take care of my books and several boxes of papers in the hands of Joseph; and pray leave me a few bottles of champagne to drink, for I am very thirsty;—but I do not insist on the last article, without you like it. I suppose you have your house full of silly women, prating scandalous things. Have you ever received my picture in oil from Sanders, London? It has been paid for these sixteen months: why do you not get it? My suite, consisting of two Turks, two Greeks, a Lutheran, and the nondescript, Fletcher, are making so much noise, that I am glad to sign myself yours, etc. etc., BYRON.

TO THE HONOURABLE MRS. BYRON

Patras, July 30, 1810.

lxx Dear Madam,—In four days from Constantinople, with a favourable wind, I arrived in the frigate at the island of Teos, from whence I took a boat to Athens, where I met my friend the Marquis of Sligo, who expressed a wish to proceed with me as far as Corinth. At Corinth we separated, he for Tripolitza, I for Patras, where I had some business with the consul, Mr. Strané, in whose house I now write.

He has rendered me every service in his power since I quitted Malta on my way to Constantinople, whence I have written to you twice or thrice. In a few days I visit the Pacha at Tripolitza, make the tour of the Morea, and return again to Athens, which at present is my head-quarters. The heat is at present intense. In England, if it reaches 98° you are all on fire: the other day, in travelling between Athens and Megara, the thermometer was at 125°!!! Yet I feel no inconvenience; of course I am much bronzed, but I live temperately, and never enjoyed better health.

Before I left Constantinople I saw the Sultan (with Mr. Adair), and the interior of the mosques, things which rarely happen to travellers. Mr. Hobhouse is gone to England: I am in no hurry to return, but have no particular communications for your country, except my surprise at Mr. Hanson's silence, and my desire that he will remit regularly. I suppose some arrangement has been made with regard to Wymondham and Rochdale. Malta is my post-office, or to Mr. Strané, consul-general, Patras, Morea. You complain of my silence—I have written twenty or thirty times within the last year: never less than twice a month, and often more. If my letters do not arrive, you must not conclude that we are eaten, or that there is a war, or a pestilence, or famine: neither must you credit silly reports, which I dare say you have in Notts, as usual. I am very well, and neither more nor less happy than I usually am; except that I am very glad to be once more alone, for I was sick of my companion,—not that he

LETTERS

was a bad one, but because my nature leads me to
solitude, and that every day adds to this disposition.
If I chose, here are many men who would wish to
join me—one wants me to go to Egypt, another to
Asia, of which I have seen enough. The greater
part of Greece is already my own, so that I shall
only go over my old ground, and look upon my old
seas and mountains, the only acquaintances I ever
found improve upon me.

I have a tolerable suite, a Tartar, two Albanians,
an interpreter, besides Fletcher; but in this country
these are easily maintained. Adair received me
wonderfully well, and indeed I have no complaints
against any one. Hospitality here is necessary, for
inns are not. I have lived in the houses of Greeks,
Turks, Italians, and English—to-day in a palace,
to-morrow in a cow-house; this day with a Pacha,
the next with a shepherd. I shall continue to write
briefly, but frequently, and am glad to hear from
you; but you fill your letters with things from the
papers, as if English papers were not found all over
the world. I have at this moment a dozen before
me. Pray take care of my books, and believe me,
my dear mother, yours, etc., BYRON.

TO THE HONOURABLE MRS. BYRON

Patras, October 2, 1810.

lxxi Dear Madam,—It is now several months since I
have received any communication from you; but at
this I am not surprised, nor indeed have I any complaint to make, since you have written frequently,

108

for which I thank you; but I very much condemn Mr. Hanson, who has not taken the smallest notice of my many letters, nor of my request before I left England, which I sailed from on this *very day* fifteen months ago. Thus one year and a quarter have passed away, without my receiving the least intelligence on the state of my affairs, and they were not in a posture to admit of neglect; and I do conceive and declare that Mr. Hanson has acted negligently and culpably in not apprising me of his proceedings; I will also add uncivilly. His letters, were there any, could not easily miscarry: the communications with the Levant are slow, but tolerably secure, at least as far as Malta, and there I left directions which I know would be observed. I have written to you several times from Constantinople and Smyrna. You will perceive by my date I am returned into the Morea, of which I have been making the tour, and visiting the Pacha, who gave me a fine horse, and paid me all possible honours and attention. I have now seen a good portion of Turkey in Europe, and Asia Minor, and shall remain at Athens, and in the vicinity, till I hear from England. I have punctually obeyed your injunctions of writing frequently, but I shall not pretend to describe countries which have been already amply treated of. I believe before this time Mr. Hobhouse will have arrived in England, and he brings letters from me, written at Constantinople. In these I mention having seen the Sultan and the mosques, and that I swam from Sestos to Abydos, an exploit of which I take care to boast.

LETTERS

I am here on business at present, but Athens is my head-quarters, where I am very pleasantly situated in a Franciscan convent.—Believe me to be, with great sincerity, yours very affectionately,   BYRON.

P.S.—Fletcher is well, and discontented as usual; his wife don't write, at least her scrawls have not arrived. You will address to Malta. Pray have you never received my picture in oil from Sanders, Vigo Lane, London?

TO MR. HODGSON

Patras, Morea, October 3, 1810.

lxxii   As I have just escaped from a physician and a fever, which confined me five days to bed, you won't expect much *allegrezza* in the ensuing letter. In this place there is an indigenous distemper, which when the wind blows from the Gulf of Corinth (as it does five months out of six), attacks great and small, and makes woful work with visitors. Here be also two physicians, one of whom trusts to his genius (never having studied)—the other to a campaign of eighteen months against the sick of Otranto, which he made in his youth with great effect.

When I was seized with my disorder, I protested against both these assassins;—but what can a help-less, feverish, toast-and-watered poor wretch do? In spite of my teeth and tongue, the English consul, my Tartar, Albanians, dragoman, forced a physician upon me, and in three days vomited and glystered me to the last gasp. In this state I made my epitaph— take it :—

> Youth, Nature, and relenting Jove,
> To keep my lamp *in* strongly strove :
> But Romanelli was so stout,
> He beat all three—and *blew* it *out*.

But Nature and Jove, being piqued at my doubts, did, in fact, at last, beat Romanelli, and here I am, well but weakly, at your service.

Since I left Constantinople, I have made a tour of the Morea, and visited Veley Pacha, who paid me great honours, and gave me a pretty stallion. H. is doubtless in England before even the date of this letter :—he bears a despatch from me to your bardship. He writes to me from Malta, and requests my journal, if I keep one. I have none, or he should have it ; but I have replied in a consolatory and exhortatory epistle, praying him to abate three and sixpence in the price of his next boke, seeing that half a guinea is a price not to be given for anything save an opera ticket.

As for England, it is long since I have heard from it. Every one at all connected with my concerns is asleep, and you are my only correspondent, agents excepted. I have really no friends in the world ; though all my old school companions are gone forth into that world, and walk about there in monstrous disguises, in the garb of guardsmen, lawyers, parsons, fine gentlemen, and such other masquerade dresses. So, I here shake hands and cut with all these busy people, none of whom write to me. Indeed I ask it not ;—and here I am, a poor traveller and heathenish philosopher, who hath perambulated the greatest part of the Levant, and seen a great quantity of very improvable land and sea, and, after all, am no better than when I set out—Lord help me!

I have been out fifteen months this very day, and I believe my concerns will draw me to England soon; but of this I will apprise you regularly from Malta. On all points Hobhouse will inform you, if you are curious as to our adventures. I have seen some old English papers up to the 15th of May. I see the *Lady of the Lake* advertised. Of course it is in his old ballad style, and pretty. After all, Scott is the best of them. The end of all scribblement is to amuse, and he certainly succeeds there. I long to read his new romance.

And how does *Sir Edgar*? and your friend Bland? I suppose you are involved in some literary squabble. The only way is to despise all brothers of the quill. I suppose you won't allow me to be an author, but I contemn you all, you dogs!—I do.

You don't know Dallas, do you? He had a farce ready for the stage before I left England, and asked me for a prologue, which I promised, but sailed in such a hurry I never penned a couplet. I am afraid to ask after his drama, for fear it should be damned —Lord forgive me for using such a word! but the pit, sir, you know the pit—they will do those things in spite of merit. I remember this farce from a curious circumstance. When Drury Lane was burnt to the ground, by which accident Sheridan and his son lost the few remaining shillings they were worth, what doth my friend Dallas do? Why, before the

fire was out, he writes a note to Tom Sheridan, the
manager of this combustible concern, to inquire
whether this farce was not converted into fuel with
about two thousand other unactable manuscripts,
which, of course, were in great peril, if not actually
consumed. Now was not this characteristic?—the
ruling passions of Pope are nothing to it. Whilst the
poor distracted manager was bewailing the loss of a
building only worth £300,000, together with some
twenty thousand pounds of rags and tinsel in the
tiring-rooms, Bluebeard's elephants, and all that—in
comes a note from a scorching author, requiring at
his hands two acts and odd scenes of a farce!!

Dear H., remind Drury that I am his well-wisher,
and let Scrope Davies be well affected towards me.
I look forward to meeting you at Newstead, and
renewing our old champagne evenings with all the
glee of anticipation. I have written by every opportunity, and expect responses as regular as those of
the liturgy, and somewhat longer. As it is impossible for a man in his senses to hope for happy days,
let us at least look forward to merry ones, which
come nearest to the other in appearance, if not in
reality ; and in such expectations I remain, etc.

TO MR. HODGSON

Athens, November 14, 1810.

My dear Hodgson,—This will arrive with an *lxxiii*
English servant whom I send homewards with some
papers of consequence. I have been journeying in
different parts of Greece for these last four months,

and you may expect me in England somewhere about April, but this is very dubious. Hobhouse you have doubtless seen; he went home in August to arrange materials for a tour he talks of publishing. You will find him well and scribbling—that is, scribbling if well, and well if scribbling. I suppose you have a score of new works, all of which I hope to see flourishing, with a hecatomb of reviews. *My* works are likely to have a powerful effect with a vengeance, as I hear of divers angry people, whom it is proper I should shoot at, by way of satisfaction. Be it so, the same impulse which made 'Otho a warrior' will make me one also. My domestic affairs being moreover considerably deranged, my appetite for travelling pretty well satiated with my late peregrinations, my various hopes in this world almost extinct, and not very brilliant in the next, I trust I shall go through the process with a creditable *sang froid* and not disgrace a line of cut-throat ancestors. [I regret in one of your letters to hear you talk of domestic embarrassments, indeed I am at present very well calculated to sympathise with you on that point. I suppose I must take to dram-drinking as a *succedaneum* for philosophy, though as I am happily not married I have very little occasion for either just yet. Talking of marriage puts me in mind of Drury, who I suppose has a dozen children by this time, all fine fretful brats; I will never forgive Matrimony for having spoiled such an excellent Bachelor.] If anybody honours my name with an inquiry tell them of 'my whereabouts,' and write if you like it. I am living alone in the Franciscan monastery with one friar (a Capuchin of course) and one frier (a bandy-legged Turkish cook), two Albanian savages, a Tartar, and a Dragoman. My only Englishman departs with this and other letters. The day before yesterday, the Waywode (or Governor of Athens), with the Mufti of Thebes (a sort of Mussulman Bishop), supped here and made themselves beastly with raw rum, and the Pàdrè of the convent being as drunk as *we*, my *Attic* feast went off with great *éclat*. I have had a present of a stallion from the Pacha of the Morea. I caught a fever going to Olympia. I was blown ashore on the Island of Salamis, in my way to Corinth through the Gulf of Ægina. I have kicked an Athenian postmaster, I have a friendship with the French consul and an Italian painter, and am on good terms with five Teutones and Cimbri, Danes and Germans, who are travelling for an Academy.—Vale! Yours ever, Μπαιρῶν.

TO THE HONOURABLE MRS. BYRON

Athens, January 14, 1811.

My dear Madam,—I seize an occasion to write, lxxiv as usual, shortly, but frequently, as the arrival of letters, where there exists no regular communication, is, of course, very precarious. I have lately made several small tours of some hundred or two miles about the Morea, Attica, etc., as I have finished my grand giro by the Troad, Constantinople, etc., and am returned down again to Athens. I believe I have mentioned to you more than once that I swam (in imitation of Leander, though without his lady) across the Hellespont, from Sestos to Abydos. Of this, and all other particulars, Fletcher, whom I have sent home with papers, etc., will apprise you. I cannot find that he is any loss; being tolerably master of the Italian and modern Greek languages, which last I am also studying with a master, I can order and discourse more than enough for a reasonable man. Besides, the perpetual lamentations after beef and beer, the stupid, bigoted contempt for everything foreign, and insurmountable incapacity of acquiring even a few words of any language, rendered him, like all other English servants, an incumbrance. I do assure you, the plague of speaking for him, the comforts he required (more than myself by far), the pilaws (a Turkish dish of rice and meat) which he could not eat, the wines which he could not drink, the beds where he could not sleep, and the long list of calamities, such as stumbling horses, want of *tea* ! ! ! etc., which assailed him would have made a lasting source of laughter to a spectator, and inconvenience to a master. After all, the man is honest enough, and, in Christendom, capable enough; but in Turkey, Lord forgive me! my Albanian soldiers, my Tartars and Janissary, worked for him and us too, as my friend Hobhouse can testify.

It is probable I may steer homewards in spring; but to enable me to do that, I must have remittances. My own funds would have lasted me very well; but I was obliged to assist a friend, who, I know, will pay me; but, in the meantime, I am out of pocket. At present I do not care to venture a winter's voyage, even if I were otherwise tired of travelling; but I am so convinced of the advantages of looking at mankind instead of reading about them, and the bitter effects of staying at home with all the narrow prejudices of an islander, that I think there should be a law amongst us to set our young men abroad, for a term, among the few allies our wars have left us.

Here I see and have conversed with French, Italians, Germans, Danes, Greeks, Turks, Americans, etc. etc. etc.; and without losing sight of my own, I can judge of the countries and manners of others. Where I see the superiority of England (which, by-the-by, we are a good deal mistaken about in many things), I am pleased, and where I find her inferior, I am at least enlightened. Now, I might have stayed, smoked in your towns, or fogged in your country, a century, without being sure of this, and without acquiring anything more useful or amusing at home. I keep no journal, nor have I any intention of scribbling my travels. I have done with authorship, and if, in my last production, I have convinced the critics of the world I was something more than they took me for, I am satisfied; nor will I hazard *that reputation* by a future effort. It is true I have some others in manuscript, but I leave them for those who come after me; and, if deemed worth publishing, they may serve to prolong my memory when I myself shall cease to remember. I have a famous Bavarian artist taking some views of Athens, etc. etc., for me. This will be better than scribbling, a disease I hope myself cured of. I hope, on my return, to lead a quiet, recluse life, but God knows and does best for us all; at least, so they say, and I have nothing to object,

as, on the whole, I have no reason to complain of my
lot. I am convinced, however, that men do more
harm to themselves than ever the devil could do to
them. I trust this will find you well, and as happy
as we can be; you will, at least, be pleased to hear I
am so, and yours ever.

TO THE HONOURABLE MRS. BYRON

Athens, February 28, 1811.

lxxv   Dear Madam,—As I have received a firman for
Egypt, etc., I shall proceed to that quarter in the
spring, and I beg you will state to Mr. Hanson that
it is necessary to further remittances. On the subject
of Newstead, I answer as before, *No.* If it is
necessary to sell, sell Rochdale. Fletcher will have
arrived by this time with my letters to that purport.
I will tell you fairly, I have, in the first place, no
opinion of funded property; if, by any particular
circumstances, I shall be led to adopt such a determination, I will, at all events, pass my life abroad,
as my only tie to England is Newstead, and, that
once gone, neither interest nor inclination lead me
northward. Competence in your country is ample
wealth in the East, such is the difference in the value
of money and the abundance of the necessaries of
life; and I feel myself so much a citizen of the world,
that the spot where I can enjoy a delicious climate,
and every luxury, at a less expense than a common
college life in England, will always be a country to
me; and such are in fact the shores of the Archipelago. This then is the alternative: if I preserve

TO MR. HODGSON

Newstead, I return ; if I sell it, I stay away. I have
had no letters since yours of June, but I have written
several times, and shall continue, as usual, on the
same plan.—Believe me yours ever,　　　Byron.

P.S.—I shall most likely see you in the course of
the summer, but, of course, at such a distance, I
cannot specify any particular month.

TO MR. HODGSON

'Volage' frigate, at sea, June 29, 1811.

In a week, with a fair wind, we shall be at　*lxxvi*
Portsmouth, and on the 2nd of July I shall have
completed (to a day) two years of peregrination,
from which I am returning with as little emotion as
I set out. I think, upon the whole, I was more
grieved at leaving Greece than England, which I am
impatient to see, simply because I am tired of a long
voyage.

Indeed, my prospects are not very pleasant. Embarrassed in my private affairs, indifferent to public,
solitary without wish to be social, with a body a little
enfeebled by a succession of fevers, but a spirit, I
trust, yet unbroken, I am returning *home* without a
hope, and almost without a desire. The first thing I
shall have to encounter will be a lawyer, the next a
creditor, then colliers, farmers, surveyors, and all the
agreeable attachments to estates out of repair and
contested coal-pits. In short, I am sick and sorry,
and when I have a little repaired my irreparable
affairs, away I shall march, either to campaign in
Spain, or back again to the East, where I can at

119

least have cloudless skies and a cessation from impertinence.

I trust to meet, or see you, in town, or at Newstead, whenever you can make it convenient—I suppose you are in love and in poetry as usual. That husband, H. Drury, has never written to me, albeit I have sent him more than one letter;—but I dare say the poor man has a family, and of course all his cares are confined to his circle.

> 'For children fresh expenses get,
> And Dicky now for school is fit.'
> WARTON.

If you see him, tell him I have a letter for him from Tucker, a regimental chirurgeon and friend of his, who prescribed for me, . . . and is a very worthy man, but too fond of hard words. I should be too late for a speech-day, or I should probably go down to Harrow. I regretted very much in Greece having omitted to carry the *Anthology* with me—I mean Bland and Merivale's.—What has *Sir Edgar* done? And the *Imitations and Translations*—where are they? I suppose you don't mean to let the public off so easily, but charge them home with a quarto. For me, I am 'sick of fops, and poesy, and prate,' and shall leave the 'whole Castalian state' to Bufo, or anybody else. But you are a sentimental and sensibilitous person, and will rhyme to the end of the chapter. Howbeit, I have written some 4000 lines, of one kind or another, on my travels.

I need not repeat that I shall be happy to see you. I shall be in town about the 8th, at Dorant's Hotel,

TO MRS. BYRON

in Albemarle Street, and proceed in a few days to
Notts, and thence to Rochdale on business.—I am,
here and there, yours, etc.

TO THE HONOURABLE MRS. BYRON

'Volage' frigate, at sea, June 25, 1811.

Dear Mother,—This letter, which shall be for- ^{lxxvii}
warded on our arrival at Portsmouth, probably about
the 4th of July, is begun about twenty-three days
after our departure from Malta.   I have just been
two years (to a day, on the 2nd of July) absent from
England, and I return to it with much the same
feelings which prevailed on my departure, viz., indifference; but within that apathy I certainly do
not comprise yourself, as I will prove by every
means in my power.   You will be good enough to
get my apartments ready at Newstead; but don't
disturb yourself, on any account, particularly mine,
nor consider me in any other light than as a visitor.
I must only inform you that for a long time I have
been restricted to an entire vegetable diet, neither
fish nor flesh coming within my regimen; so I
expect a powerful stock of potatoes, greens, and
biscuit: I drink no wine.   I have two servants,
middle-aged men, and both Greeks.   It is my intention to proceed first to town, to see Mr. Hanson,
and thence to Newstead, on my way to Rochdale.
I have only to beg you will not forget my diet,
which it is very necessary for me to observe.   I am
well in health, as I have generally been, with the

exception of two agues, both of which I quickly got over.

My plans will so much depend on circumstances, that I shall not venture to lay down an opinion on the subject. My prospects are not very promising, but I suppose we shall wrestle through life like our neighbours; indeed, by Hanson's last advices, I have some apprehension of finding Newstead dismantled by Messrs. Brothers, etc., and he seems determined to force me into selling it; but he will be baffled. I don't suppose I shall be much pestered with visitors; but if I am, you must receive them, for I am determined to have nobody breaking in upon my retirement: you know that I was never fond of society, and I am less so than before. I have brought you a shawl, and a quantity of attar of roses, but these I must smuggle, if possible. I trust to find my library in tolerable order.

Fletcher is no doubt arrived. I shall separate the mill from Mr. B——'s farm, for his son is too gay a deceiver to inherit both, and place Fletcher in it, who has served me faithfully, and whose wife is a good woman; besides, it is necessary to sober young Mr. B——, or he will people the parish with bastards. In a word, if he had seduced a dairy-maid, he might have found something like an apology; but the girl is his equal, and in high life or low life reparation is made in such circumstances. But I shall not interfere further than (like Buonaparte) by dismembering Mr. B.'s *kingdom*, and erecting part of it into a principality for field-marshal Fletcher! I hope you govern my little *empire* and its sad load of national debt with a wary hand. To drop my metaphor, I beg leave to subscribe myself, yours ever, BYRON.

P.S.—July 14.—This letter was written to be sent from Portsmouth, but, on arriving there, the squadron was ordered to the Nore, from whence I shall forward it. This I have not done before, supposing you might be alarmed by the interval mentioned in the letter being longer than expected between our arrival in port and my appearance at Newstead.

TO MR. DALLAS

'Volage' frigate, at sea, June 28, 1811.

My dear Sir,—After two years' absence (to a day, *lxxviii* on the 2nd of July, before which we shall not arrive at Portsmouth), I am retracing my way to England. I have, as you know, spent the greater part of that period in Turkey, except two months in Spain and Portugal, which were then accessible. I have seen everything most remarkable in Turkey, particularly the Troad, Greece, Constantinople, and Albania, into which last region very few have penetrated so high as Hobhouse and myself. I don't know that I have done anything to distinguish me from other voyagers, unless you will reckon my swimming from Sestos to Abydos, on May 3, 1810, a tolerable feat for a *modern*.

I am coming back with little prospect of pleasure at home, and with a body a little shaken by one or two smart fevers, but a spirit I hope yet unbroken.

My affairs, it seems, are considerably involved, and much business must be done with lawyers, colliers, farmers, and creditors. Now this, to a man who hates bustle as he hates a bishop, is a serious concern. But enough of my home department.

I find I have been scolding Cawthorn without a cause, as I found two parcels with two letters from you on my return to Malta. By these it appears you have not received a letter from Constantinople, addressed to Longman's, but it was of no consequence.

My Satire it seems is in a fourth edition, a success rather above the middling run, but not much for a production which, from its topics, must be temporary, and of course be successful at first, or not at all. At this period, when I can think and act more coolly, I regret that I have written it, though I shall probably find it forgotten by all except those whom it has offended. My friend Hobhouse's *Miscellany* has not succeeded, but he himself writes so good-humouredly on the subject, I don't know whether to laugh or cry with him. He met with your son at Cadiz, of whom he speaks highly.

Yours and Pratt's *protégé*, Blackett the cobbler, is dead, in spite of his rhymes, and is probably one of the instances where death has saved a man from damnation. You were the ruin of that poor fellow amongst you : had it not been for his patrons he might now have been in very good plight, shoe- (not verse-) making : but you have made him im: mortal with a vengeance. I write this, supposing poetry, patronage, and strong waters to have been

the death of him. If you are in town in or about
the beginning of July, you will find me at Dorant's,
in Albemarle Street, glad to see you. I have an
imitation of Horace's *Art of Poetry* ready for Cawthorn, but don't let that deter you, for I shan't inflict
it upon you. You know I never read my rhymes to
visitors. I shall quit town in a few days for Notts,
and thence to Rochdale. I shall send this the
moment we arrive in harbour, that is a week hence.—
Yours ever sincerely,   BYRON.

TO MR. HENRY DRURY

'Volage' frigate, off Ushant,
July 7, 1811.

My dear Drury,—After two years' absence (on the *lxxix*
2nd) and some odd days I am approaching your
country; the day of our arrival you will see by the
outside date of my letter; at present we are becalmed
comfortably close to Brest Harbour; I have never
been so near it since I left *Duck Puddle.* The enclosed letter is from a friend of yours, Surgeon Tucker,
whom I met with in Greece, and so on to Malta,
where he administered to me for three complaints,
viz., a . . . , a *Tertian fever,* and the *Hemor-*
rhoides, all of which I literally had at once, though
he assured me the *morbid* action of only one of these
distempers could act at a time, which was a great
comfort, though they relieved one another as regularly
as sentinels, and very nearly sent me back to Acheron,
my old acquaintance, which I left fine and flowing in
Albania. We left Malta thirty-four days ago, and

(except the Gut of Gibraltar, which we passed with an easterly wind as easy as an oil Glyster) we have had a tedious passage out.

You have never written, this comes of matrimony; Hodgson has,—so you see the balance of friendship is on the bachelor's side. I am at present well; that is, I have only two out of the three aforesaid complaints, and these I hope to be cured of, as they say one's native fogs are vastly salubrious. . . .

You will either see or hear from or of me soon after the receipt of this, as I pass through town to repair my irreparable affairs, and thence I must go to Notts and raise rents, and to Lancs and sell collieries, and back to London and pay debts, for it seems I shall neither have coals or comfort till I go down to Rochdale in person. I have brought home some marbles for Hobhouse, and for myself 'four ancient Athenian skulls dug out of Sarcophagi,' a 'phial of Attic Hemlock,' 'four live tortoises,' a greyhound (died on the passage), two live Greek servants, one an Athenian, tother a *Yaniote*, who can speak nothing but Romaic and Italian, and *myself*, as Moses in the *Vicar of Wakefield* says *slily*, and I may say it too, for I have as little cause to boast of my expedition as he of his to the fair. I wrote to you from the Cyanaean Rocks, to tell you I had swum from Sestos to Abydos; have you received my letter? . . . Hobhouse went to England to fish up his *Miscellany*, which foundered (so he tells me) in the Gulph of Lethe. I dare say it capsized with the vile goods of his contributory friends, for his own share was very portable. However, I hope he will either weigh up or set sail with a fresh cargo, and a luckier vessel. Hodgson, I suppose, is four deep by this time. What would he give to have seen, like me, the *real Parnassus*, where I robbed the Bishop of Chrisso of a book of geography? But this I only call plagiarism, as it was done within an hour's ride of Delphi.—Believe me, yours ever,   BYRON.

TO THE HONOURABLE MRS. BYRON

Reddish's Hotel, St. James's St., London,
July 23, 1811.

My dear Madam,—I am only detained by Mr. *lxxx* Hanson to sign some copyhold papers, and will give you timely notice of my approach. It is with great reluctance I remain in town. I shall pay a short visit as we go on to Lancashire on Rochdale business. I shall attend to your directions, of course, and am, with great respect, yours ever,   BYRON.

P.S.—You will consider Newstead as your house, not mine; and me only as a visitor.

TO DR. PIGOT

Newport Pagnell, August 2, 1811.

My dear Doctor,—My poor mother died yester- *lxxxi* day! and I am on my way from town to attend her to the family vault. I heard *one* day of her illness, the *next* of her death. Thank God her last moments were most tranquil. I am told she was in little pain, and not aware of her situation. I now feel the truth of Mr. Gray's observation, 'That we can only have *one* mother.' Peace be with her! I have to thank you for your expressions of regard; and as in six weeks I shall be in Lancashire on business, I may extend to Liverpool and Chester,—at least I shall endeavour.

If it will be any satisfaction, I have to inform you that in November next the Editor of the *Scourge* will be tried for two different libels on the late Mrs. B. and myself (the decease of Mrs. B. makes no difference in the proceedings); and as he is guilty, by his very foolish and unfounded assertion of a breach of privilege, he will be prosecuted with the utmost rigour.

I inform you of this, as you seem interested in the affair, which is now in the hands of the Attorney-General.

I shall remain at Newstead the greater part of this month, where I shall be happy to hear from you, after my two years' absence in the East.—I am, dear Pigot, yours very truly,   BYRON.

TO MR. SCROPE DAVIES

Newstead Abbey, August 7, 1811.

lxxxii   My dearest Davies,—Some curse hangs over me and mine. My mother lies a corpse in this house; one of my best friends is drowned in a ditch. What can I say, or think, or do? I received a letter from him the day before yesterday. My dear Scrope, if you can spare a moment, do come down to me—I want a friend. Matthews' last letter was written on *Friday*—on Saturday he was not. In ability, who was like Matthews? How did we all shrink before him? You do me but justice in saying, I would have risked my paltry existence to have preserved his. This very evening did I mean to write, inviting him, as I invite you, my very dear friend, to visit me. God forgive —— for his apathy! What will our poor Hobhouse feel? His letters breathe but of Matthews. Come to me, Scrope; I am almost desolate—left almost alone in the world—I had but you, and H., and M., and let me enjoy the survivors whilst I can. Poor M., in his letter of Friday, speaks of his intended contest for Cambridge, and a speedy journey to London. Write or come, but come if you can, or one or both.—Yours ever.

TO MR. BOLTON

Newstead Abbey, August 12, 1811.

Sir,—I enclose a rough draught of my intended *lxxxiii* will, which I beg to have drawn up as soon as possible in the firmest manner. The alterations are principally made in consequence of the death of Mrs. Byron. I have only to request that it may be got ready in a short time, and have the honour to be, your most obedient, humble servant,　BYRON.

Newstead Abbey, August 12, 1811.

DIRECTIONS FOR THE CONTENTS OF A WILL TO
BE DRAWN UP IMMEDIATELY ·

The estate of Newstead to be entailed (subject to certain deductions) on George Anson Byron, heir-at-law, or whoever may be the heir-at-law on the death of Lord B. The Rochdale property to be sold in part or the whole, according to the debts and legacies of the present Lord B.

To Nicolo Giraud of Athens, subject of France, but born in Greece, the sum of seven thousand pounds sterling, to be paid from the sale of such parts of Rochdale, Newstead, or elsewhere, as may enable the said Nicolo Giraud (resident at Athens and Malta in the year 1810) to receive the above sum on his attaining the age of twenty-one years.

To William Fletcher, Joseph Murray, and Demetrius Zograffo (native of Greece), servants, the sum of fifty pounds pr. ann. each, for their natural lives. To Wm. Fletcher, the Mill at Newstead, on condition that he payeth rent, but not subject to the caprice of the landlord. To R^t. Rushton the sum of fifty pounds per ann. for life, and a further sum of one thousand pounds on attaining the age of twenty-five years.

To J^n. Hanson, Esq., the sum of two thousand pounds sterling.

The claims of S. B. Davies, Esq., to be satisfied on proving the amount of the same.

The body of Lord B. to be buried in the vault of the garden of Newstead, without any ceremony or burial-service whatever, or any inscription, save his name and age. His dog not to be removed from the said vault.

My library and furniture of every description to my friends J^n. Cam Hobhouse, Esq., and S. B. Davies, Esq., my executors. In case of their decease, the Rev. J. Becher, of Southwell, Notts, and R. C. Dallas, Esq., of Mortlake, Surrey, to be executors.

The produce of the sale of Wymondham in Norfolk, and the late Mrs. B.'s Scotch property, to be appropriated in aid of the payment of debts and legacies.

TO MR. DALLAS

Newstead Abbey, Notts, August 12, 1811.

My dear Sir,—Peace be with the dead! Regret *lxxxiv* cannot wake them. With a sigh to the departed, let us resume the dull business of life, in the certainty that we also shall have our repose. Besides her who gave me being, I have lost more than one who made that being tolerable.—The best friend of my friend Hobhouse, Matthews, a man of the first talents, and also not the worst of my narrow circle, has perished miserably in the muddy waves of the Cam, always fatal to genius :—my poor school-fellow Wingfield, at Coimbra —within a month ; and whilst I had heard from *all three*, but not seen *one*. Matthews wrote to me the very day before his death, and though I feel for his fate, I am still more anxious for Hobhouse, who, I very much fear, will hardly retain his senses ; his letters to me since the event have been most incoherent. But let this pass—we shall all one day pass along with the rest—the world is too full of such things, and our very sorrow is selfish.

I received a letter from you, which my late occupations prevented me from duly noticing,—I hope your friends and family will long hold together.—I shall be glad to hear from you, on business, on common-place, or anything, or nothing—but death —I am already too familiar with the dead. It is strange that I look on the skulls which stand beside me (—I have always had *four* in my study—) without emotion, but I cannot strip the features of those I have known of their fleshy covering, even in idea, without a hideous sensation ; but the worms are less ceremonious. Surely the Romans did well when they burned the dead. I shall be happy to hear from you, and am, yours very sincerely,

BYRON.

TO MR. BOLTON

Newstead Abbey, August 16, 1811.

lxxxv Sir,—I have answered the queries on the margin. I wish Mr. Davies's claims to be most fully allowed, and, further, that he be one of my executors. I wish the will to be made in a manner to prevent all discussion, if possible, after my decease ; and this I leave to you as a professional gentleman.

With regard to the few and simple directions for the disposal of my *carcass*, I must have them implicitly fulfilled, as they will, at least, prevent trouble and expense,—and (what would be of little consequence to me, but may quiet the conscience of the survivors) the garden is *consecrated* ground. These directions are copied verbatim from my former will ; the alterations in other parts have arisen from the death of Mrs. B. I have the honour to be, your most obedient, humble servant,   BYRON.

TO MR. BOLTON

Newstead Abbey, August 20, 1811.

Sir,—The witnesses shall be provided from amongst *lxxxvi* my tenants, and I shall be happy to see you on any day most convenient to yourself. I forgot to mention, that it must be specified by codicil, or otherwise, that my body is on no account to be removed from the vault where I have directed it to be placed; and in case any of my successors within the entail (from bigotry, or otherwise) might think proper to remove the carcass, such proceeding shall be attended by forfeiture of the estate, which in such case shall go to my sister, the Honble. Augusta Leigh and her heirs on similar conditions.—I have the honour to be, Sir, your very obedient, humble servant, BYRON.

TO MR. DALLAS

Newstead, August 21, 1811.

Your letter gives me credit for more acute feelings *lxxxii* than I possess; for though I feel tolerably miserable, yet I am at the same time subject to a kind of hysterical merriment, or rather laughter without merriment, which I can neither account for nor conquer, and yet I do not feel relieved by it; but an indifferent person would think me in excellent spirits. 'We must forget these things,' and have recourse to our old selfish comforts, or rather comfortable selfishness. I do not think I shall return to London immediately, and shall therefore accept freely what is offered courteously—your mediation between me and Murray. I don't think my name will answer the

purpose, and you must be aware that my plaguy
Satire will bring the north and south Grub Streets
down upon the *Pilgrimage*;—but, nevertheless, if
Murray makes a point of it, and you coincide with
him, I will do it daringly; so let it be entitled, ' By
the author of *English Bards and Scotch Reviewers.*'
My remarks on the Romaic, etc., once intended to
accompany the *Hints from Horace*, shall go along
with the other, as being indeed more appropriate;
also the smaller poems now in my possession, with a
few selected from those published in Hobhouse's
Miscellany. I have found amongst my poor mother's
papers all my letters from the East, and one in
particular of some length from Albania. From this,
if necessary, I can work up a note or two on that
subject. As I kept no journal, the letters written
on the spot are the best. But of this anon, when
we have definitely arranged.

Has Murray shown the work to any one? He
may—but I will have no traps for applause. Of
course there are little things I would wish to alter,
and perhaps the two stanzas of a buffooning cast on
London's Sunday are as well left out. I much wish
to avoid identifying Childe Harold's character with
mine, and that, in sooth, is my second objection to
my name appearing in the title-page. When you
have made arrangements as to time, size, type, etc.,
favour me with a reply. I am giving you an universe
of trouble, which thanks cannot atone for. I made
a kind of prose apology for my scepticism at the
head of the MS., which, on recollection, is so much
more like an attack than a defence, that, haply, it

might better be omitted:—perpend, pronounce. After all, I fear Murray will be in a scrape, with the orthodox; but I cannot help it, though I wish him well through it. As for me, 'I have supped full of criticism,' and I don't think that the 'most dismal treatise' will stir and rouse my 'fell of hair,' till 'Birnam wood do come to Dunsinane.'

I shall continue to write at intervals, and hope you will pay me in kind. How does Pratt get on, or rather get off, Joe Blackett's posthumous stock? You killed that poor man amongst you, in spite of your Ionian friend and myself, who would have saved him from Pratt, poetry, present poverty, and posthumous oblivion. Cruel patronage! to ruin a man at his calling; but then he is a divine subject for subscription and biography; and Pratt, who makes the most of his dedications, has inscribed the volume to no less than five families of distinction.

I am sorry you don't like Harry White: with a great deal of cant, which in him was sincere (indeed it killed him as you killed Joe Blackett), certes there is poesy and genius. I don't say this on account of my simile and rhymes; but surely he was beyond all the Bloomfields and Blacketts, and their collateral cobblers, whom Lofft and Pratt have or may kidnap from their calling into the service of the trade. You must excuse my flippancy, for I am writing I know not what, to escape from myself. Hobhouse is gone to Ireland. Mr. Davies has been here on his way to Harrowgate.

You did not know Matthews: he was a man of

the most astonishing powers, as he sufficiently proved at Cambridge, by carrying off more prizes and fellowships, against the ablest candidates, than any other graduate on record ; but a most decided atheist, indeed noxiously so, for he proclaimed his principles in all societies. I knew him well, and feel a loss not easily to be supplied to myself—to Hobhouse never. —Let me hear from you, and believe me, etc.

TO MR. HODGSON

Newstead Abbey, August 22, 1811.

lxxxviii   You may have heard of the sudden death of my mother, and poor Matthews, which with that of Wingfield (of which I was not fully aware till just before I left town, and indeed hardly believed it), has made a sad chasm in my connections. Indeed the blows followed each other so rapidly that I am yet stupid from the shock ; and though I do eat, and drink, and talk, and even laugh, at times, yet I can hardly persuade myself that I am awake, did not every morning convince me mournfully to the contrary.—I shall now waive the subject,—the dead are at rest, and none but the dead can be so.

You will feel for poor Hobhouse,—Matthews was the 'god of his idolatry'; and if intellect could exalt a man above his fellows, no one could refuse him pre-eminence. I knew him most intimately, and valued him proportionably ; but I am recurring—so let us talk of life and the living.

If you should feel a disposition to come here, you will find 'beef and a sea-coal fire,' and not ungenerous wine. Whether Otway's two other requisites for an Englishman or not, I cannot tell, but probably one of them.—Let me know when I may expect you, that I may tell you when I go and when return. I have not yet been to Lancs. Davies has been here, and has invited me to Cambridge for a week in October, so that, peradventure, we may encounter glass to glass. His gaiety (death cannot mar it) has done me service; but, after all, ours was a hollow laughter.

You will write to me? I am solitary, and I never felt solitude irksome before. Your anxiety about the critique on ——'s book is amusing; as it was anonymous, certes it was of little consequence: I wish it had produced a little more confusion, being a lover of literary malice. Are you doing nothing? writing nothing? printing nothing? why not your Satire on Methodism? the subject (supposing the public to be blind to merit) would do wonders. Besides, it would be as well for a destined deacon to prove his orthodoxy.—It really would give me pleasure to see you properly appreciated. I say *really*, as, being an author, my humanity might be suspected.—Believe me, dear H., yours always.

TO MR. MURRAY

Newstead Abbey, Notts, August 23, 1811.

Sir,—A domestic calamity in the death of a near lxxxix relation has hitherto prevented my addressing you on the subject of this letter.—My friend, Mr. Dallas, has placed in your hands a manuscript poem written by

LETTERS

me in Greece, which he tells me you do not object
to publishing. But he also informed me in London
that you wished to send the MS. to Mr. Gifford.
Now, though no one would feel more gratified by the
chance of obtaining his observations on a work than
myself, there is in such a proceeding a kind of
petition for praise, that neither my pride—or whatever
you please to call it—will admit. Mr. G. is not only
the first satirist of the day, but editor of one of the
principal reviews. As such, he is the last man whose
censure (however eager to avoid it) I would deprecate
by clandestine means. You will therefore retain
the manuscript in your own care, or, if it must
needs be shown, send it to another. Though not
very patient of censure, I would fain obtain fairly any
little praise my rhymes might deserve, at all events
not by extortion, and the humble solicitations of a
bandied-about MS. I am sure a little consideration
will convince you it would be wrong.

If you determine on publication, I have some
smaller poems (never published), a few notes, and a
short dissertation on the literature of the modern
Greeks (written at Athens), which will come in at the
end of the volume.—And, if the present poem should
succeed, it is my intention, at some subsequent period,
to publish some selections from my first work,—my
Satire,—another nearly the same length, and a few
other things, with the MS. now in your hands, in two
volumes.—But of these hereafter. You will apprize
me of your determination.—I am, Sir, your very
obedient, etc.

TO MR. DALLAS

Newstead Abbey, August 25, 1811.

Being fortunately enabled to frank, I do not spare *xc* scribbling, having sent you packets within the last ten days. I am passing solitary, and do not expect my agent to accompany me to Rochdale before the second week in September; a delay which perplexes me, as I wish the business over, and should at present welcome employment. I sent you exordiums, annotations, etc. for the forthcoming quarto, if quarto it is to be: and I also have written to Mr. Murray my objection to sending the MS. to Juvenal, but allowing him to show it to any others of the calling. Hobhouse is amongst the types already: so, between his prose and my verse, the world will be decently drawn upon for its paper-money and patience. Besides all this, my *Imitation of Horace* is gasping for the press at Cawthorn's, but I am hesitating as to the *how* and the *when*, the single or the double, the present or the future. You must excuse all this, for I have nothing to say in this lone mansion but of myself, and yet I would willingly talk or think of aught else.

What are you about to do? Do you think of perching in Cumberland, as you opined when I was in the metropolis? If you mean to retire, why not occupy Miss Milbanke's "Cottage of Friendship,' late the seat of Cobbler Joe, for whose death you and others are answerable? His *Orphan Daughter* (pathetic Pratt!) will, certes, turn out a shoemaking Sappho. Have you no remorse? I think that elegant address to Miss Dallas should be inscribed on the cenotaph which Miss Milbanke means to stitch to his memory.

The newspapers seem much disappointed at his Majesty's not dying, or doing something better. I presume it is almost over. If parliament meets in October, I shall be in town to attend. I am also invited to Cambridge for the beginning of that month, but am first to jaunt to Rochdale. Now Matthews is gone, and Hobhouse in Ireland, I have hardly one left there to bid me welcome, except my inviter. At three-and-twenty I am left alone, and what more can we be at seventy? It is true I am young enough to begin again, but with whom can I retrace the laughing part of life? It is odd how few of my friends have died a quiet death,—I mean in their beds. But a quiet life is of more consequence. Yet one loves squabbling and jostling better than yawning. This *last word* admonishes me to relieve you from yours very truly, etc.

TO MR. DALLAS

Newstead Abbey, Aug. 27, 1811.

xci   I was so sincere in my note on the late Charles Matthews, and do feel myself so totally unable to do justice to his talents, that the passage must stand for the very reason you bring against it. To him all the men I ever knew were pigmies. He was an intellectual giant. It is true I loved Wingfield better; he was the earliest and the dearest, and one of the few one could never repent of having loved; but in ability—ah! you did not know Matthews!

Childe Harold may wait and welcome—books are never the worse for delay in the publication. So you have got our heir, George Anson Byron, and his sister, with you.

You may say what you please, but you are one of the *murderers* of Blackett, and yet you won't allow Harry White's genius. Setting aside his bigotry, he surely ranks next Chatterton. It is astonishing how little he was known; and at Cambridge no one thought or heard of such a man till his death rendered all notice useless. For my own part, I should have been most proud of such an acquaintance: his very prejudices were respectable. There is a sucking epic poet at Granta, a Mr. Townsend, *protégé* of the late Cumberland. Did you ever hear of him and his *Armageddon*? I think his plan (the man I don't know) borders on the sublime: though, perhaps, the anticipation of the 'Last Day' (according to you Nazarenes) is a little too daring: at least, it looks like telling the Lord what He is to do, and might remind an ill-natured person of the line,

> 'And fools rush in where angels fear to tread.'

But I don't mean to cavil, only other folks will, and he may bring all the lambs of Jacob Behmen about his ears. However, I hope he will bring it to a conclusion, though Milton is in his way.

Write to me—I dote on gossip—and make a bow to Ju—, and shake George by the hand for me; but, take care, for he has a sad sea paw.

P.S.—I would ask George here, but I don't know how to amuse him—all my horses were sold when

I left England, and I have not had time to replace them. Nevertheless, if he will come down and shoot in September, he will be very welcome : but he must bring a gun, for I gave away all mine to Ali Pacha, and other Turks. Dogs, a keeper, and plenty of game, with a very large manor, I have— a lake, a boat, house-room, and *neat wines*.

TO MR. HODGSON

Newstead Abbey, Sept. 3, 1811.

xcii   My dear Hodgson,—I will have nothing to do with your immortality; we are miserable enough in this life, without the absurdity of speculating upon another. If men are to live, why die at all? and if they die, why disturb the sweet and sound sleep that ' knows no waking'? ' Post mortem nihil est, ipsaque mors nihil'—'quæris quo jaceas post obitum loco?' ' Quo *non nata* jacent.' . . . As to revealed religion, Christ came to save men ; but a good Pagan will go to heaven, and a bad Nazarene to hell ; 'Argal' (I argue like the gravedigger) why are not all men Christians? or why are any? If mankind may be saved who never heard or dreamt, at Timbuctoo, Otaheite, Terra Incognita, etc., of Galilee and its Prophet, Christianity is of no avail; if they cannot be saved without, why are not all orthodox? It is a little hard to send a man preaching to Judæa, and leave the rest of the world—niggers and what not— dark as their complexions, without a ray of light for so many years to lead them on high ; and who will believe that God will damn men for not knowing what they were never taught? I hope I am sincere; I was so at least on a bed of sickness in a far-distant country, when I had neither friend, nor comforter, nor hope, to sustain me. I looked to death as a relief from pain, without a wish for an after-life, but a confidence that the God who punishes in this existence had left that last asylum for the weary.

ὃν ὁ Θεὸς ἀγαπάει ἀποθνήσκει νέος.

I am no Platonist, I am nothing at all; but I would sooner be a Paulician, Manichean, Spinozist, Gentile, Pyrrhonian, Zoroastian, than one of the seventy-two villanous sects who are tearing each other to pieces for the love of the Lord and hatred of each other. Talk of Galileeism? Show me the effects—are you better, wiser, kinder by your precepts? I will bring ten Mussulmans shall shame you all in goodwill towards men, prayer to God, and duty to their neighbours. And is there a ——, or a Bonze, who is not superior to a fox-hunting curate? But I will say no more on this endless theme; let me live, well if possible, and die without pain. The rest is with God, who assuredly, had He *come* or *sent*, would have made Himself manifest to nations, and intelligible to all.

I shall rejoice to see you. My present intention is to accept Scrope Davies's invitation; and then, if you accept mine, we shall meet *here* and *there*. Did you know poor Matthews? I shall miss him much at Cambridge.

143

LETTERS

TO MR. DALLAS

Newstead Abbey, Sept. 4, 1811.

xciii My dear Sir,—I am at present anxious, as Cawthorn seems to wish it, to have a small edition of the *Hints from Horace* published immediately; but the Latin (the most difficult poem in the language) renders it necessary to be very particular not only in correcting the proofs with Horace open, but in adapting the parallel passages of the imitation in such places to the original as may enable the reader not to lose sight of the allusion. I don't know whether I ought to ask you to do this, but I am too far off to do it for myself; and if you can condescend to my school-boy erudition, you will oblige me by setting this thing going, though you will smile at the importance I attach to it.—Believe me, ever yours,   BYRON.

TO MR. MURRAY

Newstead Abbey, Notts, Sept. 5, 1811.

xciv Sir,—The time seems to be past when (as Dr. Johnson said) a man was certain to 'hear the truth from his bookseller,' for you have paid me so many compliments, that, if I was not the veriest scribbler on earth, I should feel affronted. As I accept your compliments, it is but fair I should give equal or greater credit to your objections, the more so, as I believe them to be well founded. With regard to the political and metaphysical parts, I am afraid I can alter nothing; but I have high authority for my

144

errors in that point, for even the *Æneid* was a *political* poem, and written for a *political* purpose; and as to my unlucky opinions on subjects of more importance, I am too sincere in them for recantation. On Spanish affairs I have said what I saw, and every day confirms me in that notion of the result formed on the spot; and I rather think honest John Bull is beginning to come round again to that sobriety which Massena's retreat had begun to reel from its centre—the usual consequence of *un*usual success. So you perceive I cannot alter the sentiments; but if there are any alterations in the structure of the versification you would wish to be made, I will tag rhymes and turn stanzas as much as you please. As for the '*orthodox*,' let us hope they will buy, on purpose to abuse—you will forgive the one, if they will do the other. You are aware that anything from my pen must expect no quarter, on many accounts; and as the present publication is of a nature very different from the former, we must not be sanguine.

You have given me no answer to my question—tell me fairly, did you show the MS. to some of your corps?—I sent an introductory stanza to Mr. Dallas, to be forwarded to you; the poem else will open too abruptly. The stanzas had better be numbered in Roman characters. There is a disquisition on the literature of the modern Greeks, and some smaller poems to come in at the close. These are now at Newstead, but will be sent in time. If Mr. D. has lost the stanza and note annexed to it, write, and I will send it myself.—You tell me to add two cantos, but I am about to visit my *collieries* in Lancashire on the 15th instant, which is so unpoetical an employment that I need say no more.—I am, Sir, your most obedient, etc.

TO MR. DALLAS

Newstead Abbey, Sept. 7, 1811.

xcv   As Gifford has been ever my 'Magnus Apollo,' any approbation, such as you mention, would, of course, be more welcome than 'all Bocara's vaunted gold, than all the gems of Samarcand.' But I am sorry the MS. was shown to him in such a manner, and had written to Murray to say as much, before I was aware that it was too late.

Your objection to the expression 'central line' I can only meet by saying that, before Childe Harold left England, it was his full intention to traverse Persia, and return by India, which he could not have done without passing the equinoctial.

The other errors you mention, I must correct in the progress through the press. I feel honoured by the wish of such men that the poem should be continued, but to do that I must return to Greece and Asia; I must have a warm sun and a blue sky; I cannot describe scenes so dear to me by a sea-coal fire. I had projected an additional canto when I was in the Troad and Constantinople, and if I saw them again, it would go on; but under existing circumstances and *sensations,* I have neither harp, 'heart, nor voice' to proceed. I feel that *you are all right* as to the metaphysical part; but I also feel that I am sincere, and that if I am only to write 'ad captandum vulgus,' I might as well edit a magazine at once, or spin canzonettas for Vauxhall.

My work must make its way as well as it can; I know I have everything against me, angry poets and prejudices; but if the poem is a *poem*, it will surmount these obstacles, and if *not*, it deserves its fate. Your friend's Ode I have read—it is no great compliment to pronounce it far superior to Smythe's on the same subject, or to the merits of the new Chancellor. It is evidently the production of a man of taste, and a poet, though I should not be willing to say it was fully equal to what might be expected from the author of *Horæ Ionicæ*. I thank you for it, and that is more than I would do for any other Ode of the present day.

I am very sensible of your good wishes, and, indeed, I have need of them. My whole life has been at variance with propriety, not to say decency; my circumstances are become involved; my friends are dead or estranged, and my existence a dreary void. In Matthews I have lost my 'guide, philosopher, and friend'; in Wingfield a friend only, but one whom I could have wished to have preceded in his long journey.

Matthews was indeed an extraordinary man; it has not entered into the heart of a stranger to conceive such a man: there was the stamp of immortality in all he said or did;—and now what is he? When we see such men pass away and be no more—men, who seem created to display what the Creator *could make* His creatures, gathered into corruption, before

the maturity of minds that might have been the pride
of posterity, what are we to conclude? For my own
part, I am bewildered. To me he was much, to
Hobhouse everything. My poor Hobhouse doted
on Matthews. For me, I did not love quite so much
as I honoured him; I was indeed so sensible of his
infinite superiority, that, though I did not envy, I
stood in awe of it. He, Hobhouse, Davies, and myself, formed a coterie of our own at Cambridge and
elsewhere. Davies is a wit and man of the world,
and feels as much as such a character can do; but
not as Hobhouse has been affected. Davies, who is
not a scribbler, has always beaten us all in the war of
words, and by his colloquial powers at once delighted
and kept us in order. Hobhouse and myself always
had the worst of it with the other two; and even
Matthews yielded to the dashing vivacity of Scrope
Davies. But I am talking to you of men, or boys,
as if you cared about such beings.

I expect mine agent down on the 14th to proceed
to Lancashire, where I hear from all quarters that I
have a very valuable property in coals, etc. I then
intend to accept an invitation to Cambridge in
October, and shall, perhaps, run up to town. I have
four invitations—to Wales, Dorset, Cambridge, and
Chester; but I must be a man of business. I am
quite alone, as these long letters sadly testify. I
perceive, by referring to your letter, that the Ode is
from the author; make my thanks acceptable to him.
His muse is worthy a nobler theme. You will write
as usual, I hope. I wish you good evening, and am,
etc.

TO MR. HODGSON

Newstead Abbey, Sept. 9, 1811.

Dear Hodgson,—I have been a good deal in your *xcvi*
company lately, for I have been reading *Juvenal* and
Lady Jane, etc., for the first time since my return.
The Tenth Sat⁶ has always been my favourite, as
I suppose indeed of everybody's. It is the finest
recipe for making one miserable with this life, and
content to walk out of it, in any language. I should
think it might be redde with great effect to a man
dying without much pain, in preference to all the
stuff that ever was said or sung in churches. But
you are a deacon, and I say no more. Ah! you
will marry and become lethargic, like poor Hal of
Harrow, who yawns at 10 o' nights, and orders caudle
annually. I wrote an answer to yours fully some
days ago, and being quite alone and able to frank,
you must excuse this subsequent epistle, which will
cost nothing but the trouble of deciphering. I am
expectant of agents to accompany me to Rochdale, a
journey not to be anticipated with pleasure; though
I feel very restless where I am, and shall probably
ship off for Greece again; what nonsense it is to
talk of Soul, when a cloud makes it *melancholy* and
wine *mad*. Collet of *Staines*, your 'most kind host,'
has lost that girl you saw of his. She grew to five
feet eleven, and might have been God knows how
high if it had pleased Him to renew the race of
Anak; but she fell by a ptisick, a fresh proof of the
folly of begetting children. You knew Matthews.
Was he not an intellectual giant? I knew few
better or more intimately, and none who deserved

more admiration in point of ability. Scrope Davies
has been here on his way to Harrowgate; I am his
guest in October at King's, where we will 'drink
deep ere we depart.' 'Won't you, won't you, won't
you, won't you come, Mr. Mug?' We did not
amalgamate properly at Harrow; it was somehow
rainy, and then a wife makes such a damp, but in
a seat of celibacy, I will have revenge. Don't you
hate helping fish, and losing the wings of chicken?
And then, conversation is always flabby. Oh! in
the East women are in their proper sphere, and one
has—no conversation at all. My house here is a
delightful matrimonial mansion. When I wed, my
spouse and I will be so happy!—one in each wing.

I presume you are in motion from your Herefordshire station, and Drury must be gone back to
Gerund Grinding. I have not been at Cambridge
since I took my M.A. degree in 1808. *Eheu fugaces!*
I look forward to meeting you and Scrope there
with the feelings of other times. Capt Hobhouse
is at Enniscorthy in Juverna. I wish he was in
England.—Yours ever, B.

TO MR. DALLAS

Newstead Abbey, Sept. 10, 1811.

xcvii   Dear Sir,—I rather think in one of the opening
stanzas of *Childe Harold* there is this line—

' 'Tis said at times the sullen tear would start.'

Now, a line or two after, I have a repetition of the
epithet '*sullen* reverie'; so (if it be so) let us have

'speechless reverie,' or 'silent reverie'; but, at all
events, do away the recurrence.——Yours ever,

B——

TO MR. HODGSON

Newstead Abbey, Sept. 13, 1811.

My dear Hodgson,—I thank you for your song, or, *xcviii*
rather, your two songs—your new song on love, and
your *old song* on *religion*. I admire the *first* sincerely,
and in turn call upon you to *admire* the following on
Anacreon Moore's new operatic farce, or farcical
opera—call it which you will :—

> Good plays are scarce,
> So Moore writes farce ;
>   Is fame like his so brittle ?
> We knew before
> That '*Little's*' *Moore*,
> But now '*tis Moore* that's *Little*.

I won't dispute with you on the arcana of your-new
calling ; they are bagatelles, like the King of Poland's
rosary.   One remark, and I have done : the basis of
your religion is *injustice*; the *Son* of *God*, the *pure*,
the *immaculate*, the *innocent*, is sacrificed for the *guilty*.
This proves *His* heroism ; but no more does away
man's guilt than a schoolboy's volunteering to be
flogged for another would exculpate the dunce from
negligence, or preserve him from the rod.   You
degrade the Creator, in the first place, by making
Him a begetter of children ; and in the next you
convert Him into a tyrant over an immaculate and
injured Being, who is sent into existence to suffer
death for the benefit of some millions of scoundrels,

who, after all, seem as likely to be damned as ever.
As to Miracles, I agree with Hume that it is more
probable men should *lie* or be *deceived*, than that
things out of the course of nature should so happen.
Mahomet wrought miracles, Brothers the prophet
had *proselytes*, and so would Breslau, the conjurer,
had he lived in the time of Tiberius.

Besides, I trust that God is not a *Jew*, but the
God of all mankind ; and, as you allow that a virtuous
Gentile may be saved, you do away the necessity of
being a Jew or a Christian.

I do not believe in any revealed religion, because
no religion is revealed ; and if it pleases the Church
to damn me for not allowing a *nonentity*, I throw
myself on the mercy of the ' *Great First Cause, least
understood*,' who must do what is most proper; though
I conceive He never made anything to be tortured
in another life, whatever it may in this. I will neither
read *pro* nor *con*. God would have made His will
known without books, considering how very few could
read them when Jesus of Nazareth lived, had it been
His pleasure to ratify any peculiar mode of worship.
As to your immortality, if people are to live, why
die? And our carcasses, which are to rise again, are
they worth raising? I hope, if mine is, that I shall
have a better *pair of legs* than I have moved on these
two-and-twenty years, or I shall be sadly behind in
the squeeze into Paradise. Did you ever read Malthus
on Population? If he be right, war and pestilence
are our best friends, to save us from being eaten
alive, in this ' best of all possible worlds.'

I will write, read, and think no more ; indeed, I

do not wish to shock your prejudices by saying all I do think. Let us make the most of life, and leave dreams to Emanuel Swedenborg.

Now to dreams of another genus—poesies. I like your song much; but I will say no more, for fear you should think I wanted to coax you into approbation of my past, present, or future acrostics. I shall not be at Cambridge before the middle of October; but, when I go, I should certes like to see you there before you are dubbed a deacon. Write to me, and I will rejoin.—Yours ever,   BYRON.

TO MR. MURRAY

Newstead Abbey, Notts, Sept. 14, 1811.

Sir,—Since your former letter, Mr. Dallas informs me that the MS. has been submitted to the perusal of Mr. Gifford, most contrary to my wishes, as Mr. D. could have explained, and as my own letter to you did, in fact, explain, with my motives for objecting to such a proceeding. Some late domestic events, of which you are probably aware, prevented my letter from being sent before; indeed, I hardly conceived you would have so hastily thrust my productions into the hands of a stranger, who could be as little pleased by receiving them as their author is at their being offered, in such a manner, and to such a man. *xcix*

My address, when I leave Newstead, will be to 'Rochdale, Lancashire'; but I have not yet fixed the day of departure, and I will apprise you when ready to set off.

You have placed me in a very ridiculous situation, but it is past, and nothing more is to be said on the subject. You hinted to me that you wished some alterations to be made; if they have nothing to do with politics or religion, I will make them with great readiness.—I am, Sir, etc. etc.

TO MR. DALLAS

Newstead Abbey, Sept. 15, 1811.

c My dear Sir,—My agent will not be here for at least a week, and even afterwards my letters will be forwarded to Rochdale. I am sorry that Murray should *groan* on my account, tho' *that* is better than the anticipation of applause, of which men and books are generally disappointed.

The notes I sent are *merely matter* to be divided, arranged, and published *for notes* hereafter, in proper places; at present I am too much occupied with earthly cares, to waste time or trouble upon rhyme or its modern indispensables, annotations.

Pray let me hear from you, when at leisure. I have written to abuse Murray for showing the MS. to Mr. G., who must certainly think it was done by my wish, though you know the contrary.—Believe me, yours ever, B——

TO MR. MURRAY

Newstead Abbey, Sept. 16, 1811.

ci I return the proof, which I should wish to be shown to Mr. Dallas, who understands typographical arrangements much better than I can pretend to do. The printer may place the notes in his *own way*, or any *way*, so that they are out of *my way*; I care nothing about types or margins.

TO MR. DALLAS

If you have any communication to make, I shall be here at least a week or ten days longer.—I am, Sir, etc. etc.

Newstead Abbey, Sept. 16, 1811.

Dear Sir,—I send you a *motto*— *cii*

L'univers est une espèce de livre, dont on n'a lu que la première page quand on n'a vu que son pays. J'en ai feuilleté un assez grand nombre, que j'ai trouvé également mauvaises. Cet examen ne m'a point été infructueux. Je haïssais ma patrie. Toutes les impertinences des peuples divers, parmi lesquels j'ai vécu, m'ont réconcilié avec elle. Quand je n'aurais tiré d'autre bénéfice de mes voyages que celui-là, je n'en regretterais ni les frais, ni les fatigues. LE COSMOPOLITE.

If not too long, I think it will suit the book. The passage is from a little French volume, a great favourite with me, which I picked up in the Archipelago. I don't think it is well known in England ; Monbron is the author ; but it is a work sixty years old.

Good morning ! I won't take up your time.— Yours ever, BYRON.

Newstead Abbey, Sept. 17, 1811.

I can easily excuse your not writing, as you have, *ciii* I hope, something better to do, and you must pardon my frequent invasions on your attention, because I have at this moment nothing to interpose between you and my epistles.

I cannot settle to anything, and my days pass, with the exception of bodily exercise to some extent, with

uniform indolence, and idle insipidity. I have been
expecting, and still expect, my agent, when I shall
have enough to occupy my reflections in business
of no very pleasant aspect. Before my journey to
Rochdale, you shall have due notice where to address
me—I believe at the post-office of that township.
From Murray I received a second proof of the same
pages, which I requested him to show you, that anything which may have escaped my observation may
be detected before the printer lays the corner-stone
of an *errata* column.

I am now not quite alone, having an old acquaintance and school-fellow with me, so *old*, indeed, that
we have nothing *new* to say on any subject, and
yawn at each other in a sort of *quiet inquietude*. I
hear nothing from Cawthorn, or Captain Hobhouse ;
and *their quarto*—Lord have mercy on mankind !
We come on like Cerberus with our triple publications. As for *myself*, by *myself*, I must be satisfied
with a comparison to *Janus*.

I am not at all pleased with Murray for showing
the MS. ; and I am certain Gifford must see it in the
same light that I do. His praise is nothing to the
purpose : what could he say ? He could not spit in
the face of one who had praised him in every possible
way. I must own that I wish to have the impression
removed from his mind that I had any concern in
such a paltry transaction. The more I think, the
more it disquiets me ; so I will say no more about
it. It is bad enough to be a scribbler, without
having recourse to such shifts to extort praise, or
deprecate censure. It is anticipating, it is begging,

kneeling, adulating,—the devil! the devil! the devil!
and all without my wish, and contrary to my express
desire. I wish Murray had been tied to *Payne's*
neck when he jumped into the Paddington Canal,
and so tell him—*that* is the proper receptacle for
publishers. You have thoughts of settling in the
country; why not try Notts? I think there are
places which would suit you in all points, and then
you are nearer the metropolis. But of this anon.—
I am, yours, etc. BYRON.

TO MR. DALLAS

Newstead Abbey, Sept. 17, 1811.

Dear Sir,—I have just discovered some pages of *civ*
observations on the modern Greeks written at Athens,
by me, under the title of *Noctes Atticae.* They will
do to *cut up* into notes, and to be *cut up* afterwards,
which is all that notes are generally good for. They
were written at Athens, as you will see by the date.
—Yours ever, B.

TO MR. DALLAS

Newstead Abbey, Sept. 21, 1811.

I have shown my respect for your suggestions by *cv*
adopting them; but I have made many alterations
in the first proof, over and above; as, for example:

> O Thou, in *Hellas* deem'd of heavenly birth,
>   Etc., etc.,
> Since *shamed full oft* by *later lyres* on earth,
>   Mine, etc.
> Yet there *I've wander'd* by the vaunted rill;

and so on. So I have got rid of Dr. Lowth and 'drunk' to boot, and very glad I am to say so. I have also sullenised the line as heretofore, and in short have been quite conformable.

Pray write; you shall hear when I remove to Lancashire. I have brought you and my friend Juvenal Hodgson upon my back, on the score of revelation. You are fervent, but he is quite *glowing*; and if he take half the pains to save his own soul which he volunteers to redeem mine, great will be his reward hereafter. I honour and thank you both, but am convinced by neither. Now for notes. Besides those I have sent, I shall send the observations on the Edinburgh Reviewer's remarks on the modern Greek, an Albanian song in the Albanian (*not Greek*) language, specimens of modern Greek from their New Testament, a comedy of Goldoni's translated, *one scene*, a prospectus of a friend's book, and perhaps a song or two, *all* in Romaic, besides their *Pater Noster*; so there will be enough, if not too much, with what I have already sent. Have you received the *Noctes Atticae*? I sent also an annotation on Portugal. Hobhouse is also forthcoming.

TO MR. DALLAS

Newstead Abbey, Sept. 23, 1811.

Lisboa is the Portuguese word, consequently the very best. *Ulissipont* is pedantic; and as I have *Hellas* and *Eros* not long before, there would be something like an affectation of Greek terms, which I wish to avoid, since I shall have a perilous quantity of *modern* Greek in my notes, as specimens of the tongue; therefore Lisboa may keep its place. You are right about the *Hints*; they must not precede the *Romaunt*; but Cawthorn will be savage if they don't; however, keep *them* back, and *him* in *good humour*, if we can, but do not let him publish.

I have adopted, I believe, most of your suggestions, but 'Lisboa' will be an exception to prove the rule. I have sent a quantity of notes, and shall continue; and pray let them be copied; no devil can read my hand. By-the-by, I do not mean to exchange the ninth verse of the *Good Night*. I have no reason to suppose my dog better than his brother brutes, mankind; and *Argus* we know to be a fable. The *Cosmopolite* was an acquisition abroad. I do not believe it is to be found in England. It is an amusing little volume, and full of French flippancy. I read, though I do not speak the language.

I *will* be angry with Murray. It was a bookselling, back-shop, Paternoster Row, paltry proceeding; and if the experiment had turned out as it deserved, I would have raised all Fleet Street, and borrowed the giant's staff from St. Dunstan's Church, to immolate the betrayer of trust. I have written to him as he never was written to before by an author, I'll be sworn, and I hope you will amplify my wrath, till it has an effect upon him. You tell me always you have much to write about. Write it, but let us drop metaphysics;—on that point we shall never agree. I am dull and drowsy, as usual. I do nothing, and even that nothing fatigues me. Adieu.

LETTERS

Newstead Abbey, Sept. 25, 1811.

cvii   My dear Hodgson,—I fear that before the latest
of October or the first of November, I shall hardly
be able to make Cambridge. My everlasting agent
puts off his coming like the accomplishment of a
prophecy. However, finding me growing serious he
hath promised to be here on Thursday, and about
Monday we shall remove to Rochdale. I have only
to give discharges to the tenantry here (it seems the
poor creatures must be raised, though I wish it was
not necessary) and arrange the receipt of sums, and
the liquidation of some debts, and I shall be ready
to enter upon new subjects of vexation. I intend to
visit you in Granta, and hope to prevail on you to
accompany me here or there or anywhere.

My tortoises (all Athenians), my hedgehog, my
mastiff, are all purely. The tortoises lay eggs, and
I have hired a hen to hatch them. I am writing
notes for *my* quarto (Murray would have it a *quarto*),
and Hobhouse is writing text for *his* quarto; if you
call on Murray or Cawthorn you will hear news of
either. I have attacked De Pauw, Thornton, Lord
Elgin, Spain, Portugal, the *Edinburgh Review*,
travellers, painters, antiquarians and others, so you
see what a dish of sour crout controversy I shall
prepare for myself. It would not answer for me to
give way, now; as I was forced into bitterness at the
beginning, I will go through to the last. '*Væ Victis.*
If I fall, I shall fall gloriously, fighting against a host
—*Felicissima Notte a Voss. Signoria.*   B.

TO MR. DALLAS

TO MR. DALLAS

Newstead Abbey, Sept. 26, 1811.

My dear Sir,—In a stanza towards the end of *cviii*
canto 1st, there is in the concluding line,

Some bitter bubbles up, and e'en on roses *stings.*

I have altered it as follows:

Full from the heart of joy's delicious springs
Some bitter o'er the flowers its bubbling venom flings.

If you will point out the stanzas on Cintra which
you wish recast, I will send you mine answer. Be good
enough to address your letters here, and they will
either be forwarded or saved till my return. My agent
comes to-morrow, and we shall set out immediately.

The press must not proceed of course without my
seeing the proofs, as I have much to do. Pray, do
you think any alterations should be made in the
stanzas on Vathek? I should be sorry to make any
improper allusion, as I merely wish to adduce an
example of wasted wealth, and the reflection which
arose in surveying the most desolate mansion in the
most beautiful spot I ever beheld.

Pray keep Cawthorn back; he was not to begin till
November, and even that will be two months too
soon. I am so sorry my hand is unintelligible; but
I can neither deny your accusation, nor remove the
cause of it.—It is a sad scrawl, certes.—A perilous
quantity of annotation hath been sent; I think al-
:nost *enough*, with the specimens of Romaic I mean
to annex.

I will have nothing to say to your metaphysics, and

allegories of rocks and beaches; we shall all go to
the bottom together, so 'let us eat and drink, for to-
morrow,' etc. I am as comfortable in my creed as
others, inasmuch as it is better to sleep than to be
awake.

I have heard nothing of Murray; I hope he is
ashamed of himself. He sent me a vastly complimentary epistle, with a request to alter the two, and
finish another canto. I sent him as civil an answer
as if I had been engaged to translate by the sheet,
declined altering anything in sentiment, but offered
to tag rhymes, and mend them as long as he liked.

I will write from Rochdale when I arrive, if my
affairs allow me; but I shall be so busy and
savage all the time with the whole set, that my letters
will, perhaps, be as pettish as myself. If so, lay the
blame on coals and coal-heavers. Very probably I
may proceed to town by way of Newstead on my
return from Lancs. I mean to be at Cambridge in
November, so that, at all events, we shall be nearer.
I will not apologise for the trouble I have given and
do give you, though I ought to do so; but I have
worn out my politest periods, and can only say that I
am very much obliged to you.—Believe me, yours
always,   BYRON.

TO MR. DALLAS

Newstead Abbey, Oct. 11, 1811.

I have returned from Lancashire, and ascertained
that my property there may be made very valuable,
but various circumstances very much circumscribe
my exertions at present. I shall be in town on busi-

ness in the beginning of November, and perhaps at Cambridge before the end of this month; but of my movements you shall be regularly apprised. Your objections I have in part done away by alterations, which I hope will suffice; and I have sent two or three additional stanzas for both '*Fyttes.*' I have been again shocked with a *death*, and have lost one very dear to me in happier times; but 'I have almost forgot the taste of grief,' and 'supped full of horrors' till I have become callous, nor have I a tear left for an event which, five years ago, would have bowed down my head to the earth. It seems as though I were to experience in my youth the greatest misery of age. My friends fall around me, and I shall be left a lonely tree before I am withered. Other men can always take refuge in their families; I have no resource but my own reflections, and they present no prospect here or hereafter, except the selfish satisfaction of surviving my betters. I am indeed very wretched, and you will excuse my saying so, as you know I am not apt to cant of sensibility.

Instead of tiring yourself with *my* concerns, I should be glad to hear *your* plans of retirement. I suppose you would not like to be wholly shut out of society? Now, I know a large village, or small town, about twelve miles off, where your family would have the advantage of very genteel society, without the hazard of being annoyed by mercantile affluence; where *you* would meet with men of information and independence; and where I have friends to whom I should be proud to introduce you. There are, besides, a coffee-room, assemblies, etc. etc., which bring

163

people together. My mother had a house there some years, and I am well acquainted with the economy of Southwell, the name of this little commonwealth. Lastly, you will not be very remote from me ; and though I am the very worst companion for young people in the world, this objection would not apply to *you*, whom I could see frequently. Your expenses, too, would be such as best suit your inclinations, more or less, as you thought proper ; but very little would be requisite to enable you to enter into all the gaieties of a country life. You could be as quiet or bustling as you liked, and certainly as well situated as on the lakes of Cumberland, unless you have a particular wish to be *picturesque*.

Pray, is your Ionian friend in town ? You have promised me an introduction. You mention having consulted some friend on the MSS. Is not this contrary to our usual way ? Instruct Mr. Murray not to allow his shopman to call the work *Child of Harrow's Pilgrimage* !!!!! as he has done to some of my astonished friends, who wrote to inquire after my *sanity* on the occasion, as well they might. I have heard nothing of Murray, whom I scolded heartily. Must I write more notes ?—Are there not enough ?—Cawthorn must be kept back with the *Hints.*—I hope he is getting on with Hobhouse's quarto. Good evening.—Yours ever, etc.

TO MR. HODGSON
Newstead Abbey, Oct. 13, 1811.

cx You will begin to deem me a most liberal correspondent ; but as my letters are free, you will overlook their frequency. I have sent you answers in prose and verse to all your late communications; and though I am invading your ease again, I don't know why, or what to put down that you are not acquainted with already. I am growing *nervous* (how you will laugh!) —but it is true,—really, wretchedly, ridiculously, fine-ladically, *nervous.* Your climate kills me; I can neither read, write, nor amuse myself, or any one else. My days are listless, and my nights restless; I have very seldom any society, and when I have, I run out of it. At 'this present writing,' there are in the next room three *ladies,* and I have stolen away to write this grumbling letter.—I don't know that I shan't end with insanity, for I find a want of method in arranging my thoughts that perplexes me strangely; but this looks more like silliness than madness, as Scrope Davies would facetiously remark in his consoling manner. I must try the hartshorn of your company; and a session of Parliament would suit me well,— anything to cure me of conjugating the accursed verb '*ennuyer.*'

When shall you be at Cambridge? You have hinted, I think, that your friend Bland is returned from Holland. I have always had a great respect for his talents, and for all that I have heard of his character; but of me, I believe he knows nothing except that he heard my sixth form repetitions ten months together, at the average of two lines a morning, and those never perfect. I remembered him and his 'Slaves' as I passed between Capes Matapan, St. Angelo, and his Isle of Ceriga, and I always be-wailed the absence of the *Anthology.* I suppose he will now translate Vondel, the Dutch Shakspeare, and *Gysbert van Amstel* will easily be accommodated to our stage in its present state ; and I presume he saw the Dutch poem, where the love of Pyramus and Thisbe is compared to the *passion* of *Christ* ; also the love of *Lucifer* for Eve, and other varieties of Low Country literature. No doubt you will think me crazed to talk of such things, but they are all in black and white and good repute on the banks of every canal from Amsterdam to Alkmaar.—Yours ever,

B.

My poesy is in the hands of its various publishers ; but the *Hints from Horace* (to which I have subjoined some savage lines on Methodism, and ferocious notes on the vanity of the triple Editory of the *Edin. Annual Register*), my *Hints*, I say, stand still, and why?—I have not a friend in the world (but you and Drury) who can construe Horace's Latin or my English well enough to adjust them for the press, or to correct the proofs in a grammatical way. So that, unless you have bowels when you return to town (I am too far off to do it for myself), this ineffable work will be lost to the world for—I don't know how many *weeks.*

Childe Harold's Pilgrimage must wait till *Murray's* is finished. He is making a tour in Middlesex, and is to return soon, when high matter may be expected. He wants to have it in quarto, which is a cursed un-saleable size ; but it is pestilent long, and one must obey one's bookseller. I trust Murray will pass the Paddington Canal without being seduced by Payne

and Mackinlay's example,—I say Payne and Mackinlay, supposing that the partnership held good.
Drury, the villain, has not written to me; 'I am never
(as Mrs. Lumpkin says to Tony) to be gratified with
the monster's dear wild notes.'

So you are going (going indeed!) into orders. You
must make your peace with the Eclectic Reviewers
—they accuse you of impiety, I fear, with injustice.
Demetrius, the 'Sieger of Cities,' is here, with 'Gilpin
Horner.' The painter is not necessary, as the portraits he already painted are (by anticipation) very
like the new animals.—Write, and send me your
Love Song—but I want *paulo majora* from you.
Make a dash before you are a deacon, and try a *dry*
publisher.—Yours always, B.

TO MR. DALLAS

October 14, 1811.

Dear Sir,—Stanza 9th, for Canto 2nd, somewhat *cxi*
altered, to avoid a recurrence in a former stanza.

STANZA 9.

> There, thou!—whose love and life together fled,
>   Have left me here to love and live in vain:—
> Twined with my heart, and can I deem thee dead,
>   When busy Memory flashes o'er my brain?
> Well—I will dream that we may meet again,
>   And woo the vision to my vacant breast:
> If aught of young Remembrance then remain,
>   Be as it may
>   Whate'er beside Futurity's behest;
> or,—Howe'er may be
>   For me 'twere bliss enough to see thy spirit blest!

LETTERS

I think it proper to state to you, that this stanza alludes to an event which has taken place since my arrival here, and not to the death of any *male* friend.—Yours,   B.

TO MR. DALLAS
Newstead Abbey, October 16, 1811.

cxii   I am on the wing for Cambridge. Thence, after a short stay, to London. Will you be good enough to keep an account of all the MSS. you receive, for fear of omission? Have you adopted the three altered stanzas of the latest proof? I can do nothing more with them.—I am glad you like the new ones.—Of the last, and of the *trio*, I sent you a new edition—to-day a *fresh note*. The lines of the second sheet I fear must stand; I will give you reasons when we meet.—Believe me, yours ever,   BYRON.

TO MR. MOORE
Cambridge, October 27, 1811.

cxiii   Sir,—Your letter followed me from Notts to this place, which will account for the delay of my reply. Your former letter I never had the honour to receive; —be assured in whatever part of the world it had found me, I should have deemed it my duty to return and answer it in person.

The advertisement you mention I know nothing of.—At the time of your meeting with Mr. Jeffrey, I had recently entered College, and remember to have heard and read a number of squibs on the occasion; and from the recollection of these I derived all my knowledge on the subject, without the slightest idea of 'giving the lie' to an address which I never beheld. When I put my name to the production, which has occasioned this correspondence, I became responsible to all whom it might concern,—to explain where it requires explanation, and, where insufficiently or too sufficiently explicit, at all events to satisfy. My situation leaves me no choice; it rests with the injured and the angry to obtain reparation in their own way.

With regard to the passage in question, *you* were certainly *not* the person towards whom I felt personally hostile. On the contrary, my whole thoughts were engrossed by one, whom I had reason to consider as my worst literary enemy, nor could I foresee that his former antagonist was about to become his champion. You do not specify what you would wish to have done: I can neither retract nor apologise for a charge or falsehood which I never advanced.

In the beginning of the week I shall be at No. 8 St. James's Street. Neither the letter nor the friend to whom you stated your intention ever made their appearance.

Your friend, Mr. Rogers, or any other gentleman delegated by you, will find me most ready to adopt any conciliatory proposition which shall not compromise my own honour,—or, failing in that, to make the atonement you deem it necessary to require.—I have the honour to be, Sir, your most obedient, humble servant, BYRON.

LETTERS

8 St. James's Street, October 29, 1811.

cxiv   Sir,—Soon after my return to England, my friend,
Mr. Hodgson, apprised me that a letter for me was
in his possession ; but a domestic event hurrying me
from London, immediately after, the letter (which
may most probably be your own) is still *unopened in
his keeping.* If, on examination of the address, the
similarity of the handwriting should lead to such a
conclusion, it shall be opened in your presence, for
the satisfaction of all parties. Mr. H. is at present
out of town ;—on Friday I shall see him, and request
him to forward it to my address.

With regard to the latter part of both your letters,
until the principal point was discussed between us I
felt myself at a loss in what manner to reply. Was
I to anticipate friendship from one who conceived
me to have charged him with falsehood ? Were not
advances, under such circumstances, to be miscon-
strued,—not, perhaps, by the person to whom they
were addressed, but by others ? In *my* case such a
step was impracticable. If you, who conceived yourself to be the offended person, are satisfied that you
had no cause for offence, it will not be difficult to
convince me of it. My situation, as I have before
stated, leaves me no choice. I should have felt
proud of your acquaintance, had it commenced
under other circumstances ; but it must rest with you
to determine how far it may proceed after so *aus-
picious* a beginning.—I have the honour to be, etc.

TO MR. MOORE

8 St. James's Street, October 30, 1811.

Sir,—You must excuse my troubling you once cxv more upon this very unpleasant subject. It would be a satisfaction to me, and I should think to yourself, that the unopened letter in Mr. Hodgson's possession (supposing it to prove your own) should be returned *in statu quo* to the writer; particularly as you expressed yourself 'not quite easy under the manner in which I had dwelt on its miscarriage.'

A few words more, and I shall not trouble you further. I felt, and still feel, very much flattered by those parts of your correspondence which held out the prospect of our becoming acquainted. If I did not meet them in the first instance as perhaps I ought, let the situation I was placed in be my defence. You have *now* declared yourself *satisfied*, and on that point we are no longer at issue. If, therefore, you still retain any wish to do me the honour you hinted at, I shall be most happy to meet you, when, where, and how you please, and I presume you will not attribute my saying thus much to any unworthy motive.—I have the honour to remain, etc.

TO MR. DALLAS

8 St. James's Street, October 31, 1811.

Dear Sir,—I have already taken up so much of cxvi your time that there needs no excuse on your part, but a great many on mine, for the present interruption. I have altered the passages according to your wish. With this note I send a few stanzas on a subject which has lately occupied much of my thoughts. They refer to the death of one to whose name you are a *stranger*, and, consequently, cannot be interested. I mean them to complete the present volume. They relate to the same person whom I have mentioned in canto 2nd, and at the conclusion of the poem.

I by no means intend to identify myself with *Harold*, but to *deny* all connection with him. If in parts I may be thought to have drawn from myself, believe me it is but in parts, and I shall not own even to that. As to the *Monastic dome*, etc., I thought those circumstances would suit him as well as any other, and I could describe what I had seen better than I could invent. I would not be such a fellow as I have made my hero for the world.—Yours ever, B.

TO MR. MOORE

8 *St. James's Street, November* 1, 1811.

cxvii Sir,—As I should be very sorry to interrupt your Sunday's engagement, if Monday, or any other day of the ensuing week, would be equally convenient to yourself and friend, I will then have the honour of accepting his invitation. Of the professions of esteem with which Mr. Rogers has honoured me, I cannot but feel proud, though undeserving. I should be wanting to myself, if insensible to the praise of such a man ; and should my approaching interview with him and his friend lead to any degree of intimacy with both or either, I shall regard our past correspondence as one of the happiest events of my life.—I have the honour to be, your very sincere and obedient servant, · BYRON.

TO MR. HODGSON

8 *St. James's Street, November* 17, 1811.

Dear Hodgson,—I have been waiting for the *letter*, cxviii which was to be sent by you *immediately*, and must again jog your memory on the subject. I have heard from Hobhouse, who has at last sent more copy to Cawthorn for his *Travels*. I franked an enormous cover for you yesterday, seemingly to convey at least twelve cantos on any given subject. I fear the aspect of it was too *epic* for the post. From this and other coincidences I augur a publication· on your part, but what or when, or how much, you must disclose immediately.

I don't know what to say about coming down to Cambridge at present, but live in hopes. I am so completely superannuated there, and besides feel it something brazen in me to wear my magisterial habit, after all my buffooneries, that I hardly think I shall venture again. And being now an 'ἄριστον μὲν ὕδωρ' disciple I won't come within wine-shot of such determined topers as your collegiates. I have not yet subscribed to Bowen. I mean to cut Harrow 'enim unquam' as somebody classically said for a farewell sentence. I am superannuated there too, and, in short, as old at twenty-three as many men at seventy.

Do write and send this letter that hath been so long in your custody. It is of importance that M. should be certain I never received it, if it be *his*. Are you drowned that I have never heard from you, or are you fallen into a fit of perplexity? Cawthorn has declined, and the MS. is returned to him. This is all at present from yours in the faith,

Μπαιρῶν.

TO MR. HODGSON

8 *St. James's Street, Dec.* 4, 1811.

cxix   My dear Hodgson,—I have seen Miller, who will see Bland, but I have no great hopes of his obtaining the translation from the crowd of candidates. Yesterday I wrote to Harness, who will probably tell you what I said on the subject. Hobhouse has sent me my Romaic MSS., and I shall require your aid in correcting the press, as your Greek eye is more correct than mine. But these will not come to type this month, I dare say. I have put some soft lines on ye Scotch in the *Curse of Minerva*; take them:

Yet Caledonia claims some native worth, etc.

If you are not content now, I must say with the Irish drummer to the deserter who called out, 'Flog high, flog low'—'The de'il burn ye, there's no pleasing you, flog where one will.'

I have read Watson to Gibbon. He proves nothing, so I am where I was, verging towards Spinoza; and yet it is a gloomy creed, and I want a better, but there is something pagan in me that I cannot shake off. In short, I *deny nothing*, but doubt everything. The post brings me to a conclusion. Bland has just been here.—Yours ever,

BN.

TO MR. HARNESS

8 *St. James's Street, Dec.* 6, 1811.

My dear Harness,—I write again, but don't suppose cxx I mean to lay such a tax on your pen and patience as to expect regular replies. When you are inclined, write: when silent, I shall have the consolation of knowing that you are much better employed. Yesterday Bland and I called on Mr. Miller, who, being then out, will call on Bland to-day or to-morrow. I shall certainly endeavour to bring them together.— You are censorious, child; when you are a little older, you will learn to dislike everybody, but abuse nobody.

With regard to the person of whom you speak, your own good sense must direct you. I never pretend to advise, being an implicit believer in the old proverb.

This present frost is detestable. It is the first I have felt for these three years, though I longed for one in the oriental summer, when no such thing is to be had, unless I had gone to the top of Hymettus for it.

I thank you most truly for the concluding part of your letter. I have been of late not much accustomed to kindness from any quarter, and am not the less pleased to meet with it again from one where I had known it earliest. I have not changed in all my ramblings,—Harrow, and, of course, yourself, never left me, and the

'Dulces reminiscitur Argos'

attended me to the very spot to which that sentence alludes in the mind of the fallen Argive.—Our intimacy began before we began to date at all, and it rests with you to continue it till the hour which must number it and me with the things that *were*.

Do read mathematics.—I should think *X plus Y* at least as amusing as the *Curse of Kehama*, and much more intelligible. Master Southey's poems *are*, in fact, what parallel lines might be—viz. prolonged *ad infinitum* without meeting anything half so absurd as themselves.

> What news, what news? Queen Oreaca,
> What news of scribblers five?
> S——, W——, C——, L—d, and L—e?—
> All damn'd, though yet alive.

Coleridge is lecturing. 'Many an old fool,' said Hannibal to some such lecturer, 'but such as this, never.'—Ever yours, etc.

TO MR. HARNESS

St. James's Street, Dec. 8, 1811.

cxxi Behold a most formidable sheet, without gilt or black edging, and consequently very vulgar and indecorous, particularly to one of your precision; but this being Sunday, I can procure no better, and will atone for its length by not filling it. Bland

I have not seen since my last letter; but on Tuesday he dines with me, and will meet Moore, the epitome of all that is exquisite in poetical or personal accomplishments. How Bland has settled with Miller, I know not. I have very little interest with either, and they must arrange their concerns according to their own gusto. I have done my endeavours, *at your request*, to bring them together, and hope they may agree to their mutual advantage.

Coleridge has been lecturing against Campbell. Rogers was present, and from him I derive the information. We are going to make a party to hear this Manichean of poesy. Pole is to marry Miss Long, and will be a very miserable dog for all that. The present ministers are to continue, and his Majesty *does* continue in the same state; so there's folly and madness for you, both in a breath.

I never heard but of one man truly fortunate, and he was Beaumarchais, the author of *Figaro*, who buried two wives and gained three lawsuits before he was thirty.

And now, child, what art thou doing? *Reading, I trust.* I want to see you take a degree. Remember, this is the most important period of your life; and don't disappoint your papa and your aunt, and all your kin—besides myself. Don't you know that all male children are begotten for the express purpose of being graduates? and that even I am an A.M., though how I became so the *Public Orator* only can resolve. Besides, you are to be a priest; and to confute Sir William Drummond's late book about the Bible (printed, but not published), and all other

infidels whatever. Now leave Master H.'s gig, and
Master S.'s Sapphics, and become as immortal as
Cambridge can make you.

You see, Mio Carissimo, what a pestilent correspondent I am likely to become; but then you shall
be as quiet at Newstead as you please, and I won't
disturb your studies as I do now. When do you
fix the day, that I may take you up according to
contract? Hodgson talks of making a third in our
journey; but we can't stow him, inside at least.
Positively you shall go with me as was agreed, and
don't let me have any of your *politesse* to H. on the
occasion. I shall manage to arrange for both with
a little contrivance. I wish H. was not quite so fat,
and we should pack better. You will want to know
what I am doing—chewing tobacco.

You see nothing of my allies, Scrope Davies and
Matthews—they don't suit you; and how does it
happen that I—who am a pipkin of the same pottery
—continue in your good graces? Good night,—I
will go on in the morning.

Dec. 9th.—In a morning I'm always sullen, and
to-day is as sombre as myself. Rain and mist are
worse than a sirocco, particularly in a beef-eating
and beer-drinking country. My bookseller, Cawthorn, has just left me, and tells me, with a most
important face, that he is in treaty for a novel of
Madame D'Arblay's, for which 1000 guineas are
asked! He wants me to read the MS. (if he obtains
it), which I shall do with pleasure; but I should be
very cautious in venturing an opinion on her whose
Cecilia Dr. Johnson superintended. If he lends it

to me, I shall put it into the hands of Rogers and Moore, who are truly men of taste. I have filled the sheet, and beg your pardon; I will not do it again. I shall, perhaps, write again; but if not, believe, silent or scribbling, that I am, my dearest William, ever, etc.

TO MR. HODGSON

London, Dec. 8, 1811.

I sent you a sad *Tale of Three Friars* the other *cxxii* day, and now take a dose in another style. I wrote it a day or two ago, on hearing a song of former days.

'Away, away, ye notes of woe,' etc. etc.

I have gotten a book by Sir W. Drummond (printed, but not published), entitled *Œdipus Judaicus*, in which he attempts to prove the greater part of the Old Testament an allegory, particularly Genesis and Joshua. He professes himself a theist in the preface, and handles the literal interpretation very roughly. I wish you could see it. Mr. W——has lent it me, and I confess to me it is worth fifty Watsons.

You and Harness must fix on the time for your visit to Newstead; I can command mine at your wish, unless anything particular occurs in the interim. Bland dines with me on Tuesday to meet Moore. Coleridge has attacked the *Pleasures of Hope*, and all other pleasures whatsoever. Mr. Rogers was present, and heard himself indirectly *rowed* by the lecturer. We are going in a party to hear the new Art of Poetry by this reformed schismatic; and were I one of these poetical luminaries, or of sufficient consequence to be noticed by the man of lectures, I should not hear him without an answer. For you know, 'an a man will be beaten with brains, he shall never keep a clean doublet.' Campbell will be desperately annoyed. I never saw a man (and of him I have seen very little) so sensitive;—what a happy temperament! I am sorry for it; what can *he* fear from criticism? I don't know if Bland has seen Miller, who was to call on him yesterday.

To-day is the Sabbath,—a day I never pass pleasantly, but at Cambridge; and, even there, the organ is a sad remembrancer. Things are stagnant enough in town; as long as they don't retrograde, 'tis all very well. Hobhouse writes and writes and writes, and is an author. I do nothing but eschew tobacco. I wish parliament were assembled, that I may hear, and perhaps some day be heard;—but on this point I am not very sanguine. I have many plans;—sometimes I think of the East again, and dearly beloved Greece. I am well, but weakly. Yesterday Kinnaird told me I looked very ill, and sent me home happy.

Is Scrope still interesting and invalid? And how does Hinde with his cursed chemistry? To Harness I have written, and he has written, and we have all written, and have nothing now to do but write again, till death splits up the pen and the scribbler.

The Alfred has three hundred and fifty-four candidates for six vacancies. The cook has run away and left us liable, which makes our committee very plaintive. Master Brook, our head serving-man, has the gout, and our new cook is none of the best. I speak from report,—for what is cookery to a leguminous-eating ascetic?· So now you know as much of the matter as I do. Books and quiet are still there, and they may dress their dishes in their own way for me. Let me know your determination as to Newstead, and believe me, yours ever,

Μπαιρῶν.

TO MR. MOORE

December 11, 1811.

My dear Moore,—If you please, we will drop our *cxxiii* former monosyllables, and adhere to the appellations sanctioned by our godfathers and godmothers. If you make it a point, I will withdraw your name; at the same time there is no occasion, as I have this day postponed your election *sine die*, till it shall suit your wishes to be amongst us. I do not say this from any awkwardness the erasure of your proposal would occasion to *me*, but simply such is the state of the case; and, indeed, the longer your name is up, the stronger will become the probability of success, and your voters more numerous. Of course you will decide—your wish shall be my law. If my zeal has already outrun discretion, pardon me, and attribute my officiousness to an excusable motive.

I wish you would go down with me to Newstead. Hodgson will be there, and a young friend, named

Harness, the earliest and dearest I ever had from the third form at Harrow to this hour. I can promise you good wine, and, if you like shooting, a manor of 4000 acres, fires, books, your own free will, and my own very indifferent company. *Balnea, vina* . . .

Hodgson will plague you, I fear, with verse;—for my own part I will conclude, with Martial, *nil recitabo tibi*; and surely the last inducement is not the least. Ponder on my proposition, and believe me, my dear Moore, yours ever,   Byron.

TO MR. HODGSON

8 St. James's Street, Dec. 12, 1811.

cxxiv   Why, Hodgson! I fear you have left off wine and me at the same time,—I have written and written and written, and no answer! My dear Sir Edgar, water disagrees with you,—drink sack and write. Bland did not come to his appointment, being unwell, but Moore supplied all other vacancies most delectably. I have hopes of his joining us at Newstead. I am sure you would like him more and more as he develops,—at least I do.

How Miller and Bland go on, I don't know. Cawthorn talks of being in treaty for a novel of Madame D'Arblay's, and if he obtains it (at 1500 guineas!!) wishes me to see the MS. This I should read with pleasure,—not that I should ever dare to venture a criticism on her whose writings Dr. Johnson once revised, but for the pleasure of the thing. If my worthy publisher wanted a sound opinion, I should send the MS. to Rogers and Moore, as men most alive to true taste. I have had frequent letters from Wm. Harness, and *you* are silent; certes, you are not a schoolboy. However, I have the consolation of knowing that you are better employed, viz. reviewing. You don't deserve that I should add another syllable, and I won't.—Yours, etc.

P.S.—I only wait for your answer to fix our meeting.

TO MR. HARNESS

8 St. James's Street, Dec. 15, 1811.

I wrote you an answer to your last, which, on reflection, pleases me as little as it probably has pleased yourself. I will not wait for your rejoinder; but proceed to tell you, that I had just then been greeted with an epistle of ——'s, full of his petty grievances, and this at the moment when (from circumstances it is not necessary to enter upon) I was bearing up against recollections to which *his* imaginary sufferings are as a scratch to a cancer. These things combined put me out of humour with him and all mankind. The latter part of my life has been a perpetual struggle against affections which embittered the earliest portion; and though I flatter myself I have in a great measure conquered them, yet there are moments (and this was one) when I am as foolish as formerly. I never said so much before, nor had I said this now, if I did not suspect myself of having been rather savage in my letter, and wish

to inform you thus much of the cause. You know I
am not one of your dolorous gentlemen ; so now let
us laugh again.

Yesterday I went with Moore to Sydenham to
visit Campbell. He was not visible, so we jogged
homeward merrily enough. To-morrow I dine with
Rogers, and am to hear Coleridge, who is a kind of
rage at present. Last night I saw Kemble in Coriolanus ;—he *was glorious*, and exerted himself wonderfully. By good luck I got an excellent place in the
best part of the house, which was more than over-
flowing. Clare and Delawarr, who were there on the
same speculation, were less fortunate. I saw them
by accident,—we were not together. I wished for you,
to gratify your love of Shakspeare and of fine acting
to its fullest extent. Last week I saw an exhibition
of a different kind in a Mr. Coates, at the Haymarket,
who performed Lothario in a *damned* and damnable
manner.

I told you the fate of B. and H. in my last.. So
much for these sentimentalists, who console themselves for the loss—the never to be recovered
loss—the despair of the refined attachment of a
couple of drabs ! You censure *my* life, Harness,—
when I compare myself with these men, my elders
and my betters, I really begin to conceive myself a
monument of prudence—a walking statue—without
feeling or failing ; and yet the world in general hath
given me a proud pre-eminence over them in pro-
fligacy. Yet I like the men, and, God knows, ought
not to condemn their aberrations. But I own I feel
provoked when they dignify all this by the name of

184

love—romantic attachments for things marketable for a dollar!

Dec. 16*th.*—I have just received your letter;—I feel your kindness very deeply. The foregoing part of my letter, written yesterday, will, I hope, account for the tone of the former, though it cannot excuse it. I do *like* to hear from you—more than *like*. Next to seeing you, I have no greater satisfaction. But you have other duties, and greater pleasures, and I should regret to take a moment from either. H—— was to call to-day, but I have not seen him. The circumstance you mention at the close of your letter is another proof in favour of my opinion of mankind. Such you will always find them—selfish and distrustful. I except none. The cause of this is the state of society. In the world, every one is to stir for himself—it is useless, perhaps selfish, to expect anything from his neighbour. But I do not think we are born of this disposition; for you find *friendship* as a schoolboy, and *love* enough before twenty.

I went to see ——; he keeps me in town, where I don't wish to be at present. He is a good man, but totally without conduct. And now, my dearest William, I must wish you good morrow, and remain ever most sincerely and affectionately yours, etc.

TO ROBERT RUSHTON

8 *St. James's Street, Jan.* 21, 1812.

Though I have no objection to your refusal to carry *letters* to Mealey's, you will take care that the letters are taken by *Spero* at the proper time. I have also to observe, that Susan is to be treated *cxxvi* with civility, and not *insulted* by any person over whom I have the smallest control, or, indeed, by any one whatever, while I have the power to protect her. I am truly sorry to have any subject of complaint against *you* ; I have too good an opinion of you to think I shall have occasion to repeat it, after the care I have taken of you, and my favourable intentions in your behalf. I see no occasion for any communication whatever between *you* and the *women*, and wish you to occupy yourself in preparing for the situation in which you will be placed. If a common sense of decency cannot prevent you from conducting yourself towards them with rudeness, I should at least hope that your *own interest*, and regard for a master who has *never* treated you with unkindness, will have some weight.—Yours, etc., BYRON.

P.S.—I wish you to attend to your arithmetic, to occupy yourself in surveying, measuring, and making yourself acquainted with every particular relative to the *land* of Newstead, and you will *write* to me *one letter every week*, that I may know how you go on.

TO ROBERT RUSHTON

8 St. James's Street, January 25, 1812.

cxxvii Your refusal to carry the letter was not a subject of remonstrance : it was not a part of your business ; but the language you used to the girl was (as *she* stated it) highly improper.

You say that you also have something to complain of ; then state it to me immediately : it would be very unfair, and very contrary to my disposition, not to hear both sides of the question.

If anything has passed between you *before* or since my last visit to Newstead, do not be afraid to mention it. I am sure *you* would not deceive me, though *she* would. Whatever it is, *you* shall be forgiven. I have not been without some suspicions on the subject, and am certain that, at your time of life, the blame could not attach to you. You will not *consult* any one as to your answer, but write to me immediately. I shall be more ready to hear what you have to advance, as I do not remember ever to have heard a word from you before *against* any human being, which convinces me you would not maliciously assert an untruth. There is not any one who can do the least injury to you, while you conduct yourself properly. I shall expect your answer immediately.—Yours, etc.,   BYRON.

TO MR. MOORE

January 29, 1812.

My dear Moore,—I wish very much I could have cxxviii seen you; I am in a state of ludicrous tribulation . . .

Why do you say that I dislike your poesy? I have expressed no such opinion, either in *print* or elsewhere. In scribbling myself, it was necessary for me to find fault, and I fixed upon the trite charge of immorality, because I could discover no other, and was so perfectly qualified, in the innocence of

187

my heart, to 'pluck that mote from my neighbour's eye.'

I feel very, very much obliged by your approbation; but, at *this moment*, praise, even *your* praise, passes by me like 'the idle wind.' I meant and mean to send you a copy the moment of publication; but now I can think of nothing but damned, deceitful,—delightful woman, as Mr. Liston says in the *Knight of Snowdon.* — Believe me, my dear Moore, ever yours, most affectionately,   BYRON.

TO MR. ROGERS

February 4, 1812.

cxxix   My dear Sir,—With my best acknowledgments to Lord Holland, I have to offer my perfect concurrence in the propriety of the question previously to be put to ministers. If their answer is in the negative, I shall, with his Lordship's approbation, give notice of a motion for a Committee of Inquiry.   I would also gladly avail myself of his most able advice, and any information or documents with which he might be pleased to intrust me, to bear me out in the statement of facts it may be necessary to submit to the House.

From all that fell under my own observation during my Christmas visit to Newstead, I feel convinced that, if *conciliatory* measures are not very soon adopted, the most unhappy consequences may be apprehended. Nightly outrage and daily depredation are already at their height; and not only the masters of frames, who are obnoxious on account of

TO MASTER JOHN COWELL

their occupation, but persons in no degree connected with the malcontents or their oppressors, are liable to insult and pillage.

I am very much obliged to you for the trouble you have taken on my account, and beg you to believe me ever your obliged and sincere, etc.

TO MASTER JOHN COWELL

8 St. James's Street, February 12, 1812.

My dear John,—You have probably long ago for- _{cxxx} gotten the writer of these lines, who would, perhaps, be unable to recognise *yourself*, from the difference which must naturally have taken place in your stature and appearance since he saw you last. I have been rambling through Portugal, Spain, Greece, etc. etc., for some years, and have found so many changes on my return, that it would be very unfair not to expect that you should have had your share of alteration and improvement with the rest. I write to request a favour of you : a little boy of eleven years, the son of Mr. ——, my particular friend, is about to become an Etonian, and I should esteem any act of protection or kindness to him as an obligation to myself: let me beg of you then to take some little notice of him at first, till he is able to shift for himself.

I was happy to hear a very favourable account of you from a schoolfellow a few weeks ago, and should be glad to learn that your family are as well as I wish them to be. I presume you are in the upper school; —as an *Etonian*, you will look down upon a *Harrow* man; but I never, even in my boyish days, disputed your superiority, which I once experienced in a cricket match, where I had the honour of making one of eleven, who were beaten to their hearts' content by your college in *one innings.*—Believe me to be, with great truth, etc. etc.,   B.

TO MR. HODGSON

8 *St. James's Street, February* 16, 1812.

cxxxi   Dear Hodgson,—I send you a proof. Last week I was very ill and confined to bed with stone in the kidney, but I am now quite recovered. If the stone had got into my heart instead of my kidneys, it would have been all the better. The women are gone to their relatives, after many attempts to explain what was already too clear. However, I have quite recovered *that* also, and only wonder at my folly in excepting my own strumpets from the general corruption,—albeit a two months' weakness is better than ten years. I have one request to make, which is, never mention a woman again in any letter to me, or even allude to the existence of the sex. I won't even read a word of the feminine gender;—it must all be *propria quae maribus.*

In the spring of 1813 I shall leave England for ever. Everything in my affairs tends to this, and my inclinations and health do not discourage it. Neither my habits nor constitution are improved by your customs or your climate. I shall find employment in making myself a good Oriental scholar. I shall retain a mansion in one of the fairest islands, and retrace, at intervals, the most interesting portions of the East. In the meantime, I am adjusting my concerns, which will (when arranged) leave me with wealth sufficient even for home, but enough for a principality in Turkey. At present they are involved, but I hope, by taking some necessary but unpleasant steps, to clear everything. Hobhouse is expected daily in London : we shall be very glad to see him ; and, perhaps, you will come up and 'drink deep ere he depart,' if not, 'Mahomet must go to the mountain ';—but Cambridge will bring sad recollections to him, and worse to me, though for very different reasons. I believe the only human being that ever loved me in truth and entirely was of, or belonging to, Cambridge, and, in that, no change can now take place. There is one consolation in death—where he sets his seal, the impression can neither be melted nor broken, but endureth for ever. —Yours always, B.

TO MR. HODGSON

London, February 21, 1812.

My dear Hodgson,—There is a book entitled *cxxxii* ' *Galt,' his Travels in ye Archipelago,* daintily printed by Cadell and Davies, ye which I could desiderate might be criticised by you, inasmuch as ye author is a well-respected esquire of mine acquaintance, but I fear will meet with little mercy as a writer, unless a friend passeth judgment. Truth to say, ye boke is ye boke of a cock-brained man, and is full of devices crude and conceitede, but peradventure for my sake this grace may be vouchsafed unto him. Review him myself I can not, will not, and if you are likewize hard of heart, woe unto ye boke, ye which is a comely quarto.

Now then! I have no objection to review if it pleases Griffiths to send books, or rather *you*, for you know the sort of things I like to play with. You will find what I. say very serious as to my intentions. I have every reason to induce me to return to Ionia. Believe me,——Yours always,

B.

8 *St. James's Street, February 25,* 1812.

cxxxiii   My Lord,——With my best thanks, I have the honour to return the Notts letter to your Lordship. I have read it with attention, but do not think I shall venture to avail myself of its contents, as my view of the question differs in some measure from Mr. Coldham's. I hope I do not wrong him, but *his* objections to the bill appear to me to be founded on certain apprehensions that he and his coadjutors might be mistaken for the '*original advisers*' (to quote him) of the measure. For my own part, I consider the manufacturers as a much injured body of men, sacrificed to the views of certain individuals who have enriched themselves by those practices which have deprived the frame-workers of employ-ment. For instance :—by the adoption of a certain kind of frame, one man performs the work of seven —six are thus thrown out of business. But it is to be observed that the work thus done is far inferior in quality, hardly marketable at home, and hurried over with a view to exportation. Surely, my Lord, however we may rejoice in any improvement in the arts which may be beneficial to mankind, we must not allow mankind to be sacrificed to improvements in mechanism. The maintenance and well-doing of the industrious poor is an object of greater consequence to the community than the enrichment of a few monopolists by any improvement in the implements of trade, which deprives the workman of his bread, and renders the labourer 'unworthy of his hire.' My own motive for opposing the bill is founded on its palpable injustice, and its certain inefficacy. I have seen the state of these miserable men, and it is a disgrace to a civilised country. Their excesses may be condemned, but cannot be subject of wonder. The effect of the present bill would be to drive them into actual rebellion. The few words I shall venture to offer on Thursday will be founded upon these opinions formed from my own observations on the spot. By previous inquiry, I am convinced these men would have been restored to employment, and the country to tranquillity. It is, perhaps, not yet too late, and is surely worth the trial. It can never be too late to employ force in such circumstances. I believe your Lordship does not coincide with me entirely on this subject, and most cheerfully and sincerely shall I submit to your superior judgment and experience, and take some other line of argument against the bill, or be silent altogether, should you deem it more advisable. Condemning, as every

one must condemn, the conduct of these wretches, I
believe in the existence of grievances which call
rather for pity than punishment.—I have the honour
to be, with great respect, my Lord, your Lordship's
most obedient and obliged servant,   BYRON.

P.S.—I am a little apprehensive that your Lordship will think me too lenient towards these men,
and half a *frame-breaker myself.*

TO MR. HODGSON

8 *St. James's Street, March* 5, 1812.

cxxxiv   My dear Hodgson,—*We* are not answerable for
reports of speeches in the papers ; they are always
given incorrectly, and on this occasion more so than
usual, from the debate in the Commons on the same
night.   The *Morning Post* should have said *eighteen
years.*   However, you will find the speech, as spoken,
in the *Parliamentary Register,* when it comes out.
Lords Holland and Grenville, particularly the latter,
paid me some high compliments in the course of
their speeches, as you may have seen in the papers,
and Lords Eldon and Harrowby answered me.   I
have had many marvellous eulogies repeated to me
since, in person and by proxy, from divers persons
ministerial—yea, *ministerial !*—as well as opposi-
tionists ; of them I shall only mention Sir F. Burdett.
He says it is the best speech by a *lord* since the
'*Lord* knows when,' probably from a fellow-feeling
in the sentiments.   Lord H. tells me I shall beat
them all if I persevere ; and Lord G. remarked that
the construction of some of my periods are very like

TO LORD HOLLAND

Burke's!! And so much for vanity. I spoke very
violent sentences with a sort. of modest impudence,
abused everything and everybody, and put the Lord
Chancellor very much out of humour; and if I may
believe what I hear, have not lost any character by
the experiment. As to my delivery, loud and fluent
enough, perhaps a little theatrical. I could not
recognise myself or any one else in the newspapers.

I hire myself unto Griffiths, and my poesy comes
out on Saturday. Hobhouse is here; I shall tell
him to write. My stone is gone for the present, but
I fear is part of my habit. We *all* talk of a visit to
Cambridge.—Yours ever,   B.

TO LORD HOLLAND

St. James's Street, March 5, 1812.

My Lord,—May I request your Lordship to accept *cxxxv*
a copy of the thing which accompanies this note?
You have already so fully proved the truth of the
first line of Pope's couplet,

'Forgiveness to the injured doth belong,'

that I long for an opportunity to give the lie to the
verse that follows. If I were not perfectly convinced
that anything I may have formerly uttered in the
boyish rashness of my misplaced resentment had
made as little impression as it deserved to make, I
should hardly have the confidence—perhaps your
Lordship may give it a stronger and more appropriate
appellation—to send you a quarto of the same
scribbler. But your Lordship, I am sorry to observe

195

to-day, is troubled with the gout; if my book can produce a *laugh* against itself or the author, it will be of some service. If it can set you to *sleep*, the benefit will be yet greater; and as some facetious personage observed half a century ago, that 'poetry is a mere drug,' I offer you mine as a humble assistant to the *eau médicinale*. I trust you will forgive this and all my other buffooneries, and believe me to be, with great respect, your Lordship's obliged and sincere servant, BYRON.

TO MR. WILLIAM BANKES

April 20, 1812.

cxxxvi My dear Bankes,—I feel rather hurt (not savagely) at the speech you made to me last night, and my hope is, that it was only one of your *profane* jests. I should be very sorry that any part of my behaviour should give you cause to suppose that I think higher of myself, or otherwise of you than I have always done. I can assure you that I am as much the humblest of your servants as at Trin. Coll.; and if I have not been at home when you favoured me with a call, the loss was more mine than yours. In the bustle of buzzing parties there is, there can be, no rational conversation; but when I can enjoy it, there is nobody's I can prefer to your own.—Believe me ever faithfully and most affectionately yours,

BYRON.

TO MR. WILLIAM BANKES

cxxxvii My dear Bankes,—My eagerness to come to an explanation has, I trust, convinced you that whatever

196

my unlucky manner might inadvertently be, the
change was as unintentional as (if intended) it would
have been ungrateful. I really was not aware that,
while we were together, I had evinced such caprices;
that we were not so much in each other's company
as I could have wished, I well know, but I think so
acute an observer as yourself must have perceived
enough to *explain this*, without supposing any slight
to one in whose society I have pride and pleasure.
Recollect that I do not allude here to 'extended' or
'extending' acquaintances, but to circumstances you
will understand, I think, on a little reflection.

And now, my dear Bankes, do not distress me by
supposing that I can think of you, or you of me,
otherwise than I trust we have long thought. You
told me not long ago that my temper was improved,
and I should be sorry that opinion should be revoked.
Believe me, your friendship is of more account to me
than all those absurd vanities in which, I fear, you
conceive me to take too much interest. I have never
disputed your superiority, or doubted (seriously) your
good-will, and no one shall ever 'make mischief
between us' without the sincere regret on the part of
your ever affectionate, etc.

P.S.—I shall see you, I hope, at Lady Jersey's.
Hobhouse goes also.

TO MR. MOORE

March 25, 1812.

Know all men by these presents, that you, Thomas
Moore, stand indicted—no—invited, by special and *cxxxviii*

particular solicitation, to Lady Caroline Lamb's to-morrow evening, at half-past nine o'clock, where you will meet with a civil reception and decent entertainment. Pray, come—I was so examined after you this morning, that I entreat you to answer in person.—Believe me, etc.

TO MR. MOORE

Friday noon.

cxxxix   I should have answered your note yesterday, but I hoped to have seen you this morning. I must consult with you about the day we dine with Sir Francis. I suppose we shall meet at Lady Spencer's to-night. I did not know that you were at Miss Berry's the other night, or I should have certainly gone there.

As usual, I am in all sorts of scrapes, though none, at present, of a martial description.—Believe me, etc.

TO MR. MOORE

May 8, 1812.

cxl   I am too proud of being your friend, to care with whom I am linked in your estimation, and, God knows, I want friends more at this time than at any other. I am 'taking care of myself' to no great purpose. If you knew my situation in every point of view, you would excuse apparent and unintentional neglect. I shall leave town, I think; but do not you leave it without seeing me. I wish you, from my soul, every happiness you can wish yourself; and I think you have taken the road to secure it. Peace be with you! I fear she has abandoned me.—Ever, etc.

TO MR. MOORE

May 20, 1812.

On Monday, after sitting up all night, I saw Bell- cxli ingham launched into eternity, and at three the same day I saw —— launched into the country.

I believe, in the beginning of June, I shall be down for a few days in Notts. If so, I shall beat you up *en passant* with Hobhouse, who is endeavouring, like you and everybody else, to keep me out of scrapes.

I meant to have written you a long letter, but I find I cannot. If anything remarkable occurs, you will hear it from me—if good; if *bad*, there are plenty to tell it. In the meantime, do you be happy. —Ever yours, etc.

P.S.—My best wishes and respects to Mrs. Moore;—she is beautiful. I may say so even to you, for I was never more struck with a countenance.

TO BERNARD BARTON

8 St. James's St., June 1, 1812.

The most satisfactory answer to the concluding cxlii part of your letter is that Mr. Murray will republish your volume, if you still retain your inclination for the experiment, which I trust will be successful. Some weeks ago my friend Mr. Rogers showed me some of the stanzas in MS., and I then expressed my opinion

of their merit, which a further perusal of the printed
volume has given me no reason to revoke. I mention
this, as it may not be disagreeable to you to learn
that I entertained a very favourable opinion of your
powers, before I was aware that such sentiments
were reciprocal.

Waiving your obliging expressions as to my own
productions, for which I thank you very sincerely,
and assure you that I think not lightly of the praise
of one whose approbation is valuable, will you allow
me to talk to you candidly, not critically, on the subject
of yours? You will not suspect me of a wish to discourage, since I pointed out to the publisher the
propriety of complying with your wishes. I think
more highly of your poetical talents than it would,
perhaps, gratify you to hear expressed, for I believe,
from what I observe of your mind, that you are above
flattery. To come to the point, you deserve success,
but we know, before Addison wrote his *Cato*, that
desert does not always command it. But, suppose it
attained,—

> ' You know what ills the author's life assail,
> Toil, envy, want, the *patron* and the jail.'

Do not renounce writing, but never trust entirely to
authorship. If you have a possession, retain it; it will
be, like Prior's fellowship, a last and sure resource.
Compare Mr. Rogers with other authors of the day;
assuredly he is amongst the first of living poets, but
is it to that he owes his station in society, and his
intimacy in the best circles? No, it is to his prudence
and respectability; the world (a bad one, I own)

TO LORD HOLLAND

courts him because he has no occasion to court it. He is a poet, nor is he less so because he was something more. I am not sorry to hear that you are not tempted by the vicinity of Capel Loft, Esqre., though, if he had done for you what he has for the Bloomfields, I should never have laughed at his rage for patronising. But a truly constituted mind will ever be independent. That you may be so is my sincere wish, and, if others think as well of your poetry as I do, you will have no cause to complain of your readers.—Believe me, etc.

TO LORD HOLLAND

June 25, 1812.

My dear Lord,—I must appear very ungrateful, *cxliii* and have, indeed, been very negligent, but till last night I was not apprised of Lady Holland's restoration, and I shall call to-morrow to have the satisfaction, I trust, of hearing that she is well.—I hope that neither politics nor gout have assailed your Lordship since I last saw you, and that you also are 'as well as could be expected.'

The other night, at a ball, I was presented by order to our gracious Regent, who honoured me with some conversation, and professed a predilection for poetry. I confess it was a most unexpected honour, and I thought of poor Brummell's adventure, with some apprehension of a similar blunder. I have now great hope, in the event of Mr. Pye's decease, of 'warbling truth at court,' like Mr. Mallet of indifferent memory. Consider one hundred marks a year! besides the wine and the disgrace ; but then remorse would make

201

me drown myself in my own butt before the year's end, or the finishing of my first dithyrambic.—So that, after all, I shall not meditate our laureate's death by pen or poison.

Will you present my best respects to Lady Holland? and believe me hers and yours very sincerely.

TO SIR WALTER SCOTT, BART.

St. James's Street, July 6, 1812.

cxliv Sir,—I have just been honoured with your letter.— I feel sorry that you should have thought it worth while to notice the 'evil works of my nonage,' as the thing is suppressed *voluntarily*, and your explanation is too kind not to give me pain. The Satire was written when I was very young and very angry, and fully bent on displaying my wrath and my wit, and now I am haunted by the ghosts of my wholesale assertions. I cannot sufficiently thank you for your praise; and now, waiving myself, let me talk to you of the Prince Regent. He ordered me to be presented to him at a ball; and after some sayings peculiarly pleasing from royal lips, as to my own attempts, he talked to me of you and your immortalities : he preferred you to every bard past and present, and asked which of your works pleased me most. It was a difficult question. I answered, I thought the *Lay*. He said his own opinion was nearly similar. In speaking of the others, I told him that I thought you more particularly the poet of *Princes*, as *they* never appeared more fascinating than in *Marmion* and the *Lady of the Lake.* He was pleased to coincide, and to dwell on the description of your Jameses as no less royal than poetical. He spoke alternately of Homer and yourself, and seemed well acquainted with both; so that (with the exception of the Turks and your humble servant) you were in very good company. I defy Murray to have exaggerated his Royal Highness's opinion of your powers, nor can I pretend to enumerate all he said on the subject; but it may give you pleasure to hear that it was conveyed in language which would only suffer by my attempting to transcribe it, and with a tone and taste which gave me a very high idea of his abilities and accomplishments, which I had hitherto considered as confined to *manners*, certainly superior to those of any living *gentleman*.

This interview was accidental. I never went to the levee; for having seen the courts of Mussulman and Catholic sovereigns, my curiosity was sufficiently allayed; and my politics being as perverse as my rhymes, I had, in fact, 'no business there.' To be thus praised by your Sovereign must be gratifying to you; and if that gratification is not alloyed by the communication being made through me, the bearer of it will consider himself very fortunately and sincerely, your obliged and obedient servant,

BYRON.

P.S.—Excuse this scrawl, scratched in a great hurry, and just after a journey.

LETTERS

High Street, Cheltenham, Sept. 5, 1812.

clxv   Pray have the goodness to send those despatches,
and a No. of the *Edinburgh Review* with the rest.
I hope you have written to Mr. Thompson, thanked
him in my name for his present, and told him that I
shall be truly happy to comply with his request.—
How do you go on? and when is the graven image,
' with *bays and wicked rhyme upon't,*' to grace, or disgrace, some of our tardy editions?

Send me *Rokeby.* Who the deuce is he?—no
matter, he has good connections, and will be well
introduced. I thank you for your inquiries: I am
so-so, but my thermometer is sadly below the poetical
point. What will you give *me* or *mine* for a poem of
six cantos (*when complete—no* rhyme, *no* recom-
pense), as like the last two as I can make them? I
have some ideas that one day may be embodied, and
till winter I shall have much leisure.

P.S.—My last question is in the true style of Grub
Street; but, like Jeremy Diddler, I only ' ask for
information.'—Send me Adair on *Diet and Regimen,*
just republished by Ridgway.

Cheltenham, September 10, 1812.

cxlvi   My dear Lord,—The lines which I sketched off
on your hint are still, or rather *were,* in an unfinished

state, for I have just committed them to a flame more decisive than that of Drury. Under all the circumstances, I should hardly wish a contest with Philodrama—Philo-Drury—Asbestos, H——, and all the anonymes and synonymes of Committee candidates. Seriously, I think you have a chance of something much better; for prologuising is not my forte, and, at all events, either my pride or my modesty won't let me incur the hazard of having my rhymes buried in next month's Magazine, under 'Essays on the Murder of Mr. Perceval,' and 'Cures for the Bite of a Mad Dog,' as poor Goldsmith complained of the fate of far superior performances.

I am still sufficiently interested to wish to know the successful candidate; and, amongst so many, I have no doubt some will be excellent, particularly in an age when writing verse is the easiest of all attainments.

I cannot answer your intelligence with the 'like comfort,' unless, as you are deeply theatrical, you may wish to hear of Mr. Betty, whose acting is, I fear, utterly inadequate to the London engagement into which the managers of Covent Garden have lately entered. His figure is fat, his features flat, his voice unmanageable, his action ungraceful, and, as Diggory says, 'I defy him to extort that d——d muffin face of his into madness.' I was very sorry to see him in the character of the 'elephant on the slack rope'; for, when I last saw him, I was in raptures with his performance. But then I was sixteen—an age to which all London condescended to subside. After all, much better judges have admired, and may again ; but I venture to 'prognosticate a prophecy' (see the *Courier*), that he will not succeed.

So, poor dear Rogers has stuck fast on 'the brow of the mighty Helvellyn'—I hope not for ever. My best respects to Lady H. :—her departure, with that of my other friends, was a sad event for me, now reduced to a state of the most cynical solitude. ' By the waters of Cheltenham I sat down and *drank*, when I remembered thee, O Georgiana Cottage ! As for our *harps*, we hanged them up upon the willows that grew thereby. Then they said, Sing us a song of Drury Lane,' etc. ;—but I am dumb and dreary as the Israelites. The waters have disordered me to my heart's content—you *were* right, as you always are.—Believe me ever your obliged and affectionate servant, BYRON.

TO MR. MURRAY

Cheltenham, Sept. 14, 1812.

cxlvii   The parcels contained some letters and verses, all (but one) anonymous and complimentary, and very anxious for my conversion from certain infidelities into which my good-natured correspondents conceive me to have fallen. The books were presents of a *convertible* kind also,—*Christian Knowledge* and the *Bioscope*, a religious Dial of Life explained :—to the author of the former (Cadell, publisher) I beg you will forward my best thanks for his letter, his present, and, above all, his good intentions. The *Bioscope* contained a MS. copy of very excellent verses, from whom I know not, but evidently the composition of some one in the habit of writing, and of writing well. I do not know if he be the author of the *Bioscope* which accompanied them ; but whoever he is, if you can discover him, thank him from me most heartily. The other letters were from ladies, who are welcome to convert me when they please ; and if I can discover them, and they be young, as they say they are, I could convince them perhaps of my devotion. I had also a letter from Mr. Walpole on matters of this world, which I have answered.

So you are Lucien's publisher ! I am promised an interview with him, and think I shall ask *you* for a letter of introduction, as 'the gods have made him poetical.' From whom could it come with a better grace than from *his* publisher and mine? Is it not somewhat treasonable in you to have to do with a relative of the 'direful foe,' as the *Morning Post* calls his brother?

But my book on *Diet and Regimen*, where is it? I thirst for Scott's *Rokeby*; let me have your first-begotten copy. The *Anti-jacobin Review* is all very well, and not a bit worse than the *Quarterly*, and at least less harmless. By-the-by, have you secured my books? I want all the Reviews, at least the critiques, quarterly, monthly, etc., Portuguese and English, extracted, and bound up in one volume for my *old age* ; and pray, sort my Romaic books, and get the volumes lent to Mr. Hobhouse—he has had them now a long time. If anything occurs, you will favour me with a line, and in winter we shall be nearer neighbours.—
Yours, etc.,   BYRON.

LETTERS

P.S.—I was applied to to write the *Address* for Drury Lane, but the moment I heard of the contest, I gave up the idea of contending against all Grub Street, and threw a few thoughts on the subject into the fire. I did this out of respect to you, being sure you would have turned off any of your authors who had entered the lists with such scurvy competitors. To triumph would have been no glory; and to have been defeated—'sdeath!—I would have choked myself, like Otway, with a quartern loaf: so, remember I had, and have, nothing to do with it, upon *my honour* !

TO LORD HOLLAND

September 22, 1812.

cxlviii   My dear Lord,—In a day or two I will send you something which you will still have the liberty to reject if you dislike it. I should like to have had more time, but will do my best,—but too happy if I can oblige *you*, though I may offend a hundred scribblers and the discerning public.—Ever yours.

Keep *my name* a *secret*; or I shall be beset by all the rejected, and, perhaps, damned by a party.

TO LORD HOLLAND

Cheltenham, September 23, 1812.

cxlix   *Ecco !*—I have marked some passages with *double* readings—choose between them—*cut—add—reject*— or *destroy*—do with them as you will—I leave it to you and the Committee—you cannot say so called

TO LORD HOLLAND

'*a non committendo.*' What will *they* do (and I do) with the hundred and one rejected Troubadours? 'With trumpets, yea, and with shawms,' will you be assailed in the most diabolical doggerel. I wish my name not to transpire till the day is decided. I shall not be in town, so it won't much matter; but let us have a *good deliverer*. I think Elliston should be the man, or Pope; *not* Raymond, I implore you, by the love of Rhythmus!

The passages marked thus ==, above and below, are for you to choose between epithets, and such like poetical furniture. Pray write me a line, and believe me ever, etc.

My best remembrances to Lady H. Will you be good enough to decide between the various readings marked, and erase the other? or our *deliverer* may be as puzzled as a commentator, and belike repeat both. If these *versicles* won't do, I will hammer out some more endecasyllables.

P.S.—Tell Lady H. I have had sad work to keep out the Phœnix—I mean the Fire Office of that name. It has insured the theatre, and why not the *Address*?

TO LORD HOLLAND

September 24.

I send a recast of the four first lines of the con- *cl* cluding paragraph.

> This greeting o'er, the ancient rule obey'd,
> The drama's homage by her Herald paid,

LETTERS

Receive *our welcome too*, whose every tone
Springs from our hearts, and fain would win your own.
The curtain rises, etc. etc.

And do forgive all this trouble. See what it is to have to do even with the *genteelest* of us.—Ever, etc.

TO LORD HOLLAND

Cheltenham, Sept. 25, 1812.

Still 'more matter for a May morning.' Having patched the middle and end of the *Address*, I send one more couplet for a part of the beginning, which, if not too turgid, you will have the goodness to add. After that flagrant image of the *Thames* (I hope no unlucky wag will say I have set it on fire, though Dryden, in his *Annus Mirabilis*, and Churchill, in his *Times*, did it before me), I mean to insert this—

As flashing far the new Volcano shone
And swept the skies with { meteors / lightnings } not their own,
While thousands throng'd around the burning dome, etc. etc.

I think 'thousands' less flat than 'crowds collected' —but don't let me plunge into the bathos, or rise into Nat Lee's *Bedlam* metaphors. By-the-by, the best view of the said fire (which I myself saw from a house-top in Covent Garden) was at Westminster Bridge, from the reflection on the Thames.

Perhaps the present couplet had better come in after 'trembled for their homes,' the two lines after; —as otherwise the image certainly sinks, and it will run just as well.

210

TO LORD HOLLAND

The lines themselves, perhaps, may be better thus
—('choose' or 'refuse'—but please *yourself*, and
don't mind 'Sir Fretful')—

As flash'd the volumed blaze, and $\left\{\begin{array}{c}\textit{sadly}\\\text{ghastly}\end{array}\right\}$ shone
The skies with lightnings awful as their own.

The last *runs* smoothest, and, I think, best; but
you know *better* than *best*. 'Lurid' is also a less
indistinct epithet than 'livid wave,' and, if you think
so, a dash of the pen will do.

I expected one line this morning; in the meantime, I shall remodel and condense, and, if I do not
hear from you, shall send another copy.—I am ever,
etc.

TO LORD HOLLAND

September 26, 1812.

You will think there is no end to my villainous *elii*
emendations. The fifth and sixth lines I think to
alter thus—

Ye who beheld—O sight admired and mourn'd,
Whose radiance mock'd the ruin it adorn'd ;

because 'night' is repeated the next line but one;
and, as it now stands, the conclusion of the paragraph, 'worthy him (Shakspeare) and *you*,' appears
to apply the '*you*' to those only who were out of bed
and in Covent Garden market on the night of conflagration, instead of the audience or the discerning

public at large, all of whom are intended to be comprised in that comprehensive and, I hope, comprehensible pronoun.

By-the-by, one of my corrections in the fair copy sent yesterday has dived into the bathos some sixty fathom—

> When Garrick died, and Brinsley ceased to write.

Ceasing to *live* is a much more serious concern, and ought not to be first; therefore I will let the old couplet stand, with its half rhymes 'sought' and 'wrote.' Second thoughts in everything are best, but, in rhyme, third and fourth don't come amiss. I am very anxious on this business, and I do hope that the very trouble I occasion you will plead its own excuse, and that it will tend to show my endeavour to make the most of the time allotted. I wish I had known it months ago, for in that case I had not left one line standing on another. I always scrawl in this way, and smooth as much as I can, but never sufficiently; and, latterly, I can weave a nine-line stanza faster than a couplet, for which measure I have not the cunning. When I began *Childe Harold*, I had never tried Spenser's measure, and now I cannot scribble in any other.

After all, my dear Lord, if you can get a decent *Address* elsewhere, don't hesitate to put this aside. Why did you not trust your own Muse? I am very sure she would have been triumphant, and saved the Committee their trouble—''tis a joyful one' to me, but I fear I shall not satisfy even myself. After the account you sent me, 'tis no compliment to say you

would have beaten your candidates; but I mean
that, in *that* case, there would have been no occasion
for their being beaten at all.

There are but two decent prologues in our tongue
—Pope's to *Cato*—Johnson's to Drury lane. These,
with the epilogue to the *Distrest Mother*, and, I think,
one of Goldsmith's and a prologue of old Colman's
to Beaumont and Fletcher's *Philaster*, are the best
things of the kind we have.

P.S.—I am diluted to the throat with medicine
for the stone; and Boisragon wants me to try a warm
climate for the winter—but I won't.

TO LORD HOLLAND

September 27, 1812.

I have just received your very kind letter, and hope cliii
you have met with a second copy corrected and
addressed to Holland House, with some omissions
and this new couplet,

> As glared each rising flash, and ghastly shone
> The skies with lightnings awful as their own.

As to remarks, I can only say I will alter and ac-
quiesce in anything. With regard to the part which
Whitbread wishes to omit, I believe the *Address* will
go off *quicker* without it, though, like the agility of
the Hottentot, at the expense of its vigour. I leave
to your choice entirely the different specimens of
stucco-work; and a *brick* of your own will also much

improve my Babylonish turret. I should like Elliston
to have it, with your leave. 'Adorn' and 'mourn' are
lawful rhymes in Pope's *Death of the Unfortunate Lady*.
—Gray has 'forlorn' and 'mourn'—and 'torn' and
'mourn' are in Smollett's famous *Tears of Scotland*.

As there will probably be an outcry amongst the
rejected, I hope the Committee will testify (if it be
needful) that I sent in nothing to the congress whatever, with or without a name, as your Lordship well
knows. All I have to do with it is with and through
you; and though I, of course, wish to satisfy the
audience, I do assure you my first object is to comply
with your request, and in so doing to show the sense
I have of the many obligations you have conferred
upon me.—Yours ever,   B.

TO MR. MURRAY

Cheltenham, September 27, 1812.

cliv   I sent in no *Address* whatever to the Committee;
but out of nearly one hundred (this is *confidential*),
none have been deemed worth acceptance; and in
consequence of their *subsequent* application to *me*, I
have written a prologue, which *has* been received,
and will be spoken. The MS. is now in the hands of
Lord Holland.

I write this merely to say, that (however it is received by the audience) you will publish it in the
next edition of *Childe Harold*; and I only beg you at
present to keep my name secret till you hear further
from me, and as soon as possible I wish you to have
a correct copy, to do with as you think proper.

TO LORD HOLLAND

P.S.—I should wish a few copies printed off *before*, that the newspaper copies may be correct *after* the *delivery*.

TO LORD HOLLAND

September 28, 1812.

Will this do better? The metaphor is more com- *clv* plete.

<blockquote>
Till slowly ebb'd the $\left\{ \begin{array}{c} \textit{lava of the} \\ \text{spent volcanic} \end{array} \right\}$ wave,
And blackening ashes mark'd the Muse's grave.
</blockquote>

If not, we will say 'burning wave,' and instead of 'burning clime,' in the line some couplets back, have 'glowing.'

Is Whitbread determined to castrate all my *cavalry* lines? I don't see why t'other house should be spared; besides, it is the public, who ought to know better; and you recollect Johnson's was against similar buffooneries of Rich's—but, certes, I am not Johnson.

Instead of 'effects,' say 'labours'—'degenerate' will do, will it? Mr. Betty is no longer a babe, therefore the line cannot be personal.

Will this do?

<blockquote>
Till ebb'd the lava of $\left\{ \begin{array}{c} \textit{the burning} \\ \text{that molten} \end{array} \right\}$ wave,
</blockquote>

with 'glowing dome,' in case you prefer 'burning' added to this 'wave' metaphorical. The word 'fiery pillar' was suggested by the 'pillar of fire' in the

215

book of Exodus, which went before the Israelites through the Red Sea. I once thought of saying 'like Israel's pillar,' and making it a simile, but I did not know—the great temptation was leaving the epithet 'fiery' for the supplementary wave. I want to work up that passage, as it is the only new ground us prologuizers can go upon—

> This is the place where, if a poet
> Shined in description, he might show it.

If I part with the possibility of a future conflagration, we lessen the compliment to Shakspeare. However, we will e'en mend it thus—

> Yes, it shall be—the magic of that name,
> That scorns the scythe of Time, the torch of Flame,
> On the same spot, etc. etc.

There—the deuce is in it, if that is not an improvement to Whitbread's content. Recollect, it is the 'name,' and not the 'magic,' that has a noble contempt for those same weapons. If it were the 'magic,' my metaphor would be somewhat of the maddest— so the 'name' is the antecedent. But, my dear Lord, your patience is not quite so immortal—therefore, with many and sincere thanks, I am, yours ever most affectionately.

P.S.—I foresee there will be charges of partiality in the papers; but you know I sent in no *Address*; and glad both you and I must be that I did not, for, in that case, their plea had been plausible. I doubt the Pit will be testy; but conscious innocence (a novel and pleasing sensation) makes me bold.

TO MR. BANKES

TO MR. WILLIAM BANKES

Cheltenham, September 28, 1812.

My dear Bankes,—When you point out to one *clvi* how people can be intimate at the distance of some seventy leagues, I will plead guilty to your charge, and accept your farewell, but not *wittingly*, till you give me some better reason than my silence, which merely proceeded from a notion founded on your own declaration of *old*, that you hated writing and receiving letters. Besides, how was I to find out a man of many residences? If I had addressed you *now*, it had been to your borough, where I must have conjectured you were amongst your constituents. So now, in despite of Mr. N. and Lady W., you shall be as 'much better' as the Hexham post-office will allow me to make you. I do assure you I am much indebted to you for thinking of me at all, and can't spare you even from amongst the superabundance of friends with whom you suppose me surrounded.

You heard that Newstead is sold—'the sum £140,000; sixty to remain in mortgage on the estate for three years, paying interest, of course. Rochdale is also likely to do well—so my worldly matters are mending. I have been here some time drinking the waters, simply because there are waters to drink, and they are very medicinal, and sufficiently disgusting. In a few days I set out for Lord Jersey's, but return here, where I am quite alone, go out very little, and enjoy in its fullest extent the *dolce far niente*. What

217

you are about I cannot guess, even from your date;
—not daucing to the sound of the gitourney in the
Hall of the Lowthers? one of whom is here, ill, poor
thing, with a phthisic. I heard that you passed
through here (at the sordid inn where I first alighted)
the very day before I arrived in these parts. We had
a very pleasant set here; at first the Jerseys, Mel-
bournes, Cowpers, and Hollands, but all gone; and
the only persons I know are the Rawdons and
Oxfords, with some later acquaintances of less brilliant descent.

But I do not trouble them much; and as for your
rooms and your assemblies, 'they are not dreamed of
in our philosophy!!'—Did you read of a sad accident
in the Wye t'other day? A dozen drowned; and
Mr. Rossoe, a corpulent gentleman, preserved by a
boat-hook or an eel-spear, begged, when he heard his
wife was saved—no—*lost*—to be thrown in again!!
—as if he could not have thrown himself in, had he
wished it; but this passes for a trait of sensibility.
What strange beings men are, in and out of the
Wye!

I have to ask you a thousand pardons for not ful-
filling some orders before I left town; but if you
knew all the cursed entanglements I *had* to wade
through, it would be unnecessary to beg your forgiveness.—When will Parliament (the new one) meet?—
in sixty days, on account of Ireland, I presume: the
Irish election will demand a longer period for com-
pletion than the constitutional allotment. Yours, of
course, is safe, and all your side of the question.
Salamanca is the ministerial watchword, and all will

TO LORD HOLLAND

go well with you. I hope you will speak more frequently ; I am sure at least you *ought*, and it will be
expected. I see Portman means to stand again.
Good night.—Ever yours most affectionately,

Μπαίρων.

TO LORD HOLLAND

September 28.

I have altered the *middle* couplet, so as I hope clvii
partly to do away with W.'s objection. I do think,
in the present state of the stage, it had been unpardonable to pass over the horses and Miss Mudie, etc.
As Betty is no longer a boy, how can this be applied
to him ? He is now to be judged as a man. If he
acts still like a boy, the public will but be more
ashamed of their blunder. I have, you see, *now*
taken it for granted that these things are reformed.
I confess, I wish that part of the *Address* to stand ;
but if W. is inexorable, e'en let it go. I have also
new-cast the lines, and softened the hint of future
combustion, and sent them off this morning. Will
you have the goodness to add, or insert, the *approved*
alterations as they arrive ? They 'come like shadows,
so depart' ; occupy me, and, I fear, disturb you.

Do not let Mr. W. put his Address into Elliston's
hands till you have settled on these alterations. E.
will think it too long :—much depends on the speaking. I fear it will not bear much curtailing, without
chasms in the sense.

It is certainly too long in the reading ; but if Elliston
exerts himself, such a favourite with the public will

not be thought tedious.   *I* should think it so, if *he*
were not to speak it.—Yours ever, etc.

P.S.—On looking again, I doubt my idea of having
obviated W.'s objection.   To the other House allusion
is *non sequitur*—but I wish to plead for this part, because the thing really is not to be passed over.   Many
afterpieces at the Lyceum by the *same company* have
already attracted this ' Augean *Stable* '—and Johnson,
in his prologue against 'Lunn' (the harlequin manager,
Rich),—'Hunt,'—'Mahomet,' etc., is surely a fair
precedent.

TO LORD HOLLAND

September 29, 1812.

clviii   Shakspeare certainly ceased to reign in *one* of his
kingdoms, as George III. did in America, and George
IV. may in Ireland?   Now, we have nothing to do out
of our own realms, and when the monarchy was gone,
his Majesty had but a barren sceptre.   I have *cut away*,
you will see, and altered, but make it what you please;
only I do implore, for my *own* gratification, one lash
on those accursed quadrupeds—'a long shot, Sir
Lucius, if you love me.'   I have altered ' wave,' etc.,
and the ' fire,' and so forth for the timid.

Let me hear from you when convenient, and
believe me, etc.

P.S.—Do let *that* stand, and cut out elsewhere.
I shall choke, if we must overlook their d——d
menagerie.

TO LORD HOLLAND

TO LORD HOLLAND

September 30, 1812.

I send you the most I can make of it; for I am *clix*
not so well as I was, and find I 'pall in resolution.'

I wish much to see you, and will be at Tetbury by
twelve on Saturday; and from thence I go on to
Lord Jersey's. It is impossible not to allude to the
degraded state of the Stage, but I have lightened *it*,
and endeavoured to obviate your *other* objections.
There is a new couplet for Sheridan, allusive to his
Monody. All the alterations I have marked thus |,
—as you will see by comparison with the other copy.
I have cudgelled my brains with the greatest willing-
ness, and only wish I had more time to have done
better.

You will find a sort of clap-trap laudatory couplet
inserted for the quiet of the Committee, and I have
added, towards the end, the couplet you were pleased
to *like.* The whole *Address* is seventy-three lines,
still perhaps too long; and, if shortened, you will
save time, but, I fear, a little of what I meant for
sense also.

With myriads of thanks, I am ever, etc.

My sixteenth edition of respects to Lady H.—How
she must laugh at all this!

I wish Murray, my publisher, to print off some
copies as soon as your Lordship returns to town—it
will ensure correctness in the papers afterwards.

clx

> Far be from him that hour which asks in vain
> Tears such as flow for Garrick in his strain;
>
> *or,*
>
> Far be that hour that vainly asks in turn
>
> Such verse for him as { *crown'd his* / wept o'er } Garrick's urn.

Will you choose between these added to the lines on Sheridan? I think they will wind up the panegyric, and agree with the train of thought preceding them.

Now, one word as to the Committee: how could they resolve on a rough copy of an *Address* never sent in, unless you had been good enough to retain in memory, or on paper, the thing they have been good enough to adopt? By-the-by, the circumstances of the case should make the Committee less *avidus gloriae*, for all praise of them would look plaguy suspicious. If necessary to be stated at all, the simple facts bear them out. They surely had a right to act as they pleased. My sole object is one which, I trust, my whole conduct has shown; viz. that I did nothing insidious—sent in no *Address whatever*—but, when applied to, did my best for them and myself; but above all, that there was no undue partiality, which will be what the rejected will endeavour to make out. Fortunately—most fortunately—I sent in no lines on the occasion. For I am sure that had they, in that case, been preferred, it would have been asserted that *I* was known, and

222

owed the preference to private friendship. This is
what we shall probably have to encounter; but, if
once spoken and approved, we shan't be much
embarrassed by their brilliant conjectures; and, as to
criticism, an *old* author, like an old bull, grows cooler
(or ought) at every baiting.

The only thing would be to avoid a party on
the night of delivery — afterwards, the more the
better, and the whole transaction inevitably tends to
a good deal of discussion. Murray tells me there
are myriads of ironical *Addresses* ready, — *some*, in
imitation of what is called *my style*. If they are as
good as the *Probationary Odes*, or Hawkins's *Pipe of
Tobacco*, it will not be bad fun for the imitated.—
Ever, etc.

TO LORD HOLLAND

October 2, 1812.

A copy of this *still altered* is sent by the post, but *clxi*
this will arrive first. It must be 'humbler'—'*yet
aspiring*' does away the modesty, and, after all,
truth is truth. Besides, there is a puff direct altered,
to please your *plaguy renters*.

I shall be at Tetbury by 12 or 1—but send this
for you to ponder over. There are several little
things marked thus / altered for your perusal. I
have dismounted the cavalry, and, I hope, arranged
to your *general* satisfaction.—Ever, etc.

At Tetbury by noon.—I hope, after it is sent,
there will be no more elisions. It is not now so

LETTERS

long—73 lines—two less than allotted. I will alter all Committee objections, but I hope you won't permit Elliston to have any *voice* whatever,—except in speaking it.

TO MR. MURRAY

Cheltenham, Oct. 12, 1812.

clxii   I have a very *strong objection* to the engraving of the portrait, and request that it may, on no account, be prefixed; but let *all* the proofs be burnt, and the plate broken. I will be at the expense which has been incurred; it is but fair that *I* should, since I cannot permit the publication. I beg, as a particular favour, that you will lose no time in having this done, for which I have reasons that I will state when I see you. Forgive all the trouble I have occasioned you.

I have received no account of the reception of the *Address*, but see it is vituperated in the papers, which does not much embarrass an *old author*. I leave it to your own judgment to add it, or not, to your next edition when required. Pray comply *strictly* with my wishes as to the engraving, and believe me, etc.

P.S.—Favour me with an answer, as I shall not be easy till I hear that the proofs, etc., are destroyed. I hear that the *Satirist* has reviewed *Childe Harold*, in what manner I need not ask; but I wish to know if the old personalities are revived? I have a better reason for asking this than any that merely concerns myself; but in publications of that kind, others, particularly female names, are sometimes introduced.

TO LORD HOLLAND

TO LORD HOLLAND

Cheltenham, Oct. 14, 1812.

My dear Lord,—I perceive that the papers, yea, *clxiii* even Perry's, are somewhat ruffled at the injudicious preference of the Committee. My friend Perry has, indeed, *et tu Brute*-d me rather scurvily, for which I will send him, for the *M. C.*, the next epigram I scribble, as a token of my full forgiveness.

Do the Committee mean to enter into no explanation of their proceedings? You must see there is a leaning towards a charge of partiality. You will, at least, acquit me of any great anxiety to push myself before so many elder and better anonymous, to whom the twenty guineas (which I take to be about two thousand pounds *Bank* currency) and the honour would have been equally welcome. 'Honour,' I see, 'hath skill in paragraph-writing.'

I wish to know how it went off at the second reading, and whether any one has had the grace to give it a glance of approbation. I have seen no paper but Perry's and two Sunday ones. Perry is severe, and the others silent. If, however, you and your Committee are not now dissatisfied with your own judgments, I shall not much embarrass myself about the brilliant remarks of the journals. My own opinion upon it is what it always was, perhaps pretty near that of the public.—Believe me, my dear Lord, etc. etc.

P.S.—My best respects to Lady H., whose smiles will be very consolatory, even at this distance.

Cheltenham, Oct. 18, 1812.

clxiv   Will you have the goodness to get this parody of a peculiar kind (for all the first lines are *Busby's* entire) inserted in several of the papers (*correctly*— and copied *correctly ; my hand* is difficult)—particularly the *Morning Chronicle?* Tell Mr. Perry I forgive him all he has said, and may say against *my Address,* but he will allow me to deal with the Doctor—(*audi alteram partem*)—and not *betray* me. I cannot think what has befallen Mr. Perry, for of yore we were very good friends ;—but no matter, only get this inserted.

I have a poem on Waltzing for *you,* of which I make *you* a present ; but it must be anonymous. It is in the old style of *English Bards and Scotch Reviewers.*

P.S.—With the next edition of *Childe Harold* you may print the first fifty or a hundred opening lines, of the *Curse of Minerva,* down to the couplet beginning

Mortal ('twas thus she spake), etc.

Of course, the moment the *Satire* begins, there you will stop, and the opening is the best part.

TO MR. MURRAY

Oct. 19, 1812.

clxv   Many thanks, but I *must* pay the *damage,* and will thank you to tell me the amount for the engraving. I think the *Rejected Addresses* by far the best thing of the kind since the *Rolliad,* and wish *you* had published them. Tell the author 'I forgive him, were he twenty times over our satirist'; and think his imitations not at all inferior to the famous ones of Hawkins Browne. He must be a man of very lively wit, and much less scurrilous than wits often are: altogether, I very much admire the performance, and wish it all success. The *Satirist* has taken a new tone, as you will see: we have now, I think, finished with *Childe Harold's* critics. I have in *hand* a *Satire* on *Waltzing*, which you must publish anonymously: it is not long, not quite two hundred lines, but will make a very small boarded pamphlet. In a few days you shall have it.

P.S.—The editor of the *Satirist* almost ought to be thanked for his revocation; it is done handsomely, after five years' warfare.

TO MR. MURRAY

Oct. 23, 1812.

Thanks, as usual. You go on boldly; but have a care of *glutting* the public, who have by this time had enough of *Childe Harold*. *Waltzing* shall be prepared. It is rather above two hundred lines, with an introductory Letter to the Publisher. I think of publishing, with *Childe Harold*, the opening lines of the *Curse of Minerva*, as far as the first speech of Pallas,—because some of the readers like that part better than any I have ever written; and as it contains nothing to affect the subject of the subsequent portion, it will find a place as a *Descriptive Fragment*.

clxvi

The *plate* is *broken*? between ourselves, it was unlike the picture; and besides, upon the whole, the frontispiece of an author's visage is but a paltry exhibition. At all events, *this* would have been no recommendation to the book. I am sure Sanders would not have *survived* the engraving. By-the-by, the *picture* may remain with *you* or *him* (which you please), till my return. The *one* of two remaining copies is at your service till I can give you a *better*; the other must be *burned peremptorily*. Again, do not forget that I have an account with you, and *that* this is *included*. I give you too much *trouble* to allow you to incur *expense* also.

You best know how far this 'Address Riot' will affect the future sale of *Childe Harold*. I like the volume of *Rejected Addresses* better and better. The other parody which Perry has received is mine also (I believe). It is Dr. Busby's speech versified. You are removing to Albemarle Street, I find, and I rejoice that we shall be nearer neighbours. I am going to Lord Oxford's, but letters here will be forwarded. When at leisure, all communications from you will be willingly received by the humblest of your scribes. Did Mr. Ward write the review of Horne Tooke's *Life* in the *Quarterly*? It is excellent.

TO MR. MURRAY

Cheltenham, November 22, 1812.

clxvii   On my return here from Lord Oxford's, I found your obliging note, and will thank you to retain the letters, and any other subsequent ones to the same address, till I arrive in town to claim them, which will probably be in a few days. I have in charge a curious and very long MS. poem, written by Lord Brooke (the *friend* of Sir *Philip Sidney*), which I wish to submit to the inspection of Mr. Gifford, with the following queries:—first, whether it has ever been published? and secondly (if not), whether it is worth publication? It is from Lord Oxford's library, and must have escaped or been overlooked amongst the MSS. of the *Harleian Miscellany*. The writing is Lord Brooke's, except a different hand towards the close. It is very long, and in the six-line stanza. It is not for me to hazard an opinion upon its merits; but I would take the liberty, if not too troublesome, to submit it to Mr. Gifford's judgment, which, from his excellent edition of Massinger, I should conceive to be as decisive on the writings of that age as on those of our own.

Now for a less agreeable and important topic.— How came Mr. *Mac-Somebody*, without consulting you or me, to prefix the *Address* to his volume of *Dejected Addresses*? Is not this somewhat larcenous? I think the ceremony of leave might have been asked, though I have no objection to the thing itself; and leave the 'hundred and eleven' to tire themselves with 'base comparisons.' I should think the ingenious public tolerably sick of the subject, and, except the Parodies, I have not interfered, nor shall; indeed I did not know that Dr. Busby had published his Apologetical Letter and Postscript, or I should have recalled them. But, I confess, I looked upon his conduct in a different light before its appearance. I see some mountebank has taken Alderman Birch's name to vituperate Dr. Busby; he had much better have pilfered his pastry, which I should imagine the more valuable ingredient—at least for a puff.—Pray secure me a copy of Woodfall's new *Junius*, and believe me, etc.

TO MR. WILLIAM BANKES

December 26.

clxviii The multitude of your recommendations has already superseded my humble endeavours to be of use to you; and, indeed, most of my principal friends are returned. Leake from Joannina, Canning and Adair from the city of the Faithful, and at Smyrna no letter is necessary, as the consuls are always willing to do everything for personages of respectability. I have sent you *three*; one to Gibraltar, which, though of no great necessity, will, perhaps, put you on a more intimate footing with a very pleasant family there. You will very soon find out that a man of any consequence has very little occasion for any letters but to ministers and bankers, and of them we have already plenty, I will be sworn.

It is by no means improbable that I shall go in the spring; and if you will fix any place of rendezvous about August, I will *write* or *join* you.—When in Albania, I wish you would inquire after Dervise Tahiri and Vascillie (or Bazil), and make my respects to the viziers, both there and in the Morea. If you mention my name to Suleyman of Thebes, I think it will not hurt you; if I had my dragoman, or wrote

TO MR. HODGSON

Turkish, I could have given you letters of *real service*; but to the English they are hardly requisite, and the Greeks themselves can be of little advantage. Liston you know already, and I do not, as he was not then minister. Mind you visit Ephesus and the Troad, and let me hear from you when you please. I believe G. Forresti is now at Yanina; but if not, whoever is there will be too happy to assist you. Be particular about *firmauns*; never allow yourself to be bullied, for you are better protected in Turkey than anywhere; trust not the Greeks; and take some *knicknackeries* for *presents—watches, pistols*, etc. etc. to the Beys and Pachas. If you find one Demetrius, at Athens or elsewhere, I can recommend him as a good Dragoman. I hope to join you, however; but you will find swarms of English now in the Levant. —Believe me, etc.

TO MR. HODGSON

February 3, 1813.

My dear Hodgson,—I will join you in any bond *clxix* for the money you require, be it that or a larger sum. With regard to security, as Newstead is in a sort of abeyance between sale and purchase, and my Lancashire property very unsettled, I do not know how far I can give more than personal security, but what I can I will. I hear nothing of my own concerns, but expect a letter daily. Let me hear from you where you are and will be this month. I am a great admirer of the *R. A.* (*Rejected Addresses*), though I have had so great a share in the cause of their publication, and I like the *C. H.* (*Childe Harold*) imitation one of the best. Lady O. (Oxford) has heard me talk much of you as a relative of the Cokes, etc., and desires me to say she would be happy to have the pleasure of your acquaintance. You must come and see me at K——. I am sure you would like *all* here if you knew them.

The 'Agnus' is furious. You can have no idea of the horrible and absurd things she has said and done since (really from the best motives) I withdrew my homage. 'Great pleasure' is, certes, my object, but '*Why brief*, Mr. Wild?' I cannot answer for the future, but the past is pretty secure ; and in it I can number the last two months as worthy of the gods in *Lucretius.* I cannot review in the *Monthly*; in fact I can just now do nothing, at least with a pen ; and I really think the days of authorship are over with me altogether. I hear and rejoice in Bland's and Merivale's intentions. Murray has grown great, and has got him new premises in the fashionable part of town. We live here so shut out of the *monde* that I have nothing of general import to communicate, and fill this up with a 'happy new year,' and drink to you and Drury.—Ever yours, dear H.,

B.

TO MR. MURRAY

February 20, 1813.

clxx   In *Horace in London* I perceive some stanzas on Lord Elgin in which (waiving the kind compliment to myself) I heartily concur. I wish I had the

232

pleasure of Mr. Smith's acquaintance, as I could communicate the curious anecdote you read in Mr. T.'s letter. If he would like it, he can have the *substance* for his second edition; if not, I shall add it to our next, though I think we already have enough of Lord Elgin.

What I have read of this work seems admirably done. My praise, however, is not much worth the author's having; but you may thank him in my name for *his*. The idea is new—we have excellent imitations of the *Satires*, etc., by Pope; but I remember but one imitative Ode in his works, and *none* anywhere else. I can hardly suppose that *they* have lost any fame by the fate of the Farce; but even should this be the case, the present publication will again place them on their pinnacle.—Yours, etc.

TO MR. ROGERS

March 25, 1813.

I enclose you a draft for the usurious interest due *clxxi* to Lord ——'s *protégé*;—I also could wish you would state thus much for me to his Lordship. Though the transaction speaks plainly in itself for the borrower's folly and the lender's usury, it never was my intention to *quash* the demand, as I *legally* might, nor to with-hold payment of principal, or, perhaps, even *unlawful* interest. You know what my situation has been, and what it is. I have parted with an estate (which has been in my family for nearly three hundred years, and was never disgraced by being in possession of a *lawyer*, a *churchman*, or a *woman*, during that period), to liquidate this and similar demands ; and the payment of the purchase is still withheld, and may be, perhaps, for years. If, therefore, I am under the necessity of making those persons *wait* for their money (which, considering the terms, they can afford to suffer), it is my misfortune.

When I arrived at majority in 1809, I offered my own security on *legal* interest, and it was refused. *Now*, I will not accede to this. This man I may have seen, but I have no recollection of the names of any parties but the *agents* and the securities. The moment I can, it is assuredly my intention to pay my debts. This person's case may be a hard one ; but, under all circumstances, what is mine? I could not foresee that the purchaser of my estate was to demur in paying for it.

I am glad it happens to be in my power so far to accommodate my Israelite, and only wish I could do as much for the rest of the Twelve Tribes.—Ever yours, dear R.,   BN.

TO MR. MURRAY

April 21, 1813.

clxxii   I shall be in town by Sunday next, and will call and have some conversation on the subject of Westall's designs. I am to sit to him for a picture at the request of a friend of mine ; and as Sanders's is not a good one, you will probably prefer the other. I wish you to have Sanders's taken down and sent to my lodgings immediately—before my arrival. I hear that a certain malicious publication on Waltzing is attributed to me. This report, I suppose, you will take care to contradict, as the author, I am sure, will not like that I should wear his cap and bells. Mr. Hobhouse's quarto will be out immediately; pray send to the author for an early copy, which I wish to take abroad with me.

P.S.—I see the *Examiner* threatens some observations upon you next week. What can you have done to share the wrath which has heretofore been principally expended upon the Prince? I presume all your Scribleri will be drawn up in battle array in defence of the modern Tonson—Mr. Bucke, for instance.

Send in my account to Bennet Street, as I wish to settle it before sailing.

TO MR. MOORE

(*May?*) 1813.

My dear Moore,—'When Rogers' must not see clxxiii the inclosed, which I send for your perusal. I am ready to fix any day you like for our visit. Was not Sheridan good upon the whole? The 'Poulterer' was the first and best.—Ever yours, etc.

I.

When Thurlow this damn'd nonsense sent,
(I hope I am not violent),
Nor men nor gods knew what he meant,

2.

And since not ev'n our Rogers' praise
To common sense his thoughts could raise—
Why *would* they let him print his lays?

3.

*   *   *   *   *

4.

*   *   *   *   *

5.

To me, divine Apollo, grant—O !
Hermilda's first and second canto,
I'm fitting up a new portmanteau ;

6.

And thus to furnish decent lining,
My own and others' bays I'm twining—
So, gentle Thurlow, throw me thine in.

TO MR. MOORE

May 19, 1813.

clxxiv

Oh you, who in all names can tickle the town,
Anacreon, Tom Little, Tom Moore, or Tom Brown,—
For hang me if I know of which you may most brag,
Your Quarto two-pounds, or your Twopenny Post Bag ;

*   *   *   *   *

But now to my letter—to *yours* 'tis an answer—
To-morrow be with me, as soon as you can, sir,
All ready and dress'd for proceeding to spunge on
(According to compact) the wit in the dungeon—
Pray Phœbus at length our political malice
May not get us lodgings within the same palace !

TO MR. HODGSON

I suppose that to-night you're engaged with some codgers,
And for Sotheby's Blues have deserted Sam Rogers;
And I, though with cold I have nearly my death got,
Must put on my breeches, and wait on the Heathcote.
But to-morrow at four, we will both play the *Scurra*,
And you'll be Catullus, the Regent Mamurra.

Dear M.,—Having got thus far, I am interrupted
by ——.   10 o'clock.

Half-past 11.   —— is gone.   I must dress for
Lady Heathcote's.—Addio.

TO MR. HODGSON

June 6, 1813.

My dear Hodgson,—I write to you a few lines on clxxv
business.   Murray has thought proper at his own
risk, and peril, and profit (if there be any) to publish
The Giaour; and it may possibly come under your
ordeal in the *Monthly*.   I merely wish to state that
in the published copies there are additions to the
amount of ten pages, *text* and *margin* (*chiefly* the
last), which render it a little less unfinished (but
more unintelligible) than before.   If, therefore, you
review it, let it be from the published copies and not
from the first sketch.   I shall not sail for this month,
and shall be in town again next week, when I shall
be happy to hear from but more glad to see you.
You know I have no time or turn for correspondence (!).   But you also know, I hope, that I am not
the less, yours ever,   Μπαιρῶν.

LETTERS

Maidenhead, June 13, 1813.

clxxvi   I have read the *Strictures*, which are just enough, and not grossly abusive, in very fair couplets. There is a note against Massinger near the end, and one cannot quarrel with one's company, at any rate. The author detects some incongruous figures in a passage of *English Bards*, page 23, but which edition I do not know. In the *sole* copy in your possession—I mean the *fifth* edition—you may make these alterations, that I may profit (though a little too late) by his remarks :—For '*hellish* instinct,' substitute '*brutal* instinct'; '*harpies*' alter to '*felons*'; and for 'bloodhounds' write 'hell-hounds.' These be 'very bitter words, by my troth,' and the alterations not much sweeter; but as I shall not publish the thing, they can do no harm, but are a satisfaction to me in the way of amendment. The passage is only twelve lines.

You do not answer me about H.'s book; I want to write to him, and not to say anything unpleasing. If you direct to Post-Office, Portsmouth, till *called* for, I will send and receive your letter. You never told me of the forthcoming critique on *Columbus*, which is not *too* fair; and I do not think justice quite done to the *Pleasures*, which surely entitle the author to a higher rank than that assigned him in the *Quarterly*. But I must not cavil at the decisions of the *invisible infallibles*; and the article is very well written. The general horror of '*fragments*' makes me tremulous for *The Giaour*; but

238

TO MR. GIFFORD

you would publish it—I presume, by this time, to
your repentance. But as I consented, whatever be
its fate, I won't now quarrel with you, even though
I detect it in my pastry; but I shall not open a pie
without apprehension for some weeks.

The books which may be marked G. O. I will
carry out. Do you know Clarke's *Naufragia?* I
am told that he asserts the *first* volume of *Robinson
Crusoe* was written by the first Lord Oxford, when
in the Tower, and given by him to Defoe; if true,
it is a curious anecdote. Have you got back Lord
Brooke's MS.? and what does Heber say of it?
Write to me at Portsmouth.—Ever yours, etc., N.

TO MR. MURRAY

June 18, 1813.

Dear Sir,—Will you forward the enclosed answer clxxvii
to the kindest letter I ever received in my life, my
sense of which I can neither express to Mr. Gifford
himself nor to any one else?—Ever yours, N.

TO MR. GIFFORD.

June 18, 1813.

My dear Sir,—I feel greatly at a loss how to write clxxviii
to you at all—still more to thank you as I ought.
If you knew the veneration with which I have ever
regarded you, long before I had the most distant
prospect of becoming your acquaintance, literary or
personal, my embarrassment would not surprise you.

Any suggestion of yours, even were it conveyed in the less tender shape of the text of the *Baviad*, or a Monk Mason note in Massinger, would have been obeyed; I should have endeavoured to improve myself by your censure: judge then if I should be less willing to profit by your kindness. It is not for me to bandy compliments with my elders and my betters: I receive your approbation with gratitude, and will not return my brass for your gold by expressing more fully those sentiments of admiration, which, however sincere, would, I know, be unwelcome.

To your advice on religious topics I shall equally attend. Perhaps the best way will be by avoiding them altogether. The already published objectionable passages have been much commented upon, but certainly have been rather strongly interpreted. I am no bigot to infidelity, and did not expect that because I doubted the immortality of man, I should be charged with denying the existence of a God. It was the comparative insignificance of ourselves and *our world*, when placed in comparison with the mighty whole, of which it is an atom, that first led me to imagine that our pretensions to eternity might be overrated.

This, and being early disgusted with a Calvinistic Scotch school, where I was cudgelled to church for the first ten years of my life, afflicted me with this malady; for, after all, it is, I believe, a disease of the mind as much as other kinds of hypochondria.

June 22, 1813.

Yesterday I dined in company with Stael, the *clxix*
'Epicene,' whose politics are sadly changed.   She
is for the Lord of Israel and the Lord of Liverpool—a vile antithesis of a Methodist and a Tory—
talks of nothing but devotion and the Ministry, and,
I presume, expects that God and the Government
will help her to a pension.

Murray, the ἄναξ of publishers, the Anak of
stationers, has a design upon you in the paper line.
He wants you to become the staple and stipendiary
editor of a periodical work.   What say you?   Will
you be bound, like 'Kit Smart, to write for ninety-
nine years in the *Universal Visitor*'?   Seriously, he
talks of hundreds a year, and—though I hate prating
of the beggarly elements—his proposal may be to
your honour and profit, and, I am very sure, will be
to our pleasure.

I don't know what to say about 'friendship.'   I
never was in friendship but once, in my nineteenth
year, and then it gave me as much trouble as love.
I am afraid, as Whitbread's sire said to the king,
when he wanted to knight him, that I am 'too old';
but, nevertheless, no one wishes you more friends,
fame, and felicity than yours, etc.

TO MR. MOORE

4 *Benedictine Street, St. James's,*
July 8, 1813.

clxxx   I presume by your silence that I have blundered
into something noxious in my reply to your letter,
for the which I beg leave to send beforehand a
sweeping apology, which you may apply to any, or
all, parts of that unfortunate epistle.   If I err in my
conjecture, I expect the like from you, in putting our
correspondence so long in quarantine.   God He knows
what I have said ; but He also knows (if He is not as
indifferent to mortals as the *nonchalant* deities of
Lucretius) that you are the last person I want to
offend.   So, if I have,—why the devil don't you say
it at once, and expectorate your spleen ?

Rogers is out of town with Madame de Stael, who
hath published an Essay against Suicide, which, I
presume, will make somebody shoot himself ;—as
a sermon by Blinkensop, in *proof* of Christianity,
sent a hitherto most orthodox acquaintance of mine
out of a chapel-of-ease a perfect atheist.   Have you
found or founded a residence yet? and have you
begun or finished a poem ?   If you won't tell me
what *I* have done, pray say what you have done, or
left undone, yourself.   I am still in equipment for
voyaging, and anxious to hear from, or of, you *before*
I go, which anxiety you should remove more readily,
as you think I shan't cogitate about you afterwards.
I shall give the lie to that calumny by fifty foreign
letters, particularly from any place where the plague
is rife,—without a drop of vinegar or a whiff of
sulphur to save you from infection.

TO MR. MOORE

The Oxfords have sailed almost a fortnight, and my sister is in town, which is a great comfort,—for, never having been much together, we are naturally more attached to each other. I presume the illuminations have conflagrated to Derby (or wherever you are) by this time. We are just recovering from tumult and train-oil, and transparent fripperies, and all the noise and nonsense of victory. Drury Lane had a large *M. W.*, which some thought was Marshal Wellington; others, that it might be translated into Manager Whitbread; while the ladies of the vicinity of the saloon conceived the last letter to be complimentary to themselves. I leave this to the commentators to illustrate. If you don't answer this, I shan't say what *you* deserve, but I think *I* deserve a reply. Do you conceive there is no Post-Bag but the Twopenny? Sunburn me, if you are not too bad.

TO MR. MOORE

July 13, 1813.

Your letter set me at ease; for I really thought clxxxi (as I hear of your susceptibility) that I had said— I know not what—but something I should have been very sorry for, had it, or I, offended you;—though I don't see how a man with a beautiful wife—*his own* children,—quiet—fame—competency—and friends (I will vouch for a thousand, which is more than I will for a unit in my own behalf) can be offended with anything.

Do you know, Moore, I am amazingly inclined— remember I say but *inclined*—to be seriously en-

243

amoured with Lady A. F.—but this . . . has ruined
all my prospects. However, you know her; is she
clever, or sensible, or good-tempered? either *would*
do—I scratch out the *will*. I don't ask as to her
beauty—that I see; but my circumstances are mend-̄
ing, and were not my other prospects blackening,
I would take a wife, and that should be the woman,
had I a chance. I do not yet know her much, but
better than I did.

I want to get away, but find difficulty in compass-
ing a passage in a ship of war. They had better let
me go; if I cannot, patriotism is the word—'nay,
an' they 'll mouth, I 'll rant as well as they.' Now,
what are you doing?—writing, we all hope, for our
own sakes. Remember you must edite my posthumous works, with a Life of the Author, for which
I will send you Confessions, dated, 'Lazaretto,'
Smyrna, Malta, or Palermo—one can die anywhere.

There is to be a thing on Tuesday ycleped a
national *fête*. The Regent and —— are to be there,
and everybody else who has shillings enough for
what was once a guinea. Vauxhall is the scene—
there are six tickets issued for the modest women,
and it is supposed there will be three to spare. The
passports for the lax are beyond my arithmetic.

P.S.—The Stael last night attacked me most
furiously—said that I had 'no right to make love—
that I had used —— barbarously—that I had no
feeling, and was totally *in*sensible to *la belle passion*,
and *had* been all my life.' I am very glad to hear
it, but did not know it before. Let me hear from
you anon.

TO MR. MOORE

July 25, 1813.

I am not well versed enough in the ways of single *clxxxii*
woman to make much matrimonial progress.

I have been dining like the Dragon of Wantley for
this last week. My head aches with the vintage of
various cellars, and my brains are muddled as their
dregs. I met your friends the D.'s :—she sang one
of your best songs so well, that, but for the appearance of affectation, I could have cried; he reminds
me of Hunt, but handsomer, and more musical in
soul, perhaps. I wish to God he may conquer his
horrible anomalous complaint. The upper part of
her face is beautiful, and she seems much attached
to her husband. He is right, nevertheless, in leaving
this nauseous town. The first winter would in-
fallibly destroy her complexion,—and the second,
very probably, everything else.

I must tell you a story. Morris (of indifferent
memory) was dining out the other day, and complaining of the Prince's coldness to his old wassailers.
D'Israeli (a learned Jew) bored him with questions
—why this? and why that? 'Why did the Prince
act thus?'—'Why, sir, on account of Lord ——, who
ought to be ashamed of himself.'—'And why ought
Lord —— to be ashamed of himself?'—'Because
the Prince, sir, ...'—'And why, sir, did the
Prince cut *you*?'—'Because, G—d d—mme, sir,
I stuck to my principles.'—'And *why* did you stick
to your principles?'

Is not this last question the best that was ever
put, when you consider to whom? It nearly killed

Morris. Perhaps you may think it stupid, but, as
Goldsmith said about the peas, it was a very good
joke when I heard it—as I did from an ear-witness
—and is only spoilt in my narration.

The season has closed with a dandy ball;—but I
have dinners with the Harrowbys, Rogers, and Frere
and Mackintosh, where I shall drink your health in
a silent bumper, and regret your absence till 'too
much canaries' wash away my memory, or render
it superfluous by a vision of you at the opposite side
of the table. Canning has disbanded his party by
a speech from his . . .—the true throne of a Tory.
Conceive his turning them off in a formal harangue,
and bidding them think for themselves. 'I have
led my ragamuffins where they are well peppered.
There are but three of the 150 left alive, and they
are for the *Townsend* (*query*, might not Falstaff
mean the Bow Street officer? I dare say Malone's
posthumous edition will have it so) for life.'

Since I wrote last, I have been into the country.
I journeyed by night—no incident, or accident, but
an alarm on the part of my valet on the outside,
who, in crossing Epping Forest, actually, I believe,
flung down his purse before a mile-stone, with a
glow-worm in the second figure of number XIX—
mistaking it for a footpad and dark lantern. I can
only attribute his fears to a pair of new pistols
wherewith I had armed him; and he thought it
necessary to display his vigilance by calling out
to me whenever we passed anything — no matter
whether moving or stationary. Conceive ten miles,
with a tremor every furlong. I have scribbled you

a fearfully long letter. This sheet must be blank, and is merely a wrapper, to preclude the tabellarians of the post from peeping. You once complained of my *not* writing ;—I will 'heap coals of fire upon your head' by *not* complaining of your *not* reading.—Ever, my dear Moore, your'n (isn't that the Staffordshire termination?),   BYRON.

TO MR. MOORE
July 27, 1813.

When you next imitate the style of Tacitus, pray *clxxxiii* add, *de moribus Germanorum* ;—this last was a piece of barbarous silence, and could only be taken from the *Woods*, and, as such, I attribute it entirely to your sylvan sequestration at Mayfield Cottage. You will find on casting up accounts, that you are my debtor by several sheets and one epistle. I shall bring my action ;—if you don't discharge, expect to hear from my attorney. I have forwarded your letter to Ruggiero ; but don't make a postman of me again, for fear I should be tempted to violate your sanctity of wax or wafer.—Believe me ever yours *indignantly*,   BN.

TO MR. MOORE
July 28, 1813.

Can't you be satisfied with the pangs of my *clxxxiv* jealousy of Rogers, without actually making me the pander of your epistolary intrigue? This is the second letter you have enclosed to my address, notwithstanding a miraculous long answer, and a subsequent short one or two of your own. If you do

so again, I can't tell to what pitch my fury may soar.
I shall send you verse or arsenic, as likely as anything,—four thousand couplets on sheets beyond the
privilege of franking; that privilege, sir, of which
you take an undue advantage over a too susceptible
senator, by forwarding your lucubrations to every
one but himself. I won't frank *from* you, or *for*
you, or *to* you—may I be curst if I do, unless you
mend your manners. I disown you—I disclaim you
—and by all the powers of Eulogy, I will write a
panegyric upon you—or dedicate a quarto—if you
don't make me ample amends.

P.S.—I am in training to dine with Sheridan and
Rogers this evening. I have a little spite against R.,
and will shed his 'Clary wines pottle-deep.' This is
nearly my ultimate or penultimate letter; for I am
quite equipped, and only wait a passage. Perhaps
I may wait a few weeks for Sligo, but not if I can
help it.

TO MR. CROKER

Bt. Str., August 2, 1813.

Dear Sir,—I was honoured with your unexpected
and very obliging letter, when on the point of leaving
London, which prevented me from acknowledging
my obligation as quickly as I felt it sincerely. I am
endeavouring all in my power to be ready before
Saturday—and even if I should not succeed, I can
only blame my own tardiness, which will not the less
enhance the benefit I have lost. I have only to add
my hope of forgiveness for all my trespasses on your
time and patience, and with my best wishes for your

TO MR. MURRAY

public and private welfare, I have the honour to be, most truly, your obliged and most obedient servant,

BYRON.

TO MR. MURRAY

August (6?), 1813.

If you send more proofs, I shall never finish this *clxxxvi* infernal story—*Ecce signum*—thirty-three more lines enclosed! to the utter discomfiture of the printer, and, I fear, not to your advantage.   B.

TO MR. MURRAY

Half-past two in the morning, Aug. 10, 1813.

Dear Sir,—Pray suspend the *proofs*, for I am *bitten* *clxxxvii* again, and have *quantities* for other parts of the bravura.—Yours ever,   B.

P.S.—You shall have them in the course of the day.

TO MR. MOORE

Bennet Street, August 22, 1813.

As our late—I might say, deceased—correspond- *clxxxviii* ence had too much of the town-life leaven in it, we will now, *paulo majora*, prattle a little of literature in all its branches; and first of the first—criticism. The Prince is at Brighton, and Jackson, the boxer, gone to Margate, having, I believe, decoyed Yarmouth to see a milling in that polite neighbourhood. Mad°. de Stael-Holstein has lost one of her young barons, who has been carbonadoed by a vile Teutonic adjutant,—kilt and killed in a coffee-house at Scrawsenhawsen. Corinne is, of course, what all mothers must be,—but will, I venture to prophesy, do what

249

few mothers could—write an Essay upon it. She
cannot exist without a grievance—and somebody to
see, or read, how much grief becomes her. I have
not seen her since the event; but merely judge (not
very charitably) from prior observation.

In a 'mail-coach copy' of the *Edinburgh*, I perceive *The Giaour* is second article. The numbers
are still in the Leith smack—*pray which way is the
wind?* The said article is so very mild and sentimental, that it must be written by Jeffrey *in love*;—
you know he is gone to America to marry some fair
one, of whom he has been, for several *quarters*,
éperdument amoureux. Seriously—as Winifred Jenkins
says of Lismahago—Mr. Jeffrey (or his deputy) 'has
done the handsome thing by me,' and I say *nothing*.
But this I will say, if you and I had knocked one
another on the head in this quarrel, how he would
have laughed, and what a mighty bad figure we
should have cut in our posthumous works. By-the-
by, I was call'd *in* the other day to mediate between
two gentlemen bent upon carnage, and,—after a long
struggle between the natural desire of destroying one's
fellow-creatures, and the dislike of seeing men play
the fool for nothing,—I got one to make an apology,
and the other to take it, and left them to live happy
ever after. One was a peer, the other a friend un-
titled, and both fond of high play;—and one, I can
swear for, though very mild, 'not fearful,' and so
dead a shot, that, though the other is the thinnest of
men, he would have split him like a cane. They
both conducted themselves very well, and I put them
out of *pain* as soon as I could.

TO MR. MOORE

There is an American Life of G. F. Cooke, *Scurra* deceased, lately published. Such a book!—I believe, since *Drunken Barnaby's Journal*, nothing like it has drenched the press. All green-room and tap-room—drams and the drama—brandy, whisky-punch, and, *latterly*, toddy, overflow every page. Two things are rather marvellous : first, that a man should live so long drunk, and, next, that he should have found a sober biographer. There are some very laughable things in it, nevertheless ;—but the pints he swallowed, and the parts he performed, are too regularly registered.

All this time you wonder I am not gone ; so do I ; but the accounts of the plague are very perplexing— not so much for the thing itself as the quarantine established in all ports, and from all places, even from England. It is true, the forty or sixty days would, in all probability, be as foolishly spent on shore as in the ship ; but one likes to have one's choice, nevertheless. Town is awfully empty ; but not the worse for that. I am really puzzled with my perfect ignorance of what I mean to do ;—not stay, if I can help it, but where to go? Sligo is for the North ;—a pleasant place, Petersburgh, in September, with one's ears and nose in a muff, or else tumbling into one's neckcloth or pocket-kandkerchief! If the winter treated Buonaparte with so little ceremony, what would it inflict upon your solitary traveller?— Give me a *sun*, I care not how hot, and sherbet, I care not how cool, and *my* Heaven is as easily made as your Persian's. *The Giaour* is now a thousand and odd lines. 'Lord Fanny spins a thousand such

LETTERS

a day,' eh, Moore?—thou wilt needs be a wag, but I forgive it.—Yours ever, BYRON.

P.S.—I perceive I have written a flippant and rather cold-hearted letter! let it go, however. I have said nothing, either, of the brilliant sex; but the fact is, I am at this moment in a far more serious, and entirely new, scrape than any of the last twelve months, —and that is saying a good deal. It is unlucky we can neither live with nor without these women.

I am now thinking of regretting that, just as I have left Newstead, you reside near it. Did you ever see it? *Do*—but don't tell me that you like it. If I had known of such intellectual neighbourhood, I don't think I should have quitted it. You could have come over so often, as a bachelor,—for it was a thorough bachelor's mansion—plenty of wine and such sordid sensualities—with books enough, room enough, and an air of antiquity about all (except the lasses) that would have suited you, when pensive, and served you to laugh at when in glee. I had built myself a bath and a *vault*—and now I shan't even be buried in it. It is odd that we can't even be certain of a *grave*, at least a particular one. I remember, when about fifteen, reading your poems there, which I can repeat almost now;—and asking all kinds of questions about the author, when I heard that he was not dead according to the preface; wondering if I should ever see him—and though, at that time, without the smallest poetical propensity myself, very much taken, as you may imagine, with that volume. Adieu.—I commit you to the care of the gods—Hindoo, Scandinavian, and Hellenic!

P.S. 2nd.—There is an excellent review of Grimm's *Correspondence* and Mad°. de Stael in this N°. of the *E. R.* Jeffrey, himself, was my critic last year; but this is, I believe, by another hand. I hope you are going on with your *grand coup*—pray do—or that damned Lucien Buonaparte will beat us all. I have seen much of his poem in MS., and he really surpasses everything beneath Tasso. Hodgson is translating him *against* another bard. You and (I believe, Rogers) Scott, Gifford, and myself are to be referred to as judges between the twain,—that is if you accept the office. Conceive our different opinions! I think we, most of us (I am talking very impudently, you will think—*us*, indeed!), have a way of our own,—at least, you and Scott certainly have.

TO MR. MURRAY

August 26, 1813.

I have looked over and corrected one proof, but *clxxxix* not so carefully (God knows if you can read it through, but I can't) as to preclude your eye from discovering some omission of mine or *com*mission of your printer. If you have patience, look it over. Do you know anybody who can stop—I mean *point* —commas, and so forth? for I am, I hear, a sad hand at your punctuation. I have, but with some difficulty, *not* added any more to this snake of a poem, which has been lengthening its rattles every month. It is now fearfully long, being more than a canto and a half of *Childe Harold*, which contains but 882 lines per book, with all late additions inclusive.

The last lines Hodgson likes. It is not often he

does, and when he don't he tells me with great energy, and I fret and alter. I have thrown them in to soften the ferocity of our infidel, and, for a dying man, have given him a good deal to say for himself.

I was quite sorry to hear you say you stayed in town on my account, and I hope sincerely you did not mean so superfluous a piece of politeness.

Our *six* critiques!—they would have made half a *Quarterly* by themselves; but this is the age of criticism.

TO MR. MOORE

August 28, 1813.

cxc Ay, my dear Moore, 'there *was* a time'—I have heard of your tricks, when 'you was campaigning at the King of Bohemy.' I am much mistaken if, some fine London spring, about the year 1815, that time does not come again. After all, we must end in marriage; and I can conceive nothing more delightful than such a state in the country, reading the county newspaper, etc., and kissing one's wife's maid. Seriously, I would incorporate with any woman of decent demeanour to-morrow—that is, I would a month ago, but, at present. . . .

Why don't you 'parody that Ode'?—Do you think I should be *tetchy*? or have you done it, and won't tell me?—You are quite right about Giamschid, and I have reduced it to a dissyllable within this half-hour. I am glad to hear you talk of Richardson, because it tells me what you won't—that you are going to beat Lucien. At least tell me how far you have proceeded. Do you think me less interested about your works, or less sincere than our friend Ruggiero? I am not—and never was. In that thing of mine, the *English Bards*, at the time when I was angry with all the world, I never 'disparaged your parts,' although I did not know you personally;—and have always regretted that you don't give us an *entire* work, and not sprinkle yourself in detached pieces—beautiful, I allow, and quite *alone* in our language, but still giving us a right to expect a *Shah Nameh* (is that the name?) as well as gazelles. Stick to the East;—the oracle, Stael, told me it was the only poetical policy. The North, South, and West have all been exhausted; but from the East we have nothing but Southey's unsaleables,—and these he has contrived to spoil, by adopting only their most outrageous fictions. His personages don't interest us, and yours will. You will have no competitor; and, if you had, you ought to be glad of it. The little I have done in that way is merely a 'voice in the wilderness' for you; and if it has had any success, that also will prove that the public are orientalising, and pave the path for you.

I have been thinking of a story, grafted on the amours of a Peri and a mortal—something like, only more *philanthropical* than, Cazotte's *Diable Amoureux*. It would require a good deal of poesy, and tenderness is not my forte. For that, and other reasons, I have given up the idea, and merely suggest it to you, because, in intervals of your greater work, I think it a subject you might make much of. If you want any more books, there is Castellan's *Mœurs des Ottomans*, the best compendium of the kind I ever met with, in six small tomes. I am really taking a liberty by

talking in this style to my 'elders and my betters';
—pardon it, and don't *Rochefoucault* my motives.

TO MR. MOORE

August—September, I mean—1, 1813.

cxci   I send you, begging your acceptance, Castellan,
and three vols. on Turkish literature, not yet looked
into. The *last* I will thank you to read, extract what
you want, and return in a week, as they are lent to
me by that brightest of Northern constellations,
Mackintosh,—amongst many other kind things into
which India has warmed him; for I am sure your
home Scotsman is of a less genial description.

Your Peri, my dear M., is sacred and inviolable; I
have no idea of touching the hem of her petticoat.
Your affectation of a dislike to encounter me is so
flattering, that I begin to think myself a very fine
fellow. But you are laughing at me—'Stap my vitals,
Tam! thou art a very impudent person'; and, if you
are not laughing at me, you deserve to be laughed at.
Seriously, what on earth can you, or have you, to
dread from any poetical flesh breathing? It really
put me out of humour to hear you talk thus.

The Giaour I have added to a good deal; but still
in foolish fragments. It contains about 1200 lines,
or rather more—now printing. You will allow me to
send you a copy. You delight me much by telling
me that I am in your good graces, and more particularly as to temper; for, unluckily, I have the
reputation of a very bad one. But they say the Devil
is amusing when pleased, and I must have been more
venomous than the Old Serpent to have hissed or

stung in your company. It may be, and would appear to a third person, an incredible thing, but I know *you* will believe me when I say, that I am as anxious for your success as one human being can be for another's—as much as if I had never scribbled a line. Surely the field of fame is wide enough for all ; and if it were not, I would not willingly rob my neighbour of a rood of it. Now, you have a pretty property of some thousand acres there, and when you have passed your present Inclosure Bill, your income will be doubled (there's a metaphor, worthy of a Templar, namely, pert and low), while my wild common is too remote to incommode you, and quite incapable of such fertility. I send you (which return per post, as the printer would say) a curious letter from a friend of mine, which will let you into the origin of *The Giaour.* Write soon.—Ever, dear Moore, yours most entirely, etc.

P.S.—This letter was written to me on account of a *different story* circulated by some gentlewomen of our acquaintance, a little too close to the text. The part erased contained merely some Turkish names, and circumstantial evidence of the girl's detection, not very important or decorous.

TO MR. MOORE

Sept. 5, 1813.

You need not tie yourself down to a day with Tode- cxcii rini, but send him at your leisure, having anatomised him into such annotations as you want ; I do not believe that he has ever undergone that process before, which is the best reason for not sparing him now.

LETTERS

Rogers has returned to town, but not yet recovered of the *Quarterly*. What fellows these reviewers are! 'these bugs do fear us all.' They made you fight, and me (the milkiest of men) a satirist, and will end by making Rogers madder than Ajax. I have been reading *Memory* again, the other day, and *Hope* together, and retain all my preference of the former. His elegance is really wonderful—there is no such thing as a vulgar line in his book.

What say you to Buonaparte? Remember, I back him against the field, barring catalepsy and the Elements. Nay, I almost wish him success against all countries but this,—were it only to choke the *Morning Post*, and his undutiful father-in-law, with that rebellious bastard of Scandinavian adoption, Bernadotte. Rogers wants me to go with him on a crusade to the Lakes, and to besiege you on our way. This last is a great temptation, but I fear it will not be in my power, unless you would go on with one of us somewhere—no matter where. It is too late for Matlock, but we might hit upon some scheme, high life or low,—the last would be much the best for amusement. I am so sick of the other, that I quite sigh for a Cider-Cellar, or a cruise in a smuggler's sloop.

You cannot wish more than I do that the Fates were a little more accommodating to our parallel lines, which prolong *ad infinitum* without coming a jot nearer. I almost wish I were married, too— which is saying much. All my friends, seniors and juniors, are in for it, and ask me to be godfather,— the only species of parentage which, I believe, will

258

ever come to my share in a lawful way; and, in an unlawful one, by the blessing of Lucina, we can never be certain,—though the parish may. I suppose I shall hear from you to-morrow. If not, this goes as it is; but I leave room for a *P.S.*, in case anything requires an answer.—Ever, etc.

No letter—*n'importe*. Rogers thinks the *Quarterly* will be at *me* this time: if so, it shall be a war of extermination—no *quarter*. From the youngest devil down to the oldest woman of that Review, all shall perish by one fatal lampoon. The ties of nature shall be torn asunder, for I will not even spare my bookseller; nay, if one were to include readers also, all the better.

TO MR. MOORE

September 8, 1813.

I am sorry to see Toderini again so soon, for fear *cxciii* your scrupulous conscience should have prevented you from fully availing yourself of his spoils. By this coach I send you a copy of that awful pamphlet *The Giaour*, which has never procured me half so high a compliment as your modest alarm. You will (if inclined in an evening) perceive that I have added much in quantity,—a circumstance which may truly diminish your modesty upon the subject.

You stand certainly in great need of a 'lift' with Mackintosh. My dear Moore, you strangely underrate yourself. I should conceive it an affectation in any other; but I think I know you well enough to believe that you don't know your own value. However, 'tis a fault that generally mends; and, in your

LETTERS

case, it really ought. I have heard him speak of you as highly as your wife could wish ; and enough to give all your friends the jaundice.

Yesterday I had a letter from *Ali Pacha!* brought by Dr. Holland, who is just returned from Albania. It is in Latin, and begins 'Excellentissime *nec non* Carissime,' and ends about a gun he wants made for him ;—it is signed 'Ali Vizir.' What do you think he has been about? H. tells me that, last spring, he took a hostile town, where, forty-two years ago, his mother and sisters were treated as Miss Cunigunde was by the Bulgarian cavalry. He takes the town, selects all the survivors of this exploit—children, grandchildren, etc., to the tune of six hundred, and has them shot before his face. Recollect, he spared the rest of the city, and confined himself to the Tarquin pedigree,—which is more than I would. So much for 'dearest friend.'

TO MR. MOORE

Sept. 9, 1813.

cxciv   I write to you from Mr. Murray's, and I may say, from Murray, who, if you are not predisposed in favour of any other publisher, would be happy to treat with you, at a fitting time, for your work. I can safely recommend him as fair, liberal, and atten-tive, and certainly, in point of reputation, he stands among the first of 'the trade.' I am sure he would do you justice. I have written to you so much lately, that you will be glad to see so little now.— Ever, etc. etc.

TO MR. MOORE

September 27, 1813.

Thomas Moore,—(thou wilt never be called '*true* cxcv Thomas,' like he of Ercildoune,) why don't you write to me?—as you won't, I must. I was near you at Aston the other day, and hope I soon shall be again. If so, you must and shall meet me, and go to Matlock and elsewhere, and take what, in *flash* dialect, is poetically termed ' a lark,' with Rogers and me for accomplices. Yesterday, at Holland House, I was introduced to Southey—the best-looking bard I have seen for some time. To have that poet's head and shoulders, I would almost have written his Sapphics. He is certainly a prepossessing person to look on, and a man of talent, and all that, and— *there* is his eulogy.

—— read me *part* of a letter from you. By the foot of Pharaoh, I believe there was abuse, for he stopped short, so he did, after a fine saying about our correspondence, and *looked*—I wish I could revenge myself by attacking you, or by telling you that I have *had* to defend you—an agreeable way which one's friends have of recommending themselves by saying—'Ay, ay, *I* gave it Mr. Such-a-one for what he said about your being a plagiary, and a rake, and so on.' But do you know that you are one of the very few whom I never have the satisfaction of hearing abused, but the reverse;—and do you suppose I will forgive *that*?

I have been in the country, and ran away from the Doncaster Races. It is odd,—I was a visitor in the same house which came to my sire as a residence with Lady Carmarthen (with whom he adulterated before his majority—by-the-by, remember *she* was not my mamma),—and they thrust me into an old room, with a nauseous picture over the chimney, which I should suppose my papa regarded with due respect, and which, inheriting the family taste, I looked upon with great satisfaction. I stayed a week with the family, and behaved very well—though the lady of the house is young, and religious, and pretty, and the master is my particular friend. I felt no wish for anything but a poodle dog, which they kindly gave me. Now, for a man of my courses not even to have *coveted*, is a sign of great amendment. Pray pardon all this nonsense, and don't 'snub me when I'm in spirits.'—Ever yours, BN.

Here's an impromptu for you by a 'person of quality,' written last week, on being reproached for low spirits :—

When from the heart where Sorrow sits,
    Her dusky shadow mounts too high,
And o'er the changing aspect flits,
    And clouds the brow, or fills the eye :
Heed not that gloom, which soon shall sink ;
    My Thoughts their dungeon know too well—
Back to my breast the wanderers shrink,
    And bleed within their silent cell.

TO MR. HODGSON

October 1, 1813.

cxcvi My dear H.,—I leave town again for Aston on Sunday, but have messages for you. Lord Holland desired me repeatedly to bring you ; he wants to know you much, and begged me to say so ; you will

like him.   I had an invitation for you to dinner
there this last Sunday, and Rogers is perpetually
screaming because you don't call, and wanted you
also to dine with him on Wednesday last. Yesterday
we had Curran there—who is beyond all conception !
and Mackintosh and the wits are to be seen at H. H.
constantly, so that I think you would like their
society.   I will be a judge between you and the
attorned.   So B. may mention me to Lucien if he
still adheres to his opinion.   Pray let Rogers be one ;
he has the best taste extant.   Bland's nuptials delight
me ; if I had the least hand in bringing them about
it will be a subject of selfish satisfaction to me these
three weeks.   Desire Drury—if he loves me—to
kick Dwyer thrice for frightening my horses with
his flame-coloured whiskers last July.   Let the kicks
be hard, etc.

TO MR. MURRAY

Stilton, Oct. 3, 1813.

I have just recollected an alteration you may *cxcvii*
make in the proof to be sent to Aston.—Among the
lines on Hassan's Serai, not far from the beginning,
is this—

> Unmeet for Solitude to share.

Now to share implies more than *one,* and Solitude is
a single gentleman ; it must be thus—

> For many a gilded chamber 's there,
> Which Solitude might well forbear ;

and so on.—My address is Aston Hall, Rotherham.
Will you adopt this correction ? and pray accept

a Stilton cheese from me for your trouble.—Ever
yours,   B.

If the old line stands let the other run thus—

> Nor there will weary traveller halt,
> To bless the sacred bread and salt.

Note.—To partake of food—to break bread and
taste salt with your host, ensures the safety of the
guest; even though an enemy, his person from that
moment becomes sacred.

There is another additional note sent yesterday—
on the Priest in the Confessional.

P.S.—I leave this to your discretion; if anybody
thinks the old line a good one or the cheese a bad
one, don't accept either.   But, in that case, the word
share is repeated soon after in the line—

> To share the master's bread and salt;

and must be altered to—

> To break the master's bread and salt.

This is not so well, though—confound it !

TO MR. MURRAY

Oct. 12, 1813.

cxcviii   You must look *The Giaour* again over carefully;
there are a few lapses, particularly in the last page.
—'I *know* 'twas false; she could not die'; it was,
and ought to be—'*knew.*' Pray observe this and
similar mistakes.

I have received and read the *British Review*.   I

TO MR. MOORE

really think the writer in most points very right. The
only mortifying thing is the accusation of imitation.
Crabbe's passage I never saw ; and Scott I no further
meant to follow than in his *lyric* measure, which is
Gray's, Milton's, and any one's who likes it. The
Giaour is certainly a bad character, but not dangerous ; and I think his fate and his feelings will meet
with few proselytes. I shall be very glad to hear
from or of you, when you please ; but don't put yourself out of your way on my account.

TO MR. MOORE

October 2, 1813.

You have not answered some six letters of mine. cxcix
This, therefore, is my penultimate. I will write to
you once more, but, after that—I swear by all the
saints—I am silent and supercilious. I have met
Curran at Holland House—he beats everybody ;—
his imagination is beyond human, and his humour
(it is difficult to define what is wit) perfect. Then
he has fifty faces, and twice as many voices, when
he mimics—I never met his equal. Now, were I a
woman, and eke a virgin, that is a man I should
make my Scamander. He is quite fascinating. Remember, I have met him but once ; and you, who
have known him long, may probably deduct from my
panegyric. I almost fear to meet him again, lest
the impression should be lowered. He talked a
great deal about you—a theme never tiresome to
me, nor anybody else that I know. What a variety
of expression he conjures into that naturally not very

265

fine countenance of his! He absolutely changes it entirely. I have done—for I can't describe him, and you know him. On Sunday I return to ——, where I shall not be far from you. Perhaps I shall hear from you in the meantime. Good night.

Saturday morn.—Your letter has cancelled all my anxieties. I did *not suspect* you in *earnest.* Modest again! Because I don't do a very shabby thing, it seems, I 'don't fear your competition.' If it were reduced to an alternative of preference, I *should* dread you, as much as Satan does Michael. But is there not room enough in our respective regions? Go on—it will soon be my turn to forgive. To-day I dine with Mackintosh and Mrs. *Stale*—as John Bull may be pleased to denominate Corrinne—whom I saw last night, at Covent Garden, yawning over the humour of Falstaff.

The reputation of 'gloom,' if one's friends are not included in the *reputants*, is of great service; as it saves one from a legion of impertinents, in the shape of common-place acquaintance. But thou know'st I can be a right merry and conceited fellow, and rarely *larmoyant.* Murray shall reinstate your line forthwith. I believe the blunder in the motto was mine;—and yet I have, in general, a memory for *you*, and am sure it was rightly printed at first.

I do 'blush' very often, if I may believe Ladies H. and M.;—but luckily, at present, no one sees me.—Adieu.

TO MR. GIFFORD

TO MR. GIFFORD

November 12, 1813.

My dear Sir,—I hope you will consider, when I
venture on any request, that it is the reverse of a
certain Dedication, and is addressed, *not* to 'The
Editor of the *Quarterly Review*,' but to Mr. Gifford.
You will understand this, and on that point I need
trouble you no farther.

You have been good enough to look at a thing
of mine in MS.—a Turkish story; and I should feel
gratified if you would do it the same favour in its
probationary state of printing. It was written, I
cannot say for amusement, nor 'obliged by hunger
and request of friends,' but in a state of mind, from
circumstances which occasionally occur to 'us youth,'
that rendered it necessary for me to apply my mind
to something, anything but reality; and under this
not very brilliant inspiration it was composed. Being
done, and having at least diverted me from myself,
I thought you would not perhaps be offended if
Mr. Murray forwarded it to you. He has done so,
and to apologise for his doing so a second time is
the object of my present letter.

I beg you will *not* send me any answer. I assure
you very sincerely I know your time to be occupied,
and it is enough, more than enough, if you read;
you are not to be bored with the fatigue of answers.

A word to Mr. Murray will be sufficient, and send
it either to the flames or

A hundred hawkers' load,
On wings of wind to fly or fall abroad.

267

LETTERS

It deserves no better than the first, as the work of a week, and scribbled *stans pede in uno* (by-the-by, the only foot I have to stand on); and I promise never to trouble you again under forty cantos, and a voyage between each.—Believe me ever your obliged and affectionate servant,   BYRON.

TO MR. MURRAY

Nov. 12, 1813.

cci   Two friends of mine (Mr. Rogers and Mr. Sharpe) have advised me not to risk at present any single publication separately, for various reasons. As they have not seen the one in question, they can have no bias for or against the merits (if it has any) or the faults of the present subject of our conversation. You say all the last of *The Giaour* are gone—at least out of our hands. Now, if you think of publishing any new edition with the last additions which have not yet been before the reader (I mean distinct from the two-volume publication), we can add *The Bride of Abydos*, which will thus steal quietly into the world: if liked, we can then throw off some copies for the purchasers of former *Giaours*; and, if not, I can omit it in any future publication. What think you? I really am no judge of those things; and, with all my natural partiality for one's own productions, I would rather follow any one's judgment than my own.

P.S.—Pray let me have the proofs I sent *all* to-night. I have some alterations that I have thought of that I wish to make speedily. I hope the proof will be on separate pages, and not all huddled together on a mile-long ballad-singing sheet, as those of *The Giaour* sometimes are ; for then I can't read them distinctly.

TO MR. MURRAY

Nov. 13, 1813.

Will you forward the letter to Mr. Gifford with *ccii* the proof? There is an alteration I may make in Zuleika's speech, in second canto (the only one of *hers* in that canto). It is now thus—

> And curse—if I could curse—the day.

It must be—

> And mourn—I dare not curse—the day,
> That saw my solitary birth, etc. etc.

Ever yours,   B.

In the last MS. lines sent, instead of 'living heart,' correct to 'quivering heart.' It is in line ninth of the MS. passage.—Ever yours again,   B.

TO MR. MURRAY

Alteration of a line in Canto 2nd.   *cciii*
Instead of—

> And tints to-morrow with a *fancied* ray,

Print—

> And tints to-morrow with *prophetic* ray.

> The evening beam that smiles the clouds away,
> And tints to-morrow with prophetic ray ;

Or,

> And $\begin{Bmatrix} gilds \\ tints \end{Bmatrix}$ the hope of morning with its ray ;

Or,

> And gilds to-morrow's hope with heavenly ray.

I wish you would ask Mr. Gifford which of them is best, or rather *not worst.*—Ever, etc.

You can send the request contained in this at the same time with the *revise, after* I have seen the *said revise.*

TO MR. MURRAY

Nov. 13, 1813.

cciv   Certainly. Do you suppose that no one but the Galileans are acquainted with Adam, and Eve, and Cain, and Noah?—Surely, I might have had Solomon, and Abraham, and David, and even Moses. When you know that *Zuleika* is the *Persian poetical* name for *Potiphar's* wife, on whom and Joseph there is a long poem, in the Persian, this will not surprise you. If you want authority, look at Jones, D'Herbelot, *Vathek*, or the notes to the *Arabian Nights*; and, if you think it necessary, model this into a note.

Alter, in the inscription, 'the most affectionate respect,' to 'with every sentiment of regard and respect.'

TO MR. MURRAY

Nov. 14, 1813.

I sent you a note for the *ignorant*, but I really ccv
wonder at finding *you* among them. I don't care
one lump of sugar for my *poetry*; but for my *costume*,
and my *correctness* on those points (of which I think
the *funeral* was a proof), I will combat lustily.—
Yours, etc.

TO MR. MURRAY

Nov. 14, 1813.

Let the revise which I sent just now (and *not* the ccvi
proof in Mr. Gifford's possession) be returned to the
printer, as there are several additional corrections,
and two new lines in it.—Yours, etc.

TO MR. MURRAY

November 15, 1813.

Mr. Hodgson has looked over and *stopped*, or ccvii
rather *pointed*, this revise, which must be the one to
print from. He has also made some suggestions,
with most of which I have complied, as he has
always, for these ten years, been a very sincere, and
by no means (at times) flattering critic of mine. *He*
likes it (you will think *flatteringly*, in this instance)
better than *The Giaour*, but doubts (and so do I)
its being so popular; but, contrary to some others,
advises a separate publication. On this we can easily
decide. I confess I like the *double* form better.

Hodgson says, it is *better versified* than any of the others; which is odd, if true, as it has cost me less time (though more hours at a time) than any attempt I ever made.

P.S.—Do attend to the punctuation : I can't, for I don't know a comma—at least where to place one.

That Tory of a printer has omitted two lines of the opening, and *perhaps more*, which were in the MS. Will you, pray, give him a hint of accuracy? I have reinserted the *two*—but they were in the manuscript, I can swear.

TO MR. MURRAY

November 17, 1813.

ccviii That you and I may distinctly understand each other on a subject, which, like 'the dreadful reckoning when men smile no more,' makes conversation not very pleasant, I think it as well to *write* a few lines on the topic.—Before I left town for Yorkshire, you said that you were ready and willing to give five hundred guineas for the copyright of *The Giaour*; and my answer was—from which I do not mean to recede—that we would discuss the point at Christmas. The new story may or may not succeed; the probability, under present circumstances, seems to be that it may at least pay its expenses—but even that remains to be proved, and till it is proved one way or the other, we will say nothing about it. Thus then be it : I will postpone all arrangement about it, and *The Giaour* also, till Easter 1814; and you shall then, according to your own notions of fairness, make your own offer for the two. At the same time, I do not rate the last in my own estimation at half *The Giaour*; and according to your own notions of its worth and its success within the time mentioned, be the addition or deduction to or from whatever sum may be your proposal for the first, which has already had its success.

The pictures of Phillips I consider as *mine*, all three; and the one (not the Arnaout) of the two best is much at *your service*, if you will accept it as a present, from yours very truly, etc.

P.S.—The expense of engraving from the miniature send me in my account, as it was destroyed by my desire; and have the goodness to burn that detestable print from it immediately.

To make you some amends for eternally pestering you with alterations, I send you Cobbett to confirm your orthodoxy.

One more alteration of *a* into *the* in the MS.; it must be—'The *heart whose softness*,' etc.

Remember—and in the inscription, 'To the Right Honourable Lord Holland,' *without* the previous names, Henry, etc.

TO MR. MURRAY

November 20, 1813.

More work for the *Row*. I am doing my best to beat *The Giaour—no* difficult task for any one but the author.

LETTERS

TO MR. MURRAY

November 22, 1813.

ccx   I have no time to *cross*-investigate, but I believe and hope all is right. I care less than you will believe about its success, but I can't survive a single *misprint*; it *chokes* me to see words misused by the printers. Pray look over, in case of some eyesore escaping me.

P.S.—Send the earliest copies to Mr. Frere, Mr. Canning, Mr. Heber, Mr. Gifford, Lord Holland, Lady Melbourne (Whitehall), Lady Caroline Lamb (Brocket), Mr. Hodgson (Cambridge), Mr. Merivale, Mr. Ward, from the author.

TO MR. MURRAY

November 23, 1813.

ccxi   You wanted some reflections, and I send you *per Selim* (see his speech in Canto 2nd, page 46), eighteen lines in decent couplets, of a pensive, if not an *ethical* tendency. One more revise—positively the last, if decently done—at any rate the *pen*ultimate. Mr. Canning's approbation (*if* he did approve) I need not say makes me proud. As to printing, print as you will and how you will—by itself, if you like; but let me have a few copies in *sheets*.

TO MR. MURRAY

November 24, 1813.

ccxii   You must pardon me once more, as it is all for your good: it must be thus—

He makes a solitude, and calls it peace.

274

TO MR. MURRAY

'*Makes*' is closer to the passage of Tacitus, from which the line is taken, and is, besides, a stronger word than '*leaves*.'

> Mark where his carnage and his conquests cease—
> He makes a solitude, and calls it—peace.

TO MR. MURRAY

November 27, 1813.

If you look over this carefully by the *last proof* ccxiii with my corrections, it is probably right; this *you* can *do* as well or better;—I have not now time. The copies I mentioned to be sent to different friends last night, I should wish to be made up with the new *Giaours*, if it also is ready. If not, send *The Giaour* afterwards.

The *Morning Post* says *I* am the ·author of *Nourjahad*!! This comes of lending the drawings for their dresses; but it is not worth a *formal contradiction*. Besides, the criticisms on the *supposition* will, some of them, be quite amusing and furious. The *Orientalism*—which I hear is very splendid—of the melodrame (whosesoever it is, and I am sure I don't know) is as good as an advertisement for your Eastern Stories, by filling their heads with glitter.

P.S.—You will of course *say* the truth, that I am *not* the melodramist—if any one charges me in your presence with the performance.

TO MR. MURRAY

November 28, 1813.

ccxiv   Send another copy (if not too much of a request) to Lady Holland of the *Journal*, in my name, when you receive this; it is for *Earl Grey*—and I will relinquish my *own*. Also to Mr. Sharpe, Lady Holland, and Lady Caroline Lamb, copies of *The Bride* as soon as convenient.

P.S.—Mr. Ward and myself still continue our purpose; but I shall not trouble you on any arrangement on the score of *The Giaour* and *The Bride* till our return,—or, at any rate, before *May* 1814,— that is, six months from hence: and before that time you will be able to ascertain how far your offer may be a losing one: if so, you can deduct proportionably; and if not, I shall not at any rate allow you to go higher than your present proposal, which is very handsome, and more than fair.

I have had—but this must be *entre nous*—a very kind note, on the subject of *The Bride*, from Sir James Mackintosh, and an invitation to go there this evening, which it is now too late to accept.

TO MR. MURRAY

November 29, 1813.
Sunday—Monday morning—three o'clock—
in my doublet and hose,—*swearing*.

ccxv   I send you in time an errata page, containing an omission of mine, which must be thus added, as it is too late for insertion in the text. The passage is an imitation altogether from *Medea* in Ovid, and is incomplete without these two lines. Pray let this be done, and directly; it is necessary, will add one page to your book (*making*), and can do no harm, and is yet in time for the *public*. Answer me, thou oracle, in the affirmative. You can send the loose pages to those who have copies already, if they like; but certainly to all the *critical* copyholders.

P.S.—I have got out of my bed (in which, however, I could not sleep, whether I had amended this or not), and so good morning. I am trying whether *De l'Allemagne* will act as an opiate, but I doubt it.

TO MR. MURRAY

November 29, 1813.

' *You have looked at it!*' to much purpose, to allow *ccxvi* so stupid a blunder to stand; it is *not 'courage'* but '*carnage*'; and if you don't want me to cut my own throat, see it altered.

I am very sorry to hear of the fall of Dresden.

TO MR. MURRAY

Nov. 29, 1813. *Monday.*

You will act as you please upon that point; but *ccxvii* whether I go or stay, I shall not say another word on the subject till May—nor then, unless quite convenient to yourself. I have many things I wish to leave to your care, principally papers. The *vases* need not be now sent, as Mr. Ward is gone to Scotland. You are right about the errata page; place it at the beginning. Mr. Perry is a little premature in his compliments: these may do harm by exciting expectation, and I think we ought to be

LETTERS

above it—though I see the next paragraph is on the *Journal*, which makes me suspect *you* as the author of both.

Would it not have been as well to have said 'in two cantos' in the advertisement? they will else think of *fragments*, a species of composition very well for *once*, like *one ruin* in a *view*; but one would not build a town of them. The *Bride*, such as it is, is my first *entire* composition of any length (except the Satire, and be d——d to it), for the *Giaour* is but a string of passages, and *Childe Harold* is, and I rather think always will be, unconcluded. I return Mr. Hay's note, with thanks to him and you.

There have been some epigrams on Mr. Ward: one I see to-day. The first I did not see, but heard yesterday. The second seems very bad. I only hope that Mr. Ward does not believe that I had any connection with either. The Regent is the only person on whom I ever expectorated an epigram, or ever should; and even if I were disposed that way, I like and value him too well to allow my politics to contract into spleen, or to admire anything intended to annoy him or his. You need not take the trouble to answer this, as I shall see you in the course of the afternoon.

P.S.—I have said this much about the epigrams, because I live so much in the *opposite camp*, and, from my post as an engineer, might be suspected as the flinger of these hand-grenadoes; but with a worthy foe I am all for open war, and not this bush-fighting, and have not had, nor will have, anything to do with it. I do not know the author.

278

TO MR. MOORE

TO MR. MURRAY

Nov. 30, 1813.

Print this at the end of *all that is of 'The Bride of* ccxviii
Abydos,' as an errata page.   BN.

'Omitted, canto 2nd, page 47, after line 449,

> So that those arms cling closer round my neck.

Read,

> Then, if my lip once murmur, it must be
> No sigh for safety, but a prayer for thee.

TO MR. MURRAY

Tuesday evening, **Nov.** 30, 1813.

For the sake of correctness, particularly in an ccxix
errata page, the alteration of the couplet I have just
sent (half an hour ago) must take place, in spite of
delay or cancel; let me see the *proof* early to-
morrow.   I have found out *murmur* to be a neuter
verb, and have been obliged to alter the line so as to
make it a substantive, thus—

> The deepest murmur of this lip shall be
> No sigh for safety, but a prayer for thee!

Don't send the copies to the *country* till this is all
right.

TO MR. MOORE

November 30, 1813.

Since I last wrote to you, much has occurred, good, ccxx
bad, and indifferent,—not to make me forget you, but
to prevent me from reminding you of one who,
nevertheless, has often thought of you, and to whom

your thoughts, in many a measure, have frequently
been a consolation. We were once very near
neighbours this autumn; and a good and bad
neighbourhood it has proved to me. Suffice it to
say, that your French quotation was confoundedly to
the purpose, though very *unexpectedly* pertinent, as
you may imagine by what I *said* before, and my
silence since. However 'Richard's himself again,'
and except all night and some part of the morning,
I don't think very much about the matter.

All convulsions end with me in rhyme; and to
solace my midnights, I have scribbled another
Turkish story—not a Fragment—which you will
receive soon after this. It does not trench upon
your kingdom in the least, and if it did, you would
soon reduce me to my proper boundaries. You will
think, and justly, that I run some risk of losing the
little I have gained in fame by this further experiment on public patience; but I have really ceased
to care on that head. I have written this, and
published it, for the sake of the *employment*,—to
wring my thoughts from reality, and take refuge in
'imaginings,' however 'horrible'; and, as to success!
those who succeed will console me for a failure—
excepting yourself and one or two more, whom
luckily I love too well to wish one leaf of their
laurels a tint yellower. This is the work of a week,
and will be the reading of an hour to you, or even
less,—and so, let it go . . .

P.S.—Ward and I *talk* of going to Holland. I
want to see how a Dutch canal looks after the
Bosphorus. Pray respond.

TO MR. LEIGH HUNT

TO MR. MURRAY
Dec. 2, 1813.

When you can, let the couplet enclosed be inserted *ccxxi* either in the page, or in the errata page. I trust it is in time for some of the copies. This alteration is in the same part—the page *but one* before the last correction sent.

P.S.—I am afraid, from all I hear, that people are rather inordinate in their expectations, which is very unlucky, but cannot now be helped. This comes of Mr. Perry and one's wise friends; but do not *you* wind *your* hopes of success to the same pitch, for fear of accidents, and I can assure you that my philosophy will stand the test very fairly; and I have done everything to ensure you, at all events, from positive loss, which will be some satisfaction to both.

TO MR. LEIGH HUNT
4 *Bennet Street, Dec.* 2, 1813.

My dear Sir,—Few things could be more welcome *ccxxii* than your note; and on Saturday morning I will avail myself of your permission to thank you for it in person. My time has not been passed, since we met, either profitably or agreeably. A very short period after my last visit, an incident occurred, with which, I fear, you are not unacquainted, as report in many mouths and more than one paper was busy with the topic. That naturally gave me much uneasiness. Then, I nearly incurred a lawsuit on the sale of an estate; but that is now arranged: next— but why should I go on with a series of selfish and silly details? I merely wish to assure you that it was not the frivolous forgetfulness of a mind occupied by what is called pleasure (*not* in the true sense of Epicurus) that kept me away; but a perception of my *then* unfitness to share the society of those whom I value and wish not to displease. I hate being *larmoyant*, and making a serious face among those who are cheerful.

It is my wish that our acquaintance, or, if you please to accept it, friendship, may be permanent. I have been lucky enough to preserve some friends from a very early period, and I hope, as I do not (at least now) select them lightly, I shall not lose them capriciously. I have a thorough esteem for that independence of spirit which you have maintained with sterling talent, and at the expense of some suffering. You have not, I trust, abandoned the poem you were composing when Moore and I partook of your hospitality in yᵉ summer? I hope a time will come when he and I may be able to repay you in kind for the *latter*;—for the rhyme, at least in *quantity*, you are in arrear to both. Believe me very truly and affectionately yours, BYRON.

TO MR. MURRAY

Dec. 3, 1813.

ccxxiii   I send you a *scratch* or *two*, the which *heal*. The *Christian Observer* is very savage, but certainly well written—and quite uncomfortable at the naughtiness of book and author. I rather suspect you won't much like the *present* to be more moral, if it is to share also the usual fate of your virtuous volumes.

Let me see a proof of the *six* before incorporation.

TO MR. MURRAY

TO MR. MURRAY
December 3, 1813.

Look out in the Encyclopedia, article *Mecca,* ccxxiv
whether it is there or at *Medina* the Prophet is en-
tombed. If at Medina, the first lines of my alteration must run—

> Blest as the call which from Medina's dome
> Invites Devotion to her Prophet's tomb, etc.

If at Mecca, the lines may stand as before. Page 45,
canto 2nd, *Bride of Abydos.*—Yours,　　　B.

You will find this out either by article *Mecca,
Medina,* or *Mohammed.* I have no book of reference
by me.

TO MR. MURRAY

Did you look out? Is it *Medina* or *Mecca* that ccxxv
contains the *Holy* Sepulchre? Don't make me blaspheme by your negligence. I have no book of reference, or I would save you the trouble. I *blush,* as
a good Mussulman, to have confused the point.—
Yours,　　　B.

TO MR. MURRAY
Dec. 4, 1813.

I have redde through your *Persian Tales,* and ccxxvi
have taken the liberty of making some remarks on
the *blank* pages. There are many beautiful passages,
and an interesting story; and I cannot give you a
stronger proof that such is my opinion, than by the
date of the *hour—two o'clock,*—till which it has kept
me awake *without a yawn.*

The conclusion is not quite correct in *costume*:
there is no *Mussulman suicide* on record—at least

for *love*. But this matters not. The tale must have been written by some one who has been on the spot, and I wish him, and he deserves, success. Will you apologise to the author for the liberties I have taken with his MS.? Had I been less awake to, and interested in, his theme, I had been less obtrusive; but you know *I* always take this in good part, and I hope he will. It is difficult to say what *will* succeed, and still more to pronounce what *will not*. *I* am at this moment in *that uncertainty* (on our *own* score); and it is no small proof of the author's powers to be able to *charm* and *fix* a *mind's* attention on similar subjects and climates in such a predicament. That he may have the same effect upon all his readers is very sincerely the wish, and hardly the *doubt*, of yours truly, B.

TO MR. MURRAY

Monday evening, Dec. 6, 1813.

ccxxvii It is all very well, except that the lines are not numbered properly, and a diabolical mistake, page 67, which *must* be corrected with the *pen*, if no other way remains; it is the omission of '*not*' before '*disagreeable*,' in the *note* on the *amber* rosary. This is really horrible, and nearly as bad as the stumble of mine at the threshold—I mean the *misnomer* of Bride. Pray do not let a copy go without the '*not*'; it is nonsense, and worse than nonsense, as it now stands. I wish the printer was saddled with a vampire.

P.S.—It is still *hath* instead of *have* in page 20; never was any one so *misused* as I am by your devils of printers.

TO MR. MOORE

P.S.—I hope and trust the '*not*' was inserted in the first edition. We must have something—anything—to set it right. It is enough to answer for one's own bulls, without other people's.

TO MR. MOORE

December 8, 1813.

Your letter, like all the best, and even kindest ccxxviii things in this world, is both painful and pleasing. But, first, to what sits nearest. Do you know I was actually about to dedicate to you,—not in a formal inscription, as to one's *elders*,—but through a short prefatory letter, in which I boasted myself your intimate, and held forth the prospect of *your* poem; when, lo! the recollection of your strict injunctions of secrecy as to the said poem, more than *once* repeated by word and letter, flashed upon me, and marred my intents. I could have no motive for repressing my own desire of alluding to you (and not a day passes that I do not think and talk of you), but an idea that you might, yourself, dislike it. You cannot doubt my sincere admiration, waiving personal friendship for the present, which, by-the-by, is not less sincere and deep-rooted. I have you by rote and by heart; of which *ecce signum*! When I was at ——, on my first visit, I have a habit, in passing my time a good deal alone, of—I won't call it singing, for that I never attempt except to myself—but of uttering to what I think tunes, your 'Oh breathe not,' 'When the last glimpse,' and 'When he who adores thee,' with others of the same minstrel;—they are my matins and vespers. I assuredly did not intend them

285

to be overheard, but, one morning, in comes, not La
Donna, but Il Marito, with a very grave face, saying,
'Byron, I must request you won't sing any more, at
least of *those* songs.' I stared, and said, 'Certainly,
but why?'—'To tell you the truth,' quoth he, 'they
make my wife *cry*, and so melancholy, that I wish her
to hear no more of them.'

Now, my dear M., the effect must have been from
your words, and certainly not my music. I merely
mention this foolish story to show you how much I
am indebted to you for even your pastimes. A man
may praise and praise, but no one recollects but that
which pleases—at least, in composition. Though I
think no one equal to you in that department, or in
satire,—and surely no one was ever so popular in
both,—I certainly am of opinion that you have not
yet done all *you* can do, though more than enough for
any one else. I want, and the world expects, a longer
work from you; and I see in you what I never saw
in poet before, a strange diffidence of your own
powers, which I cannot account for, and which must
be unaccountable, when a *Cossac* like me can appal a
cuirassier. Your story I did not, could not, know,—
I thought only of a Peri. I wish you had confided
in me, not for your sake, but mine, and to prevent
the world from losing a much better poem than my
own, but which, I yet hope, this *clashing* will not even
now deprive them of. Mine is the work of a week,
written, *why* I have partly told you, and partly I cannot tell you by letter—some day I will.

Go on—I shall really be very unhappy if I at all
interfere with you. The success of mine is yet pro-

blematical; though the public will probably purchase a certain quantity, on the presumption of their own propensity for the *Giaour* and such 'horrid mysteries.' The only advantage I have is being on the spot; and that merely amounts to saving me the trouble of turning over books which I had better read again. If *your chamber* was furnished in the same way, you have no need to *go there* to describe—I mean only as to *accuracy*—because I drew it from recollection.

This last thing of mine *may* have the same fate, and I assure you I have great doubts about it. But, even if not, its little day will be over before you are ready and willing. Come out—'screw your courage to the sticking-place.' Except the Post Bag (and surely you cannot complain of a want of success there), you have not been *regularly* out for some years. No man stands higher,—whatever you may think on a rainy day, in your provincial retreat. 'Aucun homme, dans aucune langue, n'a été, peut-être, plus complètement le poëte du cœur et le poëte des femmes. Les critiques lui reprochent de n'avoir représenté le monde ni tel qu'il est, ni tel qu'il doit être; *mais les femmes répondent qu'il l'a représenté tel qu'elles le désirent.*'—I should have thought Sismondi had written this for you instead of Metastasio.

Write to me, and tell me of *yourself.* Do you remember what Rousseau said to some one—'Have we quarrelled? you have talked to me often, and never once mentioned yourself.'

P.S.—The last sentence is an indirect apology for my egotism,—but I believe in letters it is allowed. I wish it was *mutual.* I have met with an odd reflec-

tion in Grimm; it shall not—at least the bad part—
be applied to you or me, though *one* of us has certainly an indifferent name—but this it is :—' Many
people have the reputation of being wicked, with
whom we should be too happy to pass our lives.'
I need not add it is a woman's saying—a Mademoiselle de Sommery's.

TO MR. ASHE

4 Bennet Street, St. James's, Dec. 14, 1813.

ccxxix   Sir,—I leave town for a few days to-morrow : on
my return, I will answer your letter more at length.
Whatever may be your situation, I cannot but commend your resolution to abjure and abandon the
publication and composition of works such as those
to which you have alluded. Depend upon it, they
amuse *few*, disgrace both *reader* and *writer*, and
benefit *none*. It will be my wish to assist you, as far
as my limited means will admit, to break such a
bondage. In your answer, inform me what sum you
think would enable you to extricate yourself from the
hands of your employers, and to regain, at least, temporary independence, and I shall be glad to contribute
my mite towards it. At present, I must conclude.
Your name is not unknown to me, and I regret, for
your own sake, that you have ever lent it to the
works you mention. In saying this, I merely repeat
your *own words* in your letter to me, and have no
wish whatever to say a single syllable that may appear
to insult your misfortunes. If I have, excuse me ; it
is unintentional. Yours, etc.,   BYRON.

Dec. 22, 1813.

My dear Sir,—I am indeed 'in your debt,'—and, *ccxxx*
what is still worse, am obliged to follow *royal* example
(he has just apprised *his* creditors that they must wait
till ye meeting), and intreat your indulgence for, I
hope, a very short time. The nearest relation and
almost ye only friend I possess, has been in London
for a week, and leaves it to-morrow with me for her
own residence.—I return immediately; but we meet
so seldom, and are so *minuted* when we meet at all,
that I give up all engagements till *now*, without reluctance. On my return, I must see you to console
myself for my past disappointments. I should feel
highly honoured in Mr. B——'s permission to make
his acquaintance, and *there* you are in *my* debt—
for it is a promise of last summer which I still hope
to see performed. Yesterday I had a letter from
Moore:—you have probably heard from him lately;
but if not, you will be glad to learn that he is the
same in heart, head, and health.

TO MR. MURRAY

December 27, 1813.

Lord Holland is laid up with the gout, and would *ccxxxi*
feel very much obliged if you could obtain, and send
as soon as possible, Madame D'Arblay's (or even
Miss Edgeworth's) new work. I know they are not
out; but it is perhaps possible for your *Majesty* to
command what we cannot with much suing purchase,
as yet. I need not say that when you are able or
willing to confer the same favour on me, I shall be

obliged. I would almost fall sick myself to get at Madame D'Arblay's writings.

P.S.—You were talking to-day of the American edition of a certain unquenchable memorial of my younger days. As it can't be helped now, I own I have some curiosity to see a copy of trans-Atlantic typography. This you will perhaps obtain, and one for yourself; but I must beg that you will not *import more*, because, *seriously*, I *do wish* to have that thing forgotten as much as it has been forgiven.

If you send to the *Globe* editor, say that I want neither excuse nor contradiction, but merely a discontinuance of a most ill-grounded charge. I never was consistent in anything but my politics; and as my redemption depends on that solitary virtue, it is murder to carry away my last anchor.

NOTES

NOTES

LETTER i. p. 1.

Addressed to a young lady whom Byron knew at Southwell (Notts), and for whom he entertained a sincere and charming friendship. Newstead was let (1804), and Mrs. Byron had gone to live at Burgage Manor, a house on Southwell Green.

This, according to Miss Pigot herself, was the manner of its beginning :—'The first time I was introduced to him was at a party at his mother's, when he was so shy that she was forced to send for him three times before she could persuade him to come into the drawing-room, to play with the young people at a round game. He was then a fat, bashful boy, with his hair combed straight over his forehead, and extremely like a miniature picture that his mother had painted by M. de Chambruland. The next morning Mrs. Byron brought him to call at our house, when he still continued shy and formal in his manner. The conversation turned upon Cheltenham, where we had been staying, the amusements there, the plays, etc. ; and I mentioned that I had seen the character of Gabriel Lackbrain very well performed. His mother getting up to go, he accompanied her, making a formal bow, and I, in allusion to the play, said, "Good-bye, Gaby." His countenance lighted up, his handsome mouth displayed a broad grin, all his shyness vanished, never to return, and, upon his mother's saying, " Come, Byron, are you ready?"—no, she might go by herself, he would stay and talk a little longer; and from that moment he used to come in and go out at all hours, as it pleased him, and in our house considered himself perfectly at home.' It was Byron himself who told Moore that, if letters of his were wanted, Miss Pigot should be asked for those of this time to her ; and in 1828, when Moore was collecting material for the *Life and Letters*, Becher took him to call on Miss Pigot and her mother.

Here are his notes on the interview :—'Their reception of me was most cordial and flattering ; made me sit in the chair which Byron used to sit in, and remarked, as a singularity, that this was the poor fellow's birthday ; he would to-day have been forty. Produced a number of his early letters and poems, and without the least reserve offered any, or all, for my use, offering to copy out for me such as I should select. . . . On parting with Mrs. Pigot, a fine, intelligent old lady, who has been bedridden for years, she kissed my hand most affectionately, and said that, much as she had always admired me as a poet, it was as the friend of Byron she valued and loved me. Her affection . . . to his memory is unbounded, and she seems unwilling to allow that he had a single fault.'

My favourite, 'The Maid of Lodi' :—This is one of Tom Dibdin's two thousand and odd ditties. Sets of it were long popular in chaps. It was married 'to an Italian air ' by Shields, and sung (no doubt with the popular alternations from sucking-dove to roaring-lion) by Braham in *The Siege of Belgrade* :—

> My heart with love is beating,
> Transported by those eyes.
> Alas ! there's no retreating—
> In vain your captive flies !
> Then why such anger cherish?
> Why turn those eyes away?
> For, if they bid me perish,
> Alas ! I must obey !

The Maid of Lodi—(which Aldiborontiphoscophornio, at the house in St. John Street, used to 'roll out' to the Great Unknown 'in a style that would have done no dishonour to almost any orchestra ')—and its like were what Byron loved in song. ' Lord Byron,' says Moore, ' though he loved simple music, had no great organisation that way.' The remark was occasioned by ' some discussion with respect to Byron's *chanting* method of repeating poetry which I professed my strong dislike of.' Also, being a musician, ' observe in general that it is the men who have the worst ear for music that *sing* out poetry in this manner, having no nice perception of the difference there ought to be between animated reading and *chant.*' It was ' the Harrow style of reading,' the Diarist adds, and his Editor (Lord John Russell) notes that it was ' very much the style of reciting of the admirers of Pope in the last century.'

Miss Pigot witnessed the very beginnings of Byron. She was reading Burns aloud one day, when says Byron, in effect :—' *Anch'*

NOTES

io son pittore—I also am a poet, by the way'; and offers to pencil down a proof of his assertion. 'In thee I fondly hoped to clasp,' and all the rest of it, he wrote, with boyish gravity. Then he repeated the copy of verse, which begins thus :—'When to this airy hall my father's voice'; and, says Moore, 'from this moment the desire of appearing in print took entire possession of him.' At the time (1806) all his ambition was 'a small volume for private circulation.' In the end . . .!

LETTER ii. p. 2.

Addressed to Henry Angelo, the famous fencing-master, author of *The School of Fencing* (1787), *Hungarian and Highland Broad Sword* (1799), *Angelo's Reminiscences* (1830), and *Angelo's Pic Nic*, 'Including Numerous Recollections of Public Characters' (1837). The present letter, which is in the Watts Collection (British Museum), is printed in *Angelo's Reminiscences*, with the remark :—'This . . . I gave to Dr. Sigmond, M.D., Dover St., who has a superior collection of autographs.'

Henry's father, Domenico Malevoli Tremamundo Angelo, a renowned professor of equitation and the sword, was an *ami intime* of Peg Woffington, who fell in love with him—(so Henry says)—at a fencing-match, and whirled him off to England in her own carriage. Here he taught the *manège* and the use of the *arme blanche*, patronised the arts, was everybody's friend, married the daughter of 'Captain Masters, Commander of the *Chester* frigate,' lived honourably, and died when he was eighty-seven, leaving his son (whom he had sent to Eton and to Paris) to reign in his stead. Like Domenico, Henry taught everybody fencing, and knew everybody worth knowing. He had, too, a talent for acting and the singing of comic songs, and he played much at Wargrave with Hell-Gate Barrymore and his following, and in London with the Margravine of Anspach. An old schoolmate (Dublin) of R. B. Sheridan's, who learned the sword of him, he was particularly associated with Bannister the actor, Rowlandson the caricaturist, Jackson the pugilist (with whom he had rooms in Bond St.), and Bate Dudley, the Fighting Parson ; fenced regularly with Edmund Kean ; was able to bet fifty pounds that he had dined at the same table with the Prince of Wales ('twas in 1806, at the Neapolitan Club), and to win his wager on the authority of 'Anacreon Moore'; and was, in short, as jovial, buxom, and flourishing a blade as his state in society could show. His acquaintance with Byron began at Harrow ('From his Lordship's affability and pleasant manners I knew

LETTERS

more of him than of many I attended there at the time '); and at
the Albany, years afterwards, he used to play single-stick daily (at
half a guinea a lesson) with the poet, for the express purpose of
giving his pupil 'a fine breathing sweat,' and taking down his fat.
Angelo has several stories to tell of Byron :—how he (Angelo) hunted
down a quotation for him, and so enabled him to win a bet ; how they
met at Newmarket the day that Captain Barclay walked his match
with Wood, and how Byron drove him to Cambridge (Theodore
Hook was of the party), gave him dinner, saw him and Hook to
the coach, and 'sent to St. John's College for the good beer it was
noted for, when, filling two tumblers, he handed them up himself
to us, laughing at the many people who were wondering at his
being so very busy waiting on the outside passengers'; how
Byron 'gave me an order on Mr. Murray (whom I had first the
pleasure of knowing near forty years since, when at the Rev. Dr.
Thompson's, Kensington) for several of his books, *Childe Harold*,
etc.,' . . . and 'I did not at the time request his signature on the
title-page'; how 'I,' Henry Angelo, collected portraits of pugilists
and players, from Slack and Betterton downwards, and therewith
composed him a certain famous screen, which John Murray the
Second bought at the sale in Piccadilly, and which abides in Albemarle
Street unto this day.   On the whole, Angelo retained so good and
moving a memory of his pupil that he cannot recall that time at Cambridge, the 'pleasure' of which was so 'greatly enhanced' by Lord
Byron's 'affability and cordial reception,' without a little attempt
at the *cri du cœur* and the *note émue*.   'What must be my feelings
now,' he writes (1830), 'when recollecting the scene of that evening
—his obliging condescension, our parting, the coach driving off,
his huzzas, and the twisting of his hat!   Such feelings can never
be obliterated.'   In effect, *Sunt lacrimae rerum.* . . .

LETTER iii. p. 3.
Addressed to Miss Pigot's brother, who studied medicine at
Edinburgh, and became a doctor.
My amiable Alecto :—The writer's mother, who at this time had
taken to the use of fireirons as a means of marking her sense of
displeasure with her son.   She was Catharine, only child and heiress
of George Gordon of Gight, and she married John Byron, in 1785,
the year after the death of his first wife, Amelia d'Arcy, Baroness
Conyers, a daughter of the fourth Earl of Holderness, with whom,
as Marchioness of Carmarthen, he had eloped some years before.

NOTES

In person she was dumpy and plain, in disposition passionate, in temper furious and tyrannical, in mind a superstitious dullard, and in manners a naturally awkward and untrained provincial. But she was a fortune; and John Byron, a handsome scamp, who was head over ears in debt, had small difficulty in making her and her money his own. This, from what Moore calls 'an authentic source' (it reads like the family lawyer), is how he carried out his part of the marriage contract :—

'At the time of the marriage, Miss Gordon was possessed of about £3000 in money, two shares of the Aberdeen Banking Company, the estates of Gight and Monkshill, and the superiority of two salmon-fishings on Dee. Soon after the arrival of Mr. and Mrs. Byron Gordon in Scotland, it appeared that Mr. Byron had involved himself very deeply in debt, and his creditors commenced legal proceedings for the recovery of their money. The cash in hand was soon paid away,—the bank shares were disposed of at £600 (now worth £5000)—timber on the estate was cut down and sold to the amount of £1500—the farm of Monkshill and superiority of the fishings, affording a freehold qualification, were disposed of at £480; and, in addition to these sales, within a year after the marriage, £8000 was borrowed upon a mortgage on the estate, granted by Mrs. Byron Gordon to the person who lent the money. In March 1786 a contract of marriage in the Scotch form was drawn up and signed by the parties. In the course of the summer of that year Mr. and Mrs. Byron left Gight, and never returned to it; the estate being, in the following year, sold to Lord Haddo for the sum of £17,850, the whole of which was applied to the payment of Mr. Byron's debts, with the exception of £1122, which remained as a burden on the estate (the interest to be applied to paying a jointure of £55, 11s. 1d. to Mrs. Byron's grandmother, the principal reverting, at her death, to Mrs. Byron), and £3000 vested in trustees for Mrs. Byron's separate use, which was lent to Mr. Carsewell of Ratharllet, in Fifeshire.'

In the summer of 1786 she accompanied her husband to France; and, returning to England towards the end of 1787, took a furnished house in Holles Street, and there gave birth to her only child in the late January of 1788. From London she went to Aberdeen, where she was presently joined by Captain Byron. Of course they could not agree; and, after an attempt at life in separate lodgings (at opposite ends of the same street), during which they visited and took tea together, they ceased from speaking, and John Byron, who simply wanted her money, soon left for London. He returned in no great while, and, having squeezed her to the amount of a few pounds more, again departed, and died the next year (1791) at Valenciennes: leaving his foolish, ill-bred, ill-conditioned, ill-served, yet adoring widow to expend the full amount of her very

emotional temperament and habit on the 'lame brat,' their child.
He was a lively boy, but very sensitive and shy, and 'in my sullen
moods . . . a devil.' What chance had such a son with such a
mother? With him, it is told, on first-hand authority, 'she would
pass from passionate caresses to the actual repulsion of disgust,'
and 'the next moment she would devour him with kisses again,
and swear his eyes were as beautiful as his father's.' In 1798, on
Byron's accession to the title, the pair removed to Newstead ; and
there she placed her son in the hands of an ignoble quacksalver,
whose treatment of the poor boy's malformation—(it consisted
chiefly in twisting and wrenching the foot, and in screwing it up in
a wooden engine)—inflicted on him many hours of futile and ex-
cruciating agony. By the summer of 1799, however, it was borne
in upon her, 'daft Gordon' as she was, that the practice of this
ignorant brute had failed ; so she removed to London, took a
house in Sloane Terrace, gave her son to the care of Dr. Baillie,
and—having been placed, for some occult reason, on the Civil
List for a pension of £300 a year—sent him to a private school at
Dulwich. At Dulwich Byron might have done well enough, had
he been left alone ; but patience and tact and self-restraint were
not in his mother's nature. She disgusted Lord Carlisle, who was
her son's guardian, so that in no great while that highly respectable
nobleman was moved to wash his hands of both his ward and his
ward's mother ; while, as for the Dulwich school, she so exerted
her ill-timed and capricious fondness that, when Byron left it for
Harrow, he was, says the kindly and painstaking Glennie, 'as
little prepared as it is natural to suppose from two years of
elementary instruction, thwarted by every art that could estrange
the mind of youth from preceptor, from school, and from serious
study.' Years wrought no change, save for the worse, in her ; and
though Byron, by the time at which the present letter was written,
had contrived to get his own temper fairly well in hand, and was
often able to listen to her rants in silence, the scenes between
them were many and painful (the comic aspect of the situation is
presented with admirable wit and tact in Disraeli's *Venetia*). 'It
is told,' says Moore, 'as a curious proof of their opinions of each
other's violence, that, after parting one evening in a tempest of this
kind, they were known each to go privately that night to the
apothecary's, inquiring anxiously whether the other had been to
purchase poison, and cautioning the vendor of drugs not to attend
to such an application, if made.' On the present occasion, as we
have seen, Byron took refuge in flight.

NOTES

Mrs. Byron died at Newstead—which her son had appropriated 'almost exclusively' to her use, and to which he insisted on coming as a guest—in the July of 1811. She had grown extremely corpulent, and had been 'of late indisposed, but not to any alarming degree'; when (so Moore reports) 'a fit of rage, brought on . . . by reading over the upholsterer's bills, was the ultimate cause of her death.' The *Volage* had landed Byron but a very few days before the news of her seizure was conveyed to him ; but he reached Newstead too late to see her again in life. On the morning of the funeral he boxed, they say, with Rushton. But everybody has his way of working off an emotion. And Byron, despite the extraordinary quality of his relations with his mother, was passionately grieved by her loss. It was with many tears that he told her maid, who found him watching beside the bed of death, that he 'had but one friend in the world, and she was gone.' And there can be no manner of doubt that Mrs. Byron was immensely fond of him in her way, at the same time that in her way she was immensely proud of him.

Harness told Moore that Mrs. Byron collected what actors call the 'notices' of her son's works, pasted them in a book, and wrote comments on them which were neither so unlettered nor so unintelligent as one might have expected.

LETTER v. p. 6.

The enclosed stanzas :—Probably the lines ' To Mary,' afterwards included in *Fugitive Pieces* (see *post*, p. 300, Note to Letter vii.) :—

> Racked by the flames of jealous rage,
> By all her torments deeply curst,
> Of hell-born passions far the worst,
> What hope my pangs can now assuage.

For the whole poem, see Vol. v., Appendix to *Hours of Idleness*. Of the girl to whom it was addressed, Moore notes that she ' was of a humble, if not equivocal, station in life; that she had long, light golden hair, of which he used to show a lock, as well as her picture, among his friends ; and that the verses in his *Hours of Idleness*, entitled "To Mary, On Receiving her Picture," were addressed to her.'

LETTER vii. p. 9.

My Poetics :—Byron was preparing a volume—(*Fugitive Pieces*) —for the press as early as the January of 1806. It was printed for

him by Ridge of Newark in the November of the same year; but
the issue was burned—so thoroughly was the thing done that only
one copy is known to exist—at the request of Becher, who found a
certain number, 'To Mary' unduly voluptuous in intention and
effect. (See *ante*, p. 299, Note to Letter v.)

'*Young Moore*':—Thomas Moore was already the author of
the *Odes of Anacreon* (1800); the *Poetical Works of the late
Thomas Little, Esq.* (1801); and *Epistles, Odes, and Other Poems*
(1806), described by Jeffrey as 'a deliberate design to corrupt the
minds of maidens,' etc., one effect of which description was a
famous attempt at single combat :—

> When Little's leadless pistol met his eye,
> And Bow Street myrmidons stood laughing by.

All three were more or less 'erotic' in cast and tendency; none
was good reading for boys and girls; and on Byron, one (the
second) had, as he owned to Moore, a lasting influence. Another
book of verse to which he was greatly addicted at this time was the
Poems from the Portuguese of Luis de Camoëns (1803) of Percy
Smythe, Sixth Viscount Strangford (1780-1855):—

> Hibernian Strangford, with thine eyes of blue
> And boasted locks of red or auburn hue,
> Whose plaintive strains each love-sick miss admires :—

which he was presently (1809) to denounce, together with Little-
Moore, in *English Bards and Scotch Reviewers*, not only in
verse :—

> Mend, Strangford, mend thy morals and thy taste :—

but also in prose :—'The things given to the public as Camoëns
are no more to be found in the original Portuguese than in the
Song of Solomon.'

The Rev. John Becher (1770-1848), at whose instigation Byron
annihilated his bookling, was afterwards Prebendary of Southwell
and author (MOORE) of 'several valuable works on the Constitution
of Friendly Societies, the Regulation of Prisons and Penitentiaries,
etc.' Also, he was 'an acute and judicious critic' (MOORE), and
continually preached Shakespeare and Milton and the Bible to his
young friend (who already knew the last far better and more intimately than most men of his years), so that his influence was
altogether a good one.

NOTES

LETTER viii. p. 9.

£30,000 *richer than I was :*—This refers to the Rochdale property, of which the Fifth Lord had dispossessed his heirs by an
illegal sale. It was 'hampered with a Lawsuit,' Byron told Medwin, 'which has cost me £14,000, and is not yet finished.' In the
long-run, as we know, Byron had to part with Newstead.

You may expect to see me soon :—Byron did, in effect, return to
Southwell, but soon departed it for Harrogate with Pigot, just home
from Edinburgh. They travelled, Pigot says, 'in Lord Byron's own
carriage, with post-horses; and he sent his groom with two
saddle-horses, and a beautifully formed, very ferocious bull-mastiff
(Nelson), to meet us there.' Boatswain (who at Harrogate was
'universally admired') went on the box, with Frank, the valet.
There were theatricals—repeated soon after at Southwell—at which
Byron appears to have distinguished himself as Penruddock (in Cumberland's *Wheel of Fortune*), a favourite part with John Kemble,
and Tristram Fickle in Allingham's farce, *The Weathercock*; Byron
wrote his lines 'To a Fair Quaker'; Nelson had to be pistolled
('to the great regret of Byron'); Pigot, who was rather bored—('it is
not in my nature to be happy without either female society or study,'
he told his sister)—rode Byron's horse Sultan, and Byron 'was very
good in trying to amuse me as much as possible'; they dined in
the public room, but 'soon retired,' for 'Byron was no more a
friend to drinking than myself'; and all the rest. And Byron
supplemented Pigot to his sister in the following note:—

My dear Bridget,—I have only just dismounted from my *Pegasus*, which
has prevented me from descending to *plain* prose in an epistle of greater
length to your *fair* self. You regretted, in a former letter, that my poems
were not more extensive; I now for your satisfaction announce that I have
nearly doubled them, partly by the discovery of some I conceived to be
lost, and partly by some new productions. We shall meet on Wednesday
next; till then believe me yours affectionately,   BYRON.

P.S.—Your brother John is seized with a poetic mania, and is now
rhyming away at the rate of three lines *per hour*—so much for *inspiration*!
Adieu!'

LETTER xi. p. 12.

My dearest Clare :—This, Byron's lifelong, perhaps his only,
friend, was John Fitzwilliam, Second Earl (1792-1851), son of a
famous Lord Chancellor of Ireland. He was educated at Harrow
and at Christ Church, Oxford, and in 1830-34 was Governor of

LETTERS

Bombay. Clare is the Lycus of 'Childish Recollections' in *Hours of Idleness*, and the apostrophe to Lycus originally ended thus:—

> For ever to possess a friend in thee,
> Was bliss unhoped, though not unsought by me.
> Thy softer soul was form'd for love alone,
> To ruder passions and to hate unknown;
> Thy mind, in union with thy beauteous form,
> Was gentle, but unfit to stem the storm.
> That face, an index of celestial worth,
> Proclaim'd a heart abstracted from the earth.
> Oft, when depress'd with sad foreboding gloom,
> I sat reclined upon our favourite tomb,
> I 've seen those sympathetic eyes o'erflow
> With kind compassion for thy comrade's woe;
> Or when less mournful subjects form'd our themes,
> We tried a thousand fond romantic schemes,
> Oft hast thou sworn, in friendship's soothing tone,
> Whatever wish was mine must be thine own.

Clare and Byron saw little of each other after 1811-12. They met, however, in Italy in 1821. Here is Byron on the event:—

'"There is a strange coincidence sometimes in the little things of this world, Sancho," says Sterne in a letter (if I mistake not), and so I have often found it. Page 128, article 91, of this collection of scattered things (*Detached Thoughts*), I had alluded to my friend Lord Clare in terms such as my feelings suggested. About a week or two afterwards I met him on the road between Imola and Bologna, after not having met for seven or eight years. He was abroad in 1814, and came home just as I set out in 1816. This meeting annihilated for a moment all the years between the present time and the days of *Harrow*. It was a new and inexplicable feeling, like rising from the grave, to me. Clare, too, was much agitated —more in *appearance* than even myself; for I could feel his heart beat to his fingers' ends, unless, indeed, it was the pulse of my own which made me think so. He told me that I should find a note from him left at Bologna. I did. We were obliged to part for our different journeys, he for Rome, I for Pisa, but with the promise to meet again in spring. We were but five minutes together, and on the public road; but I hardly recollect an hour of my existence which could be weighed against them. He had heard that I was coming on, and had left his letter for me at Bologna, because the people with whom he was travelling could not wait longer. Of all I have ever known, he has always been the least altered in everything from the excellent qualities and kind affections which attached me to him so strongly at school. I should hardly have thought it possible for society (or the world, as it is called) to leave a being with so little of the leaven of bad passions. I do not speak from personal experience only, but from all I have ever heard of him from others, during absence and distance.'

302

NOTES

Thus, too, Mme. Guiccioli, of a second encounter :—

'Lord Clare's visit also occasioned him extreme delight. He had a great affection for Lord Clare, and was very happy during the short visit that he paid him at Leghorn. The day on which they separated was a melancholy one for Lord Byron. "I have a presentiment that I shall never see him more," he said, and his eyes filled with tears. The same melancholy came over him during the first weeks that succeeded to Lord Clare's departure, whenever his conversation happened to fall upon this friend.'

I have written to Delawarr:—George John, Fifth Earl of Delawarr, P.C., D.C.L. (1791-1869), a Harrow and Cambridge (Trinity) friend, the Euryalus of 'Childish Recollections,' was Lord Chancellor in 1858, and resigned in 1859. Murray's Editor (1837) notes that the 'Delawarrs' have been Barons by the male line from 1342, their ancestor, Sir Thomas West, having been summoned to parliament as Lord West, the 16th Edward II. In a note to *Hours of Idleness*, he also quotes as follows from 'some hitherto unpublished letters of Lord Byron' :—'Harrow, Oct. 25, 1804.—I am happy enough and comfortable here. My friends are not numerous, but select. Among the principal I rank Lord Delawarr, who is very amiable, and my particular friend.' 'Nov. 2, 1804.—Lord Delawarr is considerably younger than me, but the most good-tempered, amiable, clever fellow in the universe. To all which he adds the quality (a good one in the eyes of women) of being remarkably handsome. Delawarr and myself are, in a manner, connected ; for one of my forefathers, in Charles the First's time, married into their family.'

LETTER xii. p. 13.

My dear Bankes :—William John Bankes was educated at Trinity College, Cambridge; sat for Truro (1810-12), Cambridge University (1821-25), Marlborough (1829-32), and Dorset (1833-34) ; travelled and adventured with Giovanni Finati (b. *c.* 1787), the Ferrarese, who, 'under the assumed name of Mahomet, made the campaign against the Wahabees for the recovery of Mecca and Medina', published (1830) a translation (from the Italian) of Finati's *Narrative* (which was dedicated to him) ; and died at Venice, 1855. Bankes was a particular friend of Skinner Matthews ; and, says Byron, 'while he stayed (at Trinity) he ruled the roast, or rather the *roasting,*'—(he was, says Rogers, a very brilliant and potent talker)—'and was father of all mischief.'

The portrait of Pomposus:—Dr. Butler, who succeeded (1805) Dr. Drury (1750-1834), 'The dear Preceptor of my early days,' in

303

the head-mastership of Harrow. Byron, who wanted Mark Drury in his father's seat, loved not the 'upstart pedant,' who kept Mark Drury out of it. His reference is to the piece called 'Childish Recollections,' in *Hours of Idleness* :—

> Pomposus fills his magisterial chair,
> Pomposus governs,—but, my Muse, forbear,
> Contempt, in silence, be the pedant's lot.

It appears, however, that, had he reprinted the *Hours*, his sketch on Butler had been changed :—

> If once my Muse a harsher portrait drew,
> Warm with her wrongs, and deemed the likeness true,
> By cooler judgment taught, her fault she owns, etc.

Collegiate rhymes :—See 'Thoughts suggested by a College Examination,' Text and Notes, in *Hours of Idleness.*

The celebrated author of 'The Man of Feeling' :—It is worth noting of Mackenzie (1745-1831) and the *Lord Woodhouselee* (1747-1813)—'at the head of the Scotch Literati,'—of Letter xiv., that through them the Byron of *Hours of Idleness* (Newark, 1807) touches hands with the Burns of *Poems, Chiefly in the Scottish Dialect* (Kilmarnock, 1786). Mackenzie wrote warmly of both books ; while Alexander Fraser Tytler, called Lord Woodhouselee on his elevation to the bench of the Court of Session, author of *Elements of General History* (1801), *Memoirs of the Life of Henry Home, Lord Kames* (1807), and other works of good enough repute in their day, sat on that ' Jury of literati' to which Burns submitted the materials of his First Edinburgh Edition (1787), suggested changes and emendations to him which were not often to the advantage of his verse, and assisted him in passing his Fourth (and last) Edinburgh Edition (1794) for the press.

LETTER xv. p. 17.
Mr. Falkner was Mrs. Byron's landlord at Southwell.

LETTER xvi. p. 18.
The gravity of old Boatswain :—The Newfoundland, Boatswain, is one of the world's dogs now and these many years. Byron nursed the poor beast through an attack of rabies—('he more than once with his bare hand wiped away,' says Moore, 'the slaver from the dog's lips during the paroxysms')—and buried him in the garden at Newstead, under a famous inscription :—

NOTES

Near this spot
Are deposited the Remains of one
Who possessed Beauty without Vanity,
Strength without Insolence,
Courage without Ferocity,
And all the Virtues of Man without his Vices.
This Praise, which would be unmeaning Flattery
If inscribed over human ashes,
Is but a just tribute to the Memory of
BOATSWAIN, a Dog,
Who was born at Newfoundland, May 1803,
And died at Newstead Abbey, November 18, 1808.

' Boatswain is dead,' we shall find him writing to Hodgson. ' He expired in a state of madness on the 18th, after suffering much, yet retaining all the gentleness of his nature to the last, never attempting to do the least injury to any one near him.'

Make a long speech and conclude it with a 1 2 3 4 5 6 7:—a trick he had of repeating a set of numerals when he found himself at a loss for words.

LETTER xvii. p. 18.

The hero of my Cornelian :—Eddlestone, the Cambridge chorister (' my musical protégé'), who had given Byron—(they had a romantic attachment for each other)—a cornelian heart. Eddlestone left Cambridge, and went into trade (apparently through Byron's influence), but died of phthisis in the May of 1811. Thereafter Byron wrote thus to Mrs. Pigot at Southwell :—

Cambridge, Oct. 28, 1811.

Dear Madam,—I am about to write to you on a silly subject, and yet I cannot well do otherwise. You may remember a *cornelian*, which some years ago I consigned to Miss Pigot, indeed *gave* to her, and now I am going to make the most selfish and rude of requests. The person who gave it to me, when I was very young, is *dead*, and though a long time has elapsed since we met, as it was the only memorial I possessed of that person (in whom I was very much interested), it has acquired a value by this event I could have wished it never to have borne in my eyes. If, therefore, Miss Pigot should have preserved it, I must, under these circumstances, beg her to excuse my requesting it to be transmitted to me at No. 8. St. James's Street, London, and I will replace it by something she may remember me by equally well. As she was always so kind as to feel interested in the fate of him that formed the subject of our conversation, you may tell her that the giver of that cornelian died in May last of a consumption, at the age of twenty-one, making the sixth, within four months, of friends and relatives that I have lost between May and the end of August.—Believe me, dear Madam, yours very sincerely,   BYRON.

P.S.—I go to London to-morrow.

LETTERS

The trinket 'was, of course, returned, and Lord Byron, at the same time, reminded that he had left it with Miss Pigot as a deposit, *not* a gift.'—MOORE. See Letter xviii.

Don't much admire lampoons:—See 'Granta, a Medley,' in *Hours of Idleness.*

LETTER xviii. p. 21.

In short, we shall put Lady E. Butler and Miss Ponsonby to the blush :—The famous couple known indifferently as the 'Ladies of Llangollen' and the 'Ladies of the Vale.' 'It was about the year 1779 that Lady Eleanor Butler and Miss Ponsonby first associated themselves to live in retirement. It was thought desirable to separate two individuals who appeared to encourage each other's eccentricities, and after their first departure together, they were brought back to their respective relations, but soon effected a second elopement.'—MOORE. Lady Eleanor died at Llangollen in June 1829; Miss Ponsonby survived her till the December of 1831. They had lived together in the Vale for half a century. 'It is very singular,' writes John Murray the Second (23rd August 1829) to his son, 'that the ladies, intending to *retire* from the world, absolutely brought *all the world* to visit them, for after a few years of seclusion their strange story was the universal subject of conversation, and there has been no person of rank, talent, and importance in any way who did not procure introductions to them. All that was passing in the world they had fresh as it arose, and in four hours' conversation with Miss Ponsonby one day, when we were alone, and during three the next, when Mrs. M. and my daughters were with me, I found that she knew everybody and everything, and was, at the age of eighty, or nearly so, a most inexhaustible fund of entertaining instruction and lively communication.' The cottage, Murray adds, was 'fitted up with ancient oak, presented by different friends, from old castles and monasteries, none of it of less antiquity than 1200 years.' This about the twelve centuries one may believe or not. But there is no reason, I think, for doubting Miss Ponsonby's word, the last which Murray quotes, that 'during the whole fifty years, she never knew a moment that hung heavy upon her, and no sorrow but from the loss of friends.'

LETTER xix. p. 24.

P.S.—Lord Carlisle :—See *ante*, p. 296, Note to Letter iii., and *post*, p. 330, Note to Letter xxxix.

NOTES

LETTER XX. p. 25.

To Mr. Crosby:—Crosby was the publisher of *Monthly Literary Recreations*, a 'Magazine of General Information and Amusement'; and the thirteenth Number (July 1807) of this print set forth a review of *Hours of Idleness*:—'The young and noble author of these poems introduces them to public notice with a degree of modesty which does honour to his feelings as a poet and a lord. . . . Many are dedicated to a subject which all ages, all nations, civilised and unpolished, *etc.* . . . The poem entitled *The Tear* is one of his happiest effusions, *etc.* . . . Truth compels us to acknowledge that the lines 'To Mary on Receiving her Picture' teem with fire and genuine, *etc.* . . . The young bard, *etc.* . . . *Lachin-y-Gair* is written with fire, *etc.* . . . *Childish Recollections*, one of the most solid foundations . . . manly nature . . . pleasing melancholy . . . flowing harmony . . . companions of his youthful studies and enjoyments . . . orphan and brotherless state . . . inexpressible charm . . . the whole of this production. . . . The young poet, *etc. etc. etc.*' To this same number of *M. L. R.* Byron contributed his review of Wordsworth.

LETTER xxi. p. 27.

Bosworth Field:—These verses were never published.

Hutton's Account:—William Hutton (*c.* 1723-1815), F.S.A. Edin., was a Birmingham bookseller, who wrote a *History of Birmingham to* 1780; a *History of Blackpool*; a *Journey from Birmingham to London*; and *The Battle of Bosworth Field between Richard III. and Henry, Earl of Richmond* (Birmingham, 1788).

LETTER xxii. p. 28.

On Sunday next, etc.:—'This plan (which he never put in practice) had been talked of by him before he left Southwell, and is thus noticed in a letter of his fair correspondent to her brother:—" How can you ask if Lord B. is going to visit the Highlands in the summer? Why, don't *you* know that he never knows his own mind for ten minutes together? I tell him he is as fickle as the winds, and as uncertain as the waves."'—MOORE.

Last week I swam in the Thames:—This was Leigh Hunt's first glimpse of Byron. He witnessed the performance in part, and he 'noticed a respectable, manly-looking person, who was eyeing something in the distance' (Byron's head). The 'manly-looking' one was Gentleman Jackson. (See *post*, p. 316, Note to Letter xxxi.)

LETTERS

LETTER xxiii. p. 30.

My cousin, Captain **Bettesworth :—**'Captain George Edward Byron Bettesworth, born in 1781, was the son of a clergyman in the north of England. In the short space of eight years from his first entering the service as a boy he had risen by his merit to the post of Commander. When the above letter was written he had just been appointed to the *Tartar* frigate, in which he was killed in the May following, while engaging with some Danish gunboats off Bergen. He had recently married Lady Hannah Althea Grey, sister to Earl Grey; who afterwards married the Right Hon. Edward Ellice.'—MOORE.,

Another poem of 250 *lines :—*This was *English Bards and Scotch Reviewers.*

*Praised to the skies :—*See *The Critical Review,* 3rd Series, vol. xii. p. 47.

Another Periodical :—The Satirist: A Monthly Meteor, ran from 1807 to 1812, and reviewed *Hours of Idleness* in its first issue (October 1807). 'If the noble Lord,' it says, 'had not presented his *Hours of Idleness,* no human being would have guessed the quantity of time he had spent in *doing nothing.*' Finally, 'The rest of the verses are of the same stamp as the earlier ones, and completely prove, that although *George Gordon, Lord Byron, a minor,* may be a gentleman, an orator, or a statesman, unless he improves wonderfully, he never can be a poet.'

LETTER xxiv. p. 32.

*My dear Sir :—*Henry Joseph Thomas Drury (1778-1841), the son of Byron's 'Dear Preceptor,' was born at Harrow—(he was a master there for many years)—and was educated at Eton and at King's (Cambridge), of which he was duly a Fellow. He was one of the men—Hodgson, Matthews, Hobhouse, Scrope Davies—who composed what one is now at liberty to call 'the Byron Set'; Byron, who read with him, had a very great regard for him ; and he, for his part (he called a son of his, afterwards Admiral Drury, 'Byron'), returned the regard with interest. In 1828-29 he was a candidate for the Head Mastership of Harrow ; but though he was backed by some hundreds of good men—(as Butler of Shrewsbury, Peel, and Sumner)—he was 'most unexpectedly beaten' by Longley (afterwards Archbishop of Canterbury), 'a young man who had only quite recently taken his degree.' Having lived to see his son the Rev. Henry (afterwards Archdeacon Drury) edit the *Arundines Cami* (1841), he died at Harrow, whither his

308

NOTES

old schoolmate Hodgson, ever his friend and correspondent, by this time Provost of Eton, posted to administer the Sacrament to him : 'just before his death,' in the presence of the Head Master, Dr. Wordsworth, now (1878) Bishop of Lincoln.'—(JAMES T. HODGSON, *Memoir of the Rev. Francis Hodgson*, 1878.)

My Worthy Preceptor :—Dr. Butler, the Pomposus of 'Childish Recollections.'

Tatersall :—John Cecil Tatersal, a Harrow schoolmate, who took orders, and died (of consumption) at twenty-four.

And ' so on' :—Francis Calvert, Seventh Earl of Baltimore (1731-1771), married Diana Egerton, daughter of the Duke of Bridge-water, and was tried at Kingston Assize (26th March 1767) 'for a Rape on the Body of Sarah Woodcock,' together with Elizabeth Griffinburg and Ann Harvey, otherwise Darby, 'as accessories before the fact, for procuring, aiding, and abetting him in the said Rape.' He pleaded Sarah's consent, and was acquitted. He was author of *A Tour in the East in the Years* 1763 *and* 1764 . . . ; of *Select Pieces of Oriental Wit, Poetry, and Wisdom* (London, 1767) ; *Gaudia Poetica Latina Anglica et Gallica Lingua Composita* (Augustae, 1770) ; and of *Celestes et Inferi* (Venice, 1771). Also, he was the hero of a very scandalous romance ' with eight beautiful Plates,' *Injured Innocence, or The Rape of Sarah Woodcock. A Tale* ' by S—— J—— Esq., of Magdalen College, Oxford. New York : Printed for the Booksellers.' (n. d.).

LETTER XXV. p. 34.

To Mr. Dallas :—Robert Charles Dallas (1754-1824), 'author' (Moore says) 'of some novels, popular, I believe, in their day,' was the son of a doctor, was born at Dallas Castle, and was educated at Musselburgh and at Kingston (under James Elphinstone). He read law at the Inner Temple ; but, on attaining his majority, he went to Jamaica, where he had property, and for some time lived there and in the U.S.A. Returning to England, he turned author, and published *Miscellaneous Writings* (1797 : 'Consisting of *Poems; Lucretia*, a Tragedy ; and *Moral Essays*, with a Vocabulary of the Passions') ; *Percival, or Nature Vindicated* (1801), a novel ; *Elements of Self-Knowledge* (1802) ; *Aubrey* (1804) ; *Tales Illustrative of the Simple and the Surprising* (1805) ; and much else. He was a sort of connexion ('Captain George Anson Byron of the Royal Navy, father of the present Lord Byron, had married a sister of Mr. Dallas.'—MOORE) ; and at this time he introduced himself to Byron's notice in a solemn letter about *Hours*

309

LETTERS

of Idleness : a letter in which he cited, being aggressively, and even ponderously, moral, the good Lord Lyttelton as an example and the wicked Lord Lyttelton as the other thing, and wrote himself down generally the well-meaning, officious, wordy, pompous, and extremely self-satisfied person he was. Byron replied—delighted to be taken seriously, yet with his tongue most plainly in his cheek ; and Dallas was presently privileged to assist in the publication of *English Bards and Scotch Reviewers.* Four years after, on Byron's return from the East, Dallas was still further privileged, and assisted in the publication of *Childe Harold,* which Byron gave him, and on which he received the profits (£800), as he presently received, in the same way, the profits on *The Corsair* (1813). Then the pair drifted apart ; and after Missolonghi Dallas produced an account of Byron against which Hanson and Hobhouse, the poet's executors, procured an injunction, on the strength of certain letters to the Hon. Mrs. Byron which were set forth in its pages. This was just before Dallas's death, when the book was republished in Paris (1824), as *Recollections of the Life of Lord Byron from the Year* 1808 *to the end of* 1814. It was edited by the Rev. A. R. C. Dallas (the writer's son); contains an account of the dispute with Hobhouse, together with a Memoir; and has been of service in the preparation of this Volume.

A furious Philippic:—See *The Eclectic Review* for November 1807. Here is a sample of the rubbish :—' The notice we take of this publication regards the author rather than the book ; the book is a collection of juvenile pieces, some of very moderate merit, and others of very questionable morality ; but the author is a *nobleman* ! It is natural that, as commoners, we should feel a solemn reverence for hereditary rank ; and then as critics, we should hail the slightest indication of poetical talent that gleams from beneath a coronet. Powerfully as we are actuated by these sentiments, we shall not suffer this superior dignity, or these unnatural symptoms of intellect to overwhelm us with astonishment ; but duly estimating that authority which our hoary age and important function intitle us to assume, and reflecting on the juvenility of this adventurous lord, we shall furnish him with a few admonitions,' *etc. etc.*

An excellent compound of a ' Brainless' and a ' Stanhope' :— These, says Moore, are ' characters in the novel called *Percival.*'

LETTER xxvi. p. 36.
I did study ' The Spirit of Laws' and ' The Laws of Nations' :—

NOTES

The Spirit of Laws appears to be Nugent's translation (London, 1748) of Montesquieu's *l'Esprit des Lois*. The *Laws of Nations* may be the second discourse of Matthew Tindal (1657-1733), *Of the Laws of Nations and the Rights of Kings* (London, 1694).

Moore has noted, in connexion with this letter, that Byron's sentiment for his University was precisely that of Milton, Dryden, and Gray before him, and was paralleled by that of Locke and Gibbon for Oxford.

LETTER XXVII. p. 38.

My dear Harness:—William Harness (1790-1869) was Byron's junior at Harrow. Harness was weak and lame when he entered the school ; and Byron fought his battles for him. They fell out, but were reconciled : so that Byron was moved to dedicate the First and Second *Harold* to him, but did not 'for fear it should injure him in his profession.' Writing some years after Harrow, Byron speaks thus of both the estrangement and the friendship :—
'We both seem perfectly to recollect, with a mixture of pleasure and regret, the hours we once passed together, and I assure you, most sincerely, they are numbered among the happiest of my brief chronicle of enjoyment. I am now *getting into years*, that is to say, I was *twenty* a month ago, and another year will send me into the world to run my career of folly with the rest. I was then just fourteen,—you were almost the first of my Harrow friends, certainly the *first* in my esteem, if not in date ; but an absence from Harrow for some time, shortly after, and new connexions on your side, and the difference in our conduct (an advantage decidedly in your favour) from that turbulent and riotous disposition of mine, which impelled me into every species of mischief,—all these circumstances combined to destroy an intimacy, which affection urged me to continue, and memory compels me to regret. But there is not a circumstance attending that period, hardly a sentence we exchanged, which is not impressed on my mind at this moment. I need not say more,—this assurance alone must convince you, had I considered them as trivial, they would have been less indelible. How well I recollect the perusal of your "first flights"! There is another circumstance you do not know ;—the *first lines* I ever attempted at Harrow were addressed to *you*. You were to have seen them ; but Sinclair had the copy in his possession when we went home ;—and, on our return, we were *strangers*. They were destroyed, and certainly no great loss ; but you will perceive from this circumstance my opinions at an age when we cannot be hypo-

311

LETTERS

crites. I have dwelt longer on this theme than I intended, and I shall now conclude with what I ought to have begun. We were once friends,—nay, we have always been so, for our separation was the effect of chance, not of dissension. I do not know how far our destinations in life may throw us together, but if opportunity and inclination allow you to waste a thought on such a harebrained being as myself, you will find me at least sincere, and not so bigoted to my faults as to involve others in the consequences. Will you sometimes write to me? I do not ask it often; and if we meet, let us be what we *should* be, and what we *were*.'—(MOORE.)

In a letter to Moore, written after Byron's death, Harness gives this pleasant and particular account of their friendship:—' A coolness afterwards arose, which Byron alludes to in the first of the accompanying letters, and we never spoke during the last year of his remaining at school, nor till after the publication of his *Hours of Idleness*. Lord Byron was then at Cambridge; I, in one of the upper forms at Harrow. In an English theme I happened to quote from the volume, and mention it with praise. It was reported to Byron that I had, on the contrary, spoken slightingly of his work and of himself, for the purpose of conciliating the favour of Dr. Butler, the master, who had been severely satirised in one of the poems. Wingfield, who was afterwards Lord Powerscourt, a mutual friend of Byron and myself, disabused him of the error into which he had been led, and this was the occasion of the first letter of the collection. Our intimacy was renewed, and continued from that time till his going abroad. Whatever faults Lord Byron might have had towards others, to myself he was always uniformly affectionate. I have many slights and neglects towards him to reproach myself with; but I cannot call to mind a single instance of caprice or unkindness, in the whole course of our friendship, to allege against him.'

In effect, Harness was one of the friends whose portraits Byron had painted by Sanders ere his departure for the East. He remembered the Harrow days so well that at Rogers's table he was able to quote to Moore, who was then (1828-29) engaged upon the *Life and Letters*, such a 'strain of unpremeditated art' as this of Byron's, 'roared out' at a schoolmate who was a violent Bonapartist:—

> Bold Robert Speer was Bony's bad precursor.
> Bob was a bloody dog, but Bonaparte a worser.

He visited at Newstead in 1812, when Byron was correcting the

NOTES

proofs of the First and Second *Harold*. There he met Francis Hodgson (see *post*, p. 319, Note to Letter xxxv.), who was ' at work in getting out the ensuing number of *The Monthly Review*,' and for three weeks—weeks of late hours at both ends of the day—' the general talk was of poets and poetry, and who could or who could not write,' though it occasionally strayed into very serious discussions on religion ' (see Note to Letter xxxv., *ut sup.*). In due course Harness took orders and a country curacy; but Byron was never afraid of the cloth—(conspicuous among his early friends are Becher, Harness, Hodgson, and Drury, parsons all)—and the intimacy continued unimpaired till 1816 and the Exile, after which it died a natural death. Harness, a person of elegant taste, had always found Byron's poetry ' a little too "strong" for him '; being Boyle Lecturer at Cambridge, he took occasion to speak of *Cain* as he thought it deserved; and two years after came the end. But though he found Byron's Venetian life still ' stronger ' than Byron's poetry, he never ceased from being Byron's champion; and the few pages in which he discusses the Marriage, and the Separation, and the Characters of the parties thereto, are uncompromisingly Byronian, at the same time that they are sane and liberal enough to make you wish that he had written many more.

For the rest, he lived an active, blameless, useful life: as minister (1825) of Regent Square Chapel, St. Pancras, where he stayed for twenty years; as Morning Preacher at Trinity Chapel, Conduit Street, and Minister and Evening Lecturer at St. Ann's, Soho; and as Minister of Brompton Chapel, in which capacity he compassed the building of All Souls', Knightsbridge. He edited Shakespeare and Massinger, wrote much for *Blackwood*, and published a certain amount of timid, unexceptionable verse. Moreover, being extremely popular as a preacher, and withal ' a gentleman of the Old School,' he went everywhere and saw everybody. His lifelong friend (they knew each other as babies) was Mary Russell Mitford, whose *Life* he lived to write; but Sir Walter, Crabbe, Rogers, Sydney Smith, the Kembles, the Derbys, the Lansdownes, Daniel Webster, Washington Irving, the Berrys, Lydia White, Father Mathew, Talfourd, Joanna Baillie, Milman, Dickens, Thackeray, Crabb Robinson—at one or the other time he knew them all. In the end, being very old, he fell down a stone stair in the Deanery at Battle, and was taken up dead.

His *Literary Life* (1871) was written by the Rev. A. G. Lestrange, his collaborator in *The Life of Mary Russell Mitford*. I am indebted to it for the substance of this Note.

LETTER xxviii. p. 39.

A most violent attack :—The famous criticism in *The Edinburgh Review*, which Byron always attributed to Brougham, and which Mr. Jeaffreson believes to have been the work of an incensed don. It is printed (Vol. v.) as an Appendix to *English Bards*.

The partisans of Lord Holland and Co. :—That is, the Edinburgh Reviewers acknowledged no merit anywhere save in a Whig. Henry Richard Vassall Holland, Third Baron, a nephew of Charles James Fox (1773-1840), was educated at Eton and Oxford. In 1797 he married Elizabeth Vassall, the divorced wife of Sir Godfrey Webster, to whom he had already paid £6000 damages as defendant in an action for *crim. con.* The 'constant protector of all oppressed races and persecuted sects' (MACAULAY), he did good work against the Slave Trade, the Corn Laws, and the Criminal Code ; took the other side in the matter of the War and the isolation of Napoleon ; and served on the Ministries of Earl Grey and Lord Melbourne. Also, he wrote gracefully about Spanish literature and his uncle Fox, and edited the Waldegrave *Memoirs.* A good talker, a capital mimic, an engaging and accomplished host, to Sheridan he is 'the only public man I have any attachment for' ; his Holland House parties are historical ; and in 1833 Ticknor 'cannot help agreeing with Scott that he is the most agreeable man I have ever met,' the reason being that 'to the great resources of his knowledge he adds a *laissez-aller*, arising from his remarkable good-nature which is irresistible.' Of Lord Holland in Parliament, Holcroft, writing in 1799, remarks that 'He has not sufficient vehemence of feeling to become a man of genius' ; while to Byron (1813) he is 'impressive from sense and sincerity.' As we shall see, he believed himself justified in what he writes to Becher, and in the Text and Notes of *English Bards* he trounced the Holland House set with all the strength that was in him. Afterwards, being convinced of his error, he was on excellent terms with Lord Holland, to whom he was introduced by Rogers, and to whom he dedicated *The Bride of Abydos* (1813), 'With Every Sentiment of Regard and Respect.'

PAYNE KNIGHT :—Richard Payne Knight (' Phallus Knight,' as Walpole calls him) wrote *The Landscape* (1794) ; *The Progress of Civil Society* (1796) ; *An Account of the Remains of the Warship of Priapus*, etc. (1796) ; and *Carmina Homerica* (1808-20). His verse and his theories are parodied in the Twenty-first *Anti-Jacobin* :—

> There laughs the sky, there Zephyr's frolic train,
> And light-winged loves, and blameless pleasures reign :

NOTES

> There where two souls congenial ties unite,
> No hireling *Bonzes* chant the mystic rite. . . .
> There in each grove, each sloping bank along,
> And flowers, and shrubs, and odorous herbs among, *etc.*

He was born in 1750, and on his death in 1824 he bequeathed to the British Museum a collection of bronzes, gems, and coins valued at £30,000 to £60,000.

LETTER XXIX. p. 40.

Pratt, the gleaner, author, poet, etc. :—This was Samuel Jackson Pratt (1749-1814). Born at St. Ives (Bucks), he began, it appears, as a parson, but, getting into trouble over women, and quarrelling with his parents, he turned actor, playing under the noble name of Courtney Melmoth in Dublin, and failing (1774) at Covent Garden in Hamlet and in Philaster. After this he took to scribbling—still as Courtney Melmoth; went into partnership (*c.* 1776) with a Bath bookseller named Clinch; and coming to London some time afterwards, fell in with Wolcot, Beattie, Colman, and Æschylus Potter, and took so valiantly to scribbling prose and verse that three columns of the British Museum Catalogue are filled with the titles of his works: among them *Sympathy: a Poem* (1788), of which there were four editions within the year, and eleven by 1807; *The Pupils of Pleasure* (1776), translated into French and German, and abused as 'licentious'; *The Fair Circassian* (1781), a play which, as acted by Miss Farren, afterwards Countess of Derby, went through three editions within the year; and *Gleanings in England* (1799), which is trounced in a letter by Charles Lamb. He is best remembered as the discoverer of Blackett, the cobbler-bard, of whom he published *Specimens* in 1809 and the *Remains* in 1811.

In the MS. of *English Bards* Pratt is thus presented :—

> In verse most stale, unprofitable, flat,
> Come let us change the scene and 'glean' with Pratt;
> In him an author's luckless lot behold,
> Condemned to make the books which once he sold:
> Degraded Man! again resume thy trade—
> The votaries of the Muse are ill-repaid,
> Though daily puffs once more invite to buy
> A new edition of thy *Sympathy.*

But the engaging Dallas, who was a personal friend, prevailed upon the writer to suppress his verses, together with a rider in prose :—'Mr. Pratt, once a Bath bookseller, now a London author, has written as much, to as little purpose, as any of his

315

LETTERS

scribbling contemporaries. Mr. P.'s *Sympathy* is in rhyme; but his prose productions are the most voluminous.'

Hanson, my agent:—Hanson's first (published) appearance in Byron's history is as his client's escort to Dr. Glennie's school at Dulwich. According to Mrs. Leigh, there was talk (*c.* 1818) of taking Byron's affairs out of his hands; but nothing came of it, and in 1824 he went with Hobhouse to Doctors Commons for the proving of Byron's will. A series of early letters, from Byron to Hanson, which I regret that I cannot publish, shows the pair to have been on familiar, even friendly terms.

Hanson's eldest daughter—'Mary Anne (a good girl),' B.—married the Earl of Portsmouth (7th March 1814), when Byron gave away the bride. In 1828 the Earl was declared *non compos mentis* at the time of the marriage, and it was dissolved. (See *post*, Letter to Lady ——, 28 March 1823.)

My Lancashire property:—See *ante*, p. 301, Note to Letter viii. Hanson was ever for the sale of Newstead, Byron as steadily against it. But in 1818 Mrs. Leigh writes to Hodgson that 'Mr. Hanson has lately returned from Venice, having been there to sign and seal away our dear, lamented Abbey.'

LETTER xxx. p. 42.

Beside Mr. Hobhouse:—See *post*, p. 321, Note to Letter xxxv.

The 'Revenge':—Young's tragedy (1721), in which Byron loved to enact the part of the impassioned Zanga.

LETTER xxxi. p. 42.

Dear Jack:—John Jackson (1759-1845), better known as Gentleman Jackson, 'Sole Prop and Ornament of Pugilism' (MOORE), Champion of England from 1795 to 1803, when he retired. The son of that London builder, 'by whom the arch was thrown over the old Fleet Ditch,' Jackson was backed by Harvey Combe, Lord Mayor, and four times member for the City of London, and fought no more than thrice in the Ring:—in 1788, when he beat Fewteral of Birmingham at Smithson Bottom, near Croydon, in the presence of the Prince of Wales; in 1789, when he was beaten by the Brewer of Ingleston, who threw him so heavily as to dislocate his ankle and break the small bone of an arm; and in 1795, when at Hornchurch, Essex, he beat the renowned Mendoza in ten and a half minutes. Yet for over thirty years he was the most picturesque and commanding figure in the sporting world, and exercised an influence unique in its annals. The truth is, he was a **vast** deal more than an accomplished boxer and teacher of boxing and a brilliant all-

round athlete. He was also a man of character and integrity
—polite, agreeable, reputable, a capital talker, a person of tact
and energy and charm. It was at his Rooms in Bond St.—('long
the most attractive lounge in the West End')—that the Pugilistic
Club was founded (1814), which was to the Ring, for the ten or a
dozen years of its authority, what the M.C.C. is to the world of
cricket now; no mill of moment was possible unless he held the
watch or served as referee; he instituted the practice of making a
purse for the beaten man, and generally took round the hat himself; he selected and commanded the body of pugilists—Spring,
Cribb, Tom Belcher, Richmond, Tom Oliver, and the rest—which
kept order at the Coronation of George IV. Byron had always a
great regard for Jackson; walked with him at Cambridge, and told
an excited remonstrant that 'Jackson's manners are infinitely
superior to those of the fellows of my college whom I meet at the
high table' (J. W. CLARK); had him to stay at Newstead and
at Brighton (always paying the chaise both ways); wrote him
friendly letters; and, as late as 1823, described him in a note to *Don
Juan* (xi. 19) as 'my old friend and corporeal pastor and master,
John Jackson, Esq.'—(he was always MR. Jackson to the Profession
and the Press, just as—so 'tis said—a late political leader was
always 'MR. Parnell' to the members of his party)—and hoped that
he 'still retained the strength and symmetry of his model of a form,
together with his good humour and athletic as well as mental accomplishments.' And two years before Byron wrote thus, Pierce
Egan notes, with all his wonted enthusiasm in the matter of fancy
types, that 'MR. JOHN JACKSON still continues to increase in the
estimation of the *Fancy* in general, at his rooms, No. 13 Bond
Street, London, INDEPENDENT OF ALL PARTIES, yet whose most
anxious endeavour is to please all parties from the highest to the
lowest connected with the Prize Ring.' In 1820 Jackson was presented with 'a service of plate of the most magnificent description
. . . to which all ranks contributed, from the prince to the prize-
fighter.' In 1824 he gave up his Rooms, 'and retired into private
life, occupying a house in Grosvenor Street West, where he still
(1841) resides, enjoying the unabated confidence of his old friends.'
A great monument—a couchant lion and a naked athlete (weeping)
—subscribed by his pupils, marks his place in Brompton Cemetery.

In 1818, when Moore wanted to get up the slang of the Fancy
for *Tom Cribb's Memorial* (of which 2000 copies were sold in less
than a week), Scrope Davies asked him to meet Jackson at dinner,
and told him that his opposite was making £1000 a year by teaching

LETTERS

the use of ' the raw uns ' through the gloves. Moore ' got very little out of' his fellow-guest (he really learned his flash from the ass, Pierce Egan), but promised to go with Jackson and Davies to see the fight between Turner and the Nonpareil at Crawley Downs (4th December 1818). Thus does he tell the tale :— ' Breakfasted with Davies at seven. Walked to Jackson's house in Grosvenor Street ; a very neat establishment for a boxer. Were off in our chaise at eight. The immense crowds of carriages, pedestrians, *etc.*, all along the road—*the respect paid to Jackson everywhere highly comical.* He sung some flash songs '—(his own *On the High-Toby Spice Flash the Muzzle*, no doubt, among them)—' on the way, and I contrived to muster up one or two myself, much to Scrope Davies's surprise and diversion. The scene of action beyond Crawley, thirty-two miles from town ; the combatants Randall and Turner, the former an Irishman, which was lucky, as it gave me some sort of interest in the contest. The thing altogether not so horrid as I expected.' (It lasted two hours and twenty minutes, and Keats, who saw it, ' tapped his fingers on the window pane,' to give Cowden Clarke an idea of the rapidity of the Nonpareil's hits) ' Turner's face was a good deal de-humanised, but Randall the conqueror had hardly a scratch. . . . A beautiful sunshine broke out . . . and *had there been a proportionate mixture of women in the immense ring formed by the crowd, it would have been a very brilliant spectacle.*'

To be done with Jackson :—He ' showed me ' (MOORE, 23rd Feb. 1828) two or three letters of Lord B., which I copied out. Said he had often seen B.'s foot, which had been turned round with instruments, the limb altogether a little wasted ; could run very fast. In talking of his courage, said nobody could be more fearless ; showed great spirit always ' in coming up to the blows.'

LETTER xxxiii. p. 43.
To the Honourable Mrs. Byron :—The writer's mother. ' Thus addressed always by Lord Byron, but without any right to the distinction.'—MOORE.
I do not know that I resemble Jean Jacques Rousseau :— Mrs. Byron had a fancy that her son, before he was twenty, was like Rousseau ; and, says Byron in one of his journals (*Detached Thoughts*), ' Mme. de Stael used to say so too in 1813, and *The Edinburgh Review* has something of the same sort in its critique on the fourth Canto of *Childe Harold*. I can't see any resemblance :—he wrote prose ; I verse : he was of the people ; I of the aristocracy : he was a philosopher ; I am none : he

published his first work at forty; I mine at eighteen: his first
essay brought him universal applause; mine the contrary: he
married his housekeeper; I could not keep house with my wife:
he thought all the world in a plot against him; my little world
seems to think me in a plot against it, if I may judge by their
abuse in print and coterie: he liked botany; I like flowers, herbs,
and trees, but know nothing of their pedigrees: he wrote music;
I limit my knowledge of it to what I catch by *ear*—I never could
learn anything by *study*, not even a *language*—it was all by rote
and ear, and memory: he had a *bad* memory; I *had*, at least,
an excellent one (ask Hodgson the poet—a good judge, for he
has an astonishing one): he wrote with hesitation and care; I
with rapidity, and rarely with pains: *he* could never ride, nor
swim, nor "was cunning of fence"; *I* am an excellent swimmer,
a decent, though not at all a dashing, rider (having staved in a
rib at eighteen, in the course of scampering), and was sufficient
of fence, particularly of the Highland broadsword,—not a bad
boxer, when I could keep my temper, which was difficult, but
which I strove to do ever since I knocked down Mr. Purling, and
put his knee-pan out (with the gloves on), in Angelo's and Jackson's rooms in 1806, during the sparring,—and I was, besides, a
very fair cricketer,—one of the Harrow eleven, when we played
against Eton in 1805. Besides, Rousseau's way of life, his
country, his manners, his whole character, were so very different,
that I am at a loss to conceive how such a comparison could have
arisen, as it has done three several times, and all in rather a
remarkable manner. I forgot to say that *he* was also short-
sighted, and that hitherto my eyes have been the contrary, to such
a degree that, in the largest theatre of Bologna, I distinguished
and read some busts and inscriptions, painted near the stage, from
a box so distant and so *darkly* lighted, that none of the company
(composed of young and very bright-eyed people, some of them in
the same box) could make out a letter, and thought it was a
trick, though I had never been in that theatre before. Altogether, I think myself justified in thinking the comparison not
well founded. I don't say this out of pique, for Rousseau was
a great man; and the thing, if true, were flattering enough;—but
I have no idea of being pleased with the chimera.'

LETTER XXXV. p. 45.

My dear Hodgson:—Francis Hodgson (1781-1852) was the son
of James Hodgson, Rector of Keston, and Master (by the grace

LETTERS

of Jenkinson, first **Lord** Liverpool) of **Whitgift's** foundation at
Croydon. Here **he learned his** rudiments ; and in 1794 he **was
sent to** Eton, where he had **for schoolfellows Henry Drury, Scrope**
Davies, Charles Skinner Matthews, **Sumner, afterwards Archbishop
of Canterbury,** and William Lamb, **afterwards Lord Melbourne.**
In **1799** he went **(naturally) to** King's, **and there he fore-**
gathered with Denman, Merivale, and Robert Bland. In 1806 he
got a mastership at Eton ; and from **1808 to 1814 he was a tutor** at
King's. He appears to have fallen in with Byron in **1807,** and the
friendship grew apace, till in **1809 you find him a guest at New-**
stead. Like most **of the Byron set, and to a greater degree than
any but Byron** himself, he was fluent in rhyme. One of his critics
remarks that he '**literally** appears to think in **verse** ' ; he certainly
'**dropped into poetry'** with an ease and with an air which must have
been uncommon even in that scribbling age ; and in this same year,
having already translated Juvenal (1807), and **been pleasantly con-**
trasted with Gifford, and done a great deal of reviewing **for the**
Critical and the *Monthly,* of which last he was practically Editor,
he published his *Lady Jane Grey,* **a** *Tale* *in* *Two Books: With*
Miscellaneous Poems in English and **Latin,** the harbinger **of a**
whole cloud of published verses, **and began to write for the**
Quarterly (Gifford was an old friend of his father's). **In this**
same year, too, **he** intercepted and detained Moore's challenge **to
the author** of *English Bards,* and made that friendship possible
which began (at a dinner **at** Rogers's) soon after Byron's return.
In 1811 he is found calling **on** his noble friend **to cut** short his
tour and make love and verse at home :—

> Return, my Byron, to Britannia's fair,
>   To that soft pow'r which shares the bliss it yields ;
> Return to Freedom's pure and vigorous air,
>   To Love's own groves and Glory's native fields.

The tour being done, he bursts anew into apostrophic song :—

> Alone, my Byron, at Harrovian springs—
> Yet not alone—thy joyous Hodgson sings, etc.

Indeed, the two were on terms of peculiar intimacy. Hodgson
was deeply concerned for Byron's soul, and at Newstead Harness
heard him argue for Christianity to such a purpose and in such a
spirit that he could not, 'at a distance of more than fifty years,'
recall the experience 'without a deep feeling of admiration for the
judicious zeal and affectionate earnestness (often speaking with
tears in his eyes) which Dr. Hodgson evinced in his advocacy of

the truth.' In the same spirit, when Byron found that Hodgson, who had engaged to pay his father's debts, was unable to marry until that engagement was fulfilled, he gave him a thousand pounds, posted to Oxford to see the young lady's mother, and succeeded in making the marriage (1815).

In 1814 Hodgson made the acquaintance of Mrs. Leigh, with whom he was soon on the friendliest and the most confidential terms—(they continued till the end)—and broke ground with Miss Milbanke by writing to her the particulars of a certain appearance in the Senate House, when Byron was received by the assembled youth with peal on peal of 'the most rapturous applause.' In 1816 he came to London at Mrs. Leigh's request, and wrote twice to Lady Byron in the interest of peace and his friend. It was to no purpose, as we know, and Byron went into banishment. Out of it he writes thus of Hodgson, who had taken orders, and had been presented (1816) to the living of Bakewell, in Derbyshire :—

'I hear that Hodgson is your neighbour. . . . You will find him an excellent-hearted fellow, as well as one of the cleverest; a little, perhaps, too much japanned by preferment in the Church and the tuition of youth, as well as inoculated with the disease of domestic felicity, besides being overrun with fine feelings about women and constancy . . . but otherwise a very worthy man. . . . Pray remember me to him, and say I know not which to envy most—his neighbourhood, him, or you.'

Hodgson, on his part, too much japanned or not, was ever a devout Byronian. He was one of the mourners at Hucknall, and for some time thought of writing his dead friend's life. He abandoned the idea as soon as he heard that the work had been assigned to Moore, and gave that writer (who speaks of him with unfailing cordiality, and notes that he is considered 'a blessing' to his parish) all the help he could. In 1836 Lord Melbourne offered him the Archdeaconry of Derby; in 1838 he married (his first wife, a sister of Mrs. Henry Drury, had died some five or six years before) a daughter of his old friend Denman ; in 1840 he was made Provost of Eton. The story of his work in this last capacity need not here be told. Enough that he died in harness; that he wrote verses (as Byron said he would write verses) 'to the end of the chapter'; and that he left behind him none but friends or admirers, or both. (See JAMES T. HODGSON, *Memoir*, etc., London, 1878.)

My volunteer correspondent:—Nothing is discoverable concerning the mysterious Haynes.

Hobhouse is on his way up to town :—The son of a man of fortune, who contested Bristol, sat for Grampound, and in

LETTERS

1812 was made a baronet, John Cam Hobhouse was born at
Redland (near Bristol), and was partly educated at a local dis-
senting school, whence he was sent to Westminster (on the advice
of his father's friend, the Marquess of Lansdowne), and so to
Trinity College, Cambridge. There he met Byron, and 'after
hating me,' the latter writes, 'for two years, because I wore a
white hat and a *grey* coat, and rode a *grey* horse (as he himself
says), took me into his good graces, because I had written some
poetry.' At Cambridge, Byron adds, 'he did great things.' That
is, 'he founded the Cambridge "Whig Club"'—(this Hobhouse
denied with heat, like the good Radical he was)—'and the Amicable
Society, which was dissolved in consequence of the members constantly quarrelling, and made himself very popular with "us
youth," and no less formidable to all tutors, professors, and heads
of colleges.' Being a man of wit and parts, with a genuine
tincture of letters, he began, of course, by making verses. The
lines on Bowles in the First Edition of *English Bards* are his :—

> 'Stick to thy sonnets, man !—at least they sell.
> Or take the only path that open lies
> For modern worthies who would hope to rise :
> Fix on some well-known name, and, bit by bit,
> Pare off the merits of his worth and wit ;
> On each alike employ the critic's knife,
> And when a comment fails, prefix a life ;
> Hint certain failings, faults before unknown,
> Review forgotten lies, and add your own ;
> Let no disease, let no misfortune 'scape,
> And print, if luckily deform'd, his shape :
> Thus shall the world, quite undeceived at last,
> Cleave to their present wits, and quit their past ;
> Bards once revered no more with favour view,
> But give their modern sonneteers their due ;
> Thus with the dead may living merit cope,
> Thus Bowles may triumph o'er the shade of Pope ':—

and in 1809, he published a certain miscellany—(Skinner Matthews,
with whom, as his most intimate friend, he was very often at variance, used to call it the *Miss-sell-any*)—of *Imitations and Translations from the Antient and Modern Classics; Together with Original
Poems Never Before Published.* But from Falmouth onward,
despite the desperate terms in which Byron presents him :—

> Hobhouse, muttering fearful curses,
> As the hatchway down he rolls,
> Now his breakfast, now his verses,
> Vomits forth, and d——ns our souls :—

322

NOTES

he appears to have left rhyme to his friend; for he set forth the results of their expedition, as he perceived them, in a solid volume of stout and serviceable prose. This was the book now known as *Travels in Albania, Roumelia, and Other Provinces of Turkey* (1812), which went into a Second Edition in a year or so, and was reprinted in 1855. A constant guest at Newstead, he was present (as best man) at the Marriage (2nd January 1815: it was to him that the bride addressed the often-quoted 'If I am not happy, it will be my own fault'); and he served his friend most loyally through those troubled and desperate days which preceded the Exile (25th April 1816). In the summer of the same year he joined that friend at Diodati; and some circumstances of their life are set forth in the *Swiss Journal*—(addressed to Augusta Leigh)—extracts from which were published by Moore. (It was at this time that, as he tells you at the very outset of his *Italy* (1859), he saw Byron 'deface with great care' the 'atheist and philanthropist written in Greek,' which Shelley had inscribed after his own name in an inn-album.) In 1817, after a round of travel, he rejoined Byron at La Mira, and found him deep in the Fourth *Harold*. 'It'—the first draft—'was much shorter than it afterwards became, and it did not remark on several objects which appeared to me peculiarly worthy of notice. I made a list of these objects, and, in conversation with him, gave him reasons for the selection. The result was the poem as it now appears, and he then engaged me to write notes for the whole canto.' Most of this work was done at Venice—'where I had the advantage of consulting the Ducal Library'; and in the sequel the commentary grew to so great a bulk that only a part could be attached to the poem, the rest of it being published separately (*Historical Illustrations to the Fourth Canto of 'Childe Harold'; Containing Dissertations on the Ruins of Rome, and an Essay on Italian Literature*, London, 1818). Byron's regard for the writer was instantly attested by his Dedication (2nd January 1818) of his magnificent achievement 'to one whom I have known long and accompanied far, whom I have found wakeful over my sickness and kind in my sorrow, glad in my prosperity and firm in my adversity, true in counsel and trusty in peril—to a friend often tried and never found wanting;—to' John Cam Hobhouse, already (1816) the dedicatee of *The Siege of Corinth*.

There was another meeting (at Pisa) in 1822. These were the years of *Cain*, the *Vision*, the *Juan* (Hobhouse was one of that 'cursed puritanical committee' which on moral grounds objected to the publication of this last), Missolonghi; and then, in the July of

323

1824, he, as Byron's intimate and executor, took a boat, and boarded the *Florida* in Sandgate Creek. 'Three dogs' (he writes) 'that had belonged to my friend were playing on the deck. I could hardly bear to look at them. . . . I cannot describe what I felt during the five or six hours of our passage. I was the last person who shook hands with Byron when he left England in 1816. I recollected his waving his cap to me, as the packet bounded off on a curling wave, from the pier-head at Dover, and here I was now coming back to England with his corpse.' It was John Murray, not Hobhouse himself, who, writing in Hobhouse's name and without Hobhouse's instructions, was politely snubbed by Dean Ireland in the matter of a place for Byron in the Abbey among his peers. But Hobhouse was responsible for all the other circumstances of the obsequies : from the disembarkation of the coffin at the London Docks Buoy—('There were many boats round the ship . . . and the shore was crowded with spectators')—and the passage of the barge to Westminster Stairs, to the deposition in the little church at Hucknall Torkard, which, with the churchyard, was 'so crowded that we could scarcely follow the body up the aisle.' ('I was told,' he adds, 'that the place was crowded till a late hour in the evening, and that the vault was not closed till the next morning.') When he left Hucknall Torkard the Corporation of Nottingham offered him the freedom of the city ; but 'I had no inclination for the ceremonies with which the acceptance of the honour,' etc., and 'I therefore declined it.'

And his work as Byron's friend and champion was in nowise done when he turned his back upon Hucknall Churchyard. With his share in the destruction of the MS. of Byron's *Memoir*, as with his action in defence of Byron's reputation in 1830-31, it will be convenient to deal elsewhere. In this place I shall but sketch his part in that very scandalous incident in the story of Westminster Abbey—the closing of its doors upon the effigies of perhaps the greatest, and certainly the most famous, Englishman of his generation. Hobhouse, then, was largely instrumental in forming a Committee, and in procuring subscriptions, for the erection of a memorial to Byron ; and among those associated with him to this end were Goethe, Scott, Campbell, Rogers, Moore, Malcolm, Lockhart, Bowles, Mackintosh, Jeffrey, Stratford Canning, Charles Kemble, Isaac Disraeli, and Peel ; with Lords Holland, Sligo, Lansdowne, Cowper, Normanby, Nugent, and Dudley, the Duke of Devonshire, and the Earl and Countess of Jersey. At Hobhouse's suggestion the work was undertaken by

NOTES

Thorwaldsen, for so small a sum as a thousand pounds. But Dean
Ireland refused the Poet's statue, as he had barred out the Poet's
body; and it lay at the Custom House, unpacked, for many years.
Dr. Ireland was succeeded in 1842 by Dr. Turton, afterwards
Bishop of Ely; Byron's right to a place in Poets' Corner was denied
by Dr. Turton, as twice before by Dr. Ireland; his denial was
applauded by the then Bishop of London (Blomfield) in his place
in the House of Lords; and Hobhouse replied to his Lordship
(1844) in a pamphlet, privately printed, but reproduced as an
appendix to *Travels in Albania*, which is excellent reading
still. It was to no purpose. The Abbey doors are closed on
Byron yet; and the Thorwaldsen, after nearly half a century
of seclusion, was at last accepted by Master Whewell (largely at
the instance of the Messrs. De la Pryme) for the Library of Byron's
old college, whence it is not likely to be removed.

'A man,' says Byron, 'of learning, of talent, of steadiness, and
of honour': a man, as we can see, of singular alertness of mind,
energy of temperament, integrity of purpose, and strength of
character and will: Hobhouse is honourably remembered, apart
from the friendship which is his title to enduring fame, as an in-
fluential politician, and as a diligent, adroit, and faithful servant of
the State. An original Radical and Reformer, he began, being one
of the Rota Club, by getting committed to Newgate for a breach
of privilege; went on to be elected (with Burdett) for Westminster,
which he represented for thirteen years; was Secretary for War,
Chief Secretary for Ireland, Commissioner for Woods and Forests,
and twice President of the Board of Control; and in 1857 was
raised to the Peerage as Lord Broughton de Gyfford. Ere he died,
he found energy enough to write the five volumes of his *Memoirs
of a Long Life*. They are printed, but not published; but they
are partially known through an *Edinburgh* review (April 1871), the
work, it is understood, of the late Henry Reeve, to which I am indebted for certain facts and extracts embodied in this Note.

LETTER xxxvi. p. 47.
The 'Arch-Fiend's' name:—Francis Jeffrey, Editor of *The Edinburgh Review*. As to the 'real orthodoxy of that name,' I know
nothing.
The Carnifex of James II. :—'Bloody Jefferies.'
Hardwicke (*where Mary was confined*):—Hodgson was at this
time deep in what he called 'a poem' on the subject of Mary Queen
of Scots.

325

LETTERS

You do not tell me if Gifford, etc. :—William Gifford (1757-1826) —'the asp, Gifford,' as Mr. Swinburne calls him—began life as a shoemaker's apprentice ; had an extremely arduous and difficult youth ; raised himself to eminence and authority by sheer force of character and intelligence—both limited and in some sort vitiated, no doubt, but both indomitable and real ; and, having edited *The Anti-Jacobin* (1797-98), was made Editor of the *Quarterly*, on its establishment in 1809.   He did good service to literature in *The Baviad* (1794), *The Mæviad* (1795), *The Epistle to Peter Pindar* (1800)—(in the two first he utterly annihilated the silly set of poetasters known as the Della-Cruscans ; and in the second he checked the insolence of as bold and hard-hitting a ruffian as the journalism of the time could boast)—and, especially, in his editions of *Massinger* (1805), *Jonson* (1816), and *Ford* (1827), which contain much sound work, and set forth the results of wide reading and the operations of a clear, vigorous, clever, and less prejudiced than narrow mind.   Also his *Juvenal* (1802) has a certain spiteful merit, but is not much read now.   For his literary temper was atrocious ; his criticisms, whether aggressive or corrective, seem the effect of downright malignity ; in the long-run you are tempted to side with his victims.   Byron, however, was always a 'fervent' of Pope ; to Byron Gifford represented the Pope tradition at its best ; for Gifford Byron entertained an immense (and very fatuous) respect ('I have always considered him,' he writes to Murray a very little while before his death, 'as my literary father, and myself as his "prodigal son"') ; Byron was ever ready to submit himself to Gifford's judgment ; and to Gifford Byron 'gave *carte blanche* to strike out or alter anything at his pleasure in *The Siege of Corinth*' as it was passing through the press.   Monstrous though it seem to us now, in fact, this alliance between Leviathan and a blind-worm (so to speak) was genuine, and the sincerity of neither party to it can be impugned.   At the date of the present letter it was merely one-sided ; for Gifford scarce recked at all of Byron's existence, and Byron himself was only the poet of a lot of *juvenilia*.   But it was already possible, by reason of Byron's simplicity and good faith ; and in a very few years it became a rather potent fact.

LETTER xxxvii. p. 49.

Tell D'Egville his dress shall be returned :—James H. D'Egville was appointed Acting-Manager and Director of the Opera by Mr. Taylor (5th October 1807), and removed by the decree of arbitration signed by Lord Headfort and Mr. William Ogilvie (January

NOTES

11, 1808). D'Egville (who taught Kean dancing, by the way) was tried and found guilty in the Court of King's Bench of an assault on Edward Waters, principal Mortgagee of Mr. Taylor's share in the King's Theatre; and in *The Opera Glass* (London, 1808) Waters accuses him of being 'a professor of French republican principles.' Indeed, 'the letters Mr. Taylor wrote to the Duke of Portland are said to be pregnant with curious anecdotes of Mr. D'Egville's political conduct, in both London and Paris, in Robespierre's sanguinary days.'

LETTER xxxviii. p. 49.

One from B. Drury:—Benjamin, Henry Drury's elder brother, a Master at Eton: apparently the Drury who (according to Gronow; but the dates scarce fit) used to post to London, spend the fag-end of the night in taverns with Edmund Kean, and post to Eton back again, under Keate's nose and outside Keate's knowledge. It is further told of him (in J. T. Hodgson's *Memoir*) that he was wont to take advantage, 'to the infinite amusement of those present,' of the deafness of a certain Provost of King's, 'by making most uncomplimentary remarks to him in the style of a person conversing upon some ordinary topic': the said 'observations' being 'invariably received with the blandest courtesy.'

Robert Gregson, of pugilistic notoriety:—'Bob Gregson, P. P.' (='Poet of Pugilism'), was born (1778) in Lancashire; 'filled the situation of Captain of the Liverpool Wigan Packet for several years with credit and respect'; fought his way to the Championship of his County; came to London, and commenced pugilist; was twice beaten by Gully (1783-1863) for the Championship, once in October 1807 and again in May 1808; was beaten for the Championship by Cribb (1781-1848) in February 1809; and, retiring from the Profession, was for some time landlord of the Castle Tavern, Holborn—'Bob's Chophouse,' it was called—a headquarters of the Fancy during the brightest years of the Ring. As he couldn't make the Castle pay (he was succeeded by the eminent Tom Belcher, who could) he left London for Dublin, where he set up first 'A School for Teaching the Art of Self-defence,' and next was landlord of The Punch-House, Moor Street. He died in Liverpool in 1824. He was a boxer of tremendous energy, courage, and bottom (in his first fight with Gully as in his battle with Cribb, he had his men beaten to a standstill, so that it was feared that Gully would die, while Cribb fell down, and 'did not recover for some few minutes'); a fine figure of a man (he stood six feet one, and is reported to have sat

327

LETTERS

to Lawrence, and to have been lectured upon by Carlisle, Professor of Anatomy at the Royal Academy); a lover of tunes and verses, and no bad hand at a 'chaunt'; withal, a person of manners and sentiment. See *Tom Cribb's Memorial to Congress* :—

> My eyes ! how prettily Bob writes !
> Talk of your *Camels, Hogs*, and *Crabs*,
> And twenty more such Pidcock frights—
> Bob 's worth a hundred of these dabs, etc.

It is characteristic of the age that Ben Drury, probably a parson, and certainly an Eton Master, should be found pleading a bankrupt boxer's cause ; and it is characteristic of Byron, who was afterwards a member of the Pugilistic Club—one of the hundred-and-fifty Corinthians, that is, with whose countenance and inside whose ropes and stakes all decent mills were done,—who made, among others, the match between Dogherty and Tom Belcher, who saw (he says) all Cribb's fights, and who may very well have seen both of Gregson's with Gully, that he should be found willing, impecunious as he is, to come to a bankrupt boxer's aid. For these were the Golden Years of the Ring ; when Pugilism was to the people of England all, and more than all, that Cricket and Football are to the people of England now ; so that a trial between two famous artists—as Cribb and Molineaux, or Spring and Langan, or Painter and Oliver—would be fought in the presence of some twenty thousand men, the most of whom had ridden, or driven, or padded the hoof, a many miles to see, at the risk of broken heads and ravished pockets ; while £100,000 would change hands on the event. We have seen (*ante*, p. 316, Note to Letter xxxi.) how Mr. Jackson, the King of Milling, who did the most of any man that ever lived to make Pugilism respectable (as Jem Belcher made it artistic and heroic), kept, and deserved to keep, the best of company, and how two poets, Keats, the high-priest of beauty (and the most pugnacious of mortals), and 'Anacreon' Moore witnessed the great affair between Randall and Turner. This was in 1818, ten years after Ben Drury's appeal ; and in 1807, eleven years before it, here (according to the late Thomas Constable's *Archibald Constable and His Literary Correspondents*, Edinburgh, 1873) is how Alexander Gibson Hunter, 'Forfarshire laird and Edinburgh bookseller,' the Great Mogul's first partner, in company with 'the Bailie' (his father), fared forth on Fox Maule's coach, 'to see the great fight between Belcher and Cribb,' at what he calls 'Mosely Hurst near Hampton Court' (Moulsey was a favourite spot

NOTES

with Mr. Jackson and his lieges; for at Bushey lived H.R.H. the Duke of Clarence, and His Highness loved the sport). 'Mosely Hurst,' says Hunter, 'is the most beautiful meadow I almost ever saw, hard and smooth as velvet, and of great extent'; and although it had been bruited abroad that the ring would be pitched at Newmarket, which sent forth 'many a hundred on the wrong track,' yet had we 'fully 10,000, I suppose, present as it was, and many hundreds of carriages, horses, carts, *etc.*' Captain Barclay of Urie—(who had made the match for Cribb, and was presently to train him for the historic *reprise* with Molineaux)— 'received us, and put us across the river in a boat'; and 'among the gentlemen present were the Duke of Kent'—a familiar title, is it not? —'Mr. Wyndham (*sic*), Lord Archibald Hamilton (a famous hand, I am told), Lord Kinnaird, Mr. T. Sheridan, *etc. etc.*,' while 'the honourable Barclay (*sic*) Craven was judge.' In pushing to the ringside, the Bailie got 'made a *wild goose*' (that is, his hat was knocked over his eyes, and when he put up his hands to save it, he wasn't allowed to put them down again while a single pocket remained unvisited); and when at last we reached it, we found the circle of carts and carriages 'so close and so broad, and such a crowd and squeeze of people, that I could neither force my way through nor get back,' so 'I crawled through below the carriages, at the immense hazard of death from carriage wheels, kicks of horses, etc.' For the fight itself, enough that Cribb was a renowned 'glutton'; that Jem Belcher, the man of genius who had re-inspired and renewed the art, and who stands to Pugilism much as 'the Doctor' stands to Cricket, had lost an eye at rackets four years before, but was still capable of administering tremendous punishment; that it lasted some forty minutes; and that 'the great science and power displayed by both parties made me consider this a much less cruel and more manly and entertaining amusement than I could have believed possible.' Hunter, remember, was a Scot abroad; and in Scotland Pugilism never thrived. But in England Pugilism was a part of the nation's life and a moving factor in the nation's art and politics. When Moore had to appeal (in the Whig interest) to the general sentiment of the people, he cast his argument in the lingo of the Fancy, as in *Tom Cribb to Big Ben*—('Big Ben!' the *nom de guerre* of a famous bruiser, was a popular nickname for the Regent)—and *Tom Cribb's Memorial to Congress*. Hazlitt's account of the fight between Bill Neate and the terrific Hickman is among the classic pages of modern prose. Not by any means the worst of Keats's friend, John Hamilton Reynolds, are the verses he found at the ring-side, the Sonnet on Randall : —

Good with both hands, and only ten stone four :—

and the rest. In a famous speech Windham compared the spirit of those who watched the fight between Maddox and Richmond to that of the combatants at Talavera and Vimeira. In 1826 the Duke himself is found subscribing £30 towards a purse to be fought for under his eye, by Young Dutch Sam and another, on the course at Ascot. When Eldon, as he passed into the House for a big debate on Catholic Emancipation, stopped to shake hands with Plunkett (1828), 'That reminds me,' quoth Lyttelton to the Irishman, 'of Gregson and Gully shaking hands before they *set-to*.' It is told of Grey, the Foreign Secretary in 'the Talents,' that he sent an express, 'upon public service,' to Windham (Secretary for War) with the result of the second mill between these same two heroes. And it is told of Edmund Kean that he found the supreme moment of his Richard, when, in Hazlitt's phrase, 'he fought like one drunk with wounds,' in the last effort of a beaten boxer. A dreadful age, no doubt: for all its solid foundations, of faith and dogma in the Church and of virtue and solvency in the State, a fierce, drunken, gambling, 'keeping,' adulterous, high-living, hard-drinking, hard-hitting, brutal age. But it was Byron's; and *Don Juan* and *The Giaour* are as naturally its outcomes as *Absalom and Achitophel* is an expression of the Restoration, and *In Memoriam* a product of Victorian England.

LETTER xxxix. p. 51.

The Couplet on Lord C. may be scratched out :— 'Lord C.' is Frederick Howard (1748-1825), Fifth Earl of Carlisle, one of the Commissioners to America, 1778; Viceroy of Ireland, 1780; thanked by the House for 'the wisdom and purity of his administration,' 1782; Author of *Tragedies and Poems* (1801), *Thoughts on the Present Condition of the Stage* (1808), and so forth. A son of Isabella Byron, sister to the Wicked (Fifth) Lord, the Court of Chancery had made him Byron's guardian, and to him Byron dedicated *Hours of Idleness*. The compliment was coldly—not to say ungraciously—received. But Byron, whether he resented it or not, had no mind to quarrel, and in *English Bards* began by 'Crowning a new Roscommon in Carlisle.' Before the copy went to press, however, he had applied to Lord Carlisle for certain information (see *post*, p. 333, Note to Letter xlvii.), and had been snubbed. Also, being 'under the impression that it was customary for a young peer, on first taking his seat, to have some friend to in-

NOTES

troduce him, he wrote to remind Lord Carlisle that he should be of age at the beginning of the session, and received a mere formal, and, as it appeared to him, cold reply, acquainting him with the technical work of procedure on such occasions' (MOORE). As was inevitable, the couplet came out, and, in the end, the attack was delivered as we know it now :—

> No more will cheer with renovating smile
> The paralytic puling of Carlisle.

That Byron lived to regret his bitterness is shown by a letter to Rogers (1814) in which he asks if there is ' any chance of a possibility of making it up with Carlisle,' and by the 'young, gallant Howard' stanza in the Third *Harold* (xxix-xxxiii). With regard to the origin of the constraint between Byron and Carlisle (see *ante,* p. 298, Note to Letter iii.), Murray's Editor quotes ('from two unpublished letters ') these extracts :—

'Nov. 11, 1804. You mistake me if you think I dislike Lord Carlisle. I respect him, and might like him did I know him better. For him *my mother has an antipathy*—why, I know not. I am afraid he could be but of little use to me ; but I dare say he would assist me if he could ; so I take the will for the deed, and am obliged to him, exactly in the same manner as if he succeeded in his efforts.'—' Nov. 21, 1804. To Lord Carlisle make my warmest acknowledgments. I feel more gratitude than I can well express. I am truly obliged to him for his endeavours, and am perfectly satisfied with your explanation of his reserve, though I was hitherto afraid it might proceed from personal dislike. For the future, I shall consider him as more my friend than I have hitherto been *taught* to think.'

Yet five years afterwards the ward was so little acquainted with his guardian as not to know of the 'nervous disorder,' which afflicted Lord Carlisle, and to which—to Byron's indignation—it was supposed that 'paralytic puling' was a direct and open reference.

Couplets on Mr. Crabbe :—' I consider Crabbe and **Coleridge** as the first of these times in point of power and genius.' **Thus Byron** (1816) in his annotated copy of the suppressed Edition of *English Bards.* But it was enough for him that Crabbe wrote the heroic couplet, and was, in his way, a follower of Pope.

Gifford, Sotheby, M'Neil :—For *Gifford*, see *ante,* p. 326, Note to Letter xxxvi. Of *Sotheby* (William, F.R.S., etc.), enough to note that he adapted Wieland (1798), Virgil (1800), and Homer (1830) ; wrote tragedies—*Julian and Agnes* (1801), *The Siege of Cuzco* (1800),—and poems—*Saul* (1807), *Constance of Castile* (1810), a *Song of Triumph on the Peace* (1814) ; was (in a word) as persevering, ardent, and long-winded a writer of mediocre verse as the century has seen. *M'Neil* (Hector, 1746-1818) wrote *Scotland's Scaith* (a poor

331

enough teetotal 'poem') and *The Waes of War*. He was a vulgarly popular (Scots) poet in his day, but is chiefly remembered as the author of such songs as *Kelvin Grove* and *My Boy Tammie*.

LETTER xlvi. p. 55.

After the couplets concerning Naldi and Catalani :—See *English Bards* : 'Then let Ausonia, skilled in every art,' etc. Naldi (1765-1810), a Neapolitan buffo, sang at the King's Theatre for some fifteen years, and was especially delightful in *Cosi Fan Tutti* and *Il Fanatico per la Musica*. Angelica Catalani (1779-1849), the illustrious soprano, came out at Venice in 1795; sang all over the Continent; and crossed to London, where she became the rage, so that as much as £2000 was paid her for a single musical *fête*, in 1806.

LETTER xlvii. p. 55.

Poor Falkland's death:—Charles John, the Eighth Viscount (1768-1809), Captain, R.N., was mortally wounded in a duel by a Mr. Powell, and died the same day. The quarrel appears to have taken place in the Argyle Institution (or some such place), which was part hell and part assembly rooms. Hence the lines in *English Bards* :—

> The jovial caster 's set, and seven 's the nick,
> Or—done!—a thousand on the coming trick!
> If, mad with loss, existence 'gins to tire,
> And all your hope or wish is to expire,
> Here 's Powell's pistol ready for your life,
> And, kinder still, two Pagets for your wife.

In a note to this passage Byron writes :—'I knew the late Lord Falkland well. On Sunday night I beheld him presiding at his own table, in all the honest pride of hospitality; on Wednesday morning, at three o'clock, I saw stretched before me all that remained of courage, feeling, and a host of passions. He was a gallant and successful officer : his faults were the faults of a sailor [those of dissipation]—as such, Britons will forgive them. He died like a brave man in a better cause ; for had he fallen in like manner on the deck of the frigate to which he was just appointed, his last moments would have been held up by his countrymen as an example to succeeding heroes.' In a letter to Hanson (8th February 1809), Byron, after remarking that he is 'dunned from noon till twilight,' and that he must have money or 'quit the country,' adds this :—'If I do not get my seat immediately, I shall sail with Lord Falkland in the *Désirée* frigate for Sicily.' Yet, soon after the duel, says Moore, he 'reminded the unfortunate widow that he was to

NOTES

be godfather to her infant; the child was christened Byron-Charles-
Ferdinand-Plantagenet Cary, and after the ceremony the poet
inserted a five hundred pound note in a breakfast cup . . . not
discovered till he had left the house.'

The affidavits from Carhais, Cornwall:—To take his seat in
the Lords, Byron had to produce evidence of the marriage at
Caerhayes of his grandfather, Admiral Byron, with Miss Trevanion.
This was not easily done; for the ceremony had been performed
in a private chapel.   In the meantime Lord Carlisle (see *ante,*
p. 330, Note to Letter xxxix.) was asked for certain relevant information, which information he declined to give.

LETTER xlviii. p. 57.
London is full of the Duke's business:—The investigation into
Colonel Wardle's charges against the Duke of York and his
mistress, Mary Anne Clarke.

Carry you to the ' limner':—This was George L. Sanders (1774-
1846), a Kinghorn (Fife) man, who began as a coach-painter; for
some time painted miniatures and portraits, and gave drawing-
lessons in Edinburgh; came to London in 1807; had sittings from
the Prince of Wales, the Duke of Cumberland, and others; and
became in some sort fashionable.

LETTER xlix. p. 58.
Full of printing resolution:—That is, as regards the *Miss-sell-
any,* for which see *ante,* p. 322, Note to Letter xxxv.

LETTER l. p. 59.
Strongly recommended to me by Dr. Butler:—The Pomposus
of 'Recollections of Childhood.'   The two, as we have seen, were
reconciled ere Byron left England.

Robert and William:—Robert Rushton, son of one of Byron's
tenants, the 'little page,' and William Fletcher, the 'staunch
yeoman' of the 'Good Night' in the First *Harold.*

There is a picture in oil of me:—The full-length painted by
Sanders.   (See above, Note to Letter xlviii.)

Ask them to copy the others:—*I.e.* those of his friends.

LETTER li. p. 61.
The Cock is crowing, etc.:—This quotation is from Henry Carey's
burletta (1734) of Fielding's *Tom Thumb the Great* (1730).

NOTE:—Certain sentences in this and the following letter are
here restored from the originals in Mr. Alfred Morrison's Collection of Autographs.

LETTERS

LETTER lii. p. 62.

And ' all that,' as *Orator Henley said :*—' Henley, in one of his publications entitled *Oratory Transactions*, engaged to execute singly what would sprain a dozen of modern doctors of the tribe of Issachar—to write, read, and study twelve hours a day, and yet appear as untouched by the yoke as if he never wore it—to teach in one year what schools or universities teach in five ; and he furthermore pledged himself to persevere in his bold scheme, until he had ' put the Church, *and all that*, in danger.'—MOORE.

The great apostle, etc. :—This is ' England's wealthiest son,' the William Beckford (1759-1844) of *Vathek* (1787), that masterpiece of wit, imagination, and narrative, written at twenty-two, and in a single sitting of ' three days and two nights,' during which time ' I never took off my clothes,' so that ' the severe application made me very ill.' At the time of Byron's writing he was still the Beckford of Fonthill and its Tower, which he did not sell till 1822. But the Beckford of Cintra (1794-96) was already so completely of the past, that Byron, not long after this very Letter, could address him in these terms :—

> Here didst thou dwell, here schemes of pleasure plan,
> Beneath yon mountain's ever beauteous brow :
> But now, as if a thing unblest by Man,
> Thy fairy dwelling is as lone as thou !
> Here giant weeds a passage scarce allow
> To halls deserted, portals gaping wide :
> Fresh lessons to the thinking bosom, how
> Vain are the pleasaunces on earth supplied ;
> Swept into wrecks anon by Time's ungentle tide !

In 1822 he became the Beckford of Bath, where he built him another Tower, and shut himself up with his books, his pictures and statues, his moods and humours and caprices ; and then in 1834 he published his third book, the excellent series of letters entitled *Italy: with Sketches of Spain and Portugal.* In that year, too, he reprinted his *Biographical Memoirs of Extraordinary Painters,* written at seventeen, and still amusing reading of a kind ; and in 1835 he published his *Recollections of an Excursion to the Monasteries of Alobaça and Batalha.* This is all his literary baggage ; and from the *Recollections* onward till his death he was a resolute, invisible recluse. But at eleven he had succeeded to the worth of a million of money ; and he had sat in Parliament (once for Eccles and once for Hindon), known the greatest grief that can befall a man, lived as he would with none to say him nay, pro-

NOTES

duced such a master-story as must live as long as the French in which it was written and the English into which it was translated, and thereby approved himself the best Voltairean bred in England before the coming of Benjamin Disraeli. As to Byron's description of him, this from Moore (*Diary*: 18th October 1818) may serve to eke it out :—'Beckford wishes me to go to Fonthill with R[ogers]; anxious that I should look over his *Travels* . . . and prepare them for the press. Rogers supposes he would give me something magnificent for it,—a thousand pounds, perhaps. But if he were to give me a hundred times that sum, I would not have my name coupled with his. To be Beckford's *sub*, not very desirable.'

Ld. Courtney:—William, Eleventh Earl of Courtenay (1777-1839), High Steward of the University of Oxford, Patentee of the Subpœna Office, Court of Chancery, and Governor of the Charter House School.

NOTE :—With this letter was enclosed that foretaste of the true Byron, the *Lines to Mr. Hodgson* :—

> Huzza! Hodgson, we are going,
> Our embargo's off at last.

LETTER liv. p. 65.

The women of Cadiz :—Cf. the song in the first draft of the First *Harold*, for which were substituted the quatrains 'To Inez' :—

> Oh never talk again to me
>   Of northern climes and British ladies,
> It has not been your lot to see,
>   Like me, the lovely Girl of Cadiz.
> Although her eye be not of blue,
>   Nor fair her locks, like English lasses,
> How far its own expressive hue
>   The languid azure eye surpasses!
>
> Prometheus-like, from heaven she stole
>   The fire, that through those silken lashes
> In darkest glances seems to roll,
>   From eyes that cannot hide their flashes :
> And as along her bosom steal
>   In lengthen'd flow her raven tresses,
> You'd swear each clustering lock could feel,
>   And curl'd to give her neck caresses.
>
> Our English maids are long to woo,
>   And frigid even in possession;
> And if their charms be fair to view,
>   Their lips are slow at Love's confession.

335

LETTERS

But, born beneath a brighter sun,
  For love ordain'd the Spanish maid is,
And who,—when fondly, fairly won,—
  Enchants you like the Girl of Cadiz?

The Spanish maid is no coquette,
  Nor joys to see a lover tremble ;
And if she love, or if she hate,
  Alike she knows not to dissemble.
Her heart can ne'er be bought or sold—
  Howe'er it beats, it beats sincerely ;
And though it will not bend to gold,
  'Twill love you long and love you dearly.

The Spanish girl that meets your love
  Ne'er taunts you with a mock denial,
For every thought is bent to prove
  Her passion in the hour of trial.
When thronging foemen menace Spain.
  She dares the deed and shares the danger ;
And should her lover press the plain,
  She hurls the spear, her love's avenger.

And when, beneath the evening star,
  She mingles in the gay Bolero,
Or sings to her attuned guitar
  Of Christian knight or Moorish hero,
Or counts her beads with fairy hand
  Beneath the twinkling rays of Hesper,
Or joins devotion's choral band,
  To chaunt the sweet and hallow'd vesper ;—

In each her charms the heart must move
  Of all who venture to behold her ;
Then let not maids less fair reprove
  Because her bosom is not colder :
Through many a clime 'tis mine to roam
  Where many a soft and melting maid is,
But none abroad, and few at home,
  May match the dark-eyed Girl of Cadiz.

I have seen Sir John Carr at Seville and Cadiz:—John Carr (1772-1832) was an English attorney, who, having to travel for health, wrote books about his travels, and won the nickname of 'the Jaunting Carr' thereby. He published *The Fury of Discord, a Poem* (1803); *The Stranger in France* (1803); a three-act play, *The Sea-side Hero* (1804); *A Northern Summer* (1804); *The Stranger in Ireland* (1806); *Caledonian Sketches* (1807); and *Descriptive Travels in the Southern and Eastern Parts of Spain* (1811).

Byron, whether he went on his knees or not, is not mentioned in Sir John's book. On the other hand, if he had had his will, Sir John (by an anticipation of the fitful and fantastic methods of *Don Juan*) would have lightened the effect of the First *Harold*, the MS. of which ends with these stanzas :—

> Ye, who would more of Spain and Spaniards know,
> Sights, Saints, Antiques, Arts, Anecdotes, and War,
> Go! hie ye hence to Paternoster Row—
> Are they not written in the Book of Carr,
> Green Erin's Knight and Europe's wandering star!
> Then listen, Readers, to the Man of Ink,
> Hear what he did, and sought, and wrote afar;
> All these are coop'd within one Quarto's brink,
> This borrow, steal,—don't buy,—and tell us what you think.

> There may you read, with spectacles on eyes,
> How many Wellesleys did embark for Spain,
> As if therein they meant to colonise,
> How many troops y-cross'd the laughing main
> That ne'er beheld the said return again :
> How many buildings are in such a place,
> How many leagues from this to yonder plain,
> How many relics each cathedral grace,
> And where Giralda stands on her gigantic base.

> There may you read (O Phœbus, save Sir John!
> That these my words prophetic may not err)
> All that was said, or sung, or lost, or won,
> By vaunting Wellesley or by blundering Frere,
> He that wrote half the 'Needy Knife-Grinder.'
> Thus poesy the way to grandeur paves—
> Who would not such diplomatists prefer?
> But cease, my Muse, thy speed some respite craves,
> Leave Legates to their house, and armies to their graves.

Byron, however, was better advised. And the task of bringing Carr to book fell, in the long-run, to Edward Dubois (1774-1850), author of *Old Nick* (1801), of a volume of translations from the Greek (1799), and of an edition of *The Decameron*: whose *Old Nick's Pocket Book, or Hints for a ryghte Merrie and Conceited Tour* provoked Sir John to bring an (unsuccessful) action of damages against the publisher (1808).

Swift's Barber:—'Once stopping at an inn at Dundalk, the Dean was so much amused with a prating barber, that rather than be alone he invited him to dinner. The fellow was rejoiced at this unexpected honour, and being dressed out in his best apparel came to the inn, first inquiring of the groom what the clergyman's name was who had so kindly invited him. "What the vengeance," said the servant, "don't you know Dean Swift?" At which the barber turned pale, and running into the house fell upon his knees and entreated the Dean "not to put him into print; for that he was a poor barber, had a large family to maintain, and if his reverence put him into black and white he should lose all his customers."'—*Sheridan's Life of Swift.*—MOORE.

Pray remember me to the Drurys:—'This sort of passage,' writes Mr. Hodgson in a note on his copy of this letter, 'constantly occurs in his correspondence. Nor was his interest confined to mere remembrances and inquiries after health. Were it possible to state *all* he has done for numerous friends, he would appear amiable indeed. For myself, I am bound to acknowledge, in the fullest and warmest manner, his most generous and well-timed aid; and, were my poor friend Bland alive, he would as gladly bear the like testimony;—though I have most reason, of all men, to do so.'—MOORE.

And the Davies:—For Scrope Davies, see *post*, p. 350, Note to Letter lxvi.

LETTER lv. p. 67.
The Scene of Sir H[ew] D[alrymple]'s convention :—By the Convention of Cintra, 22nd August 1808, the French agreed to evacuate Portugal, on condition that they retained their arms, etc., and were landed on a coast of France. For the rest, 'Colonel Napier, in a note in his able *History of the Peninsular War*, notices the mistake into which Lord Byron and others were led on this subject;—the signature of the Convention, as well as all the other proceedings connected with it, having taken place at a distance of thirty miles from Cintra.'—MOORE.

Admiral Cordova's family:—This was Antonio de Córdoba y Lasso (174?-1811), born at Seville (where he died); lieutenant in 1760; captured by the English in Cuba; returned to Spain in 1763; was beaten by Jervis; joined the French fleet under Bruix; sailed from Cadiz to Brest; was stationed there till the end of the war; and returned to Spain in 1802, when he was gazetted Teniente-General. He appears to have been something of a scientific officer, for he it was who prepared the chart of the Strait of Magellan, and published a *Relacion del Ultimo Viage al Estrecho de Magellanes*, etc. (1788), together with a long *Apéndice à la Relacion . . . para*

NOTES

completar al reconocimiento del Estrecho, etc., both of which it is certain that he wrote.

The battle near Madrid:—Salamanca.

General **Castanós,** *the celebrated Spanish leader:*—Francisco Xavier de Castaños (1756-1852) born in Madrid, contrived the capitulation of Dupont (with 18,000 men) at Bailen in 1808; was beaten by Lannes at Tudela, in the same year; served under Wellington at Albuera, Salamanca, and Vittoria; and in 1815 commanded that Spanish Army of Occupation which, for divers reasons, did not enter France.

I have sent him and the boy back:—For reasons, as regards Young Rushton, which are too patent to need specifying.

So Lord Grey is married to a rustic:—' Henry Edward, Nineteenth Baron Grey de Ruthyn, married, 21st June 1809, Anna-Maria, daughter of Mr. William Kellam of Ryton-upon-Dunsmore, Warwick.'—MOORE. He died in the October of 1810.

LETTER lvii. p. 73.

Mrs. Spencer Smith:—The Florence of the Second *Harold* (xxx-xxxiii) :—

> Sweet Florence! could another ever share
> This wayward restless heart, it would be thine ;

of the charming copy of verses (Malta, 1809) :—

> O lady! when I left the shore,
> The distant shore which gave me birth ;

and of the 'Stanzas Composed During a Thunderstorm' (Plain of Zitza, 1809). Moore is ' much disposed to believe ' that Byron was not in love with Mrs. Spencer Smith as he knew her, but only with Mrs. Spencer Smith as he remembered her ; while Galt (*Life of Lord Byron*, 1830) says that she 'beguiled him of his valuable yellow diamond ring.' In any case, it matters very little now. The lady was, it appears, a sister-in-law of the defender of Acre (1764-1840). Of Sir Sidney's brother, John Spencer Smith, it is told in Edward Howard (*Rattlin the Reefer*)'s *Memoirs of Admiral Sir Sidney Smith, K.C.B.,* etc. (London, 1839), that he was at one time page to Queen Charlotte, and was 'so highly appreciated' that he 'was sent on a mission of great importance to the Court of Wurtemberg. He afterwards travelled to Constantinople, and it is confidently believed that he there converted to Christiaity, and subsequently married, a Turkish lady of high rank and of great wealth.' There is, however, no mention of Mrs. Spencer in Barrow's *Life and Correspondence* of the Admiral

339

LETTERS

(London, 1848); and it may very well be that the Smiths thought
her an adventuress, and said as little about her as they could. Of
her escape (on the night of May 2-3, 1806) from Brescia the story
is told, as Byron says, in Salvo's book :—*Travels in the year 1806
from Italy to England, through the Tyrol, Styria, Bohemia, Gallicia,
Poland, and Livonia, containing the Particulars of the Liberation
of Mrs. Spencer Smith from the hands of the French Police, and
of her subsequent flight through the Countries above mentioned.*
'Effected and written by the Marquis de Salvo, Member of the
Academy of Science and Literature of Turin, etc. London: Printed
for Richard Phillips, 1807.'

LETTER lviii. p. 74.
  The name of the Pacha is 'Ali' :—Ali Pasha (1741-1822), called
'the Lion,' born at Tepeleni, Albania. The son of a plundered
father and a very tigress of a mother, he began his career ('tis said)
by finding a treasure, with which he raised an army, and took
merciless and summary vengeance on the thieving Pasha who had
spoiled his house. Then, having slain his brother, and shut up his
mother for the crime, he took arms for the Porte against the Vizier
of Scutari, and, being rewarded for his services with a sort of lieutenancy of police, went hand and glove with the very brigands he
was commissioned to keep in check. Recalled in disfavour, he
bribed himself free again ; fought for the Porte against Austria and
Russia (1787) ; was given the Thessalian Pashalik of Trikala ; and
laying hands on Yanina, part forged, part bribed, part threatened
himself into the Pashalik thereof. He intrigued (1796 and 1807)
with Napoleon ; he took Prevyza from the French (1797) ; he subdued and massacred the Suliotes ; he sought alliance with the
English, got hold of Parga, and made himself so living a terror to
the Sultan, that his deposition was ordained, and he was at last
forced back upon, and shut up in, Yanina. In the end, he yielded
on the strength of an oath that his life would not be taken nor his
treasures forfeited, and received the bowstring there and then. His
head, being sent to Constantinople, and spiked outside the seraglio,
was cheapened by a native merchant as a good enough speculation
for the London show-market (Ali was well known in England,
where everybody read his *Harold*) ; but the scheme ' was defeated
by the piety of an old servant of the Pasha,' who bribed the execu-
tioner with a higher price, and bestowed decent sepulture on the
relic. He was at once a bloody tyrant, an admirable soldier, and
a vigorous and enlightened ruler. ' A short man,' says Hobhouse,

340

NOTES

'about five feet five inches in height, possessing a very pleasing face,
fair and round, with blue quick eyes, and not at all settled into
Turkish gravity' (*Travels*, etc.). And Byron, after calling him 'a
man of war and woes,' continues thus (Second *Harold*, lxii.) :—

> Yet in his lineaments ye cannot trace,
> While gentleness her milder radiance **throws**
> Along that aged venerable face,
> The deeds that lurk beneath, and stain him with disgrace.

Byron found in Ali's treatment of 'Giaffri, Pasha of Argyro Castro
or Scutari, I am not sure which'—(he afterwards married his
victim's daughter)—the material for stanzas 14-15 of the *Bride*;
while Galt convicts the Lion of being the original of Lambro :
wholly on the witness of his hand, whose delicacy the poet notes
in the Fourth *Juan* (stanza 45).

  The English Minister, Captain Leake :—William Martin Leake
(1777-1860): soldier, scholar, traveller, antiquary, a skilled topo-
grapher, and a fair, but dry, historian : entered the Royal Regiment
of Artillery in 1794. As Captain he was sent to Constantinople to
teach artillery practice to the Turks (1799) ; in 1800-1 he served with
the Grand Vizier's army and the Turkish force in Egypt ; with
Elgin's secretary, Hamilton, he made a general survey of Egypt ;
and went to Athens in June 1802.   In September 1802 he and
Hamilton sailed for England aboard the ship that was bringing the
Elgin Marbles ; and his MSS. were lost in the wreck of it. In 1804 he
was sent on a mission of military survey in the East ; and from
1805 to 1807 he was occupied in North Greece and the Morea.
War breaking out between England and Turkey, Leake was taken
prisoner in 1807, and through his offices with Ali Pasha a recon-
ciliation between the two countries was brought about.   In 1809
he was at Prevyza, and remained either there or at Joannina
till 1810.   He was 'officially resident at Joannina' when Byron
visited Ali. His chief works are :—*The Topography of Athens*
(London, 1821 : 2nd Edition, 1841), which was translated into
French in 1869 and 1876, and into German in 1829 and 1844 ;
Journal of a Tour in Asia Minor (London, 1824) ; *An Historical
Outline of the Greek Revolution* (London, 1825 : 2nd Edition,
1826); *Travels in the Morea*, 3 vols. (London, 1830) ; *Travels
in Northern Greece*, 4 vols. (London, 1835); and *Numismata
Hellenica* (London, 1854), with a *Supplement* in 1859. He also
edited Burckhardt's *Travels in Syria* (London, 1822).

  Leake was a great collector. His vases, gems, etc., are in the
Fitzwilliam Museum at Cambridge. The coins alone cost £5000.

LETTERS

*Sir Alexander **Ball**, the Governor:*—Born in Gloucestershire,
Alexander Ball (1757-1809) got his lieutenancy in 1778 and was
posted in 1783. He served with Rodney in the West Indies in
the War of the American Rebellion ; and during the Peace he
travelled France.   There he met Nelson, who thought him a
coxcomb for wearing epaulettes – not then a part of the uniform.
Then in the Great War he was sent to join Nelson's Squadron
(despatched from the master-fleet at Cadiz) for the pursuit of Bonaparte to Egypt. 'What,' said Nelson, 'are you come to have your
bones broken?' Ball replied that he didn't hanker after any such
experience, but that in the service of King and country his bones
must take their chance. Presently, however, the Commodore's flag-
ship, the *Vanguard*, was dismasted off Cape Ciece : when Ball took
her in tow of the *Alexander*, declined to cast her off at Nelson's
own request, and saved her from going ashore. This made the
two men friends, and friends they remained until the end. Ball
commanded the *Alexander* at the Nile, and was (Mr. Hannay tells
me) 'the real chief of the Siege of Malta.' After the capitulation he
was made Governor of the Island, and at the date of Byron's letter
he had been three weeks dead. Coleridge, who was with him for
eighteen months (1804-5) as Secretary, has an account of him in
The Friend ('Third Landing-Place'). It is (to quote the same
authority) 'ecstatic and misty,' but 'shows that he impressed the
writer as being very wise and humane.'

LETTER lx. p. 83.
Our ambassador:—Robert (afterwards Sir Robert) Adair (1763-
1855), Ambassador at Vienna (1806), Constantinople (1808-11),
Brussels (1831-5), and Berlin. The son of Sergeant-Surgeon Adair
and Lady Caroline Keppel, he went to Westminster School and
thence to Göttingen, where he fell in love with his tutor's daughter,
and thus (being an ancient Whig) suggested to George Canning
the character of Rogero (Adair was ever 'an enthusiastic admirer
of the fair sex,' Lord Albemarle says, and perhaps the name sets
forth a synonym too liberal for discussion here) and a certain
classic in *The Rovers, or The Double Arrangement* :—

> Whene'er with haggard eyes I view
>   This dungeon that I'm rotting in,
> I think on those companions true
> Who studied with me at the U-
>   -niversity of Göttingen
>   -niversity of Göttingen.

This was in the Thirtieth *Anti-Jacobin* (June 1798); but it was by no means Adair's first appearance in that print. In 1796 he had published *Part of a Letter from Robert Adair, Esq., to the Right Hon. C. J. Low: Occasioned by Mr. Burke's Mention of Lord Keppel in a Recent Publication.* Hence the description in the Eleventh Number :—

> 'Or is it he,—the youth, whose daring soul
> With *half a mission* sought the **Frozen Pole,**
> And then, returning from the **unfinished work,**
> Wrote *half a letter*—to demolish Burke?
> Studied Burke's manner,—aped his forms of speech ;
> Though when he strives his metaphors to reach,
> One luckless slip the meaning overstrains,
> And loads the blunderbuss with Bedford's brains' :—

with this note on the last line :—' This line is wholly unintelligible without a note. And we are afraid the note will be wholly incredible, unless the reader can fortunately procure the book to which it refers. In the *Part of a Letter*, which was published by **Mr. Robt.** Adair, in answer to Mr. Burke's *Letter to the D. of B.*, nothing is so remarkable as the studious imitation of Mr. Burke's style. His vehemence, and his passion, and his irony, his wild imagery, his far-sought illustrations, his rolling and **lengthened periods, and the** short, quick, pointed **sentences in which** he often condenses as much wisdom and wit as others would expand through **pages, or** through volumes,—all these are carefully kept in view by his opponent, though not always very artificially copied or applied. But imitators are liable to be led **strangely astray ; and never was there an instance of a more complete mistake of a plain meaning, than that which this** line is intended to illustrate—a **mistake no less** than that of a *coffin* for a *corpse.* **This is hard to believe or to** comprehend—but you shall hear. Mr. Burke, **in one of his** publications, had talked of the French "*unplumbing* the dead in order to destroy the living,"—by which he intended, without doubt, not metaphorically, but literally, "*stripping the dead of their* LEADEN COFFINS, *and then making them* (*not the* DEAD *but the* COFFINS) *into bullets.*" A circumstance perfectly notorious at the time the **book was** written. But this does **not** satisfy our **author.** He determines to retort Mr. Burke's own words **upon** him ; and unfortunately " reaching at a metaphor," where Mr. Burke only intended **a fact, he falls** into the little mistake above mentioned, and by a **stroke of his** pen transmutes the illustrious Head of the house of Russell into a metal, to which it is not for us to say how near or

how remote his affinity may possibly have been. He writes thus—
"If Mr. Burke had been content with 'unplumbing' a dead Russell, and hewing HIM (observe—not the coffin, but HIM—the old dead Russell himself) *into grape and canister, to sweep down the whole generation of his descendants,"* etc. etc. The thing is scarcely credible; but IT IS SO! We write with the book open before us.'

The 'half a mission' to 'the Frozen Pole' is a gibe at a journey to St. Petersburg (1791), which Adair was supposed to have made at Fox's instance, with a view to concerting measures with the Empress and her Ministers to the prejudice of Pitt. Hence, too, the parody of *Non Usitata Nec Tenui Penna*, called *A Bit of An Ode to Mr. Fox*, which appeared in the Twelfth *Anti-Jacobin* :—

> I mount, I mount into the sky,
> Sweet bird, to *Petersburg* I'll fly,
> Or, if you bid, to *Paris*.
> Fresh missions of the *Fox* and *Goose*
> Successful Treaties may produce,
> Though PITT in all miscarries.

'This idle story,' writes Adair, in an autograph statement pre-fixed to the *Life of Wilberforce* (London, 1838), and quoted by Mr. Charles Edmunds in his Edition (London, 1890) of the Poetry of *The Anti-Jacobin*—' This idle story is here accredited by Mr. Wilberforce, and inserted by his sons, without due examination. It was grounded on a journey I made to Vienna and St. Petersburg in 1791. Doctor Prettyman [*sic*], Bishop of Winchester, in a work entitled *The Life of the Right Hon. William Pitt*, published by him in 1823, brought forward the fact of my having gone upon this journey as a criminal charge against Mr. Fox, who, as he pretends, sent me upon it with the intent of counteracting some negotiations then carrying on between Great Britain and Russia at St. Petersburg. I answered his accusation, I trust successfully, in two letters published by Longman & Co. [*Two Letters from Mr. Adair to the Bp. of Winchester, in answer to the charge of a High Treasonable Misdemeanour brought by his Lordship against Mr. Fox and himself in his Life of the Rt. Hon. W. Pitt*, 8vo, 1821], and explained the circumstances which induced me in my travels in 1791 to visit the two capitals above mentioned.—ROBERT ADAIR, 1838.' The charge was first bruited by Edmund Burke, says Mr. Edmunds, in his *Letter on the Conduct of the Minority*, and was broached anew, as late as 1854, by Lord Malmesbury, in a speech to the Lords : when it was solemnly denied by Lord Campbell.

NOTES

It remains to add of Adair that he wrote the 'Margaret Nicholson' and the 'Song of Scrutina' in *The Rolliad*, an account of his *Mission to the Court of Vienna* (1844) and *Negotiations for the Peace of the Dardanelles* (1845); married a daughter of the Marquis d'Hazincourt; and died in Chesterfield Street only eight years short of a hundred old.

The Norfolk Sale:—That is, the sale of Wymondham and other copyholds situate in Norfolk, by which the writer hoped to escape the necessity of parting with Newstead.

LETTER lxi. p. 85.

No accounts from Hanson:—There are many passages, published and unpublished, to show that either Hanson did not write, or that (as is more probable) his letters miscarried, and that Byron was hurt by what he deemed his correspondent's indifference.

LETTER lxii. p. 87.

Are they not written in the 'Boke of Gell':—That is, *The Topography of Troy* (1804), by Sir William Gell (1777-1836), whom Byron reviewed in *The Monthly Review* for August 1811. Having seen the ground, he thought Sir William's survey 'hasty and imperfect,' and set forth his views of the man and the man's work in a stanza (suppressed) of the Second *Harold*:—

> Or will the gentle Dilettanti crew
> Now delegate the task to digging Gell?
> That mighty limner of a birds'-eye view,
> How like to Nature let his volumes tell.
> Who can with him the folio's limits swell
> With all the Author saw, or said he saw?
> Who can topographise or delve so well?
> No boaster he, nor impudent and raw,
> His pencil, pen, and shade, alike without a flaw.

Embrace Dwyer:—I know nothing of Dwyer, except that we shall find Byron begging Hodgson to ask Drury to kick him: because his fiery whiskers had frightened the writer's horses. 'And let the kicks be hard.'

Some Sentimental Sing-song of my own:—Hobhouse notes in his preface to *Imitations and Translations* that 'the poems signed "L. B.", are by Lord Byron'; that 'the collector of this miscellany is answerable for such as are dated from Trinity College, Cambridge'; and that 'the authors of the remainder . . . have affixed distinct signatures'—to wit, I. Z., L. T., E. B., I. H. B., F. Q., and T. L.—'to their respective contributions.' Byron's, nine in number, will be found in the section called *Occasional*

345

LETTERS

Pieces of this Edition. They include the well-known lines to Mrs. Musters (Mary Chaworth) :—

> Well! thou art happy, and I feel
> That I should thus be happy, too ;

the 'Inscription on the Monument of a Newfoundland Dog'; the *Song*, 'Fill the Goblet again'; and the 'Stanzas to a Lady'—(Mrs. Musters)—'On leaving England' :—

> 'Tis done—and, shivering in the gale,
> The bark unfurls her snowy sail ;
> And, whistling o'er the bending mast,
> Loud sings on high the fresh'ning blast ;
> And I must from this land begone
> Because I cannot love but one.

Theresa, Mariana, and Katinka :—Daughters of Theodora Macri. Theresa, the eldest, was the original 'Maid of Athens': 'rendered more famous,' says Galt (*Life, ut sup.*), by his Lordship's verses than her degree of beauty deserved.' As to Katinka, Byron, says Moore, 'has adopted this name in his description of the Seraglio in *Don Juan*, Canto vi. It was, if I recollect right, in making love to one of these girls that he had recourse to an act of courtship often practised in that country ;—namely, giving himself a wound across the breast with his dagger. The young Athenian, by his own account,' was 'in no degree moved to gratitude.'

LETTER lxiii. p. 90.

Two days ago I swam from Sestos to Abydos :—A piece of prowess of which he was vain until the end. See the stanzas *Written after Swimming from Sestos to Abydos :*—

> If, in the month of dark December,
> Leander, who was nightly wont, etc. :—

and the lines in *Don Juan* :—

> A feat on which ourselves we rather prided,
> Leander, Ekenhead, and I did.

(Ekenhead, in whose company the swim was done, was Lieutenant of the *Salsette* frigate, then lying in the Dardanelles, in which Hobhouse and Mr. Adair were presently (July 4th) to sail for England, landing Byron by the way at Zea.) Writing of the aforesaid stanza, 'By-the-by,' says Byron, 'from Abydos to Sestos would have been more correct.' He adds :—'A number of the *Salsette's* crew were known to have accomplished a greater distance ; and the only thing that surprised me was, that, as doubts had been entertained of the truth of Leander's story, no traveller, had ever

346

NOTES

endeavoured to ascertain its practicability.' The swimmers took an hour and ten minutes to cross from Europe to Asia.

Hobhouse thoughtfully remarks (*Travels*, etc.) that Byron 'had before made a more perilous, but less celebrated passage; for I recollect that, when we were in Portugal, he swam from old Lisbon to Belem Castle, and having to contend with a tide and counter current, the wind blowing freshly, was but little less than two hours in crossing.'

A passion for a married woman at Malta :—Mrs. Spencer Smith, for whom see *ante*, p. 339, Note to Letter lvii.

My Second Edition :—*English Bards*, 2nd Edition, October 1809.

You and Bland :—The Rev. Robert Bland (1779-1825) was educated at Harrow—where he afterwards became an assistant master—and at Pembroke College, Cambridge. He was, in succession, Reader and Preacher at certain London chapels; Minister to the English Church at Amsterdam; Curate of Prittlewell; and Curate of Kenilworth. He published *Edwy and Elgiva* (1805); *Translations Chiefly from the Greek Anthology, with Tales and Miscellaneous Poems* (1806) with Herman Merivale (1779-1844) and others; *The Four Slaves of Cythera, a Poetical Romance* (1809); *A Collection of the Most Beautiful Minor Poems of the Minor Poets of Greece* (1813); *Collections from the Greek Anthology* (1813); and some translations (prose) from the French in collaboration with Miss Plumptre (1813). His *Elements of Latin Hexameters and Pentameters* has run through some twenty editions, and is still, I believe, reprinted. We shall presently find Byron, who had sat under Bland at Harrow, trying to get him commissioned to translate the enormous *Charlemagne* of Lucien Buonaparte, a piece of work which in the end (1815) was done by Hodgson, in collaboration with the Rev. Dr. Butler. It is to Bland and Merivale that Byron addresses this apostrophe in *English Bards* :—

> And you, associate bards! who snatched to light
> Those gems too long withheld from modern sight ;
> Whose mingling taste combined to cull the wreath
> Where Attic flowers Aonian odours breathe,
> And all their renovated fragrance flung
> To grace the beauties of your native tongue ;
> Now let those minds, that nobly could transfuse
> The glorious spirit of the Grecian muse,
> Though soft the echo, scorn a borrowed tone:
> Resign Achaia's lyre, and strike your own.

A whimsical, ingenious, and accomplished man, with a very pretty

347

LETTERS

talent for letter-writing, and a great liking for France and the French and French acting—(he spoke and wrote French vastly better than most Englishmen of his generation, had travelled over Europe in war time, and lived willingly in Paris)—Bland died of a broken blood-vessel. (*See* J. T. Hodgson, *Memoir*, etc., *passim.*)

LETTER lxiv. p. 93.

When Mr. Adair takes leave, I am to see the Sultan :—This he did. ' During his stay at Constantinople,' says Moore, 'the English minister, Mr. Adair, being indisposed the greater part of the time, had but few opportunities of seeing him. He, however, pressed him, with much hospitality, to accept a lodging at the English palace, which Lord Byron, preferring the freedom of his homely inn, declined. At the audience granted to the ambassador, on his taking leave, by the Sultan, the noble poet attended in the train of Mr. Adair,—having shown an anxiety as to the place he was to hold in the procession, not a little characteristic of his jealous pride of rank. In vain had the minister assured him that no particular station could be allotted to him ; that the Turks, in their arrangements for the ceremonial, considered only the persons connected with the embassy, and neither attended to, nor acknowledged, the precedence which our forms assign to nobility. Seeing the young peer still unconvinced by these representations, Mr. Adair was, at length, obliged to refer him to an authority, considered infallible on such points of etiquette, the old Austrian Internuncio ;—on consulting whom, and finding his opinions agree fully with those of the English minister, Lord Byron declared himself perfectly satisfied.' For the Ambassador's reception by (1) the ' Caimakam,' and (2) that Sultan Mahmoud II., who ten years afterwards (1821) put through the Massacre of the Janizaries—(Byron and his fellow-traveller were compelled to sit out the payment of this redoubtable corps : an experience ' designed to captivate and astonish us by a display of Ottoman wealth,')—to the number of twenty thousand, see the last chapter of Hobhouse's *Travels*. The whole thing is too long to quote ; but I cannot choose but make room for Hobhouse's sketch of the great Sultan himself, the notes for which were taken ' within ten paces of the throne,' while the Eunuch Chamberlain—(who 'had not forgotten the assassination of Amurath')—' held me somewhat strictly by the right arm during the audience ':—
' The [presence-] chamber was small and dark, or rather illumined with a gloomy artificial light, reflected from the ornaments of silver, pearls, and other white brilliants, with which it is thickly

348

studded on every side and on the roof. The throne, which is supposed the richest in the world, is like a four-posted bed, but of a dazzling splendour; the lower part formed of burnished silver and pearls, and the canopy and supporters encrusted with jewels. It is in an awkward position, being in one corner of the room, and close to a fire-place. Sultan Mahmoud was placed in the middle of the throne, with his feet upon the ground . . . the seat of ceremony. He was dressed in a robe of yellow satin with a broad bodice of the darkest sable: his dagger, and an ornament on his breast, were covered with diamonds: the front of his white and blue turban shone with a large treble sprig of diamonds, which served as a buckle to a high straight plume of paradise feathers. He for the most part kept a hand on each knee, and neither moved his body nor head, but rolled his eyes from side to side, without fixing them for an instant upon the Ambassador or any other person present. Occasionally he stroked and turned up his beard, displaying a milk-white hand glittering with diamond rings. His eyebrows, eyes, and beard, being of a glossy jet black, did not appear natural, but added to that indescribable majesty which it would be difficult for any but an Oriental sovereign to assume; his face was pale, and regularly formed, except that his nose (contrary to the usual form of that feature in the Ottoman princes) was slightly turned up and pointed: his whole physiognomy was mild and benevolent, but expressive and full of dignity. He appeared to be of a short and small stature, and about thirty years old, which is somewhat more than his actual age.'

Thus Hobhouse of Mahmoud II. (reigned 1808-1839), the last of the great Sultans; who passed, after the murder of Selim and Mustapha IV., from 'the furnace of a bath,' where 'the fond fidelity of a slave' (HOBHOUSE) had hidden him from pursuit, to the chieftainship of Islam; against whom Byron was to die in the act of making war; who, though he lost Greece (1828) and had ever the worst of it with Russia, succeeded in keeping Egypt, and in achieving such administrative reforms as delayed the fall of the Ottoman Empire; and of whom the worst that can be said is that he left no man behind him, but exhausted (it would seem) the governing virtue of his house and race.

LETTER lxvi. p. 95.

The Nurse's dole in the 'Medea':—These (I am informed) are the verses, in 'the breathless passage which begins the *Medea*,' here represented :—

LETTERS

Εἴθ' ὤφελ' 'Αργοῦς μὴ διαπτάσθαι σκάφος
Κόλχων ἐς αἶαν κυανέας Συμπληγάδας,
μηδ' ἐν νάπαισι Πηλίου πεσεῖν ποτε
τμηθεῖσα πεύκη, μηδ' ἐρετμῶσαι χέρας
ἀνδρῶν ἀρίστων, οἳ τὸ πάγχρυσον δέρος
Πελίᾳ μετῆλθον. οὐ γὰρ ἂν δέσποιν' ἐμὴ
Μήδεια πύργους γῆς ἔπλευσ' 'Ιωλκίας—

*Tell Davies that Hobhouse has made excellent use of his best jokes
in many of His Majesty's Ships of War:*—Scrope Berdmore Davies,
a Cambridge friend, who went to Eton with Hodgson and Drury
and the rest, and was afterwards, according to custom, a Fellow of
King's. 'One of the cleverest men I ever knew, in conversation,
was Scrope Berdmore Davies. Hobhouse is also very good in that
line, though it is of less consequence to a man who has other ways
of showing his talents than in company. Scrope was always ready,
and often witty—Hobhouse as witty but not so ready, being more
diffident.'—*MS. Journal of Lord Byron* (MOORE). In the August
of 1811 Byron made a will, in which he named Davies and Hobhouse his executors : the two to divide ' my library and furniture
of every description.' On the 28th of the same month he executed
a codicil, by which he revoked the bequest of his ' household goods
and furniture, library, pictures, sabres, watches, plate, linen, trin-
kets, and other personal estate (except money and securities)
situate within the walls of the mansion-house and premises at his
decease—and bequeathed the same (except his wine and spirituous
liquors) to his friends, the said J. C. Hobhouse, S. B. Davies, and
Francis Hodgson, their executors, etc., to be equally divided
between them for their own use ;—and he bequeathed his wine and
spirituous liquors, which should be in the cellars and premises at
Newstead, unto his friend, the said J. Becher, for his own use, and
requested the said J. C. Hobhouse, S. B. Davies, F. Hodgson, and
J. Becher, respectively, to accept the bequest therein contained to
them respectively, as a token of his friendship.' A quaint and
pleasing picture of Davies is painted (under date of March 28, 1814)
in Byron's *MS. Journal* (MOORE) :—' Yesterday, dined *tête-à-tête*
at the *Cocoa*, with Scrope Davies—sat from six till midnight—
drank between us one bottle of champagne and six of claret,
neither of which wines ever affect me. Offered to take Scrope
home in my carriage ; but he was tipsy and pious, and I was
obliged to leave him on his knees praying to I know not what purpose or pagod. No headache, nor sickness. . . . I have heard
nothing more from Scrope Yesterday paid him four thousand

eight hundred pounds, a debt of some standing, and which I wished to have paid before.' In 1814 Davies is one of the Drury Lane Committee, presents a share to Edmund Kean, and appears as a subscriber to the Testimonial Cup. And in 1816 he, with Hobhouse, visits Byron at Diodati. After which you find him 'giving very good accounts of his (Byron's) health and spirits' to Augusta, 'though he confesses he *found* him gloomy' (Mrs. Leigh to Hodgson, 29th October 1816); and about the same time a generous inscription gives him *Parisina*.

According to Gronow (*Reminiscences*, Third Series), Davies, whom he describes as ' the life and soul of those who relished learning and genius and wit,' was a desperate gambler, and for some time played with equal daring and success. As a rule, he preferred the bank before the individual ; but on one occasion, having departed from his custom, he fairly beggared his antagonist, and reduced him to despair, when, learning that nothing was left him in the world, he restored his winnings on the spot, on the other man's promise that he would play no more. After a while, however, 'fortune deserted her old favourite,' and, 'unable to mingle any longer with the rich, the giddy, and the gay,' he retired to Paris, where he had 'few intimates,' received those whom he wished to see on a bench in the Tuileries Gardens, and occupied himself with the composition of certain 'notes on the men of his time '—(he talked of them to Murray)—the MS. of which has disappeared. 'His manners and appearance,' says this writer, 'were of the true Brummell type' : that is, 'there was nothing showy in his exterior.' A pun of his has got itself embalmed in the true Byron :—

'When Brummell was obliged to retire to France, he knew no French, and having obtained a grammar for the purpose of study, our friend Scrope Davies was asked what progress Brummell had made in French ; he responded, "that Brummell had been stopped, like Buonaparte in Russia, by the *elements*. I have put this pun into *Beppo*, *etc.*—BYRON, *Diary*, 1821:—

and a neat enough distich (on an amateur actor) is quoted in J. T. Hodgson's *Memoir* :—

> Not to be hissed delights the dunce,
> But who can hiss and groan at once?

In the same book you get the last of him, in a letter to Hodgson from Dr. Hawtrey :—' I am sure you will be sorry to hear that our old friend Scrope Davies was found dead in his bed at Paris '—(2 Rue Miroménil)—'a few days since' (24th May 1852). 'He was a most agreeable and kind-hearted person, and I shall not soon

LETTERS

forget the pleasant hours I have passed with him. He seemed quite broken down when I had a glimpse of him a few months since at Eton. I hardly knew him again, and should not have done so had he not mentioned his name.' See also Thomas Colley Grattan, *Beaten Paths and Those Who Trod Them* (London, 1862).

*The Cocoa Tree :—*A famous club in St. James's Street. It sprang out of the Cocoa Tree Chocolate House, a Tory centre in Queen Anne's time, and, Timbs says, existed as a club ' probably before 1746.' Horace Walpole appears to mention it in a letter to George Montague (1746), and Gibbon refers to it in his *Journal* (1762).

*And Hodgson has been publishing more poems :—*The *Sir Edgar—* 'A Tale in Two Cantos : With Serious Translations from the Antients and Merry Imitations of a Modern ' (London, 1810).

*Bland's ' Anthology' :—*This is *Translations chiefly from the Greek Anthology, etc.* (London, 1806). For Bland, see *ante*, p. 347, Note to Letter lxiii.

*By next Montem :—*A ceremony which, as Provost of Eton, their common friend Hodgson was afterwards (1847) to abolish.

LETTER lxvii. p. 97.

Mr. Hobhouse . . . is on his way to England :—' The ambassador,' says Hobhouse, on the last page of his *Travels*, ' had his audience of the Seraglio on the 10th of July ; on the evening of the 14th we embarked on board the *Salsette*, and after touching at the Dardanelles and at the island of Zea, where Lord Byron left the frigate on his return to Attica, we arrived on the 28th of the same month at Malta, from which place it may be recollected that the foregoing tour originally commenced.' Byron's letter, then, appears to have been written in anticipation of the ambassador's departure.

*Her ladyship, so far as I can judge, has lied :—*See the charming description in the *Letters during Mr. Wortley's Embassy* (June 17, O.S., 1717) of Belgrade Village, as the Elysian Fields :—' I am in the middle of a wood, consisting chiefly of fruit-trees, watered by a vast number of fountains famous for the excellency of their water, and divided into many shady walks upon short grass that seems to me artificial, but, I am assured, is the pure work of nature ; and within view of the Black Sea, from whence we perpetually enjoy the refreshment of cool breezes, that make us insensible of the heat of the summer,' etc.

*Lady Wortley errs strangely :—*So does Byron. Lady Mary does not contrast St. Sophia's and St. Paul's, but St. Paul's and ' the

NOTES

Valedé-Sultán' mosque : 'the largest of all built entirely of marble, the most prodigious, and, I think, the most beautiful structure I ever saw. . . . Between friends, St. Paul's Church would make a pitiful figure near it, as any of our squares,' etc.

LETTER lxviii. p. 103.

That matrimonial man :—Henry Drury was the first of the Byron group to marry. His wife was Caroline Taylor, daughter of A. W. Taylor of Boreham Wood, Hertfordshire. His sister married Merivale, his wife's sister Hodgson ; so that the secession from the aforesaid Byron group was whole-hearted and complete indeed.

Aberdeen's party split :—George Hamilton Gordon (1784-1860), Fourth Earl of Aberdeen, travelled (1802-1804) in France, Italy, Greece—(where he 'rediscovered and excavated the Pnyx')—and Asia Minor ; was elected President of the Society of Antiquaries ; and published (1822) an *Inquiry into the Principles of Grecian Architecture.* Byron was disposed to rank him with the Lord Elgin of *The Curse of Minerva* :—

> Ah ! Athens, scarce escaped from Turk and Goth,
> Hell sends a paltry Scotsman worse than both :—

and called upon him vehemently in a stanza (suppressed) of the Second *Harold* :—

> Come, then, ye classic Thanes of each degree,
> Dark Hamilton, and sullen Aberdeen,
> Come pilfer all the Pilgrim loves to see,
> All that yet consecrates the fading scene :
> Oh ! better were it ye had never been,
> Nor ye, nor Elgin.

The Russians and Turks are at it :—Two years afterwards there was a peace, when the country between the Pruth and the Dniester was ceded to Russia.

LETTER lxix. p. 105.

The Marquis of Sligo, my old fellow-collegian :—This was Howe Peter Browne (1788-1845), Second Marquess of Sligo, who in 1813 married Hester Catharine, eldest daughter of the Thirteenth Earl of Clanricarde. Like most of the men of his age, he was a patron of Pugilism, and in 1813, on the occasion of Tom Belcher's second fight with Dogherty, I find him giving five guineas at the ring-side towards a purse for the twice-beaten Irishman. Withal, he was something of an antiquary, and the vases, lachrymatories, and gold ornaments which he found in the tombs of Hellas were taken by him to Westport House, Westport, where they now are.

LETTERS

To understand what follows, one must know that at Gibraltar he had joined Lady Hester Stanhope (1776-1829), then starting on that uncommon adventure which was to stamp her one of the most notable women of her time. At Gibraltar she had arrived with her brother, Captain Stanhope; but at Gibraltar Stanhope was ordered to rejoin his regiment, and either she must have turned back, or she must have come on alone, had not Michael Bruce—the Bruce who was to contrive the escape of Lavalette with Hutchinson and Sir Robert Wilson (1815)—not undertaken to escort her on the perilous journey which she had resolved to make through European Turkey. (*Travels of Lady Hester Stanhope.* . . . 'Narrated By Her Physician,' London, 1846, i. 4.) At the Piræus, adds the Physician, 'just as we were passing the mole-head, we saw a man jump from it into the sea, whom Lord Sligo recognised to be Lord Byron himself, and, hailing him, bade him hasten to dress and to come and join us.' The sequel may be told in Moore's own words :—' It was in the course, I believe, of their first interview, at his (Lord Sligo's) table, that Lady Hester, with that lively eloquence for which she is so remarkable, took the poet briskly to task for the depreciating opinion, which, as she understood, he entertained of all female intellect. Being but little inclined, were he even able, to sustain such a heresy, against one who was in her own person such an irresistible refutation of it, Lord Byron had no other refuge from the fair orator's arguments than in assent and silence ; and this well-bred deference being, in a sensible woman's eyes, equivalent to concession, they became, from thenceforward, most cordial friends. In recalling some recollections of this period in his *Memoranda*, after relating the circumstance of his being caught bathing by an English party at Sunium, he added, "This was the beginning of the most delightful acquaintance which I formed in Greece." He then went on to assure Mr. Bruce, if ever those pages should meet his eyes, that the days they had passed together at Athens were remembered by him with pleasure.'

Further, Lord Sligo told Moore several anecdotes of Byron, which may here be reproduced. The first was recalled as a proof of the poet's consciousness of his beauty :—' He was a good deal weakened and thinned by his illness at Patras, and, on his return to Athens, standing one day before a looking-glass, he said to Lord Sligo— "How pale I look !—I should like, I think, to die of a consumption ?"—"Why of a consumption ?" asked his friend. " Because then (he answered) the women would all say, 'See that poor Byron

—how interesting he looks in dying!"'' The next is an anticipation of *The Deformed Transformed* :—' He spoke often of his mother . . . and with a feeling that seemed little short of aversion. "Some time or other," he said, " I will tell you *why* I feel thus towards her."—A few days after, when they were bathing together in the Gulf of Lepanto, he referred to this promise, and, pointing to his naked leg and foot, exclaimed—" Look there!—it is to her false delicacy at my birth I owe that deformity ; and yet as long as I can remember, she has never ceased to taunt and reproach me with it. Even a few days before we parted, for the last time, on my leaving England, she, in one of her fits of passion, uttered an imprecation upon me, praying that I might prove as ill formed in mind as I am in body!" His look and manner, in relating this frightful circumstance, can be conceived only by those who have ever seen him in a similar state of excitement.' 'The little value,' Moore goes on to say, ' he had for those relics of ancient art, in pursuit of which he saw all his classic fellow-travellers so ardent, was, like everything he ever thought or felt, unreservedly avowed by him. Lord Sligo having it in contemplation to expend some money in digging for antiquities, Lord Byron, in offering to act as his agent . . . said—" You may safely trust *me*—I am no dilettante. Your connoisseurs are all thieves ; but I care too little for these things ever to steal them."' A profession of indifference which is fully confirmed by Galt.

To Lord Sligo, too, we are probably indebted for the information that ' the system of thinning himself, which he (Byron) had begun before he left England, was continued still more rigidly abroad. While at Athens he took the hot bath for this purpose three times a week,—his usual drink being vinegar and water, and his food seldom more than a little rice.'—MOORE.

As for Byron's '*tour of the Morea*' :—' In a note upon the Advertisement prefixed to his *Siege of Corinth*, he says—" I visited all three (Tripolitza, Napoli, and Argos) in 1810-11, and in the course of journeying through the country, from my first arrival in 1809, crossed the Isthmus eight times in my way from Attica to the Morea, over the mountains, or in the other direction, when passing from the Gulf of Athens to that of Lepanto."'—MOORE.

LETTER lxx. p. 108.

My nature leads me to solitude:—Those who saw Byron about this time state that his habit was one of unchanging melancholy— even dejection. Surely a not uncommon circumstance with youth ?

LETTERS

LETTER lxxii. p. 111.

I have made a tour of the Morea and visited Veley Pacha :—A son of the redoubtable Ali : for an account of whom, and his civilities to Byron and Hobhouse, see the *Travels* (i. 93-116, Ed. 1855). ʻA lively young man,ʼ says Hobhouse, ʻand besides the Albanian, Greek, and Turkish languages, speaks Italian, an accomplishment not possessed by any other man of his high rank ʼ—(he was a pasha of three tails)—ʻin Turkey.ʼ His ottomans, being draped with scarlet, reminded Galt (who ʻperceived in him a considerable tincture of drollery,ʼ and whose description abounds in turbans and daggers and jewels) of ʻthe woolsacks in the House of Lords.ʼ He fell with his father (1822), and his cenotaph, with those of Ali and the others of his house, only two of which survived, ʻis seen at the Silivria Gate at Constantinople.ʼ—(H. *ut sup.*)

I see the ʻLady of the Lakeʼ advertised :—It was published in the May of 1810, and 20,000 copies—2050 in quarto—had been sold by the end of the year.

*He had a farce ready for the stage before I left England :—*ʼ This farce was entitled *Not at Home,* and was acted, though with moderate success, at the Lyceum, by the Drury Lane Company, in November 1809. It was afterwards printed, with a Prologue (intended to have been spoken) written by Walter Rodwell Wright, Esq., author of *Horæ Ionicæ.*ʼ—MOORE. Drury Lane the Third was burned down in 1809.

The ruling passions of Pope are nothing to it:—See Pope, *Moral Essays* (*c.* 1731-35), Epistle i. 174-9, etc. :—

> Search, then, the ruling passion : there, alone,
> The wild are constant, and the cunning known . . .
> This clue once found unravels all the rest :—

and *Moral Essays*, Epistle iii. 153-4, etc. :—

> The ruling passion, be it what it will,
> The ruling passion conquers reason still.

See also Burns in his rough and ready imitation of Goldsmithʼs *Retaliation*, the verses *Inscribed to the Right Hon. C. J. Fox* :—

> All in all [Manʼs] a problem must puzzle the devil.
> On his one Ruling Passion Sir Pope strongly labours,
> That, like thʼ old Hebrew walking-switch, eats up its neighbours :
> Human Natureʼs his show-box—your friend, would you know him?
> Pull the string Ruling Passion—the picture will show him.
> What pity, in rearing so beauteous a system,
> One trifling particular—Truth—should have missed him !
> For, spite of his fine theoretic positions,
> Mankind is a science defies definitions.

NOTES

Bluebeard's elephants:—Colman's pantomime of *Bluebeard*, Mr. Archer tells me, was produced at Drury Lane in 1808. The 'elephants' were certainly 'properties': the first real monster ever seen at a Patent Theatre being the Chunee which came out in Tom Dibdin's *Harlequin Padmanaba* (February **1811**), and was scorned by Johnson, the property-master, as something vastly inferior to his own creations. (See *post*, p. 424, Note to Letter clvii.)

LETTER lxxiii. p. 115.

The Waywode, or Governor, of Athens:—Hobhouse notes 'A visit always customary to the Waiwode, or Turkish Governor of the town, whom we found a well-mannered man, with more information than is usually possessed by those of his nation, and who, having served with our forces in the Egyptian wars, was somewhat partial to our countrymen—his name and title were Suleiman Aga.'—(*Travels*, etc., i. 243.)

The French consul and an Italian painter:—'Mr. Fauriel, the French Consul, . . . gratefully remembered, I believe, by every traveller who for twenty years past has visited the Levant' (HOB-HOUSE); and 'Mr. Lusieri, the only one remaining of the six artists settled during three years by Lord Elgin at Athens' (H.).

LETTER lxxv. p. 118.

As I have received a firman for Egypt:—In a letter to Hanson, 'I shall not return,' says Byron, 'till I have seen Jerusalem and Grand Cairo.' This, however, he was constrained to do; so that then and afterwards these cities remained unvisited.

At a less expense than a common college life in England:—At Livadia the Archon Logotheti, in whose house Byron and Hobhouse lodged, maintained an establishment of fifty persons—including several secretaries, a squad of chaplains, and a family physician—at a cost of less than £1150 a year.

LETTER lxxvii. p. 122.

Messrs. Brothers:—A firm of upholsterers, which had levied an execution at Newstead (1810) for £1600. Moore tells that Joe Murray, not being able to endure the scandal of the bill of sale by auction, pasted it over with brown paper.

LETTER lxxviii. p. 124.

Yours and Pratt's protégé:—Joseph Blackett (1786-1810), 'Cobbler Joe,' as Byron somewhere calls him, came eleventh in the family of twelve children born to a day labourer in the service of Sir John Lawson, at Tunstill, Yorks. In 1797 he went to London

LETTERS

as apprentice to his brother (a shoemaker); married at eighteen; was a widower (with child) at twenty-one; was helped by a printer called Marchant, who set up his verses gratis, and introduced him to Pratt; published a book of *Specimens* (with Pratt to the front as editor and bear-leader) at twenty-three (1809); and died in the August of the next year at Seaham, in Northumberland, where, as the county historian puts it of this 'unfortunate child of genius,' his 'last days were soothed by the generous attention of the family of Milbanke.'—MOORE. See, too, *English Bards*:—

> When some brisk youth, the tenant of a stall,
> Employs a pen less pointed than his awl,
> Leaves his snug shop, forsakes his store of shoes,
> St. Crispin quits, and cobbles for the Muse,
> Heavens! how the vulgar stare! how crowds applaud!
> How ladies read, and literati laud:—

with Byron's Note (1816):—'This was meant for poor Blackett, who was then patronised by A. J. B.; but *that* I did not know, or this would not have been written, at least I think not.' Moore adds a passage which has dropped from the present letter:—' Who would think that anybody would be such a blockhead as to sin against an express proverb:—Ne sutor ultra crepidam?

> But spare him, ye Critics, his follies are past,
> For the Cobbler is come, as he ought, to his *last*.

Which two lines, with a scratch under *last* to show where the joke lies, I beg that you will prevail on Miss Milbanke to have inserted on the tomb of her departed Blackett.'

An imitation of Horace's 'Art of Poetry':—The *Hints from Horace*, which Byron preferred before the First and Second *Harold*, which was placed in Cawthorn's hands, and printed off, but which was not published until 1831. See *post*, p. 367, Note to Letter lxxxvii.

LETTER lxxix. p. 125.
I have never been so near it since I left 'Duck Puddle':—'Duck-Puddle,' writes an old Harrovian, 'is the school swimming-bath. I suspect it was a duck-puddle to begin with, and that that is its official name. For many years past, however, the boys have called it "Ducker," which I believe to be the origin of the termination "—er," now in use all over the country for "Footer" (pure Harrow), "Soccer," "Rugger," and so on.'

LETTER lxxxi. p. 128.
The Editor of 'The Scourge' will be tried for two different Libels on the late Mrs. B. and myself:—See *The Scourge* for March

358

NOTES

1811. The libels are contained in a review of *English Bards*.
After a savage attack on the satirist of Cambridge and *The Edinburgh Review*, 'So much,' the writer goes on to say, 'for Lord
Byron's opinions on Literature and criticism ; it only remains for
us to notice the gross and laboured effusion of malignity, which
his lordship thought proper to withhold from publication till the
vessel that bore him from the shores of England was "shivering in
the gale," and was about to waft him from the reach of literary
punishment. We know the irritability of his temper and the obliquities of his feelings, etc. . . . We are unacquainted with any act of
cowardice that can be compared with that of keeping a libel *ready
cut and dried* till some favourable opportunity enabled its author to
disperse it without the hazard of personal responsibility, and under
circumstances which deprive the injured party of every means of
reparation. Had his lordship published the libel on Mr. Clarke
in his first edition, he would have at least deserved the praise
of magnanimity ; but he knew that the friends of that gentleman
are both able and willing to prove that he should not be insulted with impunity. He confined the knowledge of his lampoon, therefore, to the circle of his own immediate friends, and
left it to be given to the public as soon as he could have bid
adieu to the shores of Britain. *Whether his voyage was in
reality no further than to Paris, in search of the proofs of his
own legitimacy,* or, as he asserts, to "Afric's coasts, and Calpé's
adverse height," was of little consequence to Mr. Clarke, who felt
that to recriminate during his absence would be unworthy of his
character. . . . Considering the two parties not as writers but as men,
Mr. Clarke might confidently appeal to the knowledge and opinion
of the whole university ; but a character like his disdains comparison with that of his noble calumniator : a temper unruffled by
malignant passions, a mind superior to vicissitude, are gifts *for
which the pride of doubtful birth*, and the temporary possession of
Newstead Abbey, are contemptible equivalents. . . . It may be
reasonably asked whether to be a denizen of Berwick-upon-Tweed
be more disgraceful than to be the illegitimate descendant of a
murderer ; whether to labour in an honourable profession for the
peace and competence of maturer age be less worthy of praise than
to waste the property of others in vulgar debauchery ; whether to
be the offspring of parents whose only crime is their want of title
be not as honourable as to be the son of a profligate father, and a
mother whose days and nights are spent in the delirium of drunkenness? . . . Hated for malignity of temper and repulsiveness of

359

manner, and shunned by every man who did not wish to be considered as profligate without wit, and trifling without elegance. . . . We wish not to give currency to disgraceful tales . . . and shall neither expose the infamy of his uncle, the indiscretions of his mother, nor his personal follies and embarrassments. But let him not again obtrude himself on our attention as a moralist. . . . Another provocation may teach him, that with the *Editor of " The Scourge"* the inclination to punish, and the power to fulfil that inclination are synonimous ' (*sic*).

For the cause of all this fierceness, see the verses—('Right enough : this was well deserved and well laid on.'—B., 1816)—on Hewson Clarke (1787-1832 ?)—this scribbler edited *The Scourge*, and probably wrote the quoted article—in *English Bards* :—

> There Clarke, still striving piteously ' to please,'
> Forgetting doggrel leads not to degrees,
> A would-be satirist, a hired buffoon,
> A monthly scribbler of some low lampoon,
> Condemn'd to drudge, the meanest of the mean,
> And furbish falsehoods for a magazine,
> Devotes to scandal his congenial mind ;
> Himself a living libel on mankind.

With the postscript to the Second Edition :—

There is a youth ycleped Hewson Clarke (subaudi *esquire*), a sizer of Emanuel College, and, I believe, a denizen of Berwick-upon-Tweed, whom I have introduced in these pages to much better company than he has been accustomed to meet ; he is, notwithstanding, a very sad dog, and for no reason that I can discover, except a personal quarrel with a bear, kept by me at Cambridge to sit for a fellowship, and whom the jealousy of his Trinity contemporaries prevented from success, has been abusing me, and, what is worse, the defenceless innocent above mentioned, in the *Satirist*, for one year and some months. I am utterly unconscious of having given him any provocation ; indeed, I am guiltless of having heard his name till coupled with the *Satirist*. He has therefore no reason to complain, and I dare say that, like Sir Fretful Plagiary, he is rather *pleased* than otherwise. I have now mentioned all who have done me the honour to notice me and mine, that is, my bear and my book, except the editor of the *Satirist*, who, it seems, is a gentleman—God wot! I wish he could impart a little of his gentility to his subordinate scribblers.

LETTER lxxxii. p. 128.

*One of my best friends is **drowned in a ditch** :*—Charles Skinner Matthews, third son of John Matthews of Belmont, Herefordshire, and brother to Henry Matthews (1790-1828), author of the *Diary of an Invalid* (1819). After 1807, Matthews was one of Byron's most intimate friends, not so much at Cambridge—though they were at the university together, and he lived in Byron's rooms during the year of Byron's absence—as in London; and his influence on his junior, especially in the matter of religion, was strong and lasting. He passed from Eton to Trinity; was Ninth Wrangler in the Mathematical, then the only, Tripos in 1805; took his degree in 1806; and got the Members' Prize for a Latin essay in 1807. A really full and particular account of his drowning in the fork of the Cam above Newnham Mills—(he was bathing, and was caught in 'a bed of weeds, thick, eight feet deep,' so that 'not fifty of the strongest-bodied men in England could, without ropes, have given the slightest assistance')—is given by Henry Drury in a letter to Hodgson (J. T. HODGSON, *ut sup.*, i. 186). Drury's conclusion is that nothing but 'temerity little short of madness' could have induced Matthews to attempt the aforesaid weeds. For a brilliant and affectionate account of him, see Byron (from Ravenna) to Murray, under date of 9th October 1820.

LETTER lxxxiii. p. 129.

George Anson Byron:—The writer's cousin, the Seventh Baron. Byron thus discourses of him in his *Journal*, under date of Tuesday, 30th November, and Wednesday, 1st December 1813:— 'George is returned from afloat to get a new ship. He looks thin, but better than I expected. I like George much more than most people like their heirs. He is a fine fellow, and every inch a sailor. I would do anything, *but apostatise*, to get him on in his profession. . . . George Byron has not called to-day; I hope he will be an admiral, . . . and, perhaps, Lord Byron into the bargain. If he would but marry, I would engage never to marry myself, or cut him out of the heirship. He would be happier, and I should like nephews better than sons.'

Nicolo Giraud of Athens:—'During this period of his stay in Greece we find him forming one of those extraordinary friendships—if attachment to persons so inferior to himself can be called by that name—of which I have already mentioned two or three instances in his younger days, and in which the pride of being a protector, and the pleasure of exciting gratitude, seem to have constituted to his mind the chief, pervading charm. The person whom he now adopted in this manner, and from similar feelings to those which had inspired his early attachments to the cottage-boy near Newstead, and the young chorister at Cambridge, was a Greek youth, named Nicolo Giraud, the son, I believe, of a widow

LETTERS

lady, in whose house the artist Lusieri lodged. In this young man he appears to have taken the most lively, and even brotherly, interest;—so much so, as not only to have presented to him, on their parting, at Malta, a considerable sum of money, but to have subsequently designed for him, as the reader will learn, a still more munificent, as well as permanent, provision.'—MOORE.

Joseph Murray:—Byron's old servant—(a legacy from the Wicked Earl)—for whom he had ever the greatest affection and solicitude. 'I have more than once,' says a gentleman who was at this time a constant visitor to Newstead, 'seen Lord Byron at the dinner-table fill out a tumbler of Madeira, and hand it over his shoulder to Joe Murray, who stood behind his chair, saying with a cordiality that brightened his whole countenance, "Here, my old fellow, drink this." '—MOORE. See *ante,* p. 357, Note to Letter lxxvii.

Demetrius Zograffo, native of Greece:—'If the papers lie not (which they generally do), Demetrius Zograffo is at the head of the Athenian part of the Greek insurrection. He was my servant in 1809, 1810, 1811, 1812, at different intervals of these years (for I left him in Greece when I went to Constantinople), and accompanied me to England in 1811: he returned to Greece, spring 1812. He was a clever, but not *apparently* an enterprising man; but circumstances make men. His two sons (*then* infants) were named Miltiades and Alcibiades: may the omen be happy!'— BYRON, *MS. Journal.* See also HOBHOUSE, *Travels,* etc., *passim.*

The late Mrs. B.'s Scotch property:—'On the death of his mother, a considerable sum of money, the remains of the price of the estate of Gight, was paid into his hands by her trustee, Baron Clerk.'—MOORE.

With regard to this document, it is further noted by Moore:— In sending a copy of the Will, framed on these instructions, to Lord Byron, the solicitor accompanied some of the clauses with marginal queries, calling the attention of his noble client to points which he considered inexpedient or questionable; and as the short pithy answers to these suggestions are strongly characteristic of their writer, I shall here give one or two of the clauses in full, with the respective queries and answers annexed.

'This is the last will and testament of me, the Rt. Honble. George Gordon, Lord Byron, Baron Byron of Rochdale, in the county of Lancaster.—I desire that my body may be buried in the vault of the garden of Newstead, without any ceremony or burial-service whatever, and that no inscription, save my name and age, be

362

NOTES

written on the tomb or tablet; and it is my will that my faithful dog may not be removed from the said vault. To the performance of this my particular desire, I rely on the attention of my executors hereinafter named.'

'*It is submitted to Lord Byron whether this* clause relative *to the funeral had not better be omitted. The* substance of it can be *given in a letter from* his Lordship *to the executors, and accompany the will; and the will may state that* the funeral shall be performed in *such* manner as his Lordship *may by* letter direct, and, in default *of any* such letter, then at *the* discretion of his executors.'

'It must stand.   B.'

'I do hereby specifically order and direct that all the claims of the said S. B. Davies upon me shall be fully paid and satisfied as soon as conveniently may be after my decease, on his proving [by vouchers, or otherwise, to the satisfaction of my executors hereinafter named] the amount thereof, and the correctness of the same.'

'*If Mr. Davies has any* unsettled claims upon Lord *Byron, that* circumstance is a *reason for his not being appointed executor; each* executor *having* an *opportunity of paying himself his own debt* without *consulting his co-executors.*'

'So much the better—if possible let him be an executor.   B.'

LETTER lxxxiv. p. 131.

My poor schoolfellow Wingfield:—The Hon. John Wingfield of the Coldstream Guards, brother to Lord Powerscourt, who died of a fever in the May of this year. 'P. Hunter, Curzon, Long, and Tatersall were my principal friends. Clare, Dorset, Cᵃ. Gordon, De Bath, Claridge, and Jⁿᵒ. Wingfield were my juniors and favourites, whom I spoilt by indulgence. Of all human beings, I was, perhaps, at one time, the most attached to poor Wingfield, who died at Coimbra, 1811, before I returned to England.'—BYRON, *MS. Journal.* See also the sketch of Alonzo in 'Childish Recollections' (*Hours of Idleness*):—

> Alonzo! best and dearest of my friends,
> Thy name ennobles him who thus commends
> From this fond tribute thou canst gain no praise;
> The praise is his who now that tribute pays.
> Oh! in the promise of thy early youth,
> If hope anticipates the words of truth,
> Some loftier bard shall sing thy glorious name,
> To build his own upon thy deathless fame.
> Friend of my heart, and foremost of the list
> Of those with whom I lived supremely blest,

363

Oft have we drained the fount of ancient lore,
Though drinking deeply, thirsting still for more ;
Yet when confinement's lingering hour was done,
Our sports, our studies, and our souls were one.
In every element, unchanged, the same,
All, all that brothers should be, but the name :—

and the memorial stanzas (xci and xcii) interpolated in the First
Harold :—

And thou, my friend !—since unavailing woe
Bursts from my heart, and mingles with the strain—
Had the sword laid thee with the mighty low,
Pride might forbid e'en Friendship to complain :
But thus unlaurelled to descend in vain,
By all forgotten, save the lonely breast,
And mix unbleeding with the boasted slain,
While Glory crowns so many a meaner crest !
What hadst thou done to sink so peacefully to rest?

Oh, known the earliest, and esteemed the most !
Dear to a heart where nought was left so dear !
Though to my hopeless days for ever lost,
In dreams deny me not to see thee here !
And Morn in secret shall renew the tear
Of Consciousness awaking to her woes,
And Fancy hover o'er thy bloodless bier,
Till my frail frame return to whence it rose,
And mourned and mourner lie united in repose.

LETTER lxxxv. p. 132.

I have answered the queries on the margin :—' In the clause
enumerating the names and places of abode of the executors, the
solicitor had left blanks for the Christian names of these gentlemen, and Lord Byron, having filled up all but that of Dallas,
writes in the margin—" I forget the Christian name of Dallas—
cut him out." '—MOORE.

LETTER lxxxvi. p. 133.

My sister, the Honble. Augusta Leigh :—Byron's half-sister, the
Hon. Augusta Byron, daughter of John Byron, by Amelia Darcy,
Baroness Conyers, daughter of the Fourth Earl of Holderness,
wife of the Marquis of Caermarthen, and prospective Duchess
of Leeds. Augusta Byron—Mrs. Shelley's ' Dowdy-Goody '—seems
to have been born in 1784—(the year of her mother's death ;
though Mr. Paget, in his admirable account of the Beecher-
Stowe fiasco (*Blackwood*, January 1870 : *Paradoxes and Puzzles*,
London and Edinburgh, 1874), thinks that she may have been

NOTES

born as early as 1780)—and lived with her father at Chantilly,
and with her father and stepmother at Chantilly and in Holles
Street till the year of Byron's birth, when her grandmother,
the once beautiful Dutch girl, now the Dowager-Countess of
Holderness, took charge of her. This lady and the ingenuous
Mrs. John Byron were not friends : so that it was not until
after the Dowager-Countess's death that the brother and sister
began to see and know each other. By that time Byron was a boy
of fourteen ; but to Augusta he was ever the 'Baby Byron' she had
left in Holles Street. Henceforth, too, she was his best and
staunchest friend, the one influence in his life that made steadily
for good. 'Augusta,' he said at Genoa, 'knew all my weaknesses,
yet had love enough to bear with them'; in fact, she 'but loved
and pitied me the more because I was erring.' She never shrank
from telling him the truth, nor from excepting to such of his acts
and words as seemed to her to put him in the wrong; he left to
her and her children whatever remained of his estate, after the
performance of the trusts of his marriage settlement—'in consequence of my dear wife Lady Byron and whatever children I
may have otherwise amply provided for'; he cherished for her
an unwavering regard, which found utterance in more than one
immortal song. After the Marriage, Mrs. Leigh (she had been
the wife of Colonel Leigh of the Tenth Huzzars since 1807) was
received into high favour by her sister-in-law, was chosen to be
her companion before and after her confinement, and became
(in fact) the 'Goose' to Lady Byron's 'Pippin' and to Byron's
'Duck.' She did her utmost for both parties at the time of the
Separation. 'To me,' said Byron to Lady Blessington, 'she was,
in the hour of need, a tower of strength.' Indeed, 'her affection
was my last rallying-point, and is now the only bright spot that
the horizon of England offers to my view.' Still, when Byron went
into Exile (1816), she remained on terms of the most affectionate
intimacy with his wife, till the end (it would seem) of 1829, when
Lady Byron's insistence in appointing to the vacant trusteeship of
Byron's estate no less a person than the Stephen Lushington of the
Separation—(who could scarce be expected to prove a *persona grata*
to Byron's sister)—led to a series of protests (Morrison Collection)
from Mrs. Leigh, which the recipient either could not, or was
anxious not, to brook. Thereafter, Byron's only child, the
name-child, Augusta Ada, remained an entire stranger to her
aunt; and the ill-matched sisters met no more till 1851—the year
of Mrs. Leigh's death. It had been conveyed to her (it would

365

seem) that Lady Byron had complained, and loudly, that but for
Augusta's influence, Byron and she might have been reconciled;
and this induced Mrs. Leigh to ask a meeting. Writing from
Brighton (18th February 1851), 'I propose,' says Lady Byron, 'to
meet you at the nearest convenient Hotel on this railway'; to
'hear *in Private* whatever you might have to say to me'; but
'should I, after hearing it, wish to make any observations, you
must permit me to do so in the presence of a friend, who will
accompany me.' The meeting—(which 'cannot but be one of
suffering to me,' but . . . 'I think it right to make it')—took place
under these conditions (the 'friend' was Frederick Robertson of
Brighton) at the White Hart, Reigate. Mrs. Leigh's communication was simply to the effect that such influence as she had had
with her brother had ever been used to the advantage of his wife.
'Is that all?' said the other lady, who seems to have expected
nothing less than a peculiar version of the story of Laon and
Cythna. And, in writing to Mrs. Leigh (Brighton, April 12th,
1851), after remarking that she (Lady B.) has 'done all in her
power' to 'contribute to your peace of mind,' she 'remains under
the afflicting persuasion that it is not to be attained by such means
as you have taken.' The matter appears to end, so far as the
world is concerned, with Mrs. Leigh's reply to this curious expression of self-righteousness :—

St. J. Palace, April 26, 1851.

I feel sure that you would not willingly be unjust, and therefore after
much perplexing and deep consideration I have determined again to address
you. My great wish for an interview with you arose partly from a secret
desire to see you once more in this world, and still more to have the means
of convincing you that accusations which I had reason to believe had been
brought against me to you were unfounded, and at this, if only from the
recollection of the affection that once subsisted between us, you cannot be
surprised—I had not and never implied that I had anything to reveal to you,
with which *you* were not previously acquainted, on any other subject—nor
can I at all express to you the regret I have felt ever since those words
escaped you, showing that you imagined I had 'encouraged a bitterness of
feeling in Lord Byron towards you.' I now as solemnly declare to you as
if I were on my oath or on my death-bed that I never did so in any one
instance, but that I *invariably* did the contrary—I have letters from him,
and of my own to him (returned to me after his death) which would bear
out this assertion, and I am ready at this, or any other moment, to make
the most solemn asseveration of this, in any way that you can devise. I
would willingly see your Friend Mr. Robertson, and afford him every proof
of my veracity in my power. It was clear that he thought that I was keeping back communications that ought to be made to you, and as your confidential friend, it would be comfort to me to talk openly with him on such

NOTES

points as might tend to convince you of the truth of what I now say—and without which the remainder of my life will be still more unhappy than the miseries, of various kinds, which surround me must inevitably make me.

She died at the end of this same year; but Lady Byron, whether or not she had, as Paget insists, and it is generally believed, she had, talked Laon-and-Cythna under seal to Lushington, lived, as we shall see, to talk and think it ten years longer.

LETTER lxxxvii. p. 133.
Your mediation between me and Murray:—Longman had declined to publish *English Bards*; so, as far as the *Harold* was concerned, Longman was ruled out. And Cawthorn, who had published *English Bards*, and was just now busy with *Hints from Horace*, was not strong enough to take on the *Harold*. But a principal publisher at this time was William Miller (1769-1844). Born at Bungay, he started in life as an Art-student, on the advice of Sir Joshua himself; but he was the son of a bookseller, and in 1787 he was placed under Hookham the publisher, and three years later he set up for himself in Bond Street. In 1804 he removed to Albemarle Street, and lived there till his retirement in 1812, when he was succeeded by John Murray II. Among his publications were Walter Scott's *Dryden*, and Fox's *History of the Reign of James II.*, for which latter he paid what was then the record price of £4500. But Miller declined the *Harold*, because of Byron's strictures on Lord Elgin, whose publisher he was, and whom he would not suffer to be called a 'plunderer' in any print of *his* producing. Byron did not care a jot. 'As is usual in similar cases,' he writes to Miller, he has 'a predilection for the worst passages,' so he purposes to 'retain,' though he 'cannot venture to defend' them. Also, he can 'perfectly conceive, and indeed approve,' the publisher's reasons, whom he proceeds to assure (with a certain lack of grammar and a pleasant memory of Gil Blas and His Grace of Granada) that 'my sensations are not *Archiepiscopal* enough as yet to regret the rejection of my Homilies.' The ground thus cleared of Miller, there remained John Murray II. (see *post*, p. 370, Note to Letter lxxxix.); and as John II. had expressed a wish to publish something by Lord Byron, to John II. Dallas, who, to do him justice, saw much more in the *Harold* than he did in the *Hints*, took the two cantos. With the result we know.

My plaguy Satire will bring the north and south Grub Streets down upon the 'Pilgrimage':—Byron brought home with him the

367

LETTERS

MSS. of (1) the First and Second *Harold*, and (2) the *Hints from Horace*, 'Being an Allusion in English verse to the Epistle *Ad Pisones, De Arte Poetica*, and Intended as a Sequel to *English Bards and Scotch Reviewers*.' On Dallas's persuasion he suppressed the *Hints*, and published the *Harold* (1812), whose reception was so magnificent that, as he said, he felt he should be 'heaping coals of fire on his head' if he went on lampooning the authors of that reception. Nine years after, he took up the *Hints* again; but finding that, as Hobhouse said, it would take 'a good deal of slashing' to bring the verses up to date, he put them by once more, and they were not printed till seven years after his death (1831).

Five families of distinction:—This is a jape: repeated, too, from a Note to a certain passage in *Hints from Horace*:—'And then his inscription split into so many modicums!—"To the Duchess of Somuch, the Right Hon. So-and-So, and Mrs. and Miss Somebody, these volumes are, etc. etc."—why, this is doling out the "soft milk of dedication" in gills,—there is but a quart, and he divides it among a dozen. Why, Pratt, hadst thou not a puff left? Dost thou think six families of distinction can share this in quiet? There is a child, a book, and a dedication: send the girl to her grace, the volumes to the grocer, and the dedication to the devil.' Here is Pratt's Dedication :—

TO HER GRACE

THE DUCHESS OF LEEDS

LADY MILBANKE AND FAMILY

BENEVOLENT PATRONS

OF

THE AUTHOR

THESE VOLUMES

ARE RESPECTFULLY DEDICATED

BY

THE EDITOR.

I am sorry you don't like Harry White:—Henry Kirke White (1785-1806), the Nottingham poetaster for whom Byron—perhaps for the county's sake—professed a very strong regard, as witnesses a famous parallel in *English Bards* :—

> Unhappy White! while life was in its spring,
> And thy young muse just waved her joyous wing,
> The spoiler swept that soaring lyre away,
> Which else had sounded an immortal lay.

NOTES

> Oh ! what a noble heart was here undone,
> When Science' self destroyed her favourite son !
> Yes, she too much indulged thy fond pursuit,
> She sowed the seeds, but death has reaped the fruit.
> 'Twas thine own genius gave the final blow,
> And helped to plant the wound that laid thee low :
> So the struck eagle, stretched upon the plain,
> No more through rolling clouds to soar again,
> Viewed his own feather on the fatal dart,
> And winged the shaft that quivered in his heart ;
> Keen were his pangs, but keener far to feel,
> He nursed the pinion which impelled the steel ;
> While the same plumage that had warmed his nest
> Drank the last life-drop of his bleeding breast.

White had character, and died of consumption induced by over-study; but Southey's *Life* (1808) of him is rather read for its own sake than its subject's.

Lofft and Pratt:—Lofft is Capel Lofft (1751-1824), Byron's 'Mæcenas of shoemakers, and preface-writer-general to distressed versemen; a kind of gratis accoucheur to those who wish to be delivered of rhyme, but do not know how to bring forth.' Lofft, a Whig barrister, wrote volubly on all manner of subjects, but is best known as the discoverer and patron of Robert Bloomfield (1766-1823)—like Blackett, a cobbler, but a far better poet than Blackett—who was enabled by his means to publish *The Farmer's Boy.* Lofft encouraged, too, the muse of Robert's tailor-brother, Nathaniel, whence the couplets in the *Hints from Horace :*—

> Hark to those notes, narcotically soft,
> The cobbler-laureats sing to Capel Lofft !
> Till, lo ! that modern Midas, as he hears,
> Adds an ell growth to his egregious ears :—

with the Note (or rather Notes) explanatory :—'I beg Nathaniel's pardon : he is not a cobbler ; it is a *tailor*, but begged Capel Lofft to sink the profession in his preface to two pair of panta——psha !—of cantos, which he wished the public to try on ; but the sieve of a patron let it out, and so far saved the expense of an advertisement to his country customers, etc. etc.'

LETTER lxxxviii. p. 137.

Otway's two other requisites for an Englishman :—See *Venice Preserved*, Act II. Sc. ii. :—

> Give but an Englishman his whore and ease,
> Beef and a sea-coal fire, he's yours for ever.

LETTERS

LETTER lxxxix. p. 137.

To Mr. Murray:—John Murray (1778-1843) was the son of John M'Murray (John I. 1745-1793), who threw up a commission in the Marines to turn bookseller at 32 Fleet Street, where, under the style and title of John Murray, he succeeded Paul Sandby. John II. was but fifteen when his father died ; but he had uncommon energy and intelligence ; he made some fortunate ventures; and by the time he was thirty or so he had planned and launched *The Quarterly Review,* with Gifford as editor, and Scott and Heber, Canning and George Ellis, for contributors. It was so instant a success that it was everywhere accepted as the official Tory organ, and the shop in Fleet Street—(it was not till 1812 that John II. took over Miller's place in Albemarle Street, and became the 'Emperor of the West ')—was soon a veritable literary centre. Murray was Publisher to the Admiralty and the Board of Longitude ; but there is no department of letters in which he did not make and leave his mark. Among his authors were Henry Hallam, Lockhart (the *Scott* and the *Burns*), Campbell (*Specimens of the British Poets*), Richard Ford, 'Aristophanes' Mitchell, Plumer Ward, Crabbe, Lord Mahon, Prior (*Life of Goldsmith*), Sir John Barrow, Sir John Malcolm, Heber, Southey, Lord Rosse, Sir Humphrey Davy, Sir George Back, Greig, Sir George Head, Walter Scott, Morier (*Hajji Baba*), Hope (*Anastasius*), Washington Irving, Napier, Mme. de Staël, Wellington, Lady Caroline Lamb, Croker (Boswell's *Johnson*), George Borrow, Sir Edward Parry, Sir Alexander Burness, 'Monk' Lewis, Sir John Franklin, Malthus (*Essay on the Principle of Population*), Faraday, Babbage, Fanny Kemble, Mrs. Trollope, Carème (*The Art of French Cookery*), 'Nimrod,' Benjamin Disraeli (*Contarini Fleming* and *Gallomania*), and Mr. W. E. Gladstone (*The State in its Relation with the Church*)—to name but these. 'Tis a brilliant gathering ; but its *raisons d'etre* are conspicuous. 'I believe'—thus John II. to Napier, to whom he had offered £500 for the first volume of the *Peninsular War*—'I believe that you will not find it is in my character to make any ungenerous offer for a valuable work '; and he did himself the barest justice in the assumption. He gave Crabbe £3000 for a set of copyrights, whose interest was on the wane, and which the Longmans had refused to reconsider—and lost £1500 or so by the bargain. Washington Irving's *Columbus* and *Granada* cost him nearly £8800, which represented a deficit of £2250. To Moore, for the *Life* of Byron, he paid some £4800 in cash ; and in 1831 he stood

370

to lose £300 on the first issue, 'even if the whole were sold.'
But if he lost with one hand, he gained with the other. By 1838
Mrs. Rundell's *Art of Cookery* :—

> Along thy shelves in order shine
> The works thou deemest most divine,
> The Art of Cookery, and mine,
> My Murray :—

an early venture of his, had gone through sixty editions; the
circulation of the *Quarterly* ranged between nine and twelve thousand copies; his interest in Byron alone must have been literally
golden. For he was sagacious as well as daring. The business
(so he held) of 'a publishing bookseller' lay in his brains—not in
his shop; and if he endured a loss of £26,000 in the matter of *The
Representative*—(the ill-starred daily print which was the first in
time and the worst in fortune of Benjamin Disraeli's many enter-
prises)—he had the rectitude and the good sense to retire from
business with Constable and the Ballantynes; so that when the
crash came, he was able, not only to meet it with composure, but
also, to stand to the rescue of some fellow-traders who must have
gone under but for his hand. His authors, too,—and we have
seen what manner of men they were—were his personal friends.
He had the gift of wearing, as well as the trick of winning. And
he passed the greater part of a long, laborious, honourable life on
equal terms and in constant association with the best of his time.

It was in 1811, while John II. was still in Fleet Street, that Dallas
took him the MS. of the First and Second *Harold*; and this was
the beginning of a connexion which, though it was interrupted by
his refusal to publish *Don Juan* from the Sixth Canto onwards,
was in the end resumed, and was throughout an advantage and a
pleasure to both the parties. Poet and publisher were soon on the
best possible terms. As these volumes will show, to nobody did
Byron write with a finer felicity or a more abounding spirit than
he wrote to Murray; while as for Murray, his regard for Byron
was confessed not merely in big prices—(which he could afford to
pay, and which were simply Byron's due)—but in a hundred little
friendly offices, in a constant care for Byron's interest and Byron's
fame, and in a series of letters (for which see Dr. Smiles's *Memoir,
passim*), which show that the writer was never so happy as in seeking to make his correspondent happy by the transmission of good
news, or a good book, or good words from an admirer or a friend.
For the business relations between the two, enough to say that,
roughly speaking, Murray produced everything that Byron wrote,

with the exception of *English Bards*, the *Vision*, the *Hours*, the *Age of Bronze*, and the last cantos (eleven) of *Don Juan* (all which he bought of the Executors at a cost of £3885); that, besides what he gave Dallas for the First and Second *Harold* and *The Giaour* (£1125 in all), he paid to Byron nearly £15,000 in hard cash; that he purchased the MS. *Memoir* of Moore for £2100, and had decided to destroy it, and to be at the loss of the purchase-money, when the matter was taken out of his hands; that in answer to Leigh Hunt's attack on Byron's memory (see *post*, p. 435, Note to Letter clxxiv.) he commissioned Moore to prepare the *Life and Letters* (1830), himself contributing a good half of the matter, agreed to pay him four thousand guineas for the work, and in the long-run paid him £600 more; and that in 1837 he produced the annotated edition of the *Poems* which, in one or other of its forms, has been hitherto the sole complete Byron to be had. Murray, in fact, was Byron's publisher, even as Byron was Murray's poet; and to disassociate their several names and fames would, now or ever, be impossible.

Editor of one of the principal reviews:—To wit, *The Quarterly*.

Some smaller poems (never published):—For the names of those included in the Quarto—fourteen in number—see *post*, vol. v. Bibliographical Note to the First and Second *Harold*.

LETTER XC. p. 139.

Sending the MS. to Juvenal:—That is, Hodgson, who had published a translation of the Roman four years before.

Gasping for the press at Cawthorn's:—In an (unpublished) letter, dated Newstead, 1st September of this year, 'Mr. Cawthorn,' Byron writes, 'how does the printer proceed? Let the devil be attentive,' for 'you cannot expect a "votary of Apollo" to busy himself with proof-sheets.' Still, they must all be posted, 'as I am about to amend them,' so 'if you wish to see a radiant countenance,' etc. etc.

Miss Milbanke's 'Cottage of Friendship':—As we have seen, Miss Milbanke patronised Blackett, set him up in a cottage, and. had him buried in Seaham Churchyard.

The newspapers seem much disappointed:—In the late autumn of 1810 the death of Princess Amelia, the old King's favourite daughter, had precipitated, if it had not determined, the mental illness from which he never recovered; so that the Prince of Wales was sworn in as Regent in the early February of the next year (1811).

LETTER xci. p. 141.

Our heir, George Anson Byron, and his sister:—Julia-Maria, sister of the present Lord Byron; who married, in 1817, the Rev. Robert Heath, Fellow of St. John's College, Oxford.—MOORE.

There is a sucking epic poet at Granta:—The Rev. George Townsend of Trinity, Cambridge. See *Hints from Horace*:—

> For you, young bard, whom luckless fate may lead
> To tremble on the nod of all who read:—

and the long note attached to the passage:—'About two years ago a young man named Townsend was announced by Mr. Cumberland (in a review since deceased) as being engaged on an epic poem to be entitled *Armageddon*, etc. In 1815 Townsend published eight of the twelve books in which his epic was to have been contained. They were all he ever wrote; for, says he, in his introduction, "In the benevolence of his heart, Mr. Cumberland bestowed praise on me, certainly too abundantly and prematurely, but I hope that any deficiency on my part may be imputed to the true cause—my own inability to support a subject, under which the greatest mental powers must inevitably sink. My talents were ueither equal to my own ambition, nor his zeal to serve me."'

Townsend's *Cumberland* was the once popular dramatist and essayist (1732-1801). To the Goldsmith of *Retaliation* he was 'the Terence of England, the mender of hearts'; to Sheridan, the best character in the best of modern farces—the Sir Fretful Plagiary of *The Critic*.

LETTER xcii. p. 143.

A ——, or a Bonze:—The word is illegible in the original.—J. T. HODGSON, *Memoir*, etc., *ut sup.*

LETTER xciii. p. 145.

Massena's retreat:—From the lines of Torres Vedras; for us, according to Napier, the most ticklish moment of the campaign.

So you perceive I cannot alter the sentiments:—Writing 4th September 1811, Murray had asked Byron to reconsider his remarks on Spain and Portugal, together with certain expressions 'which may deprive me of some customers among the Orthodox': with the result that Sir Arthur Wellesley, Sir Hew Dalrymple, Lord Elgin (still 'the modern Pict'), and the rest were somewhat spared, and that in Canto ii. the existing Eighth Stanza took the place of this one:—

> Frown not upon me, churlish Priest! that I
> Look not for life, where life may never be;

I am no sneerer at thy phantasy ;
Thou pitiest me,—alas ! I envy thee,
Thou bold discoverer in an unknown sea
Of happy isles and happier tenants there ;
I ask thee not to prove a Sadducee ;
Still dream of Paradise, thou know'st not where,
But lov'st too well to bid thine erring brother share.

Did you show the MS. to some of your corps :—Murray had, in fact, submitted the MS. to Gifford (among others), and Byron resented the proceeding, inasmuch as he thought it looked like currying favour with the editor of a popular and powerful review. To be done with the matter : Gifford & Co. approved, but Murray doubted, and Dallas's expectation—('that he would make a very liberal arrangement with me for it')—caused him to doubt still more. In the end he compromised, took the poem on the half-profits system, and arranged to publish it in 'a handsome quarto edition,' thanks to which, Dallas netted £600.

LETTER XCV. p. 147.

Spin canzonettas for Vauxhall :—Vauxhall was still extremely popular, and the Popular Muse—when was she ever aught but imbecile? On the introduction of George Thomson of the *Scottish Airs*, she had long since corrupted and debilitated the Burns of those last years at Dumfries ; and she was no whit better now than then. For a proof of Figaro's *mot*, indeed—If there's anything not worth saying, *sing it*!—see the three volumes of *The Busy Bee, or Vocal Repository*, published (with portraits of Mrs. Billington, Captain Morris, and Mrs. Martyr) some twenty years before this time.

Your friend's Ode I have read :—'An Ode written by Mr. Walter Wright, on the occasion of the Duke of Gloucester's installation as Chancellor of the University of Cambridge.'—MOORE. Wright is 'the author of *Horæ Ionicæ*' of a few lines down the page ; and in a Note [B.] to *English Bards :*—

Blest is the man who dare approach the bower
Where dwelt the Muses in their natal hour. . . .
Wright, 'twas thy happy lot at once to view
Those shores of glory, and to sing them too :—

Horæ Ionicæ—(*A Poem, Descriptive of the Ionian Isles and Part of the Adjacent Coast of Greece*)—is described as 'a very beautiful poem just published . . . descriptive of the adjacent isles of Greece.' A third edition, the only one in the British Museum, was published in 1816, and includes 'a Translation of Alfieri's

NOTES

Tragedy Orestes.' Murray's Editor notes that Wright—'late consul-general for the Seven Islands' [B.]—on his return to England was 'chosen Recorder for Bury St. Edmonds.'

The *Smythe* of the sentence was William Smythe, M.A., Professor of Modern History in the University of Cambridge, hero of two couplets (both expunged) in *English Bards* :—

> Though printers condescend the press to soil
> With odes by Smythe and epic songs by Hoyle;
>
> . . . . . .
>
> So stink in dulness and so lost in shame
> That Smythe and Hodgson scarce redeem thy name.

LETTER xcvi. p. 149.

'*Juvenal*' and '*Lady Jane*' :—See *ante*, p. 319, Note to Letter xxxv.

Hal of Harrow :—The Rev. Henry Drury.

LETTER xcviii. p. 151.

Anacreon Moore's new operatic farce :—This was *M.P.*, or *The Bluestocking*, produced at the Lyceum, 9th September 1811. The author was far from proud of his work. But eight songs from it are included in his *Works*; and poor enough they are.

Malthus on Population :—The famous *Essay on the Principle of Population* (1798) of the Rev. T. R. Malthus (1766-1834).

LETTER cii. p. 155.

A little French volume, a great favourite with me :—Fougeret de Monbron (171?-1761) was born at Péronne; served in the Gardes du Corps; and wrote a *Henriade Travestie*, with *le Cosmopolite* (1750), and *Margot la Ravaudeuse* (1750). An edition of *le Cosmopolite, ou le Citoyen du Monde* was published in London in 1761.

LETTER ciii. p. 157.

I wish Murray had been tied to Payne's neck :—Payne, of the firm of Payne and Mackinlay, was a publisher (Hodgson's) who committed suicide in the Paddington Canal. In a note to the *Hints from Horace*, 'Mr. Southey,' Byron says, 'has lately tied another canister to his tail in the *Curse of Kehama*, maugre the neglect of *Madoc*, etc., and has in one instance had a wonderful effect. A literary friend of mine, walking out one lovely evening last summer, on the eleventh bridge of the Paddington canal, was alarmed by the cry of "one in jeopardy": he rushed along, collected a body of Irish haymakers (supping on butter-milk in an adjacent paddock), procured three rakes, one eel-spear, and a landing-net, and at last (*horresco referens*) pulled out—his own publisher. The unfortunate man was gone for ever, and so was a large quarto wherewith he had taken the leap, which proved, on inquiry, to have been Mr. Southey's last work. Its "alacrity of sinking,"' etc. etc. etc.

LETTER cv. p. 158.
Hobhouse is also forthcoming:—That is, with the MS. of certain Notes to the First and Second *Harold.*

LETTER cvi. p. 159.
The ninth verse of the 'Good Night' :—

> Perchance my dog will whine in vain
> Till fed by stranger hands ;
> But long ere I come back again
> He'd tear me where he stands.

Thus, in effect, it has always read.

The Giant's staff from St. Dunstan's Church :—Murray's shop at 32 Fleet Street stood over against old St. Dunstan in the West, which church was one of the sights of London for over a hundred and fifty years, by reason of a famous mechanical clock, 'the work of Thomas Harris, living at the end of Water Lane,' whereon the hours were struck by the staves of two brazen giants, put up in 1671 ('When the alarm strikes,' cries Congreve's Sir Sampson, 'they shall keep time like the figures of St. Dunstan's clock'). Says Mr. Wheatley in his excellent *London* :—'When the old clock was taken down, the two figures were bought by the Marquis of Hertford and removed'—1831—'to his lordship's villa in Regent's Park. Moxon says that the removal of the figures drew tears from Charles Lamb's eyes.' Also :—'The villa is still called St. Dunstan's, and is now (1896) occupied by Mr. H. Hucks Gibbs.' Mr. Wheatley does not fail to add that St. Dunstan's (of which John Donne was Vicar) Churchyard was a bookselling centre, where Southwick had his shop 'under the Diall,' and published *Romeo and Juliet* (1609) and *Hamlet* (1611), and where Richard Marriot published *The Compleat Angler* (1653). There, too, Campion was buried, and Simon Wadlow, landlord of the Devil Tavern, Ben Jonson's 'Sim, the King of Skinkers.' As for Number 32 itself, it had witnessed the birth (under John I.) of Langhorne's *Plutarch*, Mitford's *Greece*, Isaac Disraeli's first *Curiosities*, and Lavater's famous *Physiognomy* ; under John II., that of more books than I care to enumerate. It was now to be the starting-point of

376

NOTES

Childe Harold, and you are told by Dr. Smiles that Byron used to come in fresh from his bouts with Jackson, pick out a book on the shelves, and lunge at it with his cane till John II. (who was not of an athletic habit) was often 'glad enough to be rid of him.'

LETTER cvii. p. 160.

If I fall, I shall fall gloriously :—In the beginning, as to the end, that is, he was the 'passionate and dauntless soldier of a forlorn hope' revealed in Matthew Arnold's Essay.

LETTER cviii. p. 161.

Pray, do you think, etc. :—'Vathek' is not the book, but the writer thereof. (See *ante*, p. 334-5, Note to Letter liii.)

LETTER cx. p. 165.

More like silliness than madness :—It is told of Davies that he retorted one day on Byron with this very antithesis.

Some savage lines on Methodism :—

> Then spare our stage, ye methodistic men,
> Nor burn damn'd Drury till it rise again !
> Yet why to brain-scorch'd zealots thus appeal ?
> Can heavenly mercy dwell with earthly zeal ?
> For times of fire and faggot let them hope, etc.

Ferocious notes :—The *Edinburgh Annual Register*, 'suggested by Scott in the very dawn of his bookselling days' (LOCKHART), came into being *c.* 1810. The Editor was Scott ; Southey looked after 'the historical department' ; Scott 'and other eminent persons' stood for general literature and science ; Southey 'contributed some of the most admired of his minor poems,' and so did Scott. But 'the work' (on which the loss was for some time not less than £1000 a year) was never 'the source of anything but anxiety and disappointment to its original projectors.' For the *Ferocious notes*, see Byron's commentary on the lines :—

> But hark ye, Southey ! pray—but don't be vexed—
> Burn all your last three works—and half the next, etc. :—

in *Hints from Horace*. Southey's 'last three works' at this time were *Madoc*, *Thalaba*, and *The Curse of Kehama*.

Mrs. Lumpkin :—A slip of the pen for 'Mrs. Hardcastle.'

The Eclectic Reviewers :—They were exceeding severe on the score of doctrine. Thus Byron, in a Note to the *Hints*, refers them 'to their own pages, where they congratulated themselves on the prospect of a tilt between Mr. Jeffrey and myself, from which some

377

great good was to accrue, provided one or both were knocked on the head.'

Demetrius the ' Sieger of Cities' is here, with *' Gilpin Horner'* :—
These I take to be nicknames—(of a cast held eulogistic in a vain and amatorious age)—for Hobhouse and Davies (?).

LETTER cxiii. p. 168.

To Mr. Moore:—Thomas Moore (1779-1852) was the son of a Dublin (Catholic) Grocer ; was educated at Sheridan's old school— (Mr. Whyte's : ' I was long his favourite *show-*scholar ')—and at Trinity College, Dublin—' after the memorable act of 1793, was one of the first of the young Helots of the land, who hastened to avail themselves of the privilege of being educated at their country's university'; at fourteen, or less, was writing for the *Anthologia*, a local magazine, in which he read *The Pleasures of Memory* ; at fifteen began the practice of political satire at the mock-court (Dalkey) of King Stephen (Armytage), a singing pawnbroker ; at nineteen came to London to read law at the Middle Temple ; and before he was twenty-one had published (1800) a translation (as it were into scented soap) of the *Odes* of Anacreon, which was dedicated—through his earliest patron, Lord Moira, afterwards First Marquess of Hastings—to the Prince of Wales, and which (with his own excellent talent as an actor and singer) gave him the run of the very choicest Whig Society. It was followed (1801) by *The Poetical Works of the late Thomas Little, Esq.*—a gentleman who ' died in his one-and-twentieth year' ; who had ' given much of his time to the study of the amatory writers' ; and whose works were (therefore) 'all the productions of an age when the passions very often give a colouring too warm to the imagination ' ; and in 1803 Lord Moira got him made Registrar to the Admiralty Court at Bermuda. He had looked for better patronage, but he was ever a man to make the best of things, and he made the best of this one. That is, he went to Bermuda, found and engaged a Deputy, travelled in Canada :—

> Faintly as tolls the evening chime,
> Our voices keep tune, and our oars keep time. . . .
> Row, brothers, row, the stream runs fast,
> The rapids are near and the daylight 's past :—

and the United States ; returned to England ; published his *Odes and Epistles* (1806); and in 1807 began the *Irish Melodies* (Part x., 1834), which he sang with rare and peculiar art, which were long worth £500 a year to him, which are still singing here

NOTES

and there, and which, as translated by Gounet, and set to music
by no less a man than Hector Berlioz, had, like the twice or thrice
translated *Epicurean*, a certain part in the Romantic Renaissance
of 1830. In 1811 he married, and in 1812 he published *The Twopenny Post-Bag* (see *post*, p. 434, Note to Letter clxxiv.) and became
Avenger-General to the Whigs, who were fresh from the Great Disappointment of 1811, and who exulted in his effect, whether he
wept over a false and fallen Prince in an *Irish Melody* :—

> When first I met thee, warm and young,
>   There shone such truth about thee,
> And on thy lip such promise hung
>   I did not dare to doubt thee,
> But go, deceiver, go, etc. :—

or took note (in *The Morning Chronicle* or *The Times*) of the run
of things at Lady Hertford's :—

> The house where you know
> There's such good mutton cutlets and strong curaçoa :—

in Manchester Square, and gibed the wigs and stays and whiskers,
the moral obliquities and the physical rotundities, in evidence at
Carlton House. In 1817 he published *Lalla Rookh* ; for the copyright of which he received three thousand guineas ; which he
dedicated to Samuel Rogers from ' His very grateful and Affectionate Friend' ; and whose vogue was so instant and so far-wandered
that Luttrell was soon able to address him thus :—

> I'm told, dear Moore, your lays are sung
> (Can it be true, you lucky man ?)
> At midnight in the Persian tongue
> Along the streets of Ispahan.

In 1818 he went to Paris (with Rogers), and there produced that
excellent set of pasquils, the first *Fudge Family*. Meanwhile the
Deputy at Bermuda was found to have defaulted to the tune of
£6000, and, to escape arrest, Moore went abroad, travelled in Italy
—(he stayed a few days at Venice with Byron, who gave him the
MS. *Memoir*)—and then, retracing his steps, set up his rest in Paris,
where he abode till, having compromised his debt to the Exchequer
for £1000, he returned to England : there to publish his *Loves of
the Angels* (1823), his *Captain Rock* (1824), his *Sheridan* (1825),
his *Epicurean* (1827), his *Byron* (1830), and his *Lord Edward
Fitzgerald* (1831), to say nothing of innumerable lyrics and pasquinades. In 1835 he was put on the Civil List for a pension of
£300 ; but his last years were miserable enough. For all the

smirk in his love-songs and the sting (as of nettles) in his satire, he
was a worthy and magnanimous little man—the best of sons, the
most devout among husbands (he was horribly scandalised, you
learn from his *Diary*, by the Marianna Segati business at Venice,
and not less so by the sketch of Donna Inez in *Don Juan*), the
most affectionate of fathers ; and, having lost his only daughter in
her girlhood, he was doomed to see the death of his second son
(by consumption) at the very threshold of what promised to be an
honourable career, and to watch the ruin of his heir, who ended,
as one of the Foreign Legion, in an Algerine hospital.   Such
gleams of happiness as were his came through his countrymen,
who wore him, tinsel and all, in their heart of hearts, and never
failed to greet him with just such ovations (in terms of whisky
and sentiment) as the Modern Scot reserves for the immortal
memory of Burns.   In the long-run his mind decayed : by 1847 he
was 'sinking' (so he wrote to Rogers) 'into a mere vegetable,' and
in reading of the end your sole feeling is one of regret that it came
so late and took so long.   As to his personal qualities, a single
testimony, being Sir Walter's, will suffice :—'It would be a delightful addition to life,' he wrote in 1825, 'if Thomas Moore had
a cottage within two miles of me.'   For his poetry, it is the fashion
to decry him ; and it is a fact that his *Lalla Rookh* and his *Loves of the
Angels* (a mild Whig Paradise done by a tame, suburban Byron) are
glittering and 'conceited' enough to look tawdry, at the same time
that they are so clever, and so breathless in their cleverness, as to
be extremities of hard reading.   But none in this century has sur-
passed him as a writer of light, brilliant, and scarifying insolence ;
while he was a master of cadence, and his songs—as *Bendemeer's
Stream*, as *At the Mid-Hour of Night*, as *Doth Not a Meeting*, to
name no more—have a rhythmical quality, at once exquisite and
simple, for which you may quest in vain among the Minors of
to-day.

For his connexion with Byron : it began in 1812, under such
circumstances as are set forth below.   It was said of him that he
'dearly loved a lord' ; but to love a lord was in those days no
crime—especially in an earnest Whig ; and Sir Walter, albeit a
fine, unalterable Tory, was no more averse from aristocratic in-
timacies than (to slide to the lowest rung of the ladder) the Radical
Leigh Hunt.   In any case, Moore had kept the company of peers
—Moira, Lansdowne, Holland, and the like—since his *début* in
1800 ; and it is fair to argue that he was at least as strongly attracted by Byron's temperament and Byron's genius as he was

touched by Byron's barony. It is possible—even probable—that
Mr. Fraser Rae is justified in saying that he was jealous of Sheridan :
like himself an Irishman, a commoner like himself, and like himself—but to far more splendid purpose than himself—a practical
and social success. But in Byron's case there were no grounds
for spleen ; for Byron, who recognised him instantly, and was even
his admirer and his friend, was not less manifestly his superior in
poetry and genius than he was his superior by birth and fortune.
In any event, it is certain that his attitude towards his 'noble
friend' (which, being mannerly and correct, was Shelley's phrase,
and Scott's), while cordial in the extreme, was never (that I can
see) unduly subservient. He received the dedication of *The Corsair*
with a vast deal of pride ('They may say,' he wrote to Power, 'that
the praise is laid on with a trowel, but at least it is a golden trowel
that lays it on'); but he gave nothing in return for it but his very
mediocre *Fables for the Holy Alliance* (1823). He accepted the
MS. *Memoir* gratefully, but without humility—as a gift from friend
to friend ; and he did his best for his friend's sake to keep at least
a part of it for posterity. He avenged the memory of 'a late noble
Lion' on a certain 'small puppy dog' (see *post*, p. 438, Note to
Letter clxxiv.) with exemplary thoroughness. He took up the work
of writing the *Life* with such an independence of mind that he
began by making himself hateful to the Lady-Byronites, and went
on to scandalise the opposite faction in the end. In brief, I cannot
find that (even in his revolts in the character of a 'Domestic Man')
he was ever other than loyal to a friendship which was one of the
best things in his life.

⊢ For the occasion of its beginning we must go back to 1806, and
thence onward to 1809 and the publication of *English Bards*. In
the former year, the Irish poet, exasperated by the strictures which
Jeffrey had passed in verses (see *ante*, p. 300, Note to Letter vii.),
challenged his critic to the arbitrament of mortal combat. The
would-be duellists met at Chalk Farm—(they took a fancy to each
other on the ground)—but the affair had taken wind (through
William Spencer and Lord Fincastle) and they were arrested.
Now Jeffrey's friend was that Francis Horner whom Sir Walter
likened to Father Shandy's bull, and on him devolved the deadly
work of loading the tools. He was far too serious and too highly
cultured a Whig to know anything about firearms ; and when the
pistols were examined at Bow Street, it was found that one had a
bullet in it, but the other had not. Then 'Enter Rumour'—on this
occasion, as on many others, 'an Irish Journalist'—'painted full of

tongues,' all hoiloaing that the pistols held no bullets. 'In consequence of this,' says Moore, 'I was induced to write a letter to the editor of one of the Journals'—'almost all' had gone with Rumour —'contradicting the falsehood that had been circulated, and stating briefly the real circumstances of the case.' This contradiction Byron did not see; and in *English Bards* he took it on him to tell the tale, in prose and verse, as the world loved to hear it told :—

> Can none remember that eventful day,
> That ever glorious, almost fatal fray,
> When Little's leadless pistol met his eye,
> And Bow Street myrmidons stood laughing by?

'In 1806 Messrs. Jeffrey and Moore met at Chalk Farm. The duel was prevented by the interference of the magistracy; and, on examination, the balls of the pistols were found to have evaporated. This incident gave occasion to much waggery in the daily prints.' The First Edition of *English Bards* was anonymous; but to the Second (published in the summer of the same year) Byron put his name. This at the time Moore did not know; but when at last he learned who had belittled him, he put on his best duelling manner, and thus addressed his adversary :—

Dublin, January 1, 1810.

My Lord,—Having just seen the name of 'Lord Byron' prefixed to a work entitled *English Bards and Scotch Reviewers*, in which, as it appears to me, *the lie is given* to a public statement of mine, respecting an affair with Mr. Jeffrey some years since, I beg you will have the goodness to inform me whether I may consider your Lordship as the author of this publication.

I shall not, I fear, be able to return to London for a week or two; but, in the meantime, I trust your Lordship will not deny me the satisfaction of knowing whether you avow the insult contained in the passages alluded to.

It is needless to suggest to your Lordship the propriety of keeping our correspondence secret.—I have the honour to be, your Lordship's very humble servant, THOMAS MOORE.

22 Molesworth Street.

Byron, however, had gone abroad, and the letter got no further than Hodgson, who promised—but failed—to send it on to him. Byron returned to England in 1811, as we have seen; and in the interval Moore had (as he puts it) 'taken upon himself obligations, both as husband and father, which make most men—and especially those who have nothing to bequeath—less willing to expose themselves to danger.' All the same, the Note to the 'leadless pistol' couplet rankled, and he resolved to have it out—as peaceably as might be—with its noble author. 'The death of Mrs. Byron,' he

NOTES

remarks, 'for some time delayed my purpose. But as soon after
that event as was consistent with decorum, I addressed a letter to
Lord Byron, in which, referring to my former communication, and
expressing some doubts as to its having ever reached him, I re-
stated, in pretty nearly the same words, the nature of the insult,
which, as it appeared to me, the passage in his note was calculated
to convey. "It is now useless," I continued, "to speak of the
steps with which it was my intention to follow up that letter. The
time which has elapsed since then, though it has done away neither
the injury nor the feeling of it, has, in many respects, materially
altered my situation; and the only object which I have now in
writing to your Lordship is to preserve some consistency with that
former letter, and to prove to you that the injured feeling still
exists, however circumstances may compel me to be deaf to its
dictates at present. When I say 'injured feeling,' let me assure
your Lordship that there is not a single vindictive sentiment in my
mind towards you. I mean but to express that uneasiness, under
(what I consider to be) a charge of falsehood, which must haunt a
man of any feeling to his grave, unless the insult be retracted or
atoned for; and which, if I did *not* feel, I should, indeed, deserve
far worse than your Lordship's satire could inflict upon me." In
conclusion I added, that so far from being influenced by any angry
or resentful feeling towards him, it would give me sincere pleasure
if, by any satisfactory explanation, he would enable me to seek the
honour of being henceforward ranked among his acquaintance.'

This was answered in Letter cxiii.

My worst literary enemy:—Francis Jeffrey, who had edited the
attack on *Hours of Idleness*, and at whose head Byron hurled
full a hundred lines of *English Bards*:—

> Health to immortal Jeffrey! Once in name
> England could boast a judge almost the same, etc. :—

taking Little and his leadless pistol by the way. Byron and
Jeffrey, as Byron and Lord Holland :—

> Hard would be his lot,
> His hirelings mentioned, and himself forgot :—

lived to think very well of each other, and to show it each in his
own way: Jeffrey in his reviews of Byron's dazzling output, and
Byron in certain octaves in *Don Juan* (x. 11-19), at least one of
which is famous :—

> And all our little feuds, at least all *mine*,
> Dear Jeffrey, once my most redoubted foe

383

LETTERS

(As far as rhyme and criticism combine
    To make such puppets of us things below),
Are over : Here's a health to 'Auld Lang Syne !'
    I do not know you, and may never know
Your face—but you have acted on the whole
Most nobly, and I own it from my soul.

Your friend, Mr. Rogers :— Samuel Rogers (1763-1855), poet,
wit, banker; author of *The Pleasures of Memory* (1792), *The
Voyage of Columbus* (1812), *Jacqueline* (published with *Lara*, 1814),
Italy (1822-28), etc.   Rich as he was, he never married.   He was
content to give the best breakfasts in London ; to speak bitterly and
give generously (Campbell said :—' Borrow five hundred pounds
of Rogers, and he will never say a word against you till you want
to repay him ') ; to patronise the arts and to write, with the most
careful and fastidious pen in history—(the *Columbus* took him
fourteen years to write, the *Pleasures* seven, and the *Italy* fifteen)
—book after book of verses which are still enjoyable, howbeit a
little as wax flowers are decorative, and to which, in the end, he
fitted (at a cost of £15,000) over a hundred designs by Turner and
Stothard, renowned among the masterpieces of English illustration.
Byron, who to be sure was no critic, thought the world of him ('the
Tithonus of poesy, immortal already '), as we shall see as we go on.
But perhaps his best work is a certain epigram :—

They say Ward has no heart, but I deny it ;
He has a heart, and gets his speeches by it.

In 1812 Byron dedicated *The Giaour* to him, and he lived to
accept the dedication of *Master Humphrey's Clock* and to decline
(1850) the Laureateship, and so make way for Tennyson.

Rogers wrote nobly enough of Byron in his *Italy* ; and Byron,
though at Genoa he likened Rogers's achievement to an *hortus siccus*,
was generally lavish of regard for 'the father of present poesy.'
Remains that achievement in satire, the famous *Question and
Answer* which, as I think, might have been dictated by the Devil :—

' Nose and chin would shame a knocker,
Wrinkles that would puzzle Cocker,
Mouth which marks the envious scorner,
With a scorpion in each corner,' etc.

It was published in *Fraser* (January 1833), and will be found in
the *Miscellaneous Pieces* of this Edition.   I have somewhere read
(I forget where) that, on the occasion of a visit from Rogers, Byron,
who was excellent at what is called ' chaff,' not only gave his guest
a riotous reception, but slipped this ferocious caricature of him,

384

NOTES

this Gillray-Daumier (so to speak) under his pillow. That it was done in jest is evident. As evident is it that Rogers, despite those grave and generous verses in the *Italy*, lived to resent it, and resent it bitterly. This if we may believe—and I see no reason why we may not—the late Charles Mackay. Talking with Rogers one day, he praised Byron, as a young man would ; and Rogers as steadily dispraised. Says Mackay :—' You will at least acknowledge, sir, that he had fire.' And to him Rogers :—' Yes, *hell*-fire.' With which remark the elegant, ambitious, careful poetaster disappears.

LETTER cxiv. p. 170.

' In my reply to this'—(Letter cxiii.)—(says Moore), ' I commenced by saying that his Lordship's letter was, upon the whole, as satisfactory as I could expect. It contained all that, in the strict *diplomatique* of explanation, could be required, namely,—that he had never seen the statement which I supposed him wilfully to have contradicted,—that he had no intention of bringing against me any charge of falsehood, and that the objectionable passage of his work was not levelled personally at *me*. This, I added, was all the explanation I had a right to expect, and I was, of course, satisfied with it. I then entered into some detail relative to the transmission of my first letter from Dublin,—giving, as my reason for descending to these minute particulars, that I did not, I must confess, feel quite easy under the manner in which his Lordship had noticed the miscarriage of that first application to him. My reply concluded thus :—' As your Lordship does not show any wish to proceed beyond the rigid formulary of explanation, it is not for me to make any further advances. We Irishmen, in businesses of this kind, seldom know any medium between decided hostility and decided friendship ;—but, as any approaches towards the latter alternative must now depend entirely on your Lordship, I have only to repeat that I am satisfied with your letter, and that I have the honour to be,' etc. etc. Byron's answer—Letter cxv.—came next day.

LETTER cxv. p. 171.

Moore writes :—' Somewhat piqued, I own, at the manner in which my efforts towards a more friendly understanding,—ill-timed as I confess them to have been,—were received, I hastened to close our correspondence by a short note, saying that his Lordship had made me feel the imprudence I was guilty of, in wandering from the point immediately in discussion between us ; and I should now, therefore, only add, that if, in my last letter, I had correctly stated the substance of his explanation, our correspondence might, from this moment, cease for ever, as with that explanation I declared myself satisfied.' Byron replied as in the text:—whereupon 'I went instantly,' says Moore, 'to my friend, Mr. Rogers, who was, at that time, on a visit to Holland House, and, for the first time, informed him of the correspondence in which I had been engaged. With his usual readiness to oblige and serve, he proposed that the meeting between Lord Byron and myself should take place at his table, and requested of me to convey to the noble Lord his wish, that he would do him the honour of naming some day for that purpose.'

Letter cxvii. is Byron's answer. Moore's account of the meal, punctilious and wordy as it is, is worth quoting. 'Such,' says he, after an admiring review of Byron's conduct of the correspondence—'Such did I find Lord Byron, on my first experience of him; and such,—so open and manly-minded,—did I find him to the last. 'It was, at first, intended by Mr. Rogers that his company at dinner should not extend beyond Lord Byron and myself; but Mr. Thomas Campbell, having called upon our host that morning, was invited to join the party, and consented. Such a meeting could not be otherwise than interesting to us all. It was the first time that Lord Byron was ever seen by any of his three companions; while he, on his side, for the first time, found himself in the society of persons whose names had been associated with his first literary dreams, and to *two* of whom he looked up with that tributary admiration which youthful genius is ever ready to pay its precursors. Among the impressions which this meeting left upon me, what I chiefly remember to have remarked was the nobleness of his air, his beauty, the gentleness of his voice and manners, and—what was naturally not the least attraction—his marked kindness to myself. Being in mourning for his mother, the colour, as well of his dress as of his glossy, curling, and picturesque hair, gave more effect to the pure, spiritual paleness of his features, in the expression of which, when he spoke, there was a perpetual play of lively thought, though melancholy was their habitual character when in repose. As we had none of us been apprised of his peculiarities with respect to food, the embarrassment of our host was not a little on discovering that there was nothing upon the table which his noble guest could eat or drink. Neither meat, fish, nor wine would Lord Byron touch; and of biscuits and soda-water, which he asked for, there had been, unluckily, no provision. He professed, however, to be equally well pleased with potatoes and vinegar; and of these meagre materials contrived to make rather a hearty dinner.'

NOTES

The 'two' of Moore's statement were Moore himself and Rogers.
See *English Bards* :—

> 'Tis Little ! Young Catullus of his day :—

with the apostrophe to 'melodious Rogers' to 'strike to wonted
tunes his hallowed lyre.' But Byron had a very great respect for
the fourth at table, Thomas Campbell (1777-1844), whose *Pleasures
of Hope* (1799) he brackets (1809) with *The Pleasures of Memory*
as 'the most beautiful didactic poems in our language, if we
except Pope's *Essay on Man*' : even as he thought that of all the
men of his generation only these two could be reproached with
having written too little. Of the description, 'young Catullus,'
which he applies to the pert, essenced rhymester of those metrical
kissing-comfits (or *pastilles de serail*), the *Poems of the late Thomas
Little, Esq.*, it may here be remarked that it is one of the most
fatuous in the whole range of literary criticism.

LETTER cxvi. p. 172.
With this note I send a few stanzas :—See the Second *Harold*,
xcv.-xcviii. ; Letter cix., p. 163 :—*I have again been shocked with
a death*, etc. ; and the *Poems to Thyrza*.
As to the 'Monastic dome,' etc. See the First *Harold*, vii. :—

> The Childe departed from his father's hall :
> It was a vast and venerable pile ;
> So old, it seemed only not to fall,
> Yet strength was pillared in each massy aisle.
> Monastic dome ! condemned to uses vile !
> Where Superstition once had made her den
> Now Paphian girls were known to sing and smile ;
> And monks might deem their time was come agen,
> If ancient tales say true, nor wrong these holy men.

LETTER cxix. p. 174.
I have seen Miller, who will see Bland :—For Miller, see *ante*,
p. 367, Note to Letter lxxxvii. Bland at this time wanted to translate the *Charlemagne* of Lucien Bonaparte : a piece of work done
afterwards for Murray by Hodgson and Butler.
I have read Watson to Gibbon :—Richard Watson, afterwards
Bishop of Llandaff, assailed the Eighteenth Chapter of the *Decline
and Fall*, and wrote an *Apology for the Bible* in reply to Tom
Paine. 'At the distance of twelve years,' says Gibbon, 'I calmly
affirm my judgment of Davies, Chelsum, etc. A victory over such
antagonists was a sufficient humiliation. They, however, were
rewarded in this world. Poor Chelsum was indeed neglected ; and

LETTERS

I dare not boast the making Dr. Watson a Bishop; he is a prelate of a large mind and liberal spirit; but I enjoyed the pleasure of giving a royal pension to Mr. Davies, and of collating Dr. Apthorpe to an archiepiscopal living. Their success encouraged the zeal of Taylor the Arian, and Milner the Methodist, with many others, whom it would be difficult to remember, and tedious to rehearse.'

LETTER CXX. p. 176.
*I should think ' X plus Y ' at least as amusing as the ' Curse of Kehama,' and much more intelligible:—*The Curse of Kehama (1810) was the fourth, I believe, of those 'epics' whose frequent occurrence had already made Byron write (in *English Bards*) of a very worthy man but an extremely long-winded versifier, the ' Balladmonger Southey '(1774-1843) :—

> To him let Camoens, Milton, Tasso yield,
> Whose annual strains, like armies, take the field :—

and even long afterwards to make him write again (in *Don Juan*):—

> I know that what our neighbours call ' *longueurs*,'
>   (We've not so good a *word*, but have the *thing*,
> In that complete perfection which insures
>   An epic from Bob Southey every spring—)
> Form not the true temptation which allures
>   The reader.

At the present time of writing, Byron did in nowise hate his Southey: he did but laugh at Southey's so-called poetry, of which, by the way, the writer was inordinately vain (' I was perfectly aware,' he wrote to Murray of *Kehama*, 'that I was planting acorns, while other men were setting Turkey beans. The oak will grow,' etc.). Of Southey the man he knew nothing till 1813, when they met at Holland House. This was in September; and some two months after (November 22) Byron writes in his *Journal* thus :—' Southey, I have not seen much of. His appearance is *Epic*; and he is the only existing entire man of letters. All the others have some pursuit annexed to their authorship. His manners are mild, but not those of a man of the world, and his talents of the first order. His prose is perfect. Of his poetry there are various opinions: there is, perhaps, too much of it for the present generation ;— posterity will probably select. He has *passages* equal to anything. At present, he has *a party*, but no *public*—except for his prose writings. The *Life of Nelson* is beautiful.'

388

NOTES

But Southey, who, as young men will, had started life as a Republican, and in that character had written tragedies of *Wat Tyler* (1794) and *Inscriptions* in Martin the Regicide his honour :—

> Dost thou ask his **Crime?**
> **He had** rebelled against his king,
> **And** sat in judgment on him :—

had turned with time into so hardened and so militant a Tory that, when ' Poetical **Pye**' departed the world in this same year, he was chosen, Scott having said no in the interval, to wear the widowed wreath. Now, Byron was an aristocratic and an individual Radical ; besides, thus to forswear yourself was not his way ; and his references to Southey were for some time contemptuous enough. Still, for signs of positive and violent enmity we have to wait till the first years of the Exile, with the report, which Byron believed the Laureate to have set going in London, that at Geneva he and Shelley had 'formed a league of incest with two sisters,' Mary Godwin (1797-1851), that is, and Jane Clairmont (1797-1879), who was presently to become the mother of Allegra :—this the daughter of William Godwin (1756-1836) and Mary Wollstonecraft (1759-1797), that the daughter of William Godwin's second wife, the widow Clairmont, or Clements, whom he married in 1801. It was a piece of malignant gossip, picked up at a Genevese hotel ; but under the circumstances it was not at all unnatural. Byron, deserted by his wife, 'accused of every monstrous vice by public rumour and by private rancour,' had been fairly vomited by English society ; Shelley, notoriously an atheist and a freethinker in matters sexual, had left his wife for a woman with whom he was living in open adultery ; and, while both the ladies were young and pretty, which made things bad, both the ladies were whole or parcel Godwin, which made things worse, for had not Mr. Godwin's first wife vindicated the Rights of Women? and had not Godwin himself declined all laws, and especially the marriage law, 'the worst of all'? None the less, Byron was, very naturally, exasperated by it ; and one effect of the information that Southey was responsible for its introduction to talking England was that achievement in assault, the 'Dedication' (1818) suppressed, to Byron's chagrin, of the First and Second *Don Juan*. This, however, was very far from being the end. In 1811 appeared three cantos more, and Southey, in putting forth his ridiculous *Vision of Judgment*, attached to it an appropriate preface in which he opined that the poignancy of a deathbed repentance would nothing avail the author of such 'lascivious' stuff, talked of that author's

LETTERS

'Satanic spirit of pride and audacious impiety,' and hinted that here was a case for the Law. Byron retorted in his most savage and most scornful vein, remarking (truly enough), among other things, that there was 'something at once ludicrous and blasphemous in this arrogant scribbler of all work sitting down to deal damnation and destruction upon his fellow-creatures, with *Wat Tyler*, the Apotheosis of George the Third, and the Elegy on Martin the Regicide, all shuffled together in his writing-desk.' Southey, no more disposed than his antagonist to turn his cheek to the smiter, addressed a letter to *The London Courier* (5th January 1822), in which he explicitly denied that he had 'scattered abroad calumnies, knowing them to be such, against Lord Byron and others'; gloried in his attack on the Satanic School; defended himself with spirit and effect against the charge of being a scribbler of all work; protested that he had stuck the name of the author of *Don Juan* upon the gibbet, for reproach and infamy as long as it should endure; and ended by counselling Byron to 'attack him in rhyme' or not at all. Byron's reply was twofold. He challenged Southey, through Douglas Kinnaird; and he finished that *Vision of Judgment*, which is, by common consent, one of the master satires of the world. Of the challenge Southey never heard (Kinnaird suppressed it) till its author was dead; but he read the *Vision* in the first number of *The Liberal* that very year, and he must certainly have known that he shared with Brougham the very doubtful honour of being contemned and hated till the very end.

To end *con la bocca dolce*, here is a touch of fun from Medwin's *Journal* (1824):—'On my calling on Lord Byron one morning, he produced *The Deformed Transformed*. Handing it to Shelley, he said—"Shelley, I have been writing a Faustish kind of drama: tell me what you think of it." After reading it attentively, Shelley returned it. "Well," said Lord B., "how do you like it?" "Least," replied he, "of anything I ever saw of yours. It is a bad imitation of *Faust*, and besides, there are two entire lines of Southey's in it." Lord Byron changed colour immediately, and asked hastily, "What lines?" Shelley repeated,

"And water shall see thee,
And fear thee, and flee thee.

They are in *The Curse of Kehama*." His Lordship instantly threw the poem into the fire. He seemed to feel no chagrin at seeing it consume—at least his countenance betrayed none, and his conversation became more gay and lively than usual. Whether it was hatred of Southey, or respect for Shelley's opinion,' etc.

390

NOTES

What news of scribblers five:—That is to say, Scott, Wordsworth, Coleridge, Charles Lloyd (1775-1839), and Charles Lamb.
The two last, who had published a volume of *Poems in Blank
Verse* as early as 1798, are described—it is impossible to say why
—in a note to *English Bards* as 'the most ignoble followers of
Southey and Co.' For the original of Byron's parody, see Southey's
ballad of *Queen Orraca and the Five Martyrs of Morocco*:—

> 'What news, O King Affonso,
> What news of the Friars five?
> Have they preached to the Miramamolin;
> And are they still alive?'

It may be read on pp. 166-173 of Vol. vi. of that Complete Edition
of his *Poetical Works*, in Twelve Volumes, which, with a vain yet
touching faith in Posterity, he undertook 'to collect and edit . . .
at the age of sixty-three.'

LETTER cxxi. p. 177.

Coleridge has been lecturing against Campbell:—In the winter of
1811-12—(Mr. Ernest Coleridge informs me)—Coleridge delivered
a course of fifteen Lectures on English Poetry in the rooms of the
London Philosophical Society, Crane Court, Fleet Street. John
Payne Collier took notes of all fifteen, lost the greater part of
them, and published the rest in 1856. Apparently the attack on
Campbell is among the vanished material. (See *post*, p. 396, Note
to Letter cxxii.)

Pole is to marry Miss Long:—This was William Pole Tylney
Long Wellesley (1788-1857), afterwards (1845) Fourth Earl of
Mornington. The story of this 'most distinguished Briton' is one
so full of insolence, adultery, thriftlessness, and the right Regency
feeling for blackguardism and the Establishment, that I cannot
choose but tell it with a certain particularity. In 1812, after a pursuit which itself was something of a scandal, he married Catherine,
eldest daughter and co-heir of Sir James Tylney Long, Bart., of
Draycot, Wilts, whose names he added to his own, and thus inspired a delicious line in *Rejected Addresses*:—

> Long may Long Tilney Wellesley Long Pole live!

The lady had some £40,000 a year (her pin-money ran to £13,000)
and Wellesley had nothing; but 'the ancient and approved servants' of
the Tylney family were dismissed at once, and in the March of 1813
there was tried at Chelmsford the case of 'The King v. Wellesley
Pole Tylney Long Wellesley.' This was an action to try the right
of the public to a right of way through Wanstead Park, and in the

LETTERS

course of it Mr. Serjeant Shepherd, who was briefed for the defence, protested strongly against the right of common people to 'offend his (Pole's) princely mansion with the passage of unseemly vehicles.' In truth, the man was born magnificent; his life was of a piece throughout; he kept open house and a sumptuous table, had the finest hounds and horses on the country-side, retained an hundred and fifty servitors in Lincoln green, would have nothing but guineas in his pockets, and all the rest of it; and by 1821 he was in such straits that in 1822 he had to take his wife abroad (tradition says that he dodged the traps in a boat, and boarded the packet far out at sea). They were living at Naples when (in 1823) they met a certain Captain Bligh, of the Coldstream Guards, and his wife Helena (*née* Paterson), both of whom they had known in England. In the July of that year Mrs. Bligh left her husband's house in consequence of an intrigue with Wellesley; but Wellesley filed an affidavit of denial before the British Vice-Consul, and persuaded Mrs. Wellesley to offer the injured lady the protection of her roof. This she did, but at Florence she had to turn the injured lady out of the house. From Italy the Wellesleys went to Paris (1824), whither Mrs. Bligh had preceded them; and from Paris Mrs. Wellesley wrote to her father-in-law (Lord Maryborough, a most respectable man: elder brother to the Duke of Wellington, Master of the Mint in 1815, Master of the Buckhounds in 1828), that, if Wellesley would have done with Mrs. Bligh, she would forgive the man 'his profligate and unprincipled conduct,' and provide for the woman out of her own income. Lord and Lady Maryborough went to Paris and did their best; but it was to no purpose; so that Mrs. Wellesley took her children to England, and in the June of 1825 began to sue for a divorce in the Ecclesiastical Court. About that time, too, Wellesley and Mrs. Bligh, who had been playing at man and wife in divers *gîtes* in France and Holland, crossed to London; and on July 7 Wellesley drove Bligh to his wife's house in Clarges Street, for the purpose of getting hold of one or more of his children. He entered the house, when Bligh drove round to Mme. Vestris's, there to wait the event; but Mrs. Wellesley heard his voice, escaped (with her daughter) by the kitchen door, served him with a citation for divorce, and filed a bill in Chancery to make her children wards of the Court, after which the errant couple scuttled back to France. In the September of that year Mrs. Wellesley died, enjoining her sisters, the Misses Long, to resist to the utmost any attempt on Wellesley's part to remove the children; and in 1827—(in which year he had to pay swingeing damages to Captain Bligh, as defendant in a suit for *crim. con.*)—Wellesley brought an action against their guardian, his uncle Wellington, to recover possession of them. In delivering judgment, the Chancellor (Eldon) remarked that they had it in evidence that in July 1824 Wellesley had 'a venereal tumour removed from his eye by Dr. Southcote'; that Southcote had sworn that, to his knowledge, Wellesley when in Paris got blackguard children to come to the back of the house to teach his children to blaspheme; that Mr. Pitman, the tutor of Wellesley's choice, testified that he had 'heard the eldest infant plaintiffs use some very disgusting expressions, and utter the most coarse and vulgar oaths in French,' and the boy William, being rebuked for his obscenities, had replied that 'his father liked it'; that a letter of Wellesley's was before the Court (dated February 9, 1825) containing such phrases as 'If the fellow be a sportsman, . . . damn his infernal soul to hell'; that in another letter he bade his boys to 'study hard, but as soon as you have completed your tasks, go out in all weathers, and play hell and tommy—make as much riot as your tongues can admit—chase cats, dogs, and women, old and young, but spare my game'; and that Dr. Bulkeley, the physician who attended the Wellesleys at Naples, and who afterwards resided and travelled with them, had sworn that W. P. L. Wellesley said, in the presence of his children, 'Debauch all the women you meet with, young and old':—For all which reasons he, Eldon, would 'deserve to be hunted out of society if he hesitated for one moment to say, that he would sooner forfeit his life than permit the girl Victoria to go in the company of such a woman, or into the care and protection of a man who had the slightest connexion with that woman.' With incredible magnificence the Plaintiff returned to the charge and published *Two Letters to the Right Hon. Earl Eldon, Lord Chancellor, etc. etc. etc., with official and other documents and additional notes.* 'By the Hon. W. L. Wellesley. Third Edition. London: John Miller, Pall Mall, 1827.' His defence—'If shape that can be called which shape hath none'—is monumental. His wife, he says, 'was a most amiable woman . . . but she had not profited by education to the degree that might have been expected,' and that her letters were mostly written by her lady's-maid. He throws the blame on her sisters, who 'entertain principles and doctrines hostile to the Established Church.' The real cause of dislike is revealed elsewhere: it is that 'a few years after my marriage I was called upon to pay the young ladies their portions'—£15,000 each, *plus* interest—'making the whole amount to nearly £40,000.' He further contends that during Mrs. Wellesley's

LETTERS

minority, and afterwards, she gave 'very large sums of money' (a commodity he could properly appreciate) to Lady Catherine and the Misses Long. But it was understood that the Misses Long :— and be it remembered that 'sectarian troubles have operated upon the mind of the elder sister . . . to such a degree that it can scarcely be called rational'; while 'the younger, to a temper the most violent, adds manners the least refined':—should transfer their portions, charged on the Long estates, to himself and wife. The Longs, it would seem, were Methodists, and Wellesley, a pillar of the Establishment, hated Methodism as Sir Andrew hated a Puritan. The ladies, in fact, had sat too sedulously at the feet of one Barry, sometime resident apothecary to Sir James Long :—'A man of sectarian principles, and a great collector of sectarian tracts (it was tracts of this nature which I was in the habit of burning after my marriage; not because they were religious, but because they were wild, fanatic, and not in accordance with the true spirit of Christianity) with which he supplied the different members of the family,' etc. etc. etc. Barry, by the way, had made himself still more obnoxious to this sound Churchman by proposing that the Long estates should, in the event of there being no male issue of the Wellesley-Long marriage, be re-settled on the Misses Long, the defender of the true faith to receive an annuity of £10,000.

In 1828 Wellesley married 'the daughter of Colonel Paterson and *widow* of Captain Bligh of the Coldstream Guards' (*The Times*, 4th July 1857). But, to quote the same authority, this second union 'would appear to have been no better assorted than the first, to judge from the fact that, since her husband's accession to the title, Lady Mornington has repeatedly appeared in our columns as an applicant for relief at the metropolitan police-courts in consequence of having been left destitute by her husband, and chargeable to the parish.' In the end the old blood died of heart disease; and on 4th July 1857 an inquest was held (by Mr. Wakely) at the Coach-makers' Arms, Bentinck Street, Manchester Square:—'Dr. Probert, the Earl's medical man, said the late Earl had been very badly off so far as pecuniary affairs were concerned, and until the last two years had wanted the necessaries of life. . . . Major W. J. Richardson, a friend of the Earl, said he did not consider that he [the Earl] had been lately in pecuniary want, for his cousin, the Duke of Wellington, allowed him £10 a week': which, to be sure, was little enough 'for a man who once had £100,000 a year.'

The present ministers:—For some time past the Regent had professed himself anxious to strengthen his Government by the admission of some of his old political friends. The Whigs, however, then as always, at once 'too democratic in their principles and too aristocratic in their predilections' (LOCKHART), were bent on all or nothing. In the sequel they got nothing. The murder of Mr. Perceval was followed by the formation of Lord Liverpool's ministry, and their exclusion from power for many years.

> Nought's permanent among the human race
> Except the Whigs not getting into place :—

Thus Byron in 1823; and the Promised Land was still afar.

How I became so the 'Public Orator' only can resolve:—Prior to 1857, a nobleman, after three years' residence, was privileged to proceed, *jure natalium*, without examination, to the degree of M.A., for admission to which he was presented to the Vice-Chancellor by—not the Praelector of his College but—the Public Orator (the mouthpiece of the University), whose chief function now is the presentation of eminent personages for honorary degrees, and who, in presenting a peer to his Vice-Chancellor, would often do no more than briefly recite the aspirant's ancestry. (See Appendix A.)

Sir William Drummond's late book:—That is, the *Œdipus Judaicus* (1811) of the Right Hon. Sir W. Drummond (1770?-1828), an irreverent examination of the Old Testament, which was printed (not for publication) by A. J. Valpy (London, 1811), and was, in fact, a protest, surreptitious in form but damaging in effect, against the arrogant yet tongue-tied and undoubting clericalism of those years. For the Author : Byron admired him to the end. 'You must make his acquaintance,' he said to Lady Blessington, 'for he is certainly one of the most erudite men and admirable philosophers now living.' The fact is, 'He has all the wit of Voltaire, with a profundity that seldom appertains to wit, and writes so forcibly,' etc. Then his *Academical Questions* (1805) alone would, in its Preface, prove him 'an admirable writer.' Indeed, 'the following sentence' is, 'I think, one of the best in our language :—" Philosophy, wisdom, and liberty support each other : he who will not reason is a bigot ; he who cannot is a fool ; he who dares not is a slave." Is not the passage admirable?' In effect, it is a very spirited imitation of Johnson's second-best. Again :—'His *Odin* (1817) is really a fine poem, and has some passages that are beautiful'; while as for his 'translation of Persius' (1797), it is 'not only very literal, but preserves much of the spirit of the original.' In fact, 'he has escaped all the defects of translators' and the result is that 'his Persius resembles the

LETTERS

original in feeling and sentiment as nearly as two languages so different in idiom will admit.'

I note that Sir William, an accomplished scholar and a man of excellent parts, is thought to have matriculated at Christ Church, Oxford, in 1788; that he sat, in the Tory interest, for St. Mawes (1795-1801); that in 1801 he was sent as minister to Naples, in 1803 as ambassador to the Porte, and in 1804 to Naples back again as envoy-extraordinary. Other works of his are *Herculanensia*, etc. (1810), with Robert Walpole; a *Memoir on the Antiquity of the Zodiacs of Ernah and Dendera* (1821); and *Origines, or Remarks on the Origins of Several Empires, States, and Cities* (1824-9).

A novel of Madame D' Arblay's:—This, the lady's fourth and last, was, *The Wanderer, or Female Difficulties*, published in 1814. She expected to make £3000 by it; but, though 3600 copies were sold in six months, she made but half that sum.

LETTER cxxii. p. 179.

Mr. W—— has lent it me:—' Mr. W——' is probably the Hon. John William Ward, afterwards Fourth Earl of Dudley.

We are going in a party to hear the new Art of Poetry:—

In the evening at Coleridge's lecture. Conclusion of Milton. Not one of the happiest of Coleridge's efforts. Rogers was there, and with him was Lord Byron. He was wrapped up, but I recognised his club-foot, and, indeed, his countenance and general appearance.—HENRY CRABB ROBINSON, *Diary*, Jan. 20, 1812.

The Alfred has three hundred and fifty-four candidates for six vacancies:—The Alfred Club, in Albemarle Street, was founded in 1808, and in 1855 was amalgamated with the Oriental in Hanover Square. It seems to have been a quiet, semi-literary sort of place: a place, above all, where you met everybody: as it were a fore-runner of the Savile, and not, one would think, a fitting haunt for a Dandy and a devout patron of the Ring. Yet 'I was a member of the Alfred, too,' says Byron, discoursing of clubs in one of his memorandum-books, 'being elected while in Greece. It was pleasant; a little too sober and literary, and bored with Sotheby and Sir Francis D'Ivernois; but one met Peel, and Ward, and Valentia, and many other pleasant or known people; and it was, upon the whole, a decent resource in a rainy day, in a dearth of parties, or parliament, or in an empty season.' Thus, too, Walter Scott in a MS. note communicated to Moore:—' The Alfred, like all other clubs, was much haunted with *boars*—tusky monsters, which delight to range where men most do congregate; as they are kept at the spear's point pretty much in private society. A

396

boar, or bore, is always remarkable for something respectable ; such as wealth, character, high birth, acknowledged talent—or, in short, for something that forbids people . . . to cut him dead. . . . Old stagers in the club know and avoid the fated corner and arm-chair which he haunts; but he often rushes from his lair on the unexperienced.'

In the end the club was known as the 'Half-read'; it became 'an asylum of doting Tories and drivelling quidnuncs'; 'and,' said Alvanley, 'when the seventeenth bishop was proposed, I gave in,' for 'I really could not enter the place without being reminded of my catechism.'

LETTER cxxv. p. 184.

Yesterday I went with Moore to Sydenham:—'On this occasion another of the noble poet's peculiarities was, somewhat startlingly, introduced to my notice. When we were on the point of setting out from his lodgings in St. James's Street, it being then about mid-day, he said to the servant, who was shutting the door of the *vis-à-vis*, "Have you put in the pistols?" and was answered in the affirmative. It was difficult,—more especially, taking into account the circum-stances under which we had just become acquainted,—to keep from smiling at this singular noonday precaution.'—MOORE.

Kemble in Coriolanus:—Coriolanus was John Philip Kemble's best part, and it was in Coriolanus that he bade his farewell to the stage (1817).

An exhibition of a different kind:—The ridiculous creature known as 'Romeo,' 'Diamond,' and 'Cockadoodle-Doo' (his real name was Robert) Coates (1772-1848) had a very high opinion of himself as an actor, especially in such brilliant and romantic parts as Romeo and 'the haughty, gallant, gay Lothario,' which Rowe conveyed from Massinger into his own *Fair Penitent.* His absurd performances, which were absurdly dressed, were received with howls of joy: his death-scenes, in particular, being rapturously redemanded. In the end, he was hooted from the stage. The son of a rich West Indian (he was born in Antigua), he started at Bath, where he drove a curricle (with a brazen Cock on the bar, and the device, 'While I live I'll crow'), and sported many diamonds. He called himself the 'Celebrated Philanthropic Amateur,' got into difficulties, fled the country to Boulogne, married there (somehow), and after compounding with his creditors, returned to England, and lapsed into a becoming obscurity.

LETTER cxxviii. p. 187.

I am in a state of ludicrous tribulation:—Moore's Note to this

LETTERS

passage explains the two preceding numbers (cxxvi. and cxxvii.), and runs as follows:—'The passages here omitted contain rather *too* amusing an account of a disturbance that had just occurred in the establishment at Newstead, in consequence of the detected misconduct of one of the maid-servants, who had been supposed to stand rather too high in the favour of her master, and, by the airs of authority which she thereupon assumed, had disposed all the rest of the household to regard her with no very charitable eyes. The chief actors in the strife were this sultana and young Rushton; and the first point in dispute that came to Lord Byron's knowledge (though circumstances, far from creditable to the damsel, afterwards transpired) was, whether Rushton was bound to carry letters to "the Hut" at the bidding of this female. To an episode of such a nature I should not have thought of alluding, were it not for the two rather curious letters that follow, which show how gravely and coolly the young lord could arbitrate on such an occasion, and with what considerate leaning towards the servant whose fidelity he had proved, in preference to any new liking or fancy by which it might be suspected he was actuated towards the other.' A dispute, in fact, between a couple of servants—a maid and a man—who chose, for whatever reasons, to give themselves airs: a dispute too, in which neither was right, but Buttons was less wrong than Ribands. With the materials available, that is about all that can be said; and that is probably more than enough.

Rushton was the 'little Page' of the First *Harold*:—

> And of his train there was a little page,
> A peasant boy who served his master well;
> And often would his pranksome prate engage
> Childe Burun's ear, when his proud head did swell
> With sullen thoughts which he disdained to tell.
> Then would he smile on him, and Alwin smiled,
> When aught that from his young lips archly fell
> The gloomy film from Burun's eye beguiled.

Why do you say that I dislike your poesy:—Moore had written to Byron in praise of the First and Second *Harold*, proof-sheets of which he had seen at Rogers's house. It would seem, too, that if he had praised the new, he had done so at the expense of the old—that is to say, of *English Bards*.

I fixed upon the trite charge of immorality, because I could discover no other:—'Heigho!' he writes to Moore in 1820, 'I believe all the mischief I have ever done, or sung, has been owing to that confounded book of yours.' For the 'trite charge of immorality,' see *English Bards*:—

NOTES

Who in soft guise, surrounded by a choir
Of virgins melting, not to Vesta's fire,
With sparkling eyes, and cheek by passion flushed,
Strikes his wild lyre, whilst listening dames are hushed
'Tis Little! young Catullus of his day,
As sweet, but as immoral, in his lay!
Grieved to condemn, the muse must still be just,
Nor spare melodious advocates of lust.
Pure is the flame which o'er her altar burns
From grosser incense with disgust she turns:
Yet kind to youth, this expiation o'er,
She bids thee 'mend thy line, and sin no more.'

Damned, deceitful—delightful woman:—The *Knight of Snow-doun*, a farce by Thomas Morton (1764?-1838), was produced at Covent Garden, 5th February 1811. Liston played Macloon.

LETTER cxxix. p. 188.

The perfect propriety of the question to be put to ministers:—The occasion of this letter was Lord **Liverpool's** introduction (Thursday, 27th February 1812) in the Lords of the Frame-Breaking Bill: a measure designed 'to compel individuals in whose houses frames should be **broken** to give information thereof to the magistrates'; to apply provisions likely to secure detection, and 'to render the offence' in question 'capital.' The Bill, a temporary one, made necessary by 'transactions which had taken place and were still going on in the County of Nottingham,' had been introduced in the Commons by Mr. Secretary Ryder on the 14th, and read for the third time on the 20th February, was the occasion of Byron's maiden speech. In the present letter he is found concerting (at Rogers's suggestion) with Lord Holland as to the preliminaries of an attack on the Government. He replied to Lord **Liverpool**, and was followed by Lord Holland, who derided the Ministers for not attempting an answer to his discourse. The Lord Chancellor (Eldon), and Lords Lauderdale, Grosvenor, Harrowby, and Grenville took also part in the debate. For the effect of Byron's oratory, see **Letter** cxxxiv.; for the Speech itself, Vol. iv. of this issue.

LETTER cxxx. p. 189.

To Master John Cowell:—'Breakfasted with **Mr. Cowell**, having made his acquaintance for the purpose of gaining information about Lord Byron. Knew Byron for the first time, when he himself was a little boy, from being in the habit of playing with B.'s dogs. Byron wrote to him to school to bid him mind his prosody. Gave

399

me two or three of his letters. Saw a good deal of B. at Hastings; mentioned the anecdote about the ink-bottle striking one of the lead Muses. These Muses had been brought from Holland, and there were, I think, only eight of them arrived safe. Fletcher had brought B. a large jar of ink, and, not thinking it was full, B. had thrust his pen down to the very bottom; his anger at finding it come out all besmeared with ink made him chuck the jar out of the window, when it knocked down one of the Muses in the garden, and deluged her with ink. In 1813, when Byron was at Salt Hill, he had Cowley over from Eton, and *pouched* him no less than ten pounds. Cowell has ever since kept one of the notes. Told me a curious anecdote of Byron's mentioning to him, as if it had made a great impression on him, their seeing Shelley (as they thought) walking into a little wood at Lirici (*sic*), when it was discovered afterwards that Shelley was at that time in quite another direction. "This," said Byron, in a sort of awestruck voice, "was about ten days before his death." Cowell's imitation of his look and manner very striking. Thinks that in Byron's speech to Fletcher, when he was dying, threatening to appear to him, there was a touch of that humour and fun which he was accustomed to mix with everything.'—MOORE, *Diary*, 11th June 1828.

I had the honour, etc. :—The match was played in 1805, according to Byron; in 1806, according to those learned in cricket. (See Appendix B.)

LETTER cxxxi. p. 190.
The women are gone to their relatives :—See *ante*, p. 397, Note to Letters cxxvi., cxxvii., cxxviii.

LETTER cxxxii. p. 191.
'Galt,' his *Travels in Ye Archipelago :*—This is the *Voyages and Travels in the Years* 1809, 1810, *and* 1811. . . . *Statistical, Commercial, and Miscellaneous Observations in Gibraltar, Sardinia, Sicily, Serigo, and Turkey* (London, 1812) of John Galt (1779-1839). In 1809 Galt, who had left Greenock and the Custom House for London and Letters (he had the usual tragedy in his pocket) as early as 1804, was obliged, for his health's sake, to go South. At Gibraltar one day, 'in a withering levanter,' which confined him to the library, he saw Byron, and noted, without knowing who he was, the 'neatness and simplicity,' and at the same time the 'peculiarity of style,' which distinguished his attire, the fact that his 'physiognomy,' though disfigured by what was 'undoubtedly the occasional scowl of some unpleasant

reminiscence'—(it appears by the sequel that this 'made a stronger impression upon me than it did upon many others')—was 'prepossessing and intelligent,' while 'the general cast of his features was impressed with elegance and character.' The next day Galt took ship for Sardinia, and, when Byron and Hobhouse came aboard the packet, it seemed to him that 'in the little bustle of embarking their luggage his Lordship affected . . . more aristocracy than befitted his years on the occasion.' Also, he wouldn't put on the passenger at all (as Hobhouse did): on the contrary, he 'sat on the rail, leaning on the mizzen shrouds, inhaling, as it were, poetic sympathy from the gloomy rock, then dark and stern,' etc. About the third day out from Gibraltar 'Byron relented from his rapt mood . . . and became playful'; produced pistols, and approved himself the best shot on board at a bottle,' but not pre-eminently so'; helped the captain to catch a turtle—'I rather think two'; and did his part (we may assume) in hooking a shark, 'part of which was dressed for breakfast,' but 'tasted without relish,' for 'your shark is but a cannibal dainty.' And so on, and so on. Galt was amused by and pleased with Hobhouse, who told him bawdy stories—(stories 'more after the matter and manner of Swift than of Addison')—and was 'altogether an advantageous specimen of a well-educated English gentleman.' But Byron, who ate little, and drank less, and persisted in 'sitting amidst the shrouds and rattlings in the tranquillity of the moonlight, churming an inarticulate melody,' seemed 'almost apparitional' to him—suggested, in fact, that classic of the *genre*, a mystery in a winding-sheet crowned with a halo.' 'Tis true there were times when he was 'familiar and earthy'; but, as a rule, 'his dwelling was amidst the murk and the mist, and the home of his spirit in the abysm of the storm, and the hiding-places of guilt.' Even at two-and-twenty you couldn't meet him—or rather Galt couldn't—' without experiencing a presentiment that he was destined to execute some singular and ominous purpose.' Thus Galt, some twenty years after the event, of Byron at sea; and as Byron admitted to Lady Blessington that, while he saw that Galt was 'mild, equal, and sensible,' he 'took no pains to cultivate his acquaintance,' the sentiment may be accepted as natural, if the expression may not. But at Cagliari—(where Galt rather thinks that he may very possibly have seen the real original of Lara in the pit of the theatre)—the acquaintance ripened; on the voyage to Sicily 'the champagne was uncorked and in the finest condition'; and at Malta, despite the lack of 'a salute from the batteries'

LETTERS

(which Byron expected), it was found to be still on tap, for Byron and Hobhouse had to begin by 'begging a bed and a morsel for the night' of a particular friend of Galt's; and 'God forgive me!' says Galt, with a certain irrelevancy, 'but I partook of Byron's levity at the idea of personages so consequential wandering destitute in the streets,' etc. There is more of Malta, and there is much of Greece (Galt and Byron met again at Athens), but I shall sample Galt no further. Enough to say that after the return to England, and at a time when Byron 'could not well be said to be a celebrated character'—a time, in fact, when *Childe Harold* was known to Murray and Dallas alone—'I was frequently with him.' Then, however, came a tiff over *The Bride of Abydos* (1813), the story of which, as Galt insisted, was—not Byron's but —Galt's. Byron protested, and the tiff was ended, for the time being, by a very friendly letter which will be found under date of 11th December 1813, in Vol. ii. But the relation was not one made to last. At this time Byron, as he confessed to Lady Blessington, 'was in no frame of mind to form an impartial opinion' of Galt :—' His mildness and equanimity struck me even then ; but, to say the truth, his manner had not deference enough for my then aristocratical taste, and, finding I could not awe him into a respect sufficiently profound for my sublime self, either as a peer or an author, I felt a little grudge against him,' etc. If I add that Byron thought highly of Galt's novels (he read *The Entail* three times), and spoke very sensibly and well of the peculiar quality of his gift, I shall have said enough of Galt and Byron during Byron's life. The worst came after Byron's death, when Galt read (in Moore) an entry in one of Byron's *Diaries* that he (Galt) was 'almost the last person on whom any one would commit literary larceny.' That nettled him, and, in *The Life of Lord Byron* (1830), a work which, as we have seen, is rather well meant than well written, but which is still worth reading, he reflects (1) that *Childe Harold* was preceded by 'a poem in the Spenserian measure, which was 'called *The Unknown*,' which was 'intended to describe . . . pilgrim . . . the scenes I expected to visit,' and on which 'I was occasionally engaged . . . during the passage with Lord Byron from Gibraltar to Malta, *and he knew what I was about*; (2) that 'I wrote at Athens a burlesque poem on nearly the same subject' as *The Curse of Minerva*, that the MS. was 'sent to his Lordship in Asia Minor, and returned to me through Mr. Hobhouse,' and that 'his *Curse of Minerva* I saw for the first time in 1828 in Galignani's edition of his works';

402

and (3) that, though 'his Lordship disdained to commit any larceny on me, and no doubt the following passage from *The Giaour* is perfectly original' (follows the passage), yet 'not the most judicious action of all my youth was to publish certain,' etc. and 'his Lordship had the printed book in his possession long before,' etc., 'and may have read the following passage,' etc. etc. etc. It might be inferred from this that the creator of the inimitable Micah Balquhidder and the scarce less admirable Lady Grippy (as who should say a Glasgow Mrs. Gamp) was not remarkable for humour in private life. But, however that be, he was the only true begetter of the 'apparitional' Byron—the Byron who was as a mystery in a winding-sheet crowned with a halo, at the same time that he was 'distinguished for superior personal elegance, particularly in his bust.'

LETTER cxxxiii, p. 192.

With my best thanks :—See *ante*, p. 399, Note to Letter cxxix.

LETTER cxxxv. p. 195.

The thing which accompanies this note :—The First and Second *Harold*, published two days after Byron's maiden speech.

Anything I may formerly have uttered :—See *ante*, p. 314, Note to Letter xxviii. See also *English Bards* :—

> Illustrious Holland! Hard would be his lot,
> His hirelings mentioned and himself forgot :—

and the rest. With Byron's note (1816) to the passage :—' Bad enough, and on mistaken grounds, too.' Again, under date of 17th November 1813, Byron writes thus in his *Journal* :—' I have had a most kind letter from Lord Holland on *The Bride of Abydos*, which he likes, and so does Lady H. This is very good-natured in both, from whom I don't deserve any quarter. Yet I *did* think at the time that my cause of enmity proceeded from Holland House, and am glad I was wrong, and wish I had not been in such a hurry with that confounded Satire, of which I would suppress even the memory ; but people, now they can't get it, make a fuss, I verily believe out of contradiction.'

LETTER cxxxvii. p. 197.

I shall see you, I hope, at Lady Jersey's :—'Suppose that you were in love with a girl, and that her father refused his consent to the union, what would you do?' Thus, some time in 1782, John, Tenth Earl of Westmoreland, to Child the banker. 'Do?' was the answer : 'why, run away with her, to be sure !' That very night ('tis said), Lord Westmoreland and his interlocutor's one child eloped together, and took the road from Berkeley Square to Gretna Green. The father followed 'hot and instant in their trace,' and in the end so nearly ran them down that Lord Westmoreland had to stand up in the fleeing chaise, and shoot one of the banker's leaders : which happy yet desperate expedient enabled him to make good his retreat. Three months after the wedding, Robert Child died, bequeathing his very splendid fortune to the first daughter, who should be called Sarah, after his own dead wife. This was Lady Sarah Sophia Fane ; and on the 23rd May 1804 she married George Villiers, Fifth Earl of Jersey, twice Lord Chamberlain of the Household, twice Master of the Horse—(according to Byron, as reported by Lady Blessington, ' Pegasus was perhaps the only horse of whose points Lord Jersey couldn't be a judge')—and, Lord Malmesbury says, 'in manner and appearance le plus grand seigneur of his time.'

From the beginning to the end the Countess of Jersey, who was extremely beautiful, was the greatest of great ladies de par le monde, and wielded an influence in society which none, perhaps, but Lady Palmerston's could rival. She was one of the Committee of Lady Patronesses which decided who should, and who should not, be admitted to Almack's, the assembly rooms in King Street, St. James's Street, founded in 1769, and then 'the Seventh Heaven of the fashionable world (GRONOW): so that, after 1815, 'to be excluded from them was fatal to any one who aspired to belong to the *élite* of fashion' (LORD WILLIAM LENNOX). To Almack's, after Waterloo, Lady Jersey imported 'the favourite quadrille, which has so long remained popular' (a French print, copied into Gronow's First Set of *Reminiscences*, shows her in act to dance it, her fellows being Lord and Lady Worcester, and Clanronald Macdonald) ; and at Almack's (1819) Ticknor, who describes her 'as a beautiful creature with a great deal of talent, taste, and elegant accomplishment,' stood by on a memorable occasion when the Duke of Wellington (a great society man : whose nickname was The Beau) was announced at seven minutes past eleven of the clock, and heard her say, 'with emphasis and distinctness,' these awful words : – ' Give my compliments – Lady Jersey's compliments – to the Duke of Wellington, and say that she is very glad that the first enforcement of the rule of exclusion is such that hereafter no one can complain of its application. *He cannot be admitted.*' [It is worth noting that once before the Duke had been denied his place in Paradise, for that he came to look for it in trousers, and

NOTES

not in breeches as a reputable angel should.] Gronow, who did not
love the Countess, complains that, in 1814—when the Committee
consisted of herself, the Countess Lieven, Lady Castlereagh,
Lady Sefton, the Countess Cowper, Mrs. Drummond Burrell, and
the Princess Esterhazy,—'her bearing,' as compared to Lady
Cowper's, 'was that of a theatrical tragedy queen,' and that
'whilst attempting the sublime, she frequently made herself
simply ridiculous, being inconceivably rude, and in her manner
often ill-bred.' But there were two Lady Jerseys, it would seem;
and this one was the leader of *ton*, whom Byron described to Lady
Blessington as 'the veriest tyrant that ever governed Fashion's
fools, and compelled them to shake their caps and bells as she
willed it.' The other, the Lady Jersey of private life, was not at
all that sort of person. In the May of this same year Byron, who
was ever her devout admirer—('Does she still retain her beautiful
cream-coloured complexion and raven hair?' he asked at Genoa)
—and who was very soon to see her dancing with the Czar:—

> He wore but a starless blue coat, and in kersey-
> mere breeches, waltzed round with the Countess of Jersey,
> Who, lovely as ever, looked just as delighted
> With majesty's presence, as those she invited :—

inscribed to her the famous *Condolatory Address*:—'On the
Occasion of the Prince Regent Returning her Picture to Mrs.
Mee.' 'Don't be very angry with me,' he writes, in a note (unpublished) communicated to the Editor by the present Earl. 'If
ill-done, the shame can only be mine. . . . They were begun and
finished since ten o'clock to-night, so that, whether good or bad,
they were done in good earnest. Do with them what you please.
Whether they amuse your friends or light your fire, I shall be
content, so they don't offend *you*.' This is scarce the sort of letter
which a man would write to 'a theatrical tragedy queen'; nor is
a Siddons *manquée* suggested by Sheridan's description (1815:
reported by Lady Granville and quoted by Mr. Fraser Rae) of his
'Silence' (so he called her) as 'a pretty rushing babbling stream,
never stagnant.' [From this of Sheridan's about his 'Silence,' by
the way, you understand why Byron 'used to long to tell her that
she spoiled her looks by excessive animation,' for 'eyes, tongue,
head, and arms were all in motion at once.'] Take, too, the acutely
observed, not altogether friendly portrait which Charles Greville
painted of her after staying at Middleton in 1819 :—

405

LETTERS

1819, *January* 17th—'. . . It was very agreeable, and the house extremely comfortable. Lady Jersey is an extraordinary woman, and has many good qualities ; surrounded as she is by flatterers and admirers, she is neither proud nor conceited. She is full of vivacity, spirit, and good-nature, but the wide range of her sympathies and affections proves that she has more general benevolence than particular sensibility in her character. She performs all the ordinary duties of life with great correctness, because her heart is naturally good ; and she is, perhaps, from her temperament, exposed to fewer temptations than the generality of her sex. She is deficient in passion and in softness (which constitute the greatest charm in women), so that she excites more of admiration than of interest ; in conversation she is lively and pleasant, without being very remarkable, for she has neither wit, nor imagination, nor humour ; her understanding is active rather than strong, and her judgment is too often warped by prejudice to be sound. She has a retentive memory and a restless mind, together with a sort of intellectual arrangement, with which she appears rather to have been gifted by nature than to have derived from the cultivation of her reasoning faculties.'

It may have been a mistake in taste for Lady Jersey to identify herself (as she did) with the cause of the ill-guided and ill-starred Caroline of Brunswick (whose worst enemy her mother-in-law, the Dowager Countess, had been) ; and it may be that the Regent, in turning her picture out of his Gallery of Beauties, was within his rights as both Gentleman and King. But the enduring argument in her favour is that, despite the weight and manner of her tyranny, she so developed and consolidated her social influence that in the end, Lord Malmesbury says, she was 'almost a European personage, for no crowned head or representative of royalty ever landed in England without immediately calling on her, and being found in her *salon* during his stay.'

She died at eighty-two, having survived her husband (by some seventeen years) and her three daughters—(one of them married an Esterhazy, while the second eloped, as her grandmother before her)—and displayed to the last ' the courage and coolness for which she was famous' (MALMESBURY). These qualities were certainly conspicuous in her treatment of Byron at the lowest pitch of his fortune. On the eve of his departure into banishment, when all London was ringing with the rumour of his misdeeds, and there was scarce a voice which dared uplift itself in his defence, she took the lists for him with equal benevolence and intrepidity, ' made a party for him expressly,' and received him with a serene and gracious ' kindness,' which he remembered gratefully until the last. The 'party' was a failure. Most of the guests were uncivil or worse, and only one, Miss Mercer, afterwards Lady Keith, was

NOTES

cordial. 'Nothing short, perhaps,' says Moore, 'of that high station in society which a life as blameless as it is brilliant has secured to her, could have placed beyond all reach of misrepresentation, at that moment, such a compliment to one marked by the world's censure so deeply.' This is probably true. In any case, it was Byron's last taste of English Society, and on the lady's side 'twas well and valiantly done. Byron's own account of it was the page which Moore regretted worst of all in the MS. *Memoir*. In effect, Byron's true demon was upon him: he was within a year or two of *Beppo* and the *Vision* and the early cantos of *Don Juan*. What wildernesses of unexceptionable printed matter one would cheerfully resign, to know that this piece of his writing had escaped the grate in Albemarle Street, and would presently be given to the world!

I am indebted to Lady Jersey's grandson, the present Earl, for the copy of a rather breathless—(there are no commas in the original at Middleton)—letter, which goes far to show that Byron presented Sir Walter Scott to her. It is undated, but the year (1815) at least is fixed by the reference to the Duke of Dorset's death. Thus it runs:—

My dear Lord,—I am truly sorry for the afflicting family circumstance of Lord Whitworth's indisposition preceded as it has been by so grave a calamity as the death of the Duke of Dorset. I should feel so awkward in waiting upon Lady Jersey without the benefit of your Lordship's personal introduction that I must postpone availing myself of the invitation with which her Ladyship has honourd (*sic*) me untill (*sic*) the circumstances of your family will permit your Lordship to be my M^r. of ceremonies which I do most sincerely hope will soon be the case. I will take the chance unless I hear worse news of Lord Whitworth's health of calling on your Lordship to-morrow before twelve but do not stay at home on purpose.— Ever yours most faithfully   (Signed)   WALTER SCOTT.

Piccadilly, Thursday.
         'Right Honble LORD BYRON.'

LETTER CXXXVIII. p. 198.

Lady Caroline Lamb :—Born Ponsonby, Lady Caroline (1785-1828) was daughter to the Third Earl of Bessborough, by Henrietta Frances, daughter to the First Earl Spencer, and sister to the Beautiful Duchess, Georgiana of Devonshire. Reared in a *milieu* of uncommon state and splendour and self-indulgence, at ten years old she made verses, but could neither write nor read. Then she went to live with her grandmother, the Dowager Duchess of Devonshire, and, having an active body and a quick and apprehensive mind, learned French and Italian, dabbled in the classics, drew, painted, sang, danced, rode—became, in short, the parcel-blue and parcel-beauty who was presently to queen it at Melbourne House. At nineteen she fell in with George Lamb (1779-1848), then the penniless younger son of Penistone Lamb, First Viscount Melbourne ; and at twenty (1805), he being then his father's heir and a man six years her elder, she married him. It was a love-match more or less ; and both the parties lived to regret it. Meanwhile, she bore him a son ; and for a certain while, despite her whims and humours and frivolities—despite, too, a distribution of energy among so many points, that to read of her to-day is to conjure up a sort of Zimri-in-Petticoats—things went well enough between them. But, as Mr. Dunckley has noted of her in the admirable sketch inserted in his *Lord Melbourne*—(in ' The Queen's Prime Ministers')—her whole life 'was composed of a series of episodes in which love, or what passed for it, played a leading part.' Vain, selfish, wilful, spoiled, she was one of those bravos of the heart who, while they must still be challenging—challenging for the excitement of combat and the glory of victory—yet often lose their heads, forget their prime object, and are left hurt or dead upon the ground. And, as she was unscrupulous in attack, so was she disadvantaged by defeat to the loss, not only of dignity and self-control, but also of all self-respect and all care for others. She could jilt, it seems, without a pang—as many women can ; but she might not endure disdain—as, for that matter, what woman ever could? And, as she knew not reticence, nor cared twopence who suffered so she had her way, it is not astonishing that in a very few years her husband's regard, for all his affable, genial, affectionate nature, was something the worse for wear.

Even so, the time of real trouble was to come. In the February of 1812 Byron put forth the First and Second *Harold*, and awoke to find himself—not merely famous, but—famous as English poet never was before. Lady Caroline saw the book at Rogers's (as Moore had done), and, after disdaining the writer openly (at Lady Westmoreland's), and confiding to her Diary that she thought him ' mad, bad, and dangerous to know,' felt suddenly aware that here was a worthy opposite in the duel of sex, and (not to crack the wind of the poor metaphor) at once proceeded to call him out. Her challenge was accepted, and in the sequel her reputation was so badly winged that she never recovered the use of it. Byron dined with her the day after Lady Holland made them known. He called, she says in a statement penned in dustier and less 'sanitated' days than ours:—' Rogers and Moore were standing by me. I was on the sofa; I had just come in from riding. I was filthy and heated. When Lord Byron was announced, I flew out of the room to wash myself. When I returned, Rogers said, "Lord Byron, you are a happy man. Lady Caroline has been sitting in all her dirt with us, but when you were announced, she flew to beautify herself." Lord Byron wished to come and see me at eight o'clock when I was alone; that was my dinner-hour. I said he might. From that moment for more than nine months he almost lived at Melbourne House.' In no great while, that is, her 'goings-on' with Byron became the scandal they remained until the end. She sat with him, drove with him (in close carriages) from routs and plays, wrote verses to him, would even have had him take her jewels and pawn them for his own use—in short, did everything she could to compromise herself and him, and, above all, to absorb him—genius and love and glory and will—to the last atom. She achieved the inevitable effect. He's a fool, says an expert in human life and destiny, who pins his faith upon (among other things) a boy's love; and Byron, if he were no more a boy, was at all events too young and vain, too brilliant and too irresistible—especially too irresistible—for constancy. So, from being a goddess, Lady Caroline was in due course revealed a bore of the first magnitude: a bore who rowed you in public, and wrote you reproaches by the ream, and tried to storm your chambers in disguise, and at supper sought to mangle herself with table-knives, or essayed to cast herself out of ball-room windows. What was there for it but division? There was an interview, and there were letters. [One very frantic, desperate, and loverlike elucubration from Byron, in which the writer protests himself ready 'to obey, to honour, love, and fly with you, *when, where, and how* yourself . . . may determine': the sort of composition, in fact, which young men achieve in certain circumstances, and then make haste to blush for or to forget: is printed in Mr. Cordy Jeaffreson's *The Real Lord Byron* (i. 261-3) from a copy 'made from the original MS.'] But no sort of *modus vivendi* was possible, and, to smooth things over, Lady Bessborough took her deliberately impulsive child to Ireland, to be out of Byron's way. Still, they corresponded; and after some time, Lady Caroline intimated her intention of returning to London and her place in Byron's life and heart. The answer to this intimation, written upon paper stamped with the coronet and the initials of a detested rival (Lady Oxford, it is said), was 'that cruel letter that I have published in *Glenarvon*; it destroyed me;

I lost my brain. I was bled, leeched ; kept '—(thus the heroine to her friend, Lady Morgan, the Wild Irish Girl)—'for a week in the filthy "Dolphin" at Rock.' Here is the document, or as much of it as Lady Caroline chose to publish :—

> Lady Caroline Lamb,—I am no longer your lover ; and since you oblige me to confess it by this truly unfeminine persecution, learn that I am attached to another, whose name it would of course be dishonest to mention. I shall ever remember with gratitude the many instances I have received of the predilection you have shown in my favour. I shall ever continue your friend, if your ladyship will permit me so to style myself. And as a first proof of my regard, I offer you this advice : correct your vanity, which is ridiculous ; exert your absurd caprices on others ; and leave me in peace.—Your obedient servant,   BYRON.

A 'cruel letter'? Doubtless. But what is, what has ever been, more cruel than the man a woman has sickened of those favours which she yet insists on thrusting on his acceptance? The situation is as old as Society, and Byron's way of ending it was, and is, and will ever remain, a convention of the game :—

> The Eternal Saki from that bowl has poured
> Millions of bubbles like him, and will pour.

And for Lady Caroline, as for himself, it was not an end but a beginning. Lady Melbourne, George Lamb's mother, was always his very good friend ; he had proposed to her kinswoman, Miss Milbanke, in the autumn of the *Harold* year itself ; in 1814 he proposed again ; in the January of 1815 came the Marriage ; and on the 25th April 1816 followed the Exile. In the interval Lady Caroline had not been idle ; and, whatever her effect in the part of a Lapland Witch, whatever her share in the storm which drove her quondam lover from England, it is certain, at least, that she had him burned in effigy (she sent him an account of the proceedings), certain that she wrote and published *Glenarvon* in the year of his departure, and certain that in *Glenarvon* she did her best against his fame and him. She wrote this wretched book, so she tells you, in a page's habit, and at dead of night ; and for a motto she adapted two famous verses from *The Corsair* :—

> He left a name to all succeeding times,
> Linked with one virtue and a thousand crimes.

But when Byron had read, he had no more to say of *Glenarvon* than this :—' It seems to me, that if the authoress had written the *truth*, and nothing but the truth—the whole truth—the romance would not only have been more *romantic*, but more entertaining.

As for the likeness, the picture can't be good.—I did not sit long enough.'

His first sentence may well have given Disraeli the idea of a matchless scene in *Venetia*. For the rest, the sole change suffered by that antic disposition which was Lady Caroline's was for the worse. In 1824 it chanced that, riding out one morning, she saw a funeral pass the gates, and, asking whose it was, was told that it was Byron's. It was her first news of his death, and she took to her bed in a state of utter collapse, nor recovered till she had sent for Edward Bulwer, then a boy of twenty-one, added him to her list of opposites, given him a rival in the person of a certain Mr. Russell, 'a fashionable beau, extremely handsome, but dull, insipid, and silly,' and sent him so far off his wits with jealousy, that in the end he must have recourse to flight and the loss of twenty ounces of blood.—(DUNCKLEY.) By this time, in fact, her eccentricities had grown to such a pitch of extravagance that there was nothing for George Lamb but to leave her. This he did (1824), as amiably as he did everything; but in 1828, the year which saw him Viscount Melbourne, she died in his company forgiven and at peace.

A handful of opinions about her. I think it must be she of whom Lady Byron (July-August 1815) writes thus to 'Dearest Sis' (Augusta Leigh):—'She has never called on me, and when I made her a vis—(*sic*) with my mother, was very dignified. . . . She asked after B——!—Such a wicked-looking cat I never saw.'— (Morrison Autographs.) Disraeli, greatly daring, essayed to realise her in the Mrs. Felix Lorraine of *Vivian Grey*. After *Glenarvon* Rogers dismissed her in a famous couplet from Pope:—

> From furious Sappho scarce a milder fate,
> Poxed by her love and libelled by her hate.

'It is at least extraordinary,' Harness writes, 'that, while thus courted and admired, if his (Byron's) life were as licentious as some have represented, the only scandal which disturbed the decorum of Society'—(the Society, be it remembered, which had not long lost 'Old Q.', that indefatigable virtuoso (so to speak), which had still its Regent and its Yarmouth, its Harriet Wilson and its Mrs. Clarke, to name but these, and to which *crim. con.* was an essential of being)—'and with which Byron's name is connected, did not originate in any action of his but in the insane and unrequited passion of a woman.' Last of all, Sir Walter:—'Poor soul! if a godlike face and godlike powers could have made any excuse for devilry, to be sure she had one.' Withal she was a true histrion of the heart, had a right instinct for what she deemed the

LETTERS

beau rôle and the centre of the stage, and could play her part to suit all humours. '*That beautiful pale face is my fate*': so (as she told Scott's friend) she told herself in the beginning; and, writing to Murray (13th July 1824):—' I am sure I am very sorry I ever said one word against him.' Each of these utterances is what is called a *mot de la fin*; and each is capital of its kind.

LETTER cxxxix. p. 198.

Sir Francis:—No doubt Sir Francis Burdett (1770-1844), Member for Westminster, who had been committed to the Tower (1810) for breach of privilege, and was at this time a popular and conspicuous anti-Tory. 'Miss Berry' is, of course, Mary Berry (1763-1852), the friend of Horace Walpole, whose house was a centre of letters and polite society, and who died ' the repository of the whole literary history of fourscore years.'—HARRIET MARTINEAU.

LETTER cxli. p. 199.

Saw Bellingham launched into eternity:—Bellingham was a Liverpool broker who, being crazed by misfortune, went to the House of Commons bent on the murder of Lord Leveson Gower, but shot the Premier, Spencer Perceval, instead. He was executed on the 18th May 1812. In Byron's time, and after, it was good form to attend a hanging, as it was good form to back a boxer, and as it had once been good form to see the loose women whipped in Bridewell. Here is Moore's account of Byron's expedition:—
' He had taken a window opposite for the purpose, and was accompanied on the occasion by his old schoolfellows, Mr. Bailey and Mr. John Madocks. They went together from some assembly, and, on their arriving at the spot, about three o'clock in the morning, not finding the house that was to receive them open, Mr. Madocks undertook to rouse the inmates, while Lord Byron and Mr. Bailey sauntered, arm in arm, up the street. During this interval rather a painful scene occurred. Seeing an unfortunate woman lying on the steps of a door, Lord Byron, with some expression of compassion, offered her a few shillings; but, instead of accepting them, she violently pushed away his hand, and, starting up with a yell of laughter, began to mimic the lameness of his gait. He did not utter a word; but " I could feel," said Mr. Bailey, "his arm trembling within mine as we left her." '

Mrs. Moore:—The actress, Elizabeth Dyke (1793-1865), whom Moore had married the year before. The best of women and wives, she was long famous as the heroine (real or not) of one of her husband's prettiest and least mannered songs:—

412

NOTES

Fly from the world, O Bessy ! to me,
    Thou 'lt never find any sincerer.
I 'll give up the world, O Bessy ! for thee,
    I can never meet any that 's dearer.

LETTER cxlii. p. 199.

To Bernard Barton :—'The Quaker Poet,' Bernard Barton (1784-1849), published his *Metrical Effusions* in 1812, his *Poems by an Amateur* in 1817, his *Poems* in 1820. He was for forty years clerk in a bank at Woodbridge, and, being a very amiable and respectable man, as well as a writer of a not displeasing mediocrity, he had many distinguished friends, chief among them, as everybody knows, Charles Lamb.

LETTER cxliii. p. 201.

I was presented by order to our gracious Regent :—This, in general society, was Byron's sole meeting with the Prince. He was asked to Carlton House; but the levee was deferred, and to Carlton House he never went. In the March of this same year he had written his *Lines to a Lady Weeping*, on the report that the Princess Charlotte had burst into tears when she was told that a Whig Cabinet was impossible after Perceval's death—(they cut the Regent to the quick, and he was bitterly distressed when in the long-run he found them to be, not Moore's but, Byron's) :—

> Weep, daughter of a royal line,
>   A Sire's disgrace, a realm's decay ;
> Ah ! happy if each tear of thine
>   Could wash a father's fault away !
>
> Weep—for thy tears are Virtue's tears—
>   Auspicious to these suffering isles ;
> And be each drop in future years
>   Repaid thee by thy people's smiles !

But at this time the Prince, howbeit a man of fifty :—

> Brisk let us revel, while revel we may ;
> For the gay bloom of fifty soon passes away,
>   And then people get fat,
>   And infirm, and—all that,
> And a wig (I confess it) so clumsily sits,
> That it frightens the little Loves out of their wits :—

had not a little left him of the Florizel of early years ; his air, his grace, his manner, his talk, still made his regard delightful ; and Byron seems to have been equally gratified and flattered by his expression of interest and approval. More : savagely as he

413

wrote about his Sovereign afterwards, he recalled the experience with a certain pleasure well-nigh to the end :—

> There, too, he saw (whate'er he may be now)
>   A Prince, the prince of princes at the time,
> With fascination in his very bow,
>   And full of promise, as the spring of prime.
> Though royalty was written on his brow,
>   He had *then* the grace, too, rare in every clime,
> Of being, without alloy of fop or beau,
> A finished gentleman from top to toe.—*Don Juan*, xii. 84.

A pure predilection for poetry :—' Predilection ' is, perhaps, reminiscent of a certain phrase in the Regent's letter to the Duke of York (13th February 1812), the letter which so terribly enraged the disappointed Whigs. 'I have no predilections to indulge,' he wrote, 'no resentments to gratify,' or, as Moore translated the expression in his famous *Parody of a Celebrated Letter* :—

> I am proud to declare that I 've no predilections,
> My heart is a sieve, where some scattered affections
> Are just danced about for a moment or two,
> And the *finer* they are, the more sure to run through.
> Neither feel I resentments, nor wish there should come ill
> To mortal—except (now I think on 't) Beau Brummell,
> Who threatened last year, in a superfine passion,
> To cut *me*, and bring the old King into fashion.

I thought of poor Brummell's adventure :—For George Bryan Brummell (1778-1840), see the *Life* by Captain Jesse (Second Edition, 1886), and, above all, that little masterpiece of Barbey d'Aurevilly's, *Du Dandysme et de Georges Brummell* (1844). I hope to return to this exemplar of ' la Frivolité majestueuse.' It must here suffice me to say that his quarrel with the Regent, after twenty years of intimacy, dates from 1811, or thereabouts, and, as he did not retire into banishment till 1816, he had still some way to go. But the colossal and superb impertinence, ' Who 's your fat friend?' was at this time historical ; so that the true work of his life was done.

Mr. Pye's decease :—Henry James Pye (1745-1813), feeblest by far of all the line of Laureates, a man quite 'eminently respectable in everything but his poetry' (B.), succeeded Warton in 1790, and was himself succeeded by Robert Southey.

Mallet of indifferent memory :—This, of course, is David Malloch (1698-1765), the 'beggarly Scotsman' of a famous description, the 'tool with a wooden head' of a famous definition, who reviled Bentley to please Pope, slandered Pope to please Bolingbroke, raised the people against Byng to please the Ministry, got a

thousand pounds for a *Life of Marlborough*, of which he never
wrote a line, and is held, or was held, by some to be the poet of
Rule Britannia.

LETTER cxliv. p. 202.

To Sir Walter Scott, Bart. :—Byron began, of course, by lump-
ing Scott with Jeffrey. Both were products of Edinburgh; so both
were equally damnable, and both must be (and both were) brought
forth and scourged before the people, the one as a hackney poet—
('my crime,' says Scott, 'was having written a poem . . . for a
thousand pounds')—the other as a venal critic. Scott was no better
pleased than another man of spirit would be in the circumstances;
and soon after the publication of *English Bards* you find him writing
(7th August 1809) of 'a young whelp of a Lord Byron,' and noting
that 'it is not his Lordship's merit, though it may be his great good
fortune, that he was not born to live by his literary talents or success.'
Again (4th April 1812) he tells Joanna Baillie that *Childe Harold* is
'a clever poem, but gives no good symptoms of the writer's heart or
morals,' that 'it must require impudence at least equal to the noble
Lord's other powers, to claim sympathy for the *ennui* arising from
his being tired of his wassailers and his paramours,' etc. etc. But,
once made, the acquaintance, which was of Scott's seeking, was
never crossed by so much as the shadow of a shade. As matter of
fact, in nothing which the great and good Sir Walter ever wrote
are sanity of judgment and soundness of humanity more conspicuous than in (1) the 'interesting communication' with which,
years after the event, he 'found time, in the midst of all his
marvellous labours for the world,' to 'favour' Byron's biographer
(Appendix C); and (2) the reflections on Byron's death which he
contributed (1824) to an Edinburgh newspaper (Appendix D). They
met not often, nor corresponded very vigorously; but the understanding of these two radiant and distinguished spirits was none
the less complete for that. 'No one,' Scott writes to Murray (10th
January 1817), 'can honour Lord Byron's genius more than I do,
and no one had so great a wish to love him personally, though
personally we had not the means of becoming very intimate'; and
he goes on to regret that he had not interfered, as he might have
done, in Byron's 'family distress (deeply to be deprecated, and
in which probably he can yet be excused),' for the reason that he
'always seemed to give me credit for wishing him sincerely well.'
Thus Scott to Murray; and thus Murray, concerning Scott, to
Byron (22nd September 1818):—'The Saturday and Sunday pre-

LETTERS

vious I passed most delightfully with Walter Scott, who was incessant in his inquiries after your welfare. He entertains the noblest sentiments of regard towards you, and speaks of you with the best feelings.' I might go on, but, in the light of the two documents I purpose to quote, this is enough on the one part. On the other, I shall only note that, *English Bards and Scotch Reviewers* once off the writer's stomach, Byron never wavered in his admiration and respect for Scott. 'There was something highly gratifying to the feelings'—of the Countess of Blessington—'in witnessing the warmth and cordiality that Byron's countenance displayed in talking of Sir Walter Scott,' whom, for the rest, he 'never named but with praise and affection.' 'We don't say "Mr. Cæsar,"' he writes, by way of apology for speaking of his friend as plain Scott; the Novels, 'a literature in themselves,' are among the books he loves best and reads most; Scott's review of the Third *Harold* gives him extreme pleasure; to Scott *Cain* is dedicated, 'by his obliged friend and faithful servant,' (1821); and Scott, the 'Ariosto of the North,' of the Fourth *Harold* (1817)—'meaning thereby of all countries which are not the South,'—the 'Monarch of Parnassus, and the most English of bards' of a certain 'triangular *gradus ad Parnassum*' (1813), accepts 'with feelings of great obligation' Byron's 'very flattering proposal' to prefix the name of Walter Scott to his 'very grand and tremendous drama.' It is well at all times to remember that Byron's name, if it stank in the nostrils of Georgian London, was always sweet, and sweet enough, in those of the best good man of his time.

For the occasion of the present Letter: 'Mr. John Murray,' Scott wrote to Moore, 'happened to be in Scotland that season, and as I mentioned to him the pleasure I should have in making Lord Byron's acquaintance, he had the kindness to mention my wish to his Lordship, and this led to some correspondence.' Murray, in fact, took Byron fresh from his talk with the Prince Regent, and reported him to Scott, who wrote to Byron (3rd July 1812) the very pleasant letter printed in its place in Lockhart's *Life*, in which he took care to correct his correspondent's error in the matter of *Marmion* and the thousand pounds. Byron replied as in the text, and Scott retorted (16th July 1812) with what was practically an invitation to Scotland in general and to Abbotsford in particular. For the sequel, in Scott's own words, see Appendix C.

My politics being as perverse as my rhymes:—The Regent was no

416

longer the brilliant and engaging Whig of the Dedication prefixed
to Moore's *Anacreon* (1800). He was shaping fast to be that Tory
of Tories to whom Sir Walter was presently to dedicate the Waverley
Novels, and for that reason he was the cockshy of Whiggish wits
and an outcast from Whig society. Still, if Dallas be credible,
Byron is here a trifle disingenuous :—' I called on him ' (thus Dallas)
' on the morning for which the levee had been appointed, and found
him in a full-dress court suit of clothes, with his fine black hair in
powder, which by no means suited his countenance. I was surprised, as he had not told me that he should go to court ; and it
seemed to me as if he thought it necessary to apologise for his
intention, by his observing that he could not in decency but do it,
as the Regent had done him the honour to say that he hoped to
see him soon at Carlton House.'

Letter cxlv. p. 204.

Send me ' Rokeby.' Who the deuce is he?—*Rokeby* (published
this year) was named after the historic house of Scott's friend,
James Morritt, to whom the poem was dedicated. Hence the lines
in Letter vii. of *The Twopenny Post-Bag* (1813) :—

> Should you feel any touch of *poetical* glow,
> We've a scheme to suggest—Mr. Sc—tt, you must know
> [Who, we 're sorry to say it, now works for the Row],
> Having quitted the Borders to seek new renown,
> Is coming, by long Quarto stages, to Town ;
> And beginning with Rokeby (the job 's sure to pay)
> Means to do all the Gentlemen's Seats on the way.
> Now, the Scheme is (though none of our hackneys can beat him)
> To start a fresh Poet through Highgate to *meet* him ;
> Who, by means of quick proofs—no revises—long coaches –
> May do a few Villas before Sc—tt approaches.
> Indeed, if our Pegasus be not curst shabby,
> He 'll reach, without found'ring, at least Woburn Abbey.

This is good enough banter, to be sure. But in the general
opinion Scott was not the poet he had been ; and what Moore
really thought of the new quarto is expressed to better purpose in
a question to Power, publisher of the *Melodies* :—' Did you ever
see any songs so bad as the songs in *Rokeby*?' Yet among the
songs in *Rokeby* is *Brignall Banks*, one of the triumphs of the
Romantic Muse !

What will you give me or mine for a poem :—As we have seen,
Byron declined to receive a penny for the *Harold*. And it was Dallas
who got the five hundred guineas Murray gave for *The Giaour*.

LETTERS

Like Jeremy Diddler:—Kenney's farce, *Raising the Wind*, was produced in 1803.

Adair on Diet and Regimen:—This is the *Essay on Diet and Regimen as Indispensable to the Recovery and Preservation of Firm Health to Indolent, Studious, Delicate, and Invalid* (1804) of James M. Adair.

LETTER cxlvi. p. 204.

The lines which I sketched off on your hint:—No doubt, a potential *Address* for the opening night at the new Drury Lane.

Mr Betty:—William Henry West Betty (1791-1874), the 'Young Roscius' for whom the Town took such a craze that in 1805 Mr. Pitt adjourned the House that members might see his Hamlet. Three years later, after a round of such unwarrantable triumphs as justly scandalised Kean and the gifted Siddons, he left the stage, and went to Cambridge, but reappeared in 1812, and failed as, a few lines later, Byron says fail he must.

So, poor dear Rogers:—Rogers had started that summer on a tour in the North. He did not return till the end of the year.

LETTER cxlvii. p. 206.

The books were presents of a convertible kind also :—Both *Christian Knowledge* and *The Bioscope; or, Dial of Life explained* (1812) were the work of Granville Penn (1761-1844); 'a gentleman,' says Moore, 'descended from the family of Penn of Pennsylvania, and much distinguished for his learning and piety.' Byron's was ever a soul too precious for perdition. Here is the first attempt to save it. The Duke of Wellington's was exposed to visitations of the same solicitude.

So you are Lucien's publisher:—Lucien Bonaparte (1775-1840), Prince of Canino, had come to England in 1810, bought an estate in Shropshire, and written an epic there in four-and-twenty cantos called *Charlemagne, ou l'Église delivrée.* A translation, *Charlemagne, or the Church Delivered,* the work of Hodgson and Butler, was published (1815) in two volumes quarto: which, it is thought, no living man has read.

The ' Anti-Jacobin ' Review is all very well :—See the review of *Childe Harold* (Third Edition) in the August issue (1812) of that print. 'The pleasure,' it says, 'which we derived from the perusal of Lord Byron's former productions made us sit down with avidity to the pilgrimage of his favourite *Childe*. We cannot say, however, that our expectations of gratification have been fulfilled.

NOTES

From the form and nature of the ' Romaunt,' as it is whimsically,
and improperly, denominated, we were led to look for all the
characteristics of a regular poem. We were not a little surprised,
therefore, to find the piece destitute of plot or even of plan, its hero
a personage not only wandering over the world, without any fixed
object, but wholly unnecessary to forward any purpose of the
poem,' etc. etc.

Not a bit worse than the ' Quarterly' :—The *Quarterly* (March
1812) censures *Childe Harold* for the ' Childe,' the ' staunch
Yeoman,' and ' the little Page,' and asks :—' Why is this group of
antiques sent on a journey through Portugal and Spain during the
interval' between Cintra and Talavera? Such inconsistencies are
' by no means innocent, if they have led Lord Byron (as we suspect)
to adopt that motley mixture of obsolete and modern phraseology
by which the ease and elegance of his verses are often injured, and
to degrade the character of his work by the insertion of some
passages which will probably give offence to a considerable portion
of his readers.' In blaming his use of such words as ' moe, feere,
ne, losel, eld,' and the like, the Reviewer notes that the Author is not
always correct in his use of them, and cites (C. I. St. lxvii.), *Devices
quaint,* etc. :—' It must be supposed that he did not mean to per-
sonify devices and frolics for the purpose of afflicting them with
chilblains.' Again, on C. II. St. lxii. :—' It is plain that the noble
lord must have considered ruth as synonymous, not with pity,' but
with cruelty,' and ' in a third instance, where we are told that "*Childe*
Harold had a *mother,*" the vocal meaning of the first word has evidently a ludicrous effect, which could not have escaped the attention
of our author whilst writing in the language of his own day.' At the
same time ' we do not mean to lay any stress on the accidental heed-
lessness which originates such errors, we complain only of the
habitual negligence, of the frequent laxity of expression—of the
feeble or dissonant rhymes which almost always disfigure a too close
imitation of the language of our early poets, and of which we think
that the work before us offers too many examples.' Then we quote
' Even gods must yield,' etc. (C. II. St. iii.-vii.), which has this effect
on us :—' The common courtesy of society has, we think, very justly
proscribed the intrusive introduction of such topics as these into
conversation, and as no reader probably will open *Childe Harold*
with the view of inquiring into the religious tenets of the author, or
of endeavouring to settle his own, we cannot but disapprove, in
point of taste, these protracted meditations, as well as the disgusting objects by which some of them are suggested. We object

to them, also, because they have the effect of producing some little
traces of resemblance between the author and the hero of the piece,
a resemblance which Lord Byron has most sedulously and properly disclaimed in his preface.' . . . On the whole, however, 'the
applause which he has received has been very general, and in our
opinion, well deserved. We think that the poem exhibits some
marks of carelessness, many of caprice, but many also of sterling
genius. On the latter we have forborne to expatiate, because we
apprehend that our readers are quite as well qualified as ourselves
to estimate the merits of pleasing versification, of lively conception,
and of accurate expression.' Further, the poet ' has shown that his
confidence in his own powers is not to be subdued by illiberal and
unmerited censure ; and we are sure that it will not be diminished
by our animadversions : we are not sure that we should have better
consulted his future fame, or our own character for candour, if we
had expressed our sense of his talents in terms of more unqualified
panegyric.'

P.S.—Gave up the idea of contending against all **Grub Street :—**
This is true, but the *Address* was written by him **after all.** Lord
Holland asked him to write it, and, as we have seen (Letter clxxix.),
he declined to do so on the same grounds as these he here sets forth
to Murray. Meanwhile, Grub Street had entered (near a hundred
strong), and had been **cast out** utterly ; and Lord Holland, returning to the charge, succeeded where he **had** failed before, and
persuaded his young friend to give the Committee of Management
its desire : though in doing so Byron did actually, as he expected,
' offend a hundred scribblers and a discerning **public.** '

LETTER cxlix. p. 209.
I think Elliston should be the man :—Robert William Elliston
(1774-1831): Lamb's 'brightest of embodied spirits'; to Leigh
Hunt's mind 'the best lover on the stage, both in tragedy and
comedy' ; more than interesting as Romeo and Hamlet, and un-
equalled as Mercutio and Benedick and Hotspur, as Farquhar's
Mirabel and Archer, Cibber's Lord Townley, Rowe's Lothario,
the Duke Aranza of *The Honeymoon,* the Rover of *Wild Oats,* the
Ranger of *The Suspicious Husband,* the Falkland of *The Rivals,*
and (till Kean had played the part) the Sir Edward Mortimer of
The Iron Chest : was a member of the Drury Lane Company from
1804 until the fire in 1809, and again in 1812-15. He lives as fully
as dead actor can in some delightful pages by Charles Lamb. See,

NOTES

too, the capital sketch of him by Mr. William Archer in *Actors and Actresses of Great Britain and the United States.*

Or Pope:—Alexander Pope (1762-1835) 'had a handsome face, good person, genteel figure, and graceful action'; his voice, too, 'possessed a firmness, and in the softer tones called the soul-moving Barry to the recollection'; but 'his countenance was scarcely sufficiently expressive to give full effect to the passions of joy, grief, or disdain.' Leigh Hunt disliked him, and criticised him very sharply for the sameness of his gesture, the flatness of his conceptions, and the inexpressiveness of his face; while Elia described him ('On Some of the Old Actors') as 'the abdicated monarch of comedy and tragedy,' with peculiar reference to his Henry VIII. and his Lord Townley. He appeared at Covent Garden in 1784-5, and retired in 1827. He was a fine glutton, and could never forgive 'that monster Catalani' because she took a knife to a fricandeau. Again, to Incledon, who told him that the Yankees took no oil to their salads, 'No oil to their salads!' said the outraged feeder: '*Why did we make peace with them?*'

Not Raymond, I implore you, by the love of Rhythmus:—Raymond, 'from Dublin,' appeared at Drury Lane, 26th September 1799, as Osmond in Mat Lewis's *Castle Spectres.* Leigh Hunt preferred him vastly before Pope; and says Hazlitt, in his account of Kean's Hamlet (1814), 'We cannot speak too highly of Mr. Raymond's representation of the Ghost. It glided across the stage with the preternatural grandeur of a spirit.' But, for 'his manner of speaking the part, there is not so much to say: a spirit should not whine or shed tears.' In 1814, when Kean electrified the Town, Raymond appears to have been stage-manager at the new Drury Lane; but when Bluebeard's elephants were burned (see *ante,* p. 357. Note to Letter lxxii.) in 1809, he 'condescended to be the magician of an Eastern tale' and 'assisted pantomime' (the phrases are Leigh Hunt's; and the phrases will serve, though the date will not). Associated with him in *Bluebeard* were Bannister, Matthews, Mrs. Mountain, and Mrs. Bland: a cast which would beggar the existing stage.

LETTER cl. p. 209.
I send a recast:—Thus the four lines are printed.

LETTER cli. p. 210.
Dryden in his 'Annus Mirabilis':—

> A quay of fire ran all along the shore,
> And lightened all the river with a blaze;

421

LETTERS

The wakened tides began again to roar,
And wondering fish in shining waters gaze.

Annus Mirabilis, 922-25.

Churchill in his ' Times' :—

Her towers in dust, her Thames a Lake of fire.

The Times, 702.

As flashing far:—After divers corrections, the couplet came to this tremendous estate :—

As glared the volumed blaze, and ghastly shone
The skies with lightnings awful as their own.

Perhaps the present couplet had better come in after ' trembled for their homes' :—It does.

Sir Fretful:—' The insidious humility with which he seduces you to give a free opinion on any of his works can be exceeded only by the petulant arrogance with which he is sure to reject your observations.'—*The Critic*, i. 1. At this time Byron was at least good-natured. See Lord Holland to Rogers (22nd October 1812) :—' You cannot imagine how I grew to like Lord Byron in my critical intercourse with him. . . . He was so good-humoured, took so much pains, corrected so good-humouredly,' etc.

' Lurid' is also a less indistinct epithet than ' livid' :—There is no ' wave,' whether ' lurid ' or ' livid,' in the published *Address*.

LETTER clii. p. 211.

The fifth and sixth lines :—Thus altered, they form a part of the *Address*. The ' next line ' runs thus :—

Like Israel's pillar chase the night from heaven.

' When Garrick died' :—

Ere Garrick fled, and Brinsley ceased to write.

Thus the *Address* as printed.

The old couplet :—

Such are the names that here your plaudits sought,
When Garrick acted, and when Brinsley wrought.

Pope's to ' Cato' :—

To wake the soul by tender strokes of art,
To raise the genius and to mend the heart, etc.

Johnson's to Drury Lane:—Spoken, at the opening of the new Drury Lane in 1747, by Mr. Garrick. The English masterpiece of the *genre*.

NOTES

One of Goldsmith's:—Goldsmith wrote a Prologue 'To the Tragedy of *Zobeide*'; an Epilogue, 'Spoken by Mr. Lee Lewis, in the character of Harlequin, at his Benefit'; an Epilogue to *The Sisters*; an Epilogue 'Spoken by Miss Bulkley and Miss Catley'; and an Epilogue 'Intended for Mrs. Bulkley.' Which was Byron's choice I shall not pretend to determine.

A prologue of old Colman's:—

> While modern Tragedy, by Rule exact,
> Spins out a thin-wrought Fable, Act by Act,
> We dare to bring you one of those bold Plays.
> Wrote by rough English Wits in former Days;
> Beaumont and Fletcher! those twin stars, that run
> Their glorious Course round Shakespeare's golden Sun, etc.

LETTER cliii. p. 214.

'Adorn' and 'mourn':—In Byron:—

> Ye who beheld (Oh! sight admired and mourn'd!)
> Whose radiance mock'd the ruin it adorn'd.

In Gray:—

> Stay, O stay! nor thus forlorn,
> Leave me unblessed, unpitied, here to mourn.

In Pope:—

> By foreign hands thy humble grave adorned,
> By strangers honoured, and by strangers mourned.

In Smollett:—

> Mourn, hapless Caledonia, mourn
> Thy banished peace, thy laurels torn.

LETTER clv. p. 215.

Is Whitbread determined to castrate all my 'cavalry' lines?— Whitbread was; and certain verses written with an eye on Johnson's treatment of Rich and others in the 1747 *Address*:—

> Perhaps, where Lear has raved, and Hamlet died,
> On flying cars new sorcerers may ride:
> Perhaps (for who can guess th' effects of chance?)
> Here Hunt may box, and Mahomet may dance:—

were expunged from Byron's piece. They referred generally to that passion for real horses on the stage which made *The Cataract of the Ganges* one of the great successes of its time; and particularly to the appearance of real horses—the first at a Patent Theatre—

LETTERS

sixteen strong, at Covent Garden (18th February 1811) in the (revived) pantomime of *Bluebeard* (see *ante*, p. 357, Note to Letter lxxii.). They were held a scandalous innovation ; but they were so well trained that the piece ran forty-four nights—in those days a prodigious thing. Here they are, as preserved by Murray's Editor :—

> Nay, lower still, the Drama yet deplores
> That late she deigned to crawl upon all-fours.
> When Richard roars in Bosworth for a horse,
> If you command, the steed must come in course
> If you decree, the stage must condescend
> To soothe the sickly taste we dare not mend.
> Blame not our judgment should we acquiesce,
> And gratify you more by showing less.
> The past reproach let present scenes refute,
> Nor shift from man to babe, from babe to brute.

For the antithetic 'babe' of the last see below, Note to Letter clvii. Whitbread himself, by the way, sent in an *Address*. It had a Phoenix in it ; and, according to Sheridan, the maker described that fowl 'like a Poulterer : it was green, and red, and yellow, and blue : he did not let us off for a single feather.'

LETTER clvi. p. 217.

You heard that Newstead is sold :—Newstead, in effect, was put to auction at Garraway's in the autumn of this year, and was bought in at £90,000. It was soon afterwards sold privately, as Byron writes ; but Mr. Leigh, the purchaser, was unable to fulfil his contract, and forfeited £25,000. In the end the estate was bought by Byron's old schoolfellow, Colonel Wildman, so that in the long-run Hanson had his way.

Did you read of a sad accident :—' The party were returning from Tintern Abbey in a pleasure-boat, and were preparing to land below the bridge at Chepstow, when, on coming through the centre arch, where a barge was moored across, the rope taking the bottom of the boat, upset it. Out of the twelve of which the party consisted, seven actually perished.'—MOORE.

LETTER clvii. p. 219.

I have altered the middle couplet :—That is, of the 'cavalry lines' already quoted (see above, Note to Letter clv.) :—

> If you decree, the stage must condescend
> To soothe the sickly taste we dare not mend.

It had been unpardonable to pass over the horses and Miss Mudie :

424

NOTES

—Miss Mudie, advertised as 'The Theatrical Phenomenon,' who, following hard on the heels of Master Betty, appeared at Covent Garden, 23rd November 1805, as Peggy in *The Country Girl*, which Garrick adopted from Wycherley. 'She looked some eight years old, and was small for her age, but the season before she had played the first-rate comic character at Birmingham, Liverpool, Dublin, and other theatres.' At Covent Garden she was found grotesque, and, at the end of her Fourth Act, having told the audience, 'with the most perfect self-possession, that she had done nothing to offend,' and 'as for those who are sent here to hiss me, I will be much obliged to you to turn them out,' the poor little monster was hissed from the stage. John Kemble (this story is told in Clark Russell's *Representative Actors*), being asked if Miss Mudie were 'really the child she was said to be,' replied ('in his solemn tone of jesting'):—'*Child!* Why, sir, when I was a very young actor in the York Company, that little creature kept an inn at Tadcaster, and had a large family.'

'*Hunt*'—'*Mahomet*,' *etc.*:—See *ante*, p. 423, Note to Letter clv. Hunt was a stage-boxer, Mahomet a rope-dancer.

LETTER clix. p. 221.

There is a new couplet for Sheridan :—

> But still for living wit the wreaths may bloom,
> That only waste their odours o'er the tomb.
> Such Drury claimed and claims—nor you refuse
> One tribute to revive his slumbering Muse;
> With Garlands deck your own Menander's head,
> Nor hoard your honours idly for the dead.

Sheridan's dates at Drury Lane are these: 1777, *The School for Scandal*; 1777, *A Trip to Scarborough*; 1779, *The Critic*; and 1799, *Pizarro*. Both *The Rivals* and *The Duenna* (1775) were produced at Covent Garden.

LETTER clx. p. 222.

Far be from him :—Neither couplet was used.

Murray tells me there are myriads of ironical addresses ready :— This, I take it, refers especially to the *Rejected Addresses* of James (1775-1839) and Horatio, or Horace (1779-1849) Smith. This excellent piece of parody was written in six weeks, and offered for £20 to Murray, who declined it. Among the writers caricatured in it were Moore, Southey, Fitzgerald, Wordsworth, the incredible Laura Matilda, Cobbett, Coleridge, Matthew Lewis, Crabbe, Scott—('I

Oh! for the flow of Busby, and of Fitz,
The latter's loyalty, the former's wits,
To 'energise the objects I pursue,' etc.

Thus, too, Byron, in the letter 'To the Publisher,' prefixed by
'Horace Hornem' to the same work :—'I sat down, and with the
aid of William Fitzgerald, Esq., and a few hints from Dr. Busby
(whose recitations I attend, and am monstrous fond of Master
Busby's manner of delivering his father's late successful *Drury
Lane Address*), I composed the following hymn.'

I have a poem on Waltzing for you:—The aforesaid 'Apostrophic Hymn,' by Horace Hornem.

You may print the first fifty or a hundred opening lines, etc :—
Written at the Capuchin Convent, 1811, and prepared for publication with the *Hints from Horace.* Byron's assault upon Lord
Elgin for collecting the wonderful pieces now known as the Elgin
Marbles remained in MS. till 1828. Nor for the moment did anything come of his recommendation to Murray, as the verses thus
denoted were printed in no edition of the *Harold,* but were trans-
ferred, and then only in part, to the opening of the Third Canto
of *The Corsair* (1814).

LETTER clxv. p. 226.

The best thing of the kind since ' The Rolliad':—That famous
set of literary and political lampoons against the Pittites, *The
Rolliad, Probationary Odes,* etc., was published in 1795. It
handled the Tories in pretty much the same style as that in which
Canning and the men of *The Anti-Jacobin* were soon to handle the
Whigs; and in places is good reading still. Lowndes, who seems
to have written his note from copies belonging to Mackintosh and
Heber, says:—'The writers of *The Rolliad* were R. Tickell,
Joseph Richardson, Lord John Townsend, General Fitzpatrick,
Mr. Hare, G. Ellis, W. H. Reid, Mr. Adair, Rev. Bate Dudley, Mr.
Brummell, Mr. Boscawen, Mr. Pearce, the Bishop of Ossory, a Pre-
liminary Discourse to the Probationary Odes by Sir John Hawkins,
and the Preface by Dr. French Laurence.'

P.S.—The Editor of the 'Satirist,' etc. :—The *Satirist* for
October 1812 reviews *Childe Harold.* It begins by quoting 'the
judgment of our predecessors'—to the effect that unless Lord
Byron 'improved wonderfully, he could never be a poet'—but
goes on thus :—'It is with unaffected satisfaction we find that he
has improved wonderfully, and that he *is* a poet. Indeed, when
we consider the comparatively short interval which has elapsed,

NOTES

and contrast the character of his recent with that of his early work, we confess ourselves astonished at the intellectual progress which Lord Byron has made, and are happy to hold him up as another example of the extraordinary effects of study and cultivation, *even on minds apparently* of the most unpromising description.' . . . Follows a quotation, four stanzas long :—

> Three hosts combine to offer sacrifice,
> Three tongues prefer strange orisons on high :—

the sentiments in which are reproved with extreme severity. Indeed, the reviewer is ever concerned for the sinister cast of the poet's thoughts. 'The poems under our consideration,' he affirms, 'abound with beautiful imagery, clothed in a diction free, forcible, and various. *Childe Harold*, although avowedly a fragment, contains many passages which would do honour to any poet, of any period, in any country. At the same time we are compelled to remark, that there are others which we must strongly reprobate; and not the less so because it is the thought rather than the expression with which we quarrel.' Still, the said Satirist is not disposed to abandon Byron unpitied and unreconciled. Despair he leaves to Harold and his kind. For himself, he cherishes a hope of better things. As thus :—' It is a matter of regret that this young nobleman, endued as he certainly is with talents of no ordinary character, chooses thus to cherish, or affect to cherish, a gloominess of mind which, as we observed in the commencement of our strictures in the volume before us, is in so many instances tinctured with a very undesirable spirit; as it is not satisfied with the expression of a grief, which, however justly it may be deemed weak and feminine, may nevertheless be pardoned, but vents itself in a bitterness towards human nature generally which nothing can excuse. If so vulgar a consideration as pecuniary advantage may be supposed to operate favourably on the noble Lord's mental morbidity, we sincerely hope that the recent sale of Newsted [*sic*] Abbey for £140,000 (it having been previously estimated at only £60,000) may impart more cheerfulness and benevolence to the tone of his feelings; or, if literary fame may correct his misanthropy, and turn his feelings into a more genial current, we look for some happy changes from the effect of the Drury Lane Laurel.' And with this graceful reference to the reception of the *Address* he ends his song.

LETTER clxvi. p. 228.

I am going to Lord Oxford's:—Edward Harley (1773-1849), Fifth Earl of Oxford, succeeded his uncle in 1790, and four years

LETTERS

after married Jane Elizabeth, daughter of the Rev. James Scott, Vicar of Stokin (Hants), by whom he had five children. His country seat was Eywood House, in Herefordshire.

Did Mr. Ward, etc. :—He did.

LETTER clxvii. p. 229.

A curious and very long MS. poem :—Mr. A. H. Bullen conjectures this to be 'Lord Brooke's *Treatise of Monarchy*, which contains between six and seven hundred six-line stanzas.'

Mr. 'Mac-Somebody' : —See *The Genuine Rejected Addresses, Presented to the Committee of Management for Drury Lane Theatre.* These numbers were published, as we have seen, by B. M'Millan, and were, in fact, 'preceded by that written by Lord Byron, and adopted by the Committee.'

His Apologetical Letter and Postscript :—This is not in the British Museum, nor have I been able to find it elsewhere.

LETTER clxix. p. 232.

Lady O. (Oxford) has heard me talk much of you :—Hoppner's portrait of Lady Oxford (1774-1824)—one of his best : exhibited in 1798—shows a woman amiable as beautiful—the very woman, in fact, of the letter from Uvedale Price, with which I end this Note. It seems to have been Lady Oxford of whom Byron spoke thus at Genoa (BLESSINGTON, *Conversations*, etc., 1834) :— 'Even now the autumnal charms of Lady —— are remembered by me with more than admiration. She resembled a landscape by Claude Lorraine, with a setting sun, her beauties enhanced by the knowledge that they were shedding their last dying leaves, which threw a radiance round. A woman . . . is only grateful for her *first* and *last* conquests. The first of poor dear Lady ——'s was achieved before I entered on this world of care, but the *last*, I do flatter myself, was reserved for me, and a *bonne bouche* it was.' If this be a memory of the Countess, it is a good enough commentary on the fact that Byron took Thyrnham Court to be near the Oxfords next year ; and that he thought of going to Sicily this year in Lord Oxford's train, and did actually get as far as Portsmouth. Portsmouth was the end ; for the Oxfords were long abroad, and Byron lived his life at top speed. Death came to both these lovers in the same year. And on the occasion of her departure, Uvedale Price wrote thus (CLAYDEN, *Rogers and His Contemporaries*, i. 397-8) to Rogers, from Foxley, under date of 26th December 1824 :—

'This is a melancholy subject'—[the death, by consumption, of Lord

Aberdeen's children]—and ' I must go to another : poor Lady Oxford. I had heard with great concern of her dangerous illness, but hoped she might get through it, and was much, very much grieved to hear that it had ended fatally. I had, as you know, lived a great deal with her from the time she came into this country, immediately after her marriage, but for some years past, since she went abroad, had scarcely had any correspondence or intercourse with her, till I met her in town last spring. I then saw her twice, and both times she seemed so overjoyed to see an old friend, and expressed her joy so naturally and cordially, that I felt no less overjoyed at seeing her after so long an absence. She talked, with great satisfaction, of our meeting for a longer time this next spring, little thinking of an eternal separation. There could not, in all respects, be a more ill-matched pair than herself and Lord Oxford, or a stronger instance of the cruel sports of Venus, or, rather, of Hymen :—

> Cui placet impares
> Formas atque animos sub juga ahenea
> Sævo mittere cum joco.

It has been said that she was, in some measure, forced into the match ; had she been united to a man whom she had loved, esteemed, and respected, she herself might have been generally respected and esteemed as well as loved ; but in her situation, to keep clear of all misconduct required a strong mind or a cold heart ; perhaps both, and she had neither. Her failings were in no small degree the effect of circumstances ; her amiable qualities all her own. There was something about her in spite of her errors remarkably attaching, and that something was not merely her beauty ; "kindness has resistless charms," and she was full of affectionate kindness to those she loved, whether as friends or as lovers. As a friend, I always found her the same ; never at all changeful or capricious ; as I am not a very rigid moralist and am extremely open to kindness, " I could have better spared a better woman."'

The ' Agnus' is furious :—The ' Agnus '= Lady Caroline Lamb. ' Hell hath no fury,' etc. ; and this scorned woman knew herself replaced as well.

' Why brief,' Mr. Wild :—So in J. T. Hodgson's *Memoir*, i. 273. But see *The Life of Mr. Jonathan Wild*, Book III. Chapter viii., 'A Dialogue Matrimonial' :—*Lætitia*. ' But why b—ch ? Methinks I should be glad to know why b—ch ?'

NOTE.—I add a Postscript (J. T. HODGSON, *ut sup.*, pp. 274-5) inadvertently omitted from the present Text :—' I have no intention of continuing *Childe Harold*. There are a few additions in the "body of the book," of description, which will merely add to the number of pages in the next edition, I have taken Thyrnham Court. The business of last summer—[Lady Caroline?]—I broke off, and now the amusement of the gentle fair is writing letters literally threatening my life, and much in the style of Miss

LETTERS

Matthews in *Amelia* or Lucy in *The Beggar's Opera*. Such is the reward of restoring a woman to her family, who are treating her with the greatest kindness, and with whom I am on good terms. I am still in 'palatia Circes,' and, being no Ulysses, cannot tell into what animal I may be converted. . . . She '—[Lady Oxford?]— ' has had her share of the denunciations of the brilliant Phryne, and regards them as much as I do. I hope you will visit me at Th[yrnham], which will not be ready before spring, and I am very sure you would like my neighbours, if you knew them. If you come down now to Kington '—[Herefordshire : the residence of Hodgson's kinsmen, the Cokes]—' pray come and see me.'

LETTER clxx. p. 232.

In 'Horace in London' I perceive some stanzas, etc. :—*Horace in London* was the work of the Brothers Smith. Here, printed with a reference to *Childe Harold*, are the verses :—

> 'All who behold my mutilated pile
> Shall brand its ravager with classic rage ;
> And soon a titled hard (!) from Britain's isle
> Thy country's praise and suffrage shall engage,
> And fire with Athens' wrongs an angry age !'

LETTER clxxii. p. 234.

Some conversation on the subject of Westall's designs :—Richard Westall (1765-1836), A.R.A. 1792, R.A. 1794, the water-colourist and illustrator. The designs in question were for *Childe Harold* I. and II. Westall painted his portrait of Byron in 1814.

P.S.—I see 'The Examiner' threatens some observations upon you next week :—This was so. *The Examiner* for 18th April 1813 announced ' A word or two on Mr. Murray's (the "splendid" bookseller) judgment in the Fine Arts—next week, *if room.*' It would seem that the 'few words' never 'got themselves uttered.'

The wrath which has heretofore been principally expended upon the Prince :—See *post*, p. 435, Note to Letter clxxiv.

Mr. Bucke, for instance :—For an account of this scribbler's quarrel with Edmund Kean, see HAWKINS, *Life*, etc., II. Chapters v. and vi. 'How would you,' Sir Walter asks of Southey (4th April 1818), 'or how do you think I should, relish being the object of such a letter as Kean wrote tother day to a poor author who, though a pedantic blockhead, had at least the right to be treated as a gentleman by a copperlaced two-penny tearmouth, rendered mad by conceit and success ?' These be 'bitter words,' in truth ; but Sir Walter was a Kembleite, and Kean had driven 'Black

Jack' from the stage. The 'conceit,' as well as the 'blockheaded-ness,' appear to have resided with Bucke, whose tragedy, a sham Elizabethanism of the most fatuous type, the pitiful *Italians* (the cause of all this row), being at last produced, was played twice, and then departed the stage for ever.

LETTER clxxiii. p. 235.
' When Rogers' must not see the inclosed :—

'Among the many gay hours we passed together this spring, I remember particularly the wild flow of his spirits one evening when we had accompanied Mr. Rogers home from some early assembly, and when Lord Byron, who, according to his frequent custom, had not dined for the last two days, found his hunger no longer governable, and called aloud for "something to eat." Our repast—of his own choosing—was simple bread and cheese; and seldom have I partaken of so joyous a supper. It happened that our host had just received a presentation copy of a volume of poems. . . . In turning over the pages, we found, it must be owned, abundant matter for mirth. In vain did Mr. Rogers, in justice to the author, endeavour to direct our attention to some of the beauties of the work :—it suited better our purpose . . . to pounce only on such passages as ministered to the laughing humour that possessed us. In this sort of hunt through the volume we at length lighted on the discovery that our host, in addition to his sincere approbation of some of its contents, had also the motive of gratitude for standing by its author, as one of the poems was a warm, and, I need not add, well-deserved panegyric on himself. We were, however, too far gone in nonsense for even this eulogy, in which we both so heartily agreed, to stop us. The opening line of the poem was, as well as I can recollect, "When Rogers o'er this labour bent"; and Lord Byron undertook to read it aloud—but he found it impossible to get beyond the first two words. Our laughter had now increased to such a pitch that nothing could restrain it. Two or three times he began; but no sooner had the words "When Rogers" passed his lips, than our fit burst forth afresh,—till even Mr. Rogers himself, with all his feeling of our injustice, found it impossible not to join us; and we were, at last, all three, in such a state of inextinguishable laughter, that, had the author himself been of the party, I question much whether he could have resisted the infection.'—MOORE.

The book was Edward, Lord Thurlow's *Poems on Several Occasions* (1813). 'On the same day,' says Moore, 'I received from him the following additional scraps. The lines in italics are from the eulogy that provoked his waggish comments :—

'TO LORD THURLOW

I

' *"I lay my branch of laurel down."*
Thou "lay thy branch of *laurel* down!"
Why, what thou'st stole is not enow;

And, were it lawfully thine own,
   Does Rogers want it most, or thou?
Keep to thyself thy wither'd bough,
   Or send it back to Dr. Donne—
Were justice done to both, I trow,
   He'd have but little, and thou—none.

2

'" *Then thus to form Apollo's crown.*"

'A crown! why, twist it how you will,
   Thy chaplet must be foolscap still.
When next you visit Delphi's town,
   Inquire amongst your fellow-lodgers,
They'll tell you Phœbus gave his crown,
   Some years before your birth, to Rogers.

3

'" *Let every other bring his own.*"

'When coals to Newcastle are carried,
-   And owls sent to Athens as wonders,
From his spouse when the Regent's unmarried,
   Or Liverpool weeps o'er his blunders ;
When Tories and Whigs cease to quarrel,
   When Castlereagh's wife has an heir,
Then Rogers shall ask us for laurel,
   And thou shalt have plenty to spare.'

As to which last I need but note (1) that 'coals to Newcastle' are
in pretty much the same case as owls to the city of Athené ; (2) that
the Regent's quarrel with his wife was years and years old ; (3) that
Lord Liverpool, being an 'In,' was fair game for any 'Out' who
chose to lay hand to him ; and (4) that in the Dedication of *Don
Juan* the writer has these lines :—

   Would *he* adore a Sultan? *he* obey
   The intellectual *eunuch*, Castlereagh?

LETTER clxxiv. p. 236.
   Anacreon, Tom Little, Tom Moore, or Tom Brown :—Moore was
often called 'Anacreon,' and as often 'Little,' as in Tom Hood's
squib :—

   When I first came, d'ye see, my name
   Was *Little*—now I'm *Moore.*

It was as 'Tom Brown' that he had just taken the town by storm
with his *Twopenny Post-Bag* (4th March 1813. Fourteenth Edition,
20th April 1814), as brilliant a set of pasquils as the century has

NOTES

produced. It contains at least one mischievous allusion to Byron :—

> Or whether Lord George (the young man about town)
> Has by dint of bad poetry written them down :—

and was held by Lockhart to have damaged the London sales of *Rokeby*. (See *ante*, p. 417, Note to Letter cxlv.)

Your Quarto two-pounds :—I conjecture this to be a reference to the original form and price of the *Odes and Epistles* (1806), which was published in quarto at the very handsome figure of two pounds six shillings.

The wit in the dungeon :—James Henry Leigh Hunt (1784-1859) : presently imprisoned in Horsemonger Lane Gaol for that famous description (*Examiner*, 12th March 1813) of the Prince Regent as 'a violator of his word, a libertine over head and ears in disgrace, a despiser of domestic ties, the companion of gamblers and demi-reps,' and 'a man who has just closed half a century without one single claim on the gratitude of his country or the respect of posterity.'

Hunt was a Radical, of course, and Moore a Whig; but to abuse the Regent was to go straight to the heart of the great Whig Party, among whose members, says Moore, 'there existed . . . at this period a strong feeling of indignation at the late defection from themselves and their principles of the illustrious personage who had been so long looked up to as the friend, and patron of both.' As a good and loyal Whig, Moore himself was 'warmly—perhaps intemperately—under the influence of this feeling'; he 'regarded the fate of Mr. Hunt with more than common interest'; so, 'immediately on my arrival in town (I) paid him a visit in his prison.' Byron heard of the experience and of the prisoner's circumstances—'his trelliced flower-garden without, and his books, busts, pictures, and pianoforte within'; and being, he also, of the Whig way of thinking, requested an introduction. The visit was repeated, there was a dinner, there were presents of books; and, 'It strikes me,' Hunt wrote to his wife, with a truly amazing capacity for self-deception, 'that he and I shall become friends, literally and cordially speaking. There is something in the texture of his mind that seems to resemble mine to a thread; I think we are cut out of the same piece, only a different wear may have altered our respective naps a little.' Byron, on his part, thought the captive 'an extraordinary character. . . . Much talent, great independence of spirit, and an austere yet not repulsive aspect,' at the same time that he was 'the bigot of virtue (not

435

LETTERS

religion), and, perhaps, a trifle opinionated. . . . But withal, a valuable man, and less vain than success, and even the consciousness of preferring the right to the expedient, might excuse.' The 'respective naps' are different, to be sure; but for some time the relations between the wearers were friendly enough. It was to Byron that Hunt dedicated that achievement in affected English and shabby-genteel heroics in which, by an immortal piece of bathos, Dante's lovers, at the very crisis of their fate, are turned into a suburban milliner and her 'young man' :—

> 'May I come in?' said he ;—it made her start,—
> That *smiling* (!) voice—she coloured, pressed her heart
> A moment, as for breath, and then with free
> And usual tones said, 'Oh yes, certainly (!)' :—

and Byron, though he despised the style, yet thought the poem 'a devilish good one,' recommended it to Murray, and would have liked Moore to give it a hand in *The Edinburgh Review*. Again, Hunt says that he was much with Byron in the pre-Exile days, and when the Exile came, he broke forth in valediction and in song :—

> And so adieu, dear Byron,—dear to me
> For many a cause, disinterestedly, etc.

But by 1818 Byron's mood had grown truly critical, not to say truculent :—

'He (Hunt) is a good man, with some poetical elements in his chaos, but spoiled by the Christ-Church Hospital and a Sunday newspaper,—to say nothing of the Surrey gaol, which conceited him into a martyr. But he is a good man. . . . He believes his trash of vulgar phrases, tortured into compound barbarisms, to be *old* English. . . . He sent out his *Foliage* by Percy Shelley . . . and of all the ineffable Centaurs that was ever begotten by Self-Love upon a Nightmare, I think this monstrous Sagittary the most prodigious. He (Leigh H.) is an honest charlatan, who has persuaded himself into a belief in his own impostures, and talks Punch in pure simplicity of heart. . . . Is that * * * at the head of *your* profession in *your* eyes? I'll be cursed if he is of *mine*, or ever shall be. . . . But Leigh Hunt is a good man, and a good father—see his Odes to all the Masters Hunt ; a good husband—see his Sonnet to Mrs. Hunt ; a good friend—see his Epistles to different people ; and a great coxcomb, and a very vulgar person in everything about him.'

It is delightfully savage. But listen to Keats (4th Jan. 1819), who knew his Hunt like a book :—' In reality he is vain, egotistical, and disgusting in taste and morals. . . . He does one harm by making fine things petty, and beautiful things hateful.' By contrast this character of Byron's conveys the impression that the writer must

NOTES

have had a real regard for Hunt, however dashed with scorn, to
have countenanced the famous tour to Italy at all.

That tour was made at Shelley's suggestion, and on funds (£200)
which Shelley borrowed from Byron for the purpose. In the sequel
it proved the worst day's work he ever did. Its objects were (1)
rest and change for Hunt, and (2) the foundation of a magazine to
be written by Hunt, Shelley, and Byron. It is absurd to suppose
that such a venture could have prospered; but, as matter of fact,
no such venture was ever made. Hunt (with his wife and six
children) was bound for Pisa, where Shelley (then at Lerici) had
furnished the ground-floor of the Palazzo Lanfranchi, Byron's
house, for him. At Leghorn he was joined by Shelley and
Williams in the *Don Juan*. The party went on to Pisa, whither
Byron followed; and, a few days after, the *Don Juan*—'built in the
eclipse and rigged with curses dark'—put out to sea for the last
time. The impossible combination disappeared; and Byron was
left with Hunt (*cum suis*) on his hands, and the strong conviction
in his mind that the whole position was a mistake. In effect, the
results were disastrous all round. The host, to his discredit, was at
no particular pains to make himself agreeable to his guest; the
guest, who was at best a journalist of parts, but thought himself by
far the better poet of the two—(he was very soon to show, and in
The Liberal too, how Byron ought to write the *ottava rima*!)—was
not greatly concerned to conciliate his host, at the same time that he
looked to that host to give lavishly and ask no questions. In this,
however, the guest was disappointed. More: he had been all his
life a sponge, and for the first time in his life (as Mr. Monkhouse
has remarked in his excellent little monograph) he was made to
feel like the sponge he was. He had, as Keats says, taken
Haydon's 'silver,' and 'expostulated on the indelicacy' of a
demand for its return; and in less trying times he had had £1400
out of Shelley in a single year. Byron was not that stamp of
treasurer. He was better versed in character and life than Shelley;
and, whether or not he had contracted what he calls the 'good old-
gentlemanly vice,' it is certain that Hunt, though he accepted some
£500 of him, and lived 'for the best part of two years' at his
expense, was neither satisfied nor pleased. Thus the pike which
tries to swallow what appears to him his natural prey, but has to
give over the experience, 'distracted and amazed.' The starting
of *The Liberal* made matters worse. It was founded with Byron's
money, and fed with such Byronisms as *Heaven and Hell*, the
Vision, the translation from Pulci, and the letter to 'My dear

Roberts.' But it was a failure from the beginning, when John Hunt was fined and imprisoned for publishing the *Vision* ; and as, though it was little or nothing to Byron, it was bread of life, and more, to Hunt, nobody need be surprised, though everybody should be distressed, to find that Hunt was presently disposed—(I quote again his able and humane apologist)—to 'impute the meanest motives to everything Byron said or did.' If you lie down with dogs (in fact), you get up with fleas. Byron consorted with Hunt, and four years after Byron's death (1828) Hunt published his *Lord Byron and his Contemporaries.* He wrote this stuff because he wanted money, and he would not have written it (so he says) could he have got money by any other means ; and, with a littleness of mind and spirit unparalleled in any but a cast mistress or an embittered poetaster, he essayed to present the man on whom he had sponged 'for the best part of two years' as a cad of the first magnitude—as, in fact, as false, as selfish, as contemptible a human thing as had disgraced the century.

But by the time that this ignoble piece of bookmaking got into print, the British public had awakened to a sense of what it had lost in Byron—to a sense, too, of its own superb stupidity in Byron's case ; and, as Mr. Monkhouse says, its reception of Hunt's 'libel probably caused him more suffering than all the former attacks of the *Quarterly*'—(in which Lockhart described the thing as 'the miserable book of a miserable man ')—'*Blackwood*, and other enemies put together.' The most galling, I think, because the most contemptuous, diatribe of all came from his ex-friend, Moore. I shall quote it here in full, not from the *Satirical and Humorous Poems* (where it is signed 'T. Pidcock,' and dated from 'Exeter Change,' where the menagerie was), but from a copy, in the Morrison Autographs, in the handwriting of Augusta Leigh :—

THE 'LIVING DOG' AND THE 'DEAD LION'

THOMAS MOORE TO LEIGH HUNT

Jan. 13.

Next week will be published, as 'Lives' are the rage,
    The whole Reminiscences, wondrous and strange,
Of a small puppy dog, that lived once in the Cage
    Of the late noble Lion at Exeter Change.

Though the dog is a dog of the kind they call 'sad,'
    'Tis a puppy that much to good breeding pretends ;
And few Dogs have such opportunities had,
    Of knowing how lions behave among friends.

438

NOTES

How the Animal eats, how he snores, how he drinks,
  Is all noted down by this Boswell so small,
And 'tis plain from each sentence the puppy dog thinks
  That the Lion was no such great things after all.

Though he roar'd pretty well—this the puppy allows—
  It was all, he says, borrow'd—all second-hand roar,
And he vastly prefers his own little bow-wows
  [To] the loftiest War-note the Lion could pour.

'Tis indeed as good fun as a Cynic could ask,
  To see how this cockney-bred setter of rabbits
Takes gravely the head of the Forest to task
  And judges of Lions by Puppy Dog habits.

Nay, fed as he was (and this makes [it] a dark case)
  With sops every day from the Lion's own pan,
He lifts up his leg at the noble beast's carcase,
  And does all a Dog, so diminutive can.

However, the Book's a good book—being rich in
  Examples and warnings to Lions high-bred,
How they suffer small mongrelly curs in their kitchen,
  Who'll feed on them living, and foul them when dead.

Thus Moore, and, broadly speaking, thus the general press. An ordinary person—if one can imagine an ordinary person in such circumstances—would have imitated Captain Shandy's (proposed) method of dealing with that work which the great Lepsius composed the day he was born. But Hunt was a spirited creature in his way ; and, howbeit something saddened and surprised (above all surprised) by the terms of his reception, he at once proceeded to give proof positive that, as he told his readers, he had 'moral courage, and a great deal of it.' In Sir Walter's phrase (LANG, *Lockhart*, ii. 23), he had already 'behaved like a hyæna to Byron,' for that he had 'dug him up to girn and howl over him in the same breath'; and in a second edition he showed that he could do still worse. For in certain Appendices, while protesting that 'no man could hold in greater horror' than he did 'the violation of the *sub iisdem trabibus*—the sacred enclosure of private walls,' he essayed to justify himself on this head ; and in his Preface, retorting on a reference (LOCKHART) to his 'not very tractable children,' he ventured to 'thank God they were not tractable to' Byron, and to add this :—' I have something very awful to say on this subject in case it is forced from me.' He said not how nor when this 'something very awful' was discovered to him ; and in common charity one must infer that it was neither when he was living under Byron's roof nor when he was taking Byron's money as an outdoor pensioner.

'I have many infirmities,' he wrote, 'and nothing great in me but my sympathy with mankind.' The infirmities are patent ; but for the 'sympathy,' etc., one must go elsewhither than to *Lord Byron and His Contemporaries*. It is fair to add that Hunt wrote with true piety of Shelley—(but if, as Trelawny says, he really did prefer his own Muse before Shelley's, the density of his conceit is not to be expressed in terms of words)—and Keats ; that he lived to a green old age ; that he numbered Carlyle among his many friends ; and that another of them, Charles Dickens, was severely taken to task for presenting him as the Harold Skimpole of *Bleak House*. A person of parts, no doubt—of parts, and a certain charm, and a facile, amiable, liquorish temperament. But there was no clearer, keener vision than Keats's ; and I fear that Keats's word about Leigh Hunt must be remembered as the last.

LETTER clxxvi. p. 238.

The author detects some incongruous figures, etc. :—Of the '*Strictures*' referred to I know nothing. For the rest :—'In an article on this Satire (written for Cumberland's Review, but never printed) by that most amiable man and excellent poet, the late Rev. William Crowe, the incongruity of these metaphors is thus noticed :—" Within the space of three or four couplets, he transforms a man into as many different animals. Allow him but the compass of three lines, and he will metamorphose him from a wolf into a harpy, and in three more he will make him a bloodhound." There are also in this MS. critique some curious instances of oversight or ignorance adduced from the Satire ; such as "*Fish* from *Helicon*" —"*Attic* flowers *Aonian* odours breathe,"' etc. etc.—MOORE. The existing text of *English Bards* is printed from a copy of the Fifth Edition, revised and annotated by the author.

The forthcoming critique :—See *The Quarterly Review*, vol. ix. (1813) p. 207. The Reviewer dismisses *The Pleasures of Memory* as a poem published years before, and secure of popularity. The rest of his article is devoted to *Columbus*, of which he writes without enthusiasm, regarding the subject as unfit for verse, and protesting against the introduction of the supernatural. The thing is considered and quoted, and in the end is 'found to have beauties of no ordinary kind.' But this was not enough for Rogers, nor for the devout Byron either.

NOTES

The general horror of 'fragments,' etc. :—*Columbus* is in
fragments, and *The Giaour*, which was written in imitation of
Columbus, had been put on the town in May. It began by being a
thing of three or four hundred lines; but it grew and grew with
each Edition, and now it is fourteen hundred strong.

Do you know Clarke's 'Naufragia' :—' Clarke ' is James Stanier
Clarke (1765-1834), founder of *The Naval Chronicle* (1799-1818)
and author (among other works) of *Naufragia: or Historical
Memoirs of Shipwrecks and of the Providential Deliverance of
Vessels* (London, 1808).

LETTER clxxviii. p. 240.

A Monk Mason note in Massinger:—Monck Mason (1726-1809)
had produced an edition of Massinger (1779), and Gifford, in
editing the same good poet, had pursued him from page to page
with the aspish illiberality of which none save himself was capable.

LETTER clxxix. p. 241.

Stael, the ' Epicene' :—To Madame de Staël, as to many others—
Sheridan, Whitbread, Mackintosh, Rose, Lauderdale, Brummell—
I purpose to return, in another Volume, the Notes to this one
having grown out of all measure as it is. For the present
reference :—

> 'And ah ! what verse can grace thy stately mien,
> Guide of the world, preferment's golden queen,
> Necker's fair daughter, Stael the *Epicene* !
> Fain would the Muse—but ah ! she dares no more,
> A mournful voice from lone Guiana's shore,
> Sad Quatremer, the bold presumption checks,
> Forbid to question thy ambiguous sex.

' These lines contain the secret history of Quatremer de Quincy's
deportation. He presumed, in the council of five-hundred, to
arraign Madame de Stael's conduct, and even to hint a doubt of
her sex. He was sent to Guiana.'—CANNING, *New Morality*.—
MOORE.

A design upon you in the paper line:—It came to nought. For
' Kit Smart' (1722-1770), see JOHNSON, *Lives of the Poets*, and
BOSWELL, *Life of Johnson :*—' Old Gardner the bookseller
employed Rolt and Smart to write the Universal Visitor. There
was a formal agreement, which Allen the printer saw. They were
bound to write nothing else, were to have a third of the profits,
and the contract was for ninety-nine years.'—MOORE.

LETTERS

As Whitbread's sire said to the king:—

'But first the monarch, so polite,
Asked Mr. Whitbread if he'd be a knight?
Unwilling in the list to be enrolled,
Whitbread contemplated the knights of Peg,
Then to his generous sovereign made a leg,
And said, " He was afraid he was too old," ' etc.

Peter Pindar.—MOORE.

LETTER clxxx. p. 242.

An Essay against Suicide:—See the lady's *Essay on Suicide* (London, 1813). I know nothing of Blinkinsop.

Tumult and train-oil:—The town was illuminated for - the Battle of Vittoria.

LETTER clxxxi. p. 244.

There is to be a thing on Tuesday ycleped a national fête:—Like the illuminations, in celebration of Vittoria. Thus (more or less) *The Morning Chronicle* for Friday, July 9, 1813:—' VAUXHALL GARDENS. On Wednesday a Grand Military Fête was given at this favourite resort of the votaries of pleasure, in honour of the late glorious victory in the Peninsula . . . new devices met the eye in every direction . . . the names of Ciudad Rodrigo, Talavera, Vimeira, Almeida, Badajoz, Albuera, Barrosa and Salamanca threw their refulgent light on the warrior's title. . . . The Gardens were crowded at an early hour; among the fashionables were several of the Foreign Ambassadors, Dukes of Norfolk and Argyll, Duchess of Argyll, Earl and Countess Westmoreland, Earl and Countess Grey, Lord Burghursh [*sic*], Lord Jersey, Lord Dillon, Lord Rey, Lord Ossulston, Lord J. Somerset, Lord Alvanley, Lord Boringdon, Lord Clancarty, Lord Haberton, Lady Lake, etc.'

LETTER clxxxii. p. 245.

I have been dining like the Dragon of Wantley:—This romantic monster did worse than swallow ' poor children three As one would eat an apple' :—

All sorts of cattle this Dragon did eat,
Some say he ate up trees,
And that the forests sure he would
Devour up by degrees ;
For houses and churches were to him geese and turkies,
He ate all, and left none behind, etc.

Morris (of indifferent memory):—This was Captain Charles Morris (1745-1838), author of innumerable moral songs (*Lyra Urbanica*, 1840), but remembered chiefly for *Jenny Sutton* and

442

NOTES

The Great Plenipotentiary (both still prized among amateurs of the *genre*), and a single line in *The Contrast*:—

'O, give me the sweet shady side of Pall Mall.'

Being a Whig bard and satirist (he was responsible for such pasquinades as *Billy's Too Young to Drive Us*), he incensed the Anti-Jacobins, who introduced him with peculiar opprobrium, in a sham account of the celebration of Fox's birthday. Thus runs that part of the report (compiled, 'tis said, from the *Morning Post* and *Morning Chronicle*: 'the *Courier* being too stupid for our purpose') which concerns him:—

'We know not how far Mr. Fox might have proceeded, had he not been interrupted by a jangling of bells from the Side-table which immediately drew all eyes that way. This proceeded from Captain Morris, who had fallen asleep during Mr. Fox's Song, and was now nodding on his chair, with a large paper Cap on his head, ornamented with gilt tassels and bells, which one of the Company had dexterously whipped on unperceived. The first motion was that of indignation; but the stupid stare of the unconscious Captain, who half opened his eyes at every sound of the bells as his head rose or fell, and immediately closed them again, *somno vinoque gravatus*, had such a powerful effect on the risible faculties of the Company, that they broke, as if by consent, into the most violent and convulsive fits of laughter; Mr. Fox himself not being exempt from the general contagion. As soon as the Captain was made sensible of the cause of this uproar, he attempted to pull off the Cap, but was prevented by a Citizen from the *Corresponding Society*, who maintained that the Company had a right to be amused by the Captain in what manner they pleased; and that, as he seemed to amuse them more effectually in *that state* than in any other, he insisted, for one, on his continuing to wear the Cap. This was universally agreed to, with the exception of the Duke of Norfolk. The Captain was therefore led to the upper table, with all his "jangling honours loud upon him"! Here, as soon as he was seated, his Noble Friend called upon him for a Song. The Captain sang the *Plenipo* in his best manner. This was received with great applause; and then the Duke gave "The Defenders—of Ireland"— (*three times three*). Captain Morris then began:—

"And all the Books of Moses":—

but was interrupted, before he had finished the first line, by Mr. Tierney, who declared he would not sit there and hear anything like ridicule on the Bible.—(*Much coughing and scraping*.)—Mr. Erskine took God to witness, that he thought the Captain meant no harm;—and a gentleman from Cambridge, whose name we could not learn, said, with great *naïveté*, that it was no more than was done every day by his acquaintance. Mr. Tierney, however, persisted in his opposition to the Song, and Captain Morris was obliged to substitute *Jenny Sutton* in the place of it. But the good humour of the company was already broken in upon, and Mr. Tierney soon after left the

LETTERS

room (to which he did not return) with greater marks of displeasure in his face than we ever remember to have seen there.'

Thus, too, Kirkpatrick Sharpe—Sir Walter's friend: withal 'the unclean bird, which buildeth its nest in the corner of the temple, and defileth the holy places,' of the *Chaldee Manuscript*—in that *Vision of Liberty* which he contributed to *The Anti-Jacobin Review and Magazine* :—

> 'On a cock sparrow fed with Spanish flies,
> A swilling Captain came, with liquor mellow,
> And still the crowd in hideous uproar cries,
> "Sing us a b——dy song, thou d——d good fellow."
> Incontinent he sets himself to bellow,
> And shouts with all the strength that in him lies ;
> The Citizens exclaim, "He 's sans pareilly O " ;
> The Citizens in raptures roll their eyes,
> And drink with leathern ears the fool's lewd ribaldries.'

(Both quotations are from Mr. Edmonds's Edition of *The Poetry of the Anti-Jacobin* ; London, 1890.) The captain was for many years a parasite of that violent Whig, the Duke of Norfolk, who left him nothing in the end. He had, however, an annuity of £200 from the Regent, and, for all his reputation, is described by Moore as 'a very grave, steady person' (this is confirmed by the odd, anonymous *Memoirs of a Man of Fashion* ; London, 1821). For a pretty story of Morris and Lord Stowell and their old sweetheart, Molly Dacre (then Lady Clarke), see MOORE (*Diary*, 19th November 1829), who is also responsible for the story that the captain's widow expected £10,000 of Murray for the MS. afterwards published as *Lyra Urbanica*.

Disraeli (a learned Jew) :—Isaac Disraeli (1766-1848), Rogers's 'man with only half an intellect, who writes books that must live,' had at this time published, with some forgotten novels and verses, part of the *Curiosities of Literature* (1791-1834) and *The Calamities of Authors* (1812-13). Next year came *The Quarrels of Authors* ; and it was in memory of the last two that Byron inscribed to him *Some Observations on an Article in Blackwood's Magazine*, etc. (1819), further described as ' This additional Calamity and Quarrel.'

LETTER clxxxv. p. 248.

To Mr. Croker :—In 1809, that very able but wholly unscrupulous and characterless person, John Wilson Croker (1780-1857), sometimes called 'The Talking Potato,' had been made Secretary of the Admiralty for adroit and useful Parliamentary work on behalf

444

of the Duke of York in the business of Mrs. Clarke. Byron had
asked him for a passage to the Mediterranean in a king's ship, and,
at his request, Captain Carlton of the *Boyne*, 'just then ordered
to reinforce Sir Edward Pellew, had consented to receive Lord
Byron into his cabin for the voyage.'—MOORE. (See *infra*, Note
to Letter clxxxviii.)

LETTERS clxxxvi and clxxxvii. p. 249.

This infernal story:—See *ante*, p. 440, Note to Letter clxxvi.

LETTER clxxxviii. p. 249.

Having, I believe, decoyed Yarmouth :—

> Our next round of toasts was a fancy quite new,
> For we drank—and you'll own 'twas benevolent too—
> To those well-meaning husbands, cits, parsons, or peers,
> Whom we've, any time, honoured by courting their dears.
> This museum of wittols was comical rather;
> Old H—df—rt gave M—ss—y, and *I* gave your f—th—r.

Thus an 'Intercepted Letter' from 'G—ge, Pr—ce R—g—nt to
the E—rl of Y—rm—th'; and as matter of fact the second Marchioness of Hertford—(Isabella Anne Ingram Shepeard (*d.* 1834),
daughter and co-heir of Charles, Viscount Irwin, of Scotland)—
who had at this time 'reached the regulation age,' and was,

> (As near as one can fix
> From peerage dates) full fifty-six,

was all-powerful with the Regent, and was justly execrated of the
Whigs. They suspected her of alienating their sometime Patron's
affections from them, and of dictating that course of policy, one
effect—and not the worst—of which was their absolute exclusion
from Place; and they applauded with both hands not only such
capital chaff as the *Horace: Ode* XI. *Book* ii. ('Freely Translated
by the Pr—ce R—g—nt'):—

> Go—bid her haste hither,
> And let her bring with her
> The latest No-Popery Sermon that's going—
> Oh! let her come with her dark tresses flowing,
> All gentle and juvenile, curly and gay,
> In the manner of—Ackermann's *Dresses for May*:—

but also such ruffianism as the lines first quoted, and the well-nigh
unpresentable anacreontic, *To a Plumassier*:—

> Seek me out a fine Pea-hen;
> Such a Hen, so tall and grand,

As by Juno's side might stand,
If there were no cocks at hand.
Seek her feathers, soft as down, etc.

Her son, Francis Charles Seymour Conway, Earl of Yarmouth
(1777-1842) and Third Marquess of Hertford (1822), was fifteen
years the Prince's junior. Familiarly known as ' Red Herrings,' by
reason partly of his title and partly of the fiery hue of his
whiskers :—

Thy whiskers, too, Yarmouth—alas ! even they,
    Tho' so rosy they burn,
    Too quickly must turn
(What a heart-breaking change for thy whiskers !) to *Grey* :—

he was one of the most conspicuous, as well as one of the most
characteristic, figures of the later Georgian Age. Educated at
Eton and Oxford (Christ Church and St. Mary's Hall : he proceeded
to his M.A. degree as late as 1814), in 1798 he married Maria
Fagniani, old Q.'s (or George Selwyn's : he left her £30,000) natural
daughter, and entered the Commons as member for Orford (Suffolk). In 1802-3, after the Peace of Amiens, he took his wife to
Paris, and was presently captured with the rest of his countrymen
in France, and sent to Verdun : a special exception being made for
his Countess, who remained in the capital. [In 1842 *The Times*
(12th March) quotes *The Scotsman* to this effect :—'The wife
of the deceased Marquis was the acknowledged mistress of Marshal
Junot.' Hence, perhaps, the epithet in Moore's pasquinade :—
' His Y—rm—th's own *Frenchified* hand cut it out.' Be this as it
may, it was at Paris that was born her second son, the Lord Henry
Seymour (1805-1859), who was afterwards to found the French
Jockey Club, and of whom it is reported that neither could he
speak English, nor had he ever set foot on English ground.]
When the Whigs came in (1806), the Prince requested Fox, who
was in *private* correspondence with Talleyrand, to negotiate
Yarmouth's release ; and the Emperor, believing him to be a
personal friend of Fox's, let him out at once, and packed him off
to England to arrange terms of peace. He reached London on
4th June, and was sent back as Envoy-Extraordinary ; but in
the interval there had been *pourparlers* with Russia, Napoleon had
raised his terms, and Yarmouth was dished. His mission remained
a secret till August, when he was joined by Lord Lauderdale, who
took up the negotiations in his stead ; but neither Lauderdale (with
Yarmouth) for England nor d'Oubril for Russia was clever enough
to play bowls with Napoleon, and in the sequel they went home

NOTES

baffled and shamed. (All this on the word of *The Gentleman's Magazine*, May 1842). In 1809 Yarmouth seconded his cousin Castlereagh in the duel with Canning; in 1810 he succeeded to ' the greatest part of the disposable property of the rich and eccentric Duke of Queensberry, the putative father of his wife '—to £150,000, that is, besides real estate; in 1811 he was made Vice-Chamberlain; in 1812 he was appointed Lord Warden of the Stanneries and a member of the Privy Council, and (with his mother) was preferred by the Regent before Lords Grey and Grenville, who declined to join the new Cabinet unless the Hertfords (the Second Marquess (1743-1822) was Lord High Chamberlain) and their son were removed from the Household; in 1814 he helped to found the Pugilistic Club, and was told off to do the honours to the Emperor Alexander, who gave him the Order of St. Anne; in 1822 he succeeded to the Marquisate, and received the Garter; and in 1827, being sent, as Ambassador-Extraordinary, to invest the Czar Nicholas with the Garter at Tsarkoeseloe, he played his part with a magnificence which set the Court and City gaping. After the passing of the Reform Bill he 'took a dislike' to England, and chiefly lived abroad until his death, which made him still more notorious (if that were possible) than he had been in life. His will, indeed, was made the occasion for years of scandalous litigation. It disposed of a vast amount of property; it dealt largely with scamps and demi-reps; and it was so violently phrased that *The Times* declined to quote a number of its instructions. It is far too elaborate and long to analyse, much less to print in full; and the executors, who had their work cut out for them in any case, were moved, unwisely, to boggle at certain of its provisions. Hence an action by one Angélique Borel, who recovered £3000; hence, too, an action by Lord Hertford's valet, Nicholas Suisse, who recovered more thousands than I care to say; and hence the criminal prosecution of Suisse—first in London and then in Paris—on a charge of embezzling divers sums of money, amounting (on one count only) to as much as £100,000. For the legitimate effect of the will, it remains obscure. But, so far as I can learn, a codicil (one of thirty) revoked a large bequest to the mother of Lord Hertford's three wards, because she had formed a connexion which was displeasing to him; but those wards, the daughters of Admiral Sir Richard Strachan (scandal gave them another sire):—

> Sir Richard, longing to be at 'em,
> Stood waiting for the Earl of Chatham :—

Countess Zichy (who lived with him until the end), Countess

LETTERS

Barthold, and Princess Ruffo got £86,000, £80,000, and £40,000 respectively. Also ' Lady Strachan's maid ' took £5000 down and a life annuity of £1000 ; the servants, £16,000 to £20,000 among them ; John Wilson Croker (whose relations with the Marquis are suggested in Thackeray's Mr. Wenham and, especially, Disraeli's Mr. Rigby), £21,000 and the wine (the best of it was abroad, so he made not much by this part of the bequest) ; the executors £5000 apiece; and so on, and so on. Altogether an amazing document. 'Aware of the infamy of the character of one' of a pair of legatees, the testator 'wishes the other to be as little in the power of that person as possible, and regulates certain payments in order that the one person may have no occasion to shorten the life of the other.' This provision *The Times* made bold to reproduce. We may judge of those it let alone.

Besides being Lord Warden of the Stanneries, Lord Hertford was Steward and Vice-Admiral of the Duchy of Cornwall, Chief Commissioner of the Duchy of Cornwall, Recorder of Coventry and Bodmin, Custos Rotulorum of the County of Antrim, Vice-Admiral of the Coast of Suffolk, etc. etc. etc. Also, as the 'patron' of Aldeburgh, Bodmin, Orford, and Lisburne, he nominated eight Members of Parliament. Indeed, his chief claims to distinction are that he so lived his life as to make it as it were a sublimation of the life and spirit of his time, and was as high, as puissant, and as magnificent a being as that time could show. In this capacity he touched the imagination of two men of genius, and he exists in literature as the Monmouth of *Coningsby* and the Steyne of *Vanity Fair*. Both are masterpieces, and the one completes the other ; for Lord Monmouth produces the impression not merely of the dissolute grandee, but also of the Great Noble who is naturally and easily in the front of politics and society, has the sense of affairs, can be a statesman when he will, and on occasion can do the honours for his country as becomes the best among English gentlemen ; while Lord Steyne, with his decoration of red hair and gleaming tusks, his leg and his *grand air* and his Garter, his effect in theatres and drawing-rooms, and his general potency in intrigue, remains a perfect exemplar of the debauched patrician, the person of birth and wealth and breeding who is above all an *homme à femmes*. And on the whole, Lord Hertford was ever rather Steyne than Monmouth to the general. I seem to remember him figuring thus, 'for all he's worth,' in that blackguard thing, *The Mysteries of the Court* ; he appears (as, for that matter, who does not ?), though to no great purpose, in the *Memoirs* of Harriette

NOTES

Wilson; and there is a little book, *The Confessions of Nicholas Suisse, Late Valet to the Marquis of Hertford* (Jackson and Co., 134 New Bond Street, 1842), which I would quote, if I dared, in illustration of the repute in which he was held, and of the terms in which men spoke and thought of him. [In reading Suisse, by the way, one cannot choose but think of a certain Monsieur Fiche— ('Since Monseigneur's death he has returned to his native country, where he lives much respected, and has purchased from his prince the title of Baron Ficci')—and his desperate confidences to Mrs. Rawdon Crawley on the Pincian Hill.] In any case, he was a sterling Georgian type, a man of Byron's *monde*, a representative of the age whose mouthpiece Byron was; and that must serve as my excuse for this Note. (See further, Appendix E.)

A last touch or two. Lord Yarmouth, being robbed of certain jewels, informed the authorities that he kept them 'in his rouge-box.' Also, he is said to have kicked and caned his master for misbehaviour to a lady. The story is told in Suisse's *Confessions*, and in a lampoon of the period, *R—y—l Stripes, or a Kick from Y—rm—th to Wa—s*, etc. 'A Poem, by P—— P——, Poet Laureat (London, E. Wilson, 1812)' :—

> Lord Y——h's blood began to freeze,
> To see P——e G——e upon his knees,
>   Yet guess'd the meaning of his motions:
> And thinking this no time for speech,
> Gave him a kick across the breech,
>   Which marr'd his H——ss's devotions. . . .

> Loud roar'd the P——e, but roar'd in vain,
> L——d Y——h brandish'd high his cane,
>   And guided every r—y—l movement;
> Now up, now down, now to, and fro
> The R——t nimbly moved his toe,
> The lady much enjoy'd the show,
>   And complimented his *improvement*. . . .

> Soft pity touch'd the tender fair,
> She heard his accents of despair,
>   His piteous sighs, his deep repentance;
> And begg'd Lord Y——h to refrain,
> And give some respite to his cane,
>   And mitigate the r—y—l sentence.

> The Peer obey'd—the nymph admir'd—
> No more he laid his stick upon him;
> And Britain's blubb'ring P——e retir'd,
>   With *blushing honours* thick upon him, etc.

LETTERS

To see a milling in that polite **neighbourhood** *:*—This was the fight, for £25 a side, between Harry Harmer and Jack Ford. It came off at St. Nicholas, 23rd August 1813, and was won by Harmer (an accomplished boxer) in thirty-five minutes.

Mad^e. de Staël-Holstein has lost one of her young barons :—Her son Albert : the only man who ever had his head cut off in a duel. Mr. A. Stevens, in his *Madame de Staël* (London, 1881), vol. ii. pp. 204-5, quotes Pictet de Sergy's unpublished *Souvenirs* to this effect :—He (Albert) 'led an irregular life, and met a deplorable death at Doberan, a small city of the Duchy of Mecklenburg-Schwerin, on the coast of the Baltic Sea, a favourite resort in summer for bathing, gambling, etc. Some officers of the état-major of Bernadotte had gone to try their luck in this place of play and pleasure. They quarrelled over some louis, and a duel immediately ensued. I well remember that the Grand Duke Paul of Mecklenburg-Schwerin told me he was there at the time, and while walking with his tutors in the park, suddenly heard the clinking of swords in a neighbouring thicket. They ran to the place, and reached it in time to see the head of Albert fall, cleft by one of those long and formidable sabres which were carried by the Prussian cavalry.' A little before the event, Albert's mother had written him (he was not twenty when he died) an austere letter of rebuke :—' Except the miserable attachment which a fine face can procure, I know not a single tie that you have. M. de Montmorency is here ; you stand aloof from him. Nothing pleases you but vulgar habits, the pipe, etc. *Neither the intellect of your mother*, nor the dignified manners of your brother, nor the charm of your sister, nor the talents of M. Schlegel, attract you,' etc. etc. The biographers of the Staël are greatly excited by Byron's reference. Thus, 'the terrible news, so heartlessly mentioned by Byron' (STEVENS) ; and again, ' Byron's flippant allusion to the tragic event has brought him into much disrepute' (BELLA DUFFY, *Madame de Staël* ; London, 1887).

In a mail-coach **copy** *of the ' Edinburgh,'* etc. :—According to *The Edinburgh Review* for July 1823, *The Giaour* is 'very beautiful—or, at all events, full of spirit, character, and originality. . . . We do not think any other but Lord Byron himself could have imparted the force and the character which are conspicuous in the fragments that are now before us.' . . . The 'images are sometimes strained and unnatural—and the language sometimes harsh and neglected, or abrupt and disorderly ; but the effect of the whole is powerful and pathetic. . . . Energy of character and intensity of emotion are sublime in themselves, and attractive in the highest degree as objects of admiration ; but the admiration which they excite, when presented in combination with worthlessness and guilt, is one of the most powerful corrupters and perverters of our moral nature ; and is the more to be lamented, as it is most apt to exert its influence on the noblest characters. The poetry of Lord Byron is full of this perversion ; and it is because we conceive it capable of producing other and still more delightful sensations than those of admiration, that we wish to see it employed upon subjects less gloomy and revolting than those to which it has hitherto been almost exclusively devoted.'

The Edinburgh booksellers did their business with London by coach in the case of special copies, and by smack from Leith in that of general orders.

Gone to America to marry some fair one :—In 1814 Francis Jeffrey (1773-1850), married the daughter of John Wilkes's nephew, a Mr. Wilkes of New York. At the time of Byron's writing, Jeffrey, a sound enough critic according to his lights, had edited *The Edinburgh Review* (1802) for some ten years, and had made it the first periodical in the world. His chief faults as an editor were (1) a trick of mixing politics with criticism, so that your Tory seldom, if ever, got fair play at his hands ; and (2) a tendency to be 'high-sniffing' and superior, which prevented him from considering anybody, or anything, excepting from his own peculiar point of view, which was that of a flippant (because divinely gifted) Whig. Hence some enormous blunders and an influence which made on the whole for mischief, and was not more bitterly resented than it deserved.

An American Life of G. F. Cooke :—Dunlop's *Memoir* (1813) of George Frederick Cooke (1756-1812).

P.S. 2nd. Your 'grand coup' : — Presumably *Lalla Rookh* (1817).

LETTER CXC. p. 254.

When 'you was campaigning at the King of Bohemy' :—Thus Jerry Sneak to Major Sturgeon in Foote's farce, *The Mayor of Garratt* (1764), a piece which Byron seems to have known by heart. He probably rejoiced in it as it was played by Dowton (the Major) and Russell (Jerry), who gave in Foote what Hazlitt (1816) calls 'a perfect exhibition of comic talent.'

Why don't you 'parody that ode' : — 'The Ode of Horace, "Natis in usum laetitiae," etc.; some passages of which I told him might be parodied, in allusion to some of his late adventures :—

> Quanta laboras in Charybdi
> Digne puer meliore flamma.'

—MOORE.

Cazotte's ' Diable Amoureux' :—Paris, 1772.   So far as the East is concerned, Jacques Cazotte (1720-1792) was a right influence in romance ; for in 1790, two years before his death (by the guillotine) he translated four volumes of tales as a continuation of Galland's *Mille et une nuits.*

Castellan's ' Mœurs des Ottomans' :—Paris, 1812.

LETTER cxci. p. 256.

Three vols. on Turkish literature :—The *Letteratura Turchesca* (Venezia, 1787, 3 vols.) of Giovanni Battista Toderini.   In 1789 a translation into French, *De la Littérature des Turcs,* was published at Paris by the Abbé de Cournand.

Your Peri . . . is sacred and inviolable :—'I had already, singularly enough, anticipated this suggestion, by making the daughter of a Peri the heroine of one of my stories, and detailing the love adventures of her aërial parent in an episode.   In acquainting Lord Byron with this circumstance, in my answer to the above letter, I added, "All I ask of your friendship is—not that you will abstain from Peris on my account, for that is too much to ask of human (or, at least, author's) nature—but that, whenever you mean to pay your addresses to any of these aërial ladies, you will, at once, tell me so, frankly and instantly, and let me, at least, have my choice whether I shall be desperate enough to go on, with such a rival, or at once surrender the whole race into your hands, and take, for the future, to Antediluvians with Mr. Montgomery."' —MOORE.

A curious letter from a friend of mine :—Lord Sligo (see *ante*, p. 353, Note to Letter lxix.), whom Byron had asked to say what he knew of the origin of *The Giaour.*   Here is the letter :—

Albany, Monday, August 31, 1813.

My dear Byron,—You have requested me to tell you all that I heard at Athens about the affair of that girl who was so near being put an end to while you were there ; you have asked me to mention every circumstance, in the remotest degree relating to it, which I heard.   In compliance with your wishes, I write to you all I heard, and I cannot imagine it to be very far from the fact, as the circumstance happened only a day or two before I arrived at Athens, and, consequently, was a matter of common conversation at the time.

NOTES

The new governor, unaccustomed to have the same intercourse with the Christians as his predecessor, had of course the barbarous Turkish ideas with regard to women. In consequence, and in compliance with the strict letter of the Mohammedan law, he ordered this girl to be sewed up in a sack, and thrown into the sea,—as is, indeed, quite customary at Constantinople. As you were returning from bathing in the Piræus, you met the procession going down to execute the sentence of the Waywode on this unfortunate girl. Report continues to say, that on finding out what the object of their journey was, and who was the miserable sufferer, you immediately interfered ; and on some delay in obeying your orders, you were obliged to inform the leader of the escort, that force should make him comply ;—that, on further hesitation, you drew a pistol, and told him, that if he did not immediately obey your orders, and come back with you to the Aga's house, you would shoot him dead. On this the man turned about and went with you to the governor's house ; here you succeeded, partly by personal threats, and partly by bribery and entreaty, in procuring her pardon, on condition of her leaving Athens. I was told that you then conveyed her in safety to the convent, and despatched her off at night to Thebes, where she found a safe asylum. Such is the story I heard, as nearly as I can recollect it at present. Should you wish to ask me any further questions about it, I shall be very ready and willing to answer them. —I remain, my dear Byron, Yours very sincerely, SLIGO.

Galt declares (*Life, ut sup.*, pp. 157-8) that Byron himself ' was in fact the cause of the girl being condemned and ordered to be sewed up in a sack and thrown into the sea,' and in substance his story of the rescue is identical with Lord Sligo's. And Byron told Medwin that the girl (who belonged, he said, to his Turkish servant) died soon after reaching her City of Refuge—' perhaps of love.'

LETTER cxcii. p. 258.

Not yet recovered of the ' Quarterly' :—See *ante*, p. 440, Note to Letter clxxvi.

I quite sigh for a Cider-Cellar :—The Cider-Cellar's tavern was No. 20 Maiden Lane. It was (says Mr. Wheatley, *London*, s.v. ' Maiden Lane') 'a favourite haunt of Professor Porson, who furnished the motto which was placed over the entrance—*Honos erit huic quoque homo*,' and of Lord Campbell, Dr. Raine (master of Charter House), and others ; also, for many years, it was renowned among bloods of all degrees, for kidneys, oysters, stout, cigars, and comic songs—these of a cast which has long been obsolete. Just such a place was Thackeray's Back-Kitchen, and by just such a song as Byron might have heard any night of his life at No. 20 Maiden Lane was Colonel Newcome shocked and scandalised

LETTERS

long years after. From the Princes downwards, it should be noted, your Regency buck sang for himself at least as cheerfully as he listened to the singing of others. Also, he made play in society with any talent he may have had for mimicry and the like ; so that (*teste* Hobhouse) Kean—(*his* fancy was the Coal Hole)—entertained the party assembled to meet him at Holland House by figuring, with a handkerchief and certain fingers, a sailor dancing a hornpipe. On the same occasion, Grattan (HOBHOUSE, *Recollections*) mimicked divers Irishmen till ' Lord Holland and myself were in convulsions of laughter,' while Kean 'roared outright, Lady Holland gave way, and Miss Fox was in ecstasy.' And Holland House was (as contemporary papers might have said) 'a grand Dépôt of Intellect and Magazine of Polite Learning.'

LETTER cxciii. p. 260.

Dr. Holland :—The late Sir Henry Holland (1788-1873) went to the East after graduating at Edinburgh in 1811, and in 1815 published his *Travels in Albania, Thessaly,* etc. For 'Ali Pasba,' see *ante,* p. 340, Note to Letter lviii.

As Miss Cunigunde by the Bulgarian Cavalry :—See *Candide, ou l'Optimisme,* chapître vii. :—' On ne vous a donc pas violée ? on ne vous a point fendu le ventre, comme le philosophe Pangloss me l'avait assuré ? Si fait, dit la belle Cunégonde ; mais on ne meurt pas toujours de ces deux accidents.'

LETTER cxcv. p. 261.

I was introduced to Southey :—See *ante,* p. 388, Note to Letter cxx.

Which came to my sire as a residence with Lady Carmarthen :— I conjecture this to be Aston Manor, Rotherham. For 'Lady Carmarthen,' see *ante,* p. 296, Note to Letter iii.

LETTER cxcviii. p. 264.

I have received and read the 'British Review' :—' My Grandmother's ' (October 1813) remarks that, ' As we are really admirers of Lord Byron's genius, and think it worth watching, we will not be among the number of those who flatter him into madness, or hold up his errors to imitation. He possesses so much that is excellent, that he deserves to be told of his mistakes.' . . . The fact is that ' It has appeared to us, and we really were concerned to observe it, that Lord Byron, who need not be kept awake by the trophies of any modern competitor in verse, has had the bad taste to imitate Mr. Walter Scott. We call it bad taste, because, ready as we are to do justice to the merit of Mr. Scott, we think the style of his poetry unfit and unsafe to be imitated. . . . We have nothing to do but, in the simple discharge of our duty, to tell him that we cannot give our suffrage, such as it is, to this new method of writing poetry,' etc. etc. etc. Moreover, . . . 'The character of his Giaour is of a cast which we cannot approve' . . . being 'likely to beget a feeling in which too much of admiration enters, for a reader not well grounded in good principles to be safe under its influence. And upon the whole, we are of opinion that these heroes and heroines of the new epic are not a whit more respectable than the heroes and heroines of *The Beggar's Opera.*'

'*Crabbe's*' *passage I never saw :*—Much exercised by a certain comparison in *The Giaour* :—

> The rugged metal of the mine
> Must burn before its surface shine;
> But, plunged within the furnace flame,
> It bends and melts—though still the same :—

the Reviewer remarks that 'the first of the two similes . . . is too like the beginning of Mr. Crabbe's tale entitled *Resentment* to suffer us to doubt that it had made an impression on the metal of Lord Byron's mind.' Here are the lines from Crabbe :—

> Like smelted iron these the forms retain,
> But, once impressed, will never melt again.

LETTER cxcix. p. 266.
Murray shall reinstate your line forthwith :—' The motto to *The Giaour* ' :—

> One fatal remembrance—one sorrow that throws
> Its bleak shade alike o'er our joys and our woes, etc. :—

'which is taken from one of the *Irish Melodies*, had been quoted by him incorrectly in the first editions of the poems. He made afterwards a similar mistake in the lines from Burns, prefixed to *The Bride of Abydos.*'—MOORE.

LETTER cc. p. 267.
A thing of mine in MS. :—This was the miscalled *Bride of Abydos*, published early in the December of 1813.

LETTER cciv. p. 270.
Certainly. Do you suppose, etc. :—Murray had been questioning the propriety of making a Moslem talk about Cain.

LETTER ccxi. p. 274.
Mr. Canning's approbation :—' Mr. Canning had addressed the

LETTERS

following note to Mr. Murray:—"I received the books, and, among them, *The Bride of Abydos*. It is very, very beautiful. Lord Byron (when I met him, one day, at dinner at Mr. Ward's) was so kind as to promise to give me a copy of it. I mention this, not to save my purchase, but because I should be really flattered by the present." '—MOORE.

LETTER ccxiii. p. 275.

The 'Morning Post' says I am the author of 'Nourjahad' :— That is, *Illusion, or the Trances of Nourjahad*, 'a melodramatic spectacle in three acts by an anonymous author' (GENEST), founded upon Sidney Biddulph—Mrs. T. Sheridan—'s pretty Eastern tale. It was produced at Drury Lane, 25th November 1813, and ran forty-one nights.

LETTER ccxiv. p. 276.

Another copy of the 'Journal' :—The *Journal of Llewellyn Penrose, a Seaman* :—'A book published by Mr. Murray at this time.'—MOORE.

P.S.—Mr. Ward and I still continue our purpose :—Of going to Holland. But it was never fulfilled.

Your present proposal :—Murray had offered a thousand guineas for *The Giaour* and *The Bride*.

A very kind note :—' Lord Byron is the author of the day. Six thousand of his *Bride of Abydos* have been sold within a month.— MACINTOSH, *Life*, ii. 266.'—MOORE.

LETTER ccxvii. p. 277.

Mr. Perry is a little premature in his compliments:—Mr. Perry's *Morning Chronicle* for Monday, 29th November 1813, has this paragraph :—' Lord Byron's muse is extremely fruitful. He has another poem coming out, entitled *The Bride of Abydos*, which is spoken of in terms of the highest encomium.'

The next paragraph is on the 'Journal' :—Of Llewellyn Penrose.

The second seems very bad :—' They say Ward has no heart,' etc. See *ante*, p. 384, Note to Letter cxiii.

The Regent is the only person, etc. :—See *ante*, p. 413, Note to Letter cxliii.

LETTER ccxxii. p. 281.

An incident occurred, with which, I fear, etc. :—Conjecturally the scandal about Lady Caroline Lamb.

Then, I nearly incurred a lawsuit, etc. :—See *ante*, p. 424, Note to Letter clvi.

NOTES

LETTER ccxxiii. p. 282.

The 'Christian Observer' is very savage:—See *The Christian Observer* for November 1813. The occasion is *The Giaour*; and this is how it's done :—

'If any edict were issued to incarcerate this particular poem, something after the manner of the unfortunate female whose history it records, we should be well content to have it in prison, instead of blazoning it upon the page of criticism. . . . A somewhat opaque mass of images and sentiments, streaked here and there by the lights of genuine poetry. . . . The offences against "*morality*" in the poem are almost innumerable. It is rather peculiar to Lord Byron, among poets, as we have already had occasion to observe, to excite all the interest of his readers for thoroughly unworthy objects. . . . We beseech him not to add himself to the infamous catalogue of those who have endeavoured to make vice reputable, who have ruined their country by overthrowing its altars and expelling its gods. . . . Let him not covet a celebrity like that of him who fired the temple of Ephesus . . . but those amaranthine honours which God gives, and which the world can neither give nor take away. . . . This fine passage is followed by a lofty address to the prostrate cities of Greece; cities prostrated (let his Lordship remember) chiefly by the licentious indulgences of the people. . . . The immersion of the body is well described, p. 20. . . . Parts of it are indeed exceedingly powerful; but the great mass savours too much of Newgate and Bedlam for our expurgated pages. We do not, of course, mean to fasten any of the Giaour's sentiments upon the author. . . . He has probably seen more than one example of young men of high birth, talents, and expectancies, on whom the eye of an anxious country rested, and for whom the loftiest niche of distinction and the richest rewards of virtue and piety were prepared, sink under the burden of unsubdued tempers, licentious alliances, and enervating indulgence. He has seen these high pretenders to this world's good become objects of contempt to the world, of pity to the thoughtful, of sorrow to the pious. He has *seen* all this; nay, perhaps —— ——. But we check our pen—and will conclude with a wish devoutly felt, that his usefulness may be commensurate with his talents; and that he, who has *thus* taught us to dread vice, may go on to display the dignity and the happiness of virtue.'

LETTER ccxxvi. p. 283.

I have redde through your 'Persian Tales':—Henry Gally Knight (1786-1816) is responsible for *Ilderim, A Syrian Tale* (1816) :—

> 'I tried at Ilderim—
> Ahem':—

and for *Phrosyne, A Grecian Tale: Alashtar, an Arabian Tale* (1817). Probably these were vaguely known as 'Persian Tales' in Murray's shop, and as 'Persian Tales' were passed to Byron. He recommended Knight to publish, as we shall see ; but Knight was profoundly scandalised by certain irreverent allusions to his 'little poems' in Moore's Second Volume (1831), and wrote an angry letter to Murray (SMILES, *Memoir*, ii. 323), in which he asserted that 'whoever remained, ever so quietly and unaffectedly, the friend of Lady Byron could not escape the malignity of her lord.' For the rest, the good Knight regards Moore's Second Volume as 'neither more nor less than *Don Juan* in prose,' and cannot say how much he regrets 'to see Lord Byron's amours so openly paraded before the public. It is an indecorous exhibition, and but too likely to do harm,' etc. etc.

LETTER ccxxviii. p. 288.

A Mademoiselle de Sommery's :—Authoress of *Doutes sur différentes Opinions reçues dans la Société* (1782) ; *Lettres de Mme. la Comtesse de L—— à M. le Comte de R.* (1785), etc. She died in 1790.

LETTER ccxxix. p. 288.

To Mr. Ashe :—Thomas Ashe (1770-1835) began as an officer in the Eighty-Third Foot, and next went clerking at Bordeaux. There he seduced a girl, fought a duel with her brother, wounded him, and was laid in hold till the hurt was healed. After this, he returned to his native Dublin and was made Secretary to the Diocesan and Endowed Schools Commission, but got into debt, resigned his post, and levanted to Switzerland. He wrote, among other things, *Travels in America* (1808), *Memoirs and Confessions* (1815), and *The Spirit of 'The Book,'* or *Memoirs of Caroline, Princess of Hasburgh, A Political and Amatory Romance* (1811) ; and it is for the achievement of this last, which purports to contain letters from Caroline of Brunswick to her daughter, that Byron reproves him. On the title-page, by way of motto, is this advertisement :—as to which it is necessary to remark that '*The Book*' is the name by which that defence was known which Spencer Perceval drew up for the Princess of Wales against the charges advanced (1806-7) by Lady Douglas ; which was presented to the King at Windsor ; and which, as it was printed under circumstances of peculiar secrecy—(a masked M.P. corrected the proofs, and the whole issue was delivered at Spencer Perceval's at dead of night)—and then withheld from publication, was an object of extraordinary curiosity and suspicion till the appearance of a reprint (with additions) in 1813 :—' "The Book."— Any Person having in their possession a CERTAIN BOOK, printed by

Mr. Edwards in 1807, but *never published*, with W. Lindsell's name as the seller of the same on the Title Page, and will bring it to W. Lindsell, Bookseller, Wimpole Street, will receive a handsome gratuity.—Times Paper, 27th March 1809.' Ashe takes the highest tone in his preface:—'The subsequent letters are compiled from the purest motives—from a patriotic feeling,—and with all the affectionate devotion of a subject,—to establish the innocence of the persecuted,—to do justice to the injured,—and to substantiate the virtues of, and to wipe off the calumnious stain from those illustrious personages which public error and misconception have attached to them.' And so on. The letters, it need scarce be said, are utter rubbish.

It remains to note that at Ashe's request Byron advanced him a hundred and fifty pounds, of which seventy were paid him at the rate of ten a month, and the other eighty in a lump, on the strength of a wish of his to go to New South Wales.

LETTER ccxxxi. p. 289.

Mme. d'Arblay's (or even Miss Edgeworth's) new work:—The one was *The Wanderer* (see *ante*, p. 396, Note to Letter cxxi.); the other *Patronage* (1814).

P.S.—You were talking to-day of the American Edition:— Apparently of *English Bards and Scotch Reviewers.*

If you send to the 'Globe' editor:—I cannot explain this reference, as there is a 'solution of continuity' in the Museum file.

APPENDICES

APPENDIX A

BYRON entered Trinity College on the 1st July 1805. I am indebted to Mr. J. W. Clark for a copy of this entry in the College admission-book :—

July 1, 1805.—Admissus est nobilis Georgius Baro Byron de Londino et e Scholâ apud Harrow sub presidio Doctoris Butler ann. nat. **17**. Magistro Jones Tutore.

He was admitted to the degree of Master of Arts on 4th July 1808, with two others, and all three matriculated that same day : the reason of which irregular and extraordinary proceeding is not now discoverable.

APPENDIX B

IN Frederick Lillywhite's *Cricket Scores and Biographies of Celebrated Cricketers from 1746 to 1826* (London, 1862), i. 319-20, the date of Byron's Eton-Harrow match, which was played at Lord's, is given as 1805. Eton won by an innings and two runs. Here is the full score :—

HARROW

First Innings.			Second Innings.		
Lord Ipswich, b. Carter,	.	10	b. Heaton,	.	21
T. Farrer, Esq., b. Carter,	.	7	c. Bradley,	.	3
T. Drury, Esq., b. Carter,	.	0	st. Heaton,	.	6
—— Bolton, Esq., run out,	.	2	b. Heaton,	.	0
C. Lloyd, Esq., b. Carter,	.	0	b. Carter,	.	0
A. Shakespeare, Esq., st. Heaton,		8	run out,	.	5
Lord Byron, c. —— Barnard,	.	7	b. Carter,	.	2
Hon. T. Erskine, b. Carter,	.	4	b. Heaton,	.	8
W. Brockman, Esq., b. Heaton,	.	9	b. Heaton,	.	10
E. Stanley, Esq., not out,	.	3	c. Canning,	.	7
—— Asheton, Esq., b. Carter,		3	not out,	.	0
Byes,	.	2	Byes,	.	3
		55			65

LETTERS

ETON

APPENDIX C

COMMUNICATED to Moore, for the *Life and Letters*, by Walter Scott :—

' My first acquaintance with Byron began in a manner rather doubtful. I was so far from having anything to do with the offensive criticism in the *Edinburgh*, that I remember remonstrating against it with our friend, the editor, because I thought the *Hours of Idleness* treated with undue severity. They were written, like all juvenile poetry, rather from the recollection of what had pleased the author in others than what had been suggested by his own imagination; but, nevertheless, I thought they contained some passages of noble promise. I was so much impressed with this, that I had thoughts of writing to the author; but some exaggerated reports concerning his peculiarities, and a natural unwillingness to intrude an opinion which was uncalled for, induced me to relinquish the idea.

' When Byron wrote his famous Satire, I had my share of flagellation among my betters. My crime was having written a poem (*Marmion*, I think) for a thousand pounds; which was no otherwise true than that I sold the copyright for that sum. Now, not to mention that an author can hardly be censured for accepting such a sum as the booksellers are willing to give him, especially as the gentlemen of the trade made no complaints of their bargain, I thought the interference with my private affairs was rather beyond the limits of literary satire. On the other hand, Lord Byron paid me, in several passages, so much more praise than I deserved, that I must have been more irritable than I have ever felt upon such subjects, not to sit down contented, and think no more about the matter.

' I was very much struck, with all the rest of the world, at the vigour and force of imagination displayed in the first cantos of *Childe Harold*, and the

464

other splendid productions which Lord Byron flung from him to the public with a promptitude that savoured of profusion. My own popularity, as a poet, was then on the wane, and I was unaffectedly pleased to see an author of so much power and energy taking the field. Mr. John Murray happened to be in Scotland that season; and as I mentioned to him the pleasure I should have in making Lord Byron's acquaintance, he had the kindness to mention my wish to his Lordship, which led to some correspondence.

'It was in the spring of 1815 that, chancing to be in London, I had the advantage of a personal introduction to Lord Byron. Report had prepared me to meet a man of peculiar habits and a quick temper, and I had some doubts whether we were likely to suit each other in society. I was most agreeably disappointed in this respect. I found Lord Byron in the highest degree courteous, and even kind. We met, for an hour or two almost daily, in Mr. Murray's drawing-room, and found a great deal to say to each other. We also met frequently in parties and evening society, so that for about two months I had the advantage of a considerable intimacy with this distinguished individual. Our sentiments agreed a good deal, except upon the subjects of religion and politics, upon neither of which I was inclined to believe that Lord Byron entertained very fixed opinions. I remember saying to him, that I really thought, that if he lived a few years he would alter his sentiments. He answered, rather sharply, "I suppose you are one of those who prophesy I will turn Methodist." I replied, "No —I don't expect your conversion to be of such an ordinary kind. I would rather look to see you retreat upon the Catholic faith, and distinguish yourself by the austerity of your penances. The species of religion to which you must, or may, one day attach yourself must exercise a strong power on the imagination." He smiled gravely, and seemed to allow I might be right.

'On politics, he used sometimes to express a high strain of what is now called Liberalism; but it appeared to me that the pleasure it afforded him as a vehicle of displaying his wit and satire against individuals in office was at the bottom of this habit of thinking, rather than any real conviction of the political principles on which he talked. He was certainly proud of his rank and ancient family, and, in that respect, as much an aristocrat as was consistent with good sense and good breeding. Some disgusts, how adopted I know not, seemed to me to have given this peculiar and, as it appeared to me, contradictory cast of mind: but, at heart, I would have termed Byron a patrician on principle.

'Lord Byron's reading did not seem to me to have been very extensive either in poetry or history. Having the advantage of him in that respect, and possessing a good competent share of such reading as is little read, I was sometimes able to put under his eye objects which had for him the interest of novelty. I remember particularly repeating to him the fine poem of *Hardyknute*, an imitation of the old Scottish Ballad, with which he was so much affected, that some one who was in the same apartment asked me what I could possibly have been telling Byron by which he was so much agitated.

'I saw Byron, for the last time, in 1815, after I returned from France.

He dined, or lunched, with me at Long's in Bond Street. I never saw him so full of gaiety and good-humour, to which the presence of Mr. Mathews, the comedian, added not a little. Poor Terry was also present. After one of the gayest parties I ever was present at, my fellow-traveller, Mr. Scott of Gala, and I set off for Scotland, and I never saw Lord Byron again. Several letters passed between us—one perhaps every half-year. Like the old heroes in Homer, we exchanged gifts :—I gave Byron a beautiful dagger mounted with gold, which had been the property of the redoubted Elfi Bey. But I was to play the part of Diomed, in the *Iliad* ; for Byron sent me, some time after, a large sepulchral vase of silver. It was full of dead men's bones, and had inscriptions on two sides of the base. One ran thus :—"The bones contained in this urn were found in certain ancient sepulchres within the land walls of Athens, in the month of February 1811." The other face bears the lines of Juvenal :—

'" Expende—quot libras in duce summo invenies.
—Mors sola fatetur quantula hominum corpuscula."
JUV. x.

'To these I have added a third inscription, in these words :—"The gift of Lord Byron to Walter Scott." There was a letter with this vase more valuable to me than the gift itself, from the kindness with which the donor expressed himself towards me. I left it naturally in the urn with the bones, —but it is now missing. As the theft was not of a nature to be practised by a mere domestic, I am compelled to suspect the inhospitality of some individual of higher station,—most gratuitously exercised certainly, since, after what I have said, no one will probably choose to boast of possess-ing this literary curiosity.

'We had a good deal of laughing, I remember, on what the public might be supposed to think, or say, concerning the gloomy and ominous nature of our mutual gifts.

'I think I can add little more to my recollections of Byron. He was often melancholy,—almost gloomy. When I observed him in this humour, I used either to wait till it went off of its own accord, or till some natural and easy mode occurred of leading him into conversation, when the shadows almost always left his countenance, like the mist rising from a landscape. In conversation he was very animated.

'I met with him very frequently in society ; our mutual acquaintances doing me the honour to think that he liked to meet with me. Some very agreeable parties I can recollect,—particularly one at Sir George Beau-mont's, where the amiable landlord had assembled some persons distinguished for talent. Of these I need only mention the late Sir Humphry Davy, whose talents for literature were as remarkable as his empire over science. Mr. Richard Sharp and Mr. Rogers were also present.

'I think I also remarked in Byron's temper starts of suspicion, when he seemed to pause and consider whether there had not been a secret, and perhaps offensive, meaning in something casually said to him. In this case, I also judged it best to let his mind, like a troubled spring, work itself clear, which it did in a minute or two. I was considerably older, you will recollect, than my noble friend, and had no reason to fear his misconstruing my sentiments towards him, nor had I ever the slightest reason to doubt that they were kindly returned on his part. If I had occasion to be mortified by the display of genius which threw into the shade such pretensions as I was then supposed to possess, I might console myself that, in my own case, the materials of mental happiness had been mingled in a greater proportion.

'I rummage my brains in vain for what often rushes into my head unbidden,—little traits and sayings which recall his looks, manner, tone, and gestures; and I have always continued to think that a crisis of life was arrived in which a new career of fame was opened to him, and that had he been permitted to start upon it, he would have obliterated the memory of such parts of his life as friends would wish to forget.'

APPENDIX D

CONTRIBUTED by Walter Scott to *The Edinburgh Weekly Journal* in the year of Byron's death. Very notable is the blend of affection with pride in the '*our* Byron' eight lines from the end :—

'Amidst the general calmness of the political atmosphere, we have been stunned, from another quarter, by one of those death-notes which are pealed at intervals, as from an archangel's trumpet, to awaken the soul of a whole people at once. Lord Byron, who has so long and so amply filled the highest place in the public eye, has shared the lot of humanity. That mighty genius, which walked amongst men as something superior to ordinary mortality, and whose powers were beheld with wonder, and something approaching to terror, as if we knew not whether they were of good or of evil, is laid as soundly to rest as the poor peasant whose ideas went not beyond his daily task. The voice of just blame and of malignant censure are at once silenced; and we feel almost as if the great luminary of heaven had suddenly disappeared from the sky, at the moment when every telescope was levelled for the examination of the spots which dimmed its brightness. It is not now the question, what were Byron's faults, what his mistakes; but, how is the blank which he has left in British literature to be filled up? Not, we fear, in one generation, which, among many highly gifted persons, has produced none which approached Lord Byron, in ORIGINALITY, the first attribute of genius. Only thirty-six years old—so much already done for immortality—so much time remaining, as it seemed to us short-sighted mortals, to maintain and to extend his fame, and to atone for errors in conduct and levities in composition,—who will not grieve that such a race has been shortened, though not always keeping the straight path; such a light extinguished, though sometimes flaming to dazzle and to bewilder? One word on this ungrateful subject, ere we quit it for ever.

'The errors of Lord Byron arose neither from depravity of heart,—for Nature had not committed the anomaly of uniting to such extraordinary talents an imperfect moral sense,—nor from feelings dead to the admiration of virtue. No man had ever a kinder heart for sympathy, or a more open hand for the relief of distress; and no mind was ever more formed for the enthusiastic admiration of noble actions, providing he was convinced that the actors had proceeded on disinterested principles. . . . Remonstrances from a friend, of whose intentions and kindness he was secure, had often great weight with him; but there were few who would venture on a task so difficult. Reproof he endured with impatience, and reproach hardened him in his error; so that he often resembled the gallant war-steed, who rushes forward on the steel that wounds him. In the most painful crisis of his private life, he evinced this irritability and impatience of censure in such a degree, as almost to resemble the noble victim of the bull-fight, which is more maddened by the squibs, darts, and petty annoyances of the unworthy crowds beyond the lists, than by the lance of his nobler, and, so to speak, his more legitimate antagonist. In a word, much of that in which he erred was in bravado and scorn of his censors, and was done with the motive of Dryden's despot, "to show his arbitrary power." . . .

'As various in composition as Shakespeare himself (this will be admitted by all who are acquainted with his *Don Juan*), he has embraced every topic of human life, and sounded every string on the divine harp, from its slightest to its most powerful and heart-astounding tones. There is scarce a passion or a situation which has escaped his pen; and he might be drawn, like Garrick, between the weeping and the laughing Muse, although his most powerful efforts have certainly been devoted to Melpomene. His genius seemed as prolific as various. The most prodigal use did not exhaust his powers, nay, seemed rather to increase their vigour. Neither *Childe Harold*, nor any of the most beautiful of Byron's earlier tales, contain more exquisite morsels of poetry than are to be found scattered through the cantos of *Don Juan*, amidst verses which the author appears to have thrown off with an effort as spontaneous as that of a tree resigning its leaves to the wind. But that noble tree will never more bear fruit or blossom! It has been cut down in its strength, and the past is all that remains to us of Byron. We can scarce reconcile ourselves to the idea—scarce think that the voice is silent for ever, which, bursting so often on our ear, was often heard with rapturous admiration, sometimes with regret, but always with the deepest interest—

"All that's bright must fade,
The brightest still the fleetest!"

With a strong feeling of awful sorrow, we take leave of the subject. Death creeps upon our most serious as well as upon our most idle employments; and it is a reflection solemn and gratifying, that he found our Byron in no moment of levity, but contributing his fortune, and hazarding his life, in behalf of a people only endeared to him by their own past glories, and as fellow-creatures suffering under the yoke of a heathen oppressor. . . . To have fallen in a crusade for Freedom and Humanity, as in olden times it would have been an atonement for the blackest crimes, may in the present be allowed to expiate greater follies than even exaggerating calumny has propagated against Byron.'

APPENDICES

APPENDIX E

THE Hertfords came in for their share of the attentions of a lampooning age. Some I have quoted. Here are others, 'embedded and enjellied' in the agitation (1820) about the luckless Lady who called herself 'the Queen of this Realm.' In *The Political A-Apple-Pie, or The Extraordinary Red-Book Versified*, the letter H is illustrated by a portrait of the Marchioness—(she is said, by the way, to have presided, at Manchester House, over a committee of ladies, self-constituted to consider whether pantaloons or trousers were the more modest wear, and her decision, against *le collant*, was received with fury by the Sons of England, each of whom, like Sir Willoughby Patterne, 'had a leg')—an obese yet haughty dame in a short frock and plumes, whose appearance is a capital commentary on the lines in *The Twopenny Post-Bag*:—

> The Marchesa and he, inconvenient in more ways,
> Have taken much lately to whispering in doorways,
> Which, you know, dear, considering the *size* of the two, etc. ;

while the Marquis is chastened for his salary of £3000 a year as Lord High Chamberlain :—

> *Lord Hertford*, the loyal, good-humoured, and true,
> Had three thousand pieces with nothing to do,
> But how much HIS LADY had nobody knew ;
> For, though much beloved by the Prince of the Pie,
> Her Ladyship was most remarkably shy,
> And took what she had, as they say, 'on the sly.'

Again, her Ladyship, who was by this time more or less supplanted by the Marchioness of Conyngham, is soundly rated in *A Lecture on Various Subjects, By the Clerk of the Closet Near St. James's Place* (London, 1821). 'Shall H—tf—d stain this sacred page?' the Clerk inquires :—

> That prostitute in closing age,
> Steeped in perdition—sunk in mire,
> Slave of ambition, and desire,
> To please the King and run the round
> When C—n—g—m cannot be found.

From *A Favourite New Royal Alphabet*, etc., 'By Peter Pangloss, LL.D. and A.S.S.,' here is a character of Lord Yarmouth :—

> Y stands for Y—outh, a *youth* without doubt,
> Though forty-five winters I 've seen him about,

> Yet still he 's a youth, whose *mamma* can engender
> In *dandy of sixty* a passion so tender.
> A *fortunate* youth, too, he 's been all his life ;
> Too *lucky* at *play* to have luck in a *wife.*

His Lordship's tenderness for the lads of the Fancy (he seems to have been himself a boxer as well as a patron of the Ring) is indicated, coarsely enough, in Epistle VI. of *The Royal Letter-Bag* (1820), a poor imitation of Mr. Thomas Brown the Younger, which, however, 'met with such unexampled Success as to occasion a demand for SIX EDITIONS in less than TWO WEEKS.' And in 1819 that very moral and disreputable print, *The New Bon Ton Magazine* (II. 321-26), remarking that ' The Brighton news have given us a rum story of a royal piece of kitchen stuff,' proceeds to show Lord Yarmouth and the Regent finishing their wine above-stairs at the Pavilion, and then going down, to crown the evening, among the scullions in the kitchen, where 'the R—g—t, seated on the best elbow chair, facing Y—— on a stool, bawled loudly for supper.' Says the Veracious Chronicler :—' The kitchen table was soon clad in white, and a banquet served up . . . *and* at which G—ge played an excellent knife and fork. . . . The glasses went briskly round, the Prince and the Peer hobnobbed,' etc. ; till, at last, 'a little black wench found herself situated on the knee of the L—d Warden, and Mother Cl—k was enshrined in the arms of Royalty,' etc. etc. After which the Veracious Chronicler drops into poetry :—

> Let the M—ch—ss stay
> For ever away,
> My cook hath superior charms, etc.

This, so far as I know, is our last glimpse of ' Red Herrings ' in the course of the present work.

END OF VOL. I

Printed by T. and A. CONSTABLE, Printers to Her Majesty
at the Edinburgh University Press